CADOGAN    Dana Facaros and Michael Pauls

# Umbria

| | |
|---|---|
| Introduction | vii |
| Travel | 1 |
| Practical A–Z | 13 |
| History and Art | 33 |
| Topics | 49 |
| Perugia, Lake Trasimeno, and Assisi | 59 |
| Northern Umbria | 111 |
| The Valle Umbra: Spello to Spoleto | 133 |
| The Tiber Valley: Todi, Orvieto, Amelia | 165 |
| The Valnerina: Narni to Norcia | 199 |
| Language | 229 |
| Artistic, Architectural and Historical Terms | 237 |
| Further Reading | 240 |
| Index | 241 |

**Cadogan Guides**
West End House, 11 Hills Place,
London W1R 1AG, UK
*becky.kendall@morrispub.co.uk*

Distributed in North America by
**The Globe Pequot Press**
246 Goose Lane, PO Box 480, Guilford
Connecticut 06437–0480

Text first published 1989
Updated 2000 for this edition by Nicky Swallow
Copyright © Dana Facaros and Michael Pauls 2000
Illustrations © Horatio Monteverde 1996

Book and cover design by Animage
Cover photographs by John Ferro Sims
Maps © Cadogan Guides, drawn by Map Creation Ltd

Editorial Director: Vicki Ingle
Series Editor: Linda McQueen

Editor: Fiona Beddall
Proofreading: Linda McQueen
Indexing: Judith Wardman
Production: Rupert Wheeler Book Production Services

A catalogue record for this book is available from the British Library
ISBN 1–86011–959–X

Printed and bound in England by Cambridge University Press

All rights reserved. No part of this publication may
be reproduced, stored in a retrieval system, or
transmitted, in any form or by any means, elec-
tronic or mechanical, including photocopying and
recording, or by any information storage and
retrieval system except as may be expressly
permitted by the UK 1988 Copyright Design &
Patents Act and the USA 1976 Copyright Act or in
writing from the publisher. Requests for permission
should be addressed to Cadogan Guides, West End
House, 11 Hills Place, London W1R 1AG.

## About the Authors

Dana Facaros and Michael Pauls are professional travel writers. They have written over 30 Cadogan Guides, including all the Italy series. For three years they and their two children lived in a tiny Umbrian hilltop village, where they suffered massive overdoses of food, art and wine, and enjoyed every minute of it. They reckon they could now whip 98 per cent of the world's non-Italian population in Italian Trivial Pursuit (except for the sports questions). They now live in Ireland.

## About the Updater

Nicky Swallow, a professional musician, has lived in Florence for 18 years. Her enthusiasm for Italian life has led to an intimate knowledge of Tuscany and Umbria, where she has travelled extensively. She is a regular contributor to travel guides and magazines.

## Updater's Acknowledgements

Thanks to Helen Holubov for her help with checking out the facts.

## Please help us to keep this guide up to date

We have done our best to ensure that the information in this guide is correct at the time of going to press. But places and facilities are constantly changing, and standards and prices in hotels and restaurants fluctuate. We would be delighted to receive any comments concerning existing entries or omissions, as well as suggestions for new features. Authors of the best letters will be offered a copy of the Cadogan Guide of their choice.

## Please Note

The author and publishers have made every effort to ensure the accuracy of the information in the book at the time of going to press. However, they cannot accept any responsibility for any loss, injury or inconvenience resulting from the use of information contained in this guide.

# Contents

Introduction ix  The Best of Umbria ix
A Few Suggestions viii

## Travel 1–12

Getting There from the
UK and Ireland 2
Getting There from the
USA and Canada 4
Passports and Customs
Formalities 5
Getting Around 6
By Train 6

By Coach and Bus 7
By Taxi 8
By Car 8
By Motorbike or Bicycle 9
Disabled Travellers 9
Courses for Foreigners and
Specialist Holidays 11

## Practical A–Z 13–32

Climate and When to Go 14
Festivals 14
Food and Drink 17
Embassies and Consulates 22
Insurance and Health 22
Lavatories 22
Money and Banks 22
Official Holidays 23
Opening Hours and
Museums 24

Packing 24
Photography 25
Police Business 25
Post Offices 25
Purchasing a House 35
Telephones 26
Shopping 26
Sports and Activities 27
Tourist Information 28
Where to Stay 28

## History and Art 33–48

History 34  Art in Umbria 45

## Topics 49–58

After the Earthquakes:
Art versus People 50
Guelphs and Ghibellines 51
St Francis of Assisi 52

Landscapes and Nature 55
Umbria's Totem Tubers 57
The Ultimate Umbrian
Accessory 58

## Perugia, Lake Trasimeno, and Assisi 59–110

| | | | |
|---|---|---|---|
| Perugia | 60 | Città della Pieve | 88 |
| Around Perugia: | | Panicale and Around | 90 |
| Torgiano, Deruta and Corciano | 80 | Assisi | 91 |
| Lake Trasimeno | 82 | West of Assisi | 109 |
| South of Lake Trasimeno | 88 | | |

## Northern Umbria 111–32

| | | | |
|---|---|---|---|
| Umbertide and Around | 112 | Gubbio | 121 |
| Montone | 114 | Down the Via Flaminia | 130 |
| Morra | 114 | Gualdo Tadino | 131 |
| Città di Castello | 115 | Nocera Umbra | 132 |

## The Valle Umbra: Spello to Spoleto 133–64

| | | | |
|---|---|---|---|
| Spello | 134 | Around Montefalco: | |
| Foligno | 139 | Into the Monti Martani | 148 |
| Bevagna | 143 | Trevi and the Tempietto | |
| Montefalco | 145 | del Clitunno | 148 |
| | | Spoleto | 152 |

## The Tiber Valley: Todi, Orvieto, Amelia 165–98

| | | | |
|---|---|---|---|
| Todi | 166 | Hills, Lakes and Gardens | |
| Around Todi | 175 | Around Orvieto | 190 |
| Orvieto | 176 | Amelia | 194 |
| | | Around Amelia | 196 |

## The Valnerinia: Narni to Norcia 199–228

| | | | |
|---|---|---|---|
| Narni | 201 | Cascia | 219 |
| Terni | 208 | Norcia and the Monti Sibellini | 221 |
| Up the Valley and Into the | | | |
| Mountains | 214 | | |

| Language | 229–36 |
| --- | --- |

| Architectural, Artistic and Historical Terms | 237–9 |
| --- | --- |

| Further Reading | 240 |
| --- | --- |

| Index | 241–8 |
| --- | --- |

## Maps and Plans

| Umbria | *inside front* | Spoleto | 153 |
| --- | --- | --- | --- |
| Perugia, Lake Trasimeno, | | The Tiber Valley | 166 |
| and Assisi | 60 | Todi | 169 |
| Assisi | 92–3 | Orvieto | 177 |
| Northern Umbria | 113 | The Valnerinia | 200 |
| The Valle Umbra | 135 | Perugia | *inside back* |

# Introduction

*It realized all my dreams of Italy.*

Samuel Rogers

We've been debating whether or not this book should come with a warning label reading, 'Beware: Umbria can get seriously under your skin.' It happens almost imperceptibly, and you'll probably only realize that you've been bagged when you leave and cross over the border into Lazio, the Marche or even Tuscany: somehow, after Umbria, they seem less solid and reliable, more busy and badgered. The reason for this subtle increase in atmospheric pressure, on the authority of a spiky-haired Turinese motorcyclist who roared into our village one day, is because 'Umbria has best karma in Italy'.

That this little region, the 'Green Heart of Italy', is bewitchingly beautiful has something to do with it. Umbria may not have a coastline, or mountains as spectacular as the Alps or Dolomites, but the gentler charms of its wooded hills, lush valleys and placid lakes—the landscapes of Perugino—are the visual equivalent of the centre of your favourite chocolate. And it comes spiked with art; the regional tourist board claims that Umbria has the densest quantity of works in Italy, and it may even be true. Perugia, Assisi, Orvieto, Gubbio, Spoleto, Città di Castello, Todi and a hundred smaller towns are crammed with ancient, medieval and Renaissance treasures (just don't come here for Baroque or anything later; in much of Umbria, time stopped around 1530). You could even consider the towns themselves as works of art, pink and white dream cities piled on silvery hills of olives and vineyards. There's art in the kitchen, too: no one in this nation of fussy eaters is as fussy or traditional as an Umbrian. You may never get any *nuova cucina*, but the food, even in the cheapest trattorias, is the most consistently delicious and reliable in Italy. For gastronomic enlightenment, Umbrian style, try the fresh truffles, homemade pasta, wild asparagus or a bottle of blood-red Sagrantino di Montefalco.

In spite of all these sensual delights, Umbria's most important contributions to civilization have been spiritual and otherworldly. As the nun on the bus put it, 'Umbria speaks in silences.' It is Italy's cradle of saints and mystics, having produced a baker's dozen or so, including Benedict, the founder of western monasticism, and Francis, the most gentle of spiritual revolutionaries. It is his lingering influence that makes Umbria a centre that holds in the Italian whirlwinds of fashion, fame and political kerfuffles. Isolated from outside influences, the only region neither to touch the sea nor to border another country, Umbria in its miniature time-warp may be conservative in its ways (though not in its politics—its other nickname is 'Red Umbria'), but it is also an immensely kind, sweet-tempered, hospitable, and wise place to be.

## A Few Suggestions

Umbria, with a population of little more 800,000, covers less than three per cent of the total area of Italy. But it manages to fit in a lot of geography in that compact space. 43 per cent of this is forested hills or mountains, and travelling times are longer than you might expect. The Umbria Marche **map** (1:200,000) published by the Touring Club Italiano is a good investment, especially for touring in out-of-the-way spots.

Small as it is, visiting all Umbria from a single base is exhausting, although if that's what you're determined to do, the regional capital **Perugia** is your best bet: besides its central location, Perugia has the most in the way of **public transport**. Don't overlook this, even if you have a car; if you want to spend a day in one of the larger hill towns, relaxing on a bus or train (provided that you get a seat—on trains you can book ahead) and not having to park has distinct advantages, especially in the summer or during a festival.

If this is your first visit to Umbria, a short list of **must-sees** would include the extraordinary art cities of Perugia, Assisi, Spoleto, Orvieto and Gubbio; the Cascate delle Marmore, Italy's most beautiful waterfall (on a Sunday afternoon); a day around Lake Trasimeno (including a visit to Isola Maggiore and an overview from Città della Pieve), and an excursion up to the Piano Grande in the foothills of the Sibilline mountains. A slightly longer list would add Todi, Città di Castello, the Tempietto di Clitunno, Spello, Montefalco, Trevi, Bevagna, Narni, Norcia, the abbey of San Pietro in Valle, and Amelia. But there are dozens of other places that are just as lovely. Besides its old Grand Tourist sites, Umbria is so rich in smaller sites that it lends itself perfectly to micro-tourism, concentrating on the little things around your base (combined with long walks in the lovely countryside, and long lazy Umbrian lunches). The locals are invariably a fount of friendly advice if you want to explore.

## The Best of Umbria

### Roman and Etruscan Sites

**Perugia** (gates, tombs and museum). **Assisi** (Temple of Minerva—only complete Roman temple façade). **Spello** (Roman gates). Roman ruins at **Carsulae** near San Gemini. **Orvieto** (Etruscan tombs).

### Early Medieval Art and Architecture

**Lugnano in Teverina** (Santa Maria Assunta). **Terni** (San Salvatore) and **Ferentillo** (San Pietro in Valle). **Spoleto** (San Pietro, Cathedral, San Salvatore). **Bevagna** (San Salvatore and San Michele). **Foligno** (Cathedral façade and Santa Maria Infraportas). **Tempietto di Clitunno**. **Spello** (Santa Claudio). **Perugia** (Sant'Angelo).

### High Medieval Art and Architecture

**Perugia** (Palazzo dei Priori, Fontana Maggiore, many churches). **Assisi** (great hoard of trecento frescoes in San Francesco, many good churches). The thoroughly medieval city of **Gubbio**.

### Renaissance

Renaissance art somehow seems especially rarefied out in the provinces. **Orvieto** (cathedral frescoes by Angelico and Signorelli). **Città della Pieve** (Perugino). **Perugia** (Pinacoteca, San Bernardino, and others).

### Nature and Scenery

Southern Umbria's **Piano Grande** around **Norcia**, in the shadow of the snow-capped **Monti Sibillini**. Also the **Cascata delle Marmore**, the **Valnerina** north of Arrone and any of the side roads through the mountains.

## Wine

For the best of Umbrian DOC wines, and some of the most ravishing scenery, **Tuoro** and **Passignano** on Lake Trasimeno. **Perugia** (wines: Colli del Trasimeno and Colli Perugini). **Orvieto** (wine: Orvieto Classico).

## Curiosities

The unexpected, unique side of Umbria doesn't jump out at you; you'll have to look for it. **Orvieto**, for one of the world's most remarkable wells, **Pozzo di San Patrizio**, and a dip over the border into Lazio for the **Bomarzo Monster Park**, a Renaissance 'Sacred Wood' full of strange stone creatures. If you're still game, **Terni** for the paintings of **Orneore Metelli**, a shoemaker who never learned the lessons of perspective, and **Ferentillo** up the Valnerina road for the **Chinese and Napoleonic mummies.**

Getting There from the UK and Ireland 2

Getting There from the USA and Canada 4

Passports and
    Customs Formalities 5

Getting Around 6

  By Train 6

  By Coach and Bus 7

  By Taxi 8

# Travel

  By Car 8

  By Motorbike or Bicycle 9

Disabled Travellers 9

Courses for Foreigners and Specialist Holidays 11

## By Air

**Rome** is the closest airport to Umbria, with direct flights from half a dozen British airports, including 14 flights a week from London Stansted on low-price Go Airlines, which can cost as little as £100 return. From London Heathrow or London Gatwick there are several regular Alitalia and British Airways flights to **Milan** connecting with a twice-daily service to Perugia (operated by Alitalia). British Airways also have direct flights from Manchester to Milan. The low-cost airlines Ryanair, Go and Buzz also fly to Milan; fares vary between £90 and £200, but must include a Saturday night stay. Other possibilities include Ryanair's cheap flights to **Ancona** in the Marche, with frequent train links to Umbria, or Meridiana's direct flights from London to **Florence**, or Go's flights to **Bologna**. For train connections from the airports, *see* p.6. Also of interest are Sulga buses (✆ 075 500 9641), which will take you directly from Rome's Fiumicino airport to Perugia in three and half hours.

From Ireland, there are direct flights most weeks from Dublin and Cork on either Alitalia or Aer Lingus to Milan and Rome, from where you can pick up a connecting flight to Perugia. Keep your eye open for bargains and charters in the papers.

The carriers listed below have a variety of **discounts** if booked in advance. Apex fares have fixed arrival and departure dates, and the stay in Italy must include at least one Saturday night. Children under the age of two usually travel free, and both British Airways and Alitalia offer cheaper tickets on some flights for students and those under 26. Alitalia in particular often has promotional perks like rental cars (Jetdrive), or discounts on domestic flights within Italy, on hotels, or on tours. A Superapex return fare (booked at least two weeks in advance) between London and Milan will vary between £120 and £490 (exclusive of tax).

You can find some of the best last-minute bargains of all on the **Internet**. Try *www.lastminute.com, www.travelocity.com* or *www.cheapflights.com.*

### *main carriers*

| | |
|---|---|
| **Alitalia** | London, ✆ 08705 448 259; Dublin, ✆ 01 844 6035, *www.alitalia.co.uk* |
| **British Airways** | General number for the UK, ✆ 0345 222 111, *www.british-airways.com* |
| **Aer Lingus** | Belfast, ✆ 0645 737747; Dublin, ✆ 01 705 3333, *www.aerlingus.ie* |
| **Meridiana** | London, ✆ 020 7839 2222, *www.meridiana.it* |
| **Ryanair** | ✆ 0870 156 9569 or 01 609 7800 from Ireland, *www.ryanair.com* |
| **Go** | ✆ 0845 605 4321, *www.go-fly.com* |
| **Buzz** | ✆ 0870 240 7070, *www.buzzaway.com* |

### *discounts and special deals*

| | |
|---|---|
| **Italflights** | 125 High Holborn, London WC1V 6QA, ✆ 020 7405 6771. |
| **Italia Nel Mondo** | 6 Palace Street, London SW1E 5HY, ✆ 020 7828 9171. |
| **Italy Sky Bus** | 37 Harley Street, London W1N 1DB, ✆ 020 7631 3444. |
| **Italy Sky Shuttle** | 227 Shepherds Bush Road, London W6 7NL, ✆ 020 8748 1333. |
| **Budget Travel** | 154 Lower Baggot Street, Dublin 2, ✆ 01 661 1866. |
| **United Travel** | Stillorgan Bowl, Stillorgan, County Dublin ✆ 01 288 4346. |

Besides saving 25 per cent on regular flights, young people under 26 have the choice of flying on special discount charters.

**USIT Campus Travel**, 52 Grosvenor Gardens SW1, London SW1 0AG, ✆ 020 7730 3402, *www.campustravel.co.uk,* with branches at most UK universities, including: Bristol, ✆ 0117 929 2494; Manchester, ✆ 0161 833 2046; Edinburgh, ✆ 0131 668 3303; Birmingham, ✆ 0121 414 1848; Oxford, ✆ 01865 242 067; Cambridge, ✆ 01223 324 283.

**STA Travel**, 6 Wright's Lane, London W8 6TA, ✆ 020 7361 6161, and many other branches in the UK, including: Bristol, ✆ 0117 929 4399; Leeds, ✆ 0113 244 9212; Manchester, ✆ 0161 834 0668; Oxford, ✆ 01865 792 800; Cambridge, ✆ 01223 366 966.

**USIT**, Aston Quay, Dublin 2, ✆ 01 679 8833. **Ireland**'s largest student travel agent. Cork, ✆ 021 270 900; Belfast, ✆ 01232 324 073; Galway, ✆ 091 565 177; Limerick, ✆ 061 415 064; Waterford, ✆ 051 72601.

**Europe Student Travel**, 6 Campden Street, London W8, ✆ 020 7727 7647 (catering to non-students as well).

## By Train

Note that the train costs more than the cheapest air fares and takes a lot longer. From London's Waterloo Station it's about 19–20 hours by train to Perugia, and you'll have to change trains twice—in Paris and in Rome. The fare is around £280 second class return, £390 first class, travelling by Eurostar on the London–Paris leg of the journey. These trains require reservations and a *couchette*, and if you take along a good book are a fairly painless way of getting there. Order tickets from the **International Rail Centre**, Victoria Station, London SW1, ✆ 0990 848 848; for **Eurostar**, EPS House, Waterloo Station, London SE1, ✆ 0345 881 881.

Discounts are available for senior citizens, families and children, and anyone under 26. Get them from the International Rail Centre (*see* above) and throughout Europe at student offices (CTS in Italy) in main railway stations. If you have a Senior Citizen Railcard, another £5 will get you a Rail Europe Senior Card, good for a discount on fares within Europe. Within Italy itself there are several other discount tickets and passes available for under-26s (*see* p.7), which you can obtain from **Wasteels**, adjacent to Platform 2, Victoria Station, London SW1V 1JT, ✆ 020 7834 7066.

## By Car

Driving to Italy from the UK is a rather lengthy and expensive proposition, and if you're only staying for a short period you should figure your costs against Alitalia's or other airlines' fly-drive scheme. No matter how you cross the Channel, it is a good two-day drive, about 1,600km, from Calais to Perugia. Ferry information is available at any travel agent or direct from the ferry companies. You can cut many of the costly motorway tolls by going from Dover to Calais, through France, to Basle, Switzerland, and then through the Gotthard Tunnel under the Alps; in the summer you can save the steep tunnel tolls by taking one of the passes.

To bring your car into Italy, you need your car registration document (log book), valid driving licence and valid insurance (a Green Card is not necessary, but you'll need one if you go through Switzerland). Make sure everything is in excellent working order or your slightly bald tyre may enrich the coffers of the Swiss or Italian police—it's not uncommon to be stopped for no reason and have your car searched until the police find something to stick a fine on. Also beware that spare parts for some non-Italian cars are difficult to come by, almost impossible for pre-1988 Japanese models.

Foreign-plated cars are no longer entitled to free breakdown service by the **Italian Auto Club** (ACI), but their prices are fair. Phone ACI on ✆ 06 44 77 to find out the current rates. At the time of writing the motorway tunnel tolls are:

**Fréjus Tunnel**, from Modane (France) to Bardonècchia. L30,000–L59,000.

**Gran San Bernardo**, from Bourg St Pierre (Switzerland) to Aosta. Cars L34,000 single, L47,000 return. Motorcycles L19,000 single, L25,000 return.

The **Mont Blanc Tunnel** is still closed indefinitely. There is talk of it reopening in September 2000, but at the time of writing this is not confirmed.

## Getting There from the USA and Canada

*By Air*

Alitalia flies direct to Italy from both the USA and Canada. From the United States there are direct Alitalia and British Airways flights to Rome and Milan, the latter connecting twice daily to Perugia (operated by Alitalia). Your travel agent may find a much cheaper fare from your home airport by way of London, Brussels, Paris, Frankfurt or Amsterdam. There are frequent trains from Rome to Umbria (*see* p.6) and a Sulga bus direct from Fiumicino airport to Perugia, ✆ 075 500 9641.

To be eligible for low-cost or Apex fares you'll have to have fixed arrival and departure dates and spend at least a week in Italy, but no more than 90 days. Superapex, the cheapest normal fares available, must be purchased at least 14 days (or sometimes 21 days) in advance and there are penalties to pay if you change your flight dates. At the time of writing the lowest mid-week Superapex between New York and Milan off-season is around $508, rising to the $900 zone in summer.

To sweeten the deal, Alitalia in particular often has promotional perks like rental cars (Jetdrive), or discounts on domestic flights within Italy, on hotels, or on tours. Ask your travel agent. Children under the age of two usually travel for free and both British Airways and Alitalia offer cheaper tickets on some flights for students and the under-26s.

*major carriers*

| | |
|---|---|
| **Alitalia** | USA, ✆ (800) 223 5730; Canada, ✆ (800) 563 5954. |
| **Lufthansa** | USA, ✆ (800) 645 3880. |
| **Delta** | USA, ✆ (800) 241 414. |
| **Air Canada** | USA, ✆ (888) 247 2262; Canada, ✆ (800) 555 1212. |
| **KLM** | USA, ✆ (800) 374 7747; Canada, ✆ (800) 361 5330. |
| **TWA** | ✆ (800) 892 4141. |
| **British Airways** | USA, ✆ (800) 247 9297; Canada, ✆ (800) 668 1055. |

**New Frontiers**, USA, ✆ (800) 366 6387; Canada, in Montreal, ✆ (514) 526 8444.

**Travel Avenue**, USA, ✆ (800) 333 3335.

**Air Brokers International**, USA, ✆ (800) 883 3273. Discounter.

**Last Minute Travel Club**, USA, ✆ (800) 527 8646. Annual membership fee gets you cheap standby deals.

**Encore Travel Club**, USA, ✆ (800) 444 9800. Scheduled flight discount club.

### student and youth travel

**STA Travel**, in the USA, New York, ✆ (212) 627 3111, or toll-free ✆ (800) 777 0112.

**Council Travel**, 205 East 42nd Street, New York, NY 10017, ✆ (800) 743 1823. Major specialist in student and charter flights; branches all over the USA.

**Travel Cuts**, 187 College Street, Toronto, Ontario M5T 1P7, ✆ (416) 979 2406. Canada's largest student travel specialists; branches in most provinces.

### By Train

*See* above, p.3, for notes on travelling to Italy by train. For information on Italian rail passes and special deals, contact:

**Wasteels**, 5728 Major Boulevard, Suite 308, Orlando, FL 32819, ✆ (407) 351 2537.

**CIT Tours Corporation**, 15 West 44th Street, 10th floor, New York, NY 10036, ✆ (800) 248 7245, 📠 (888) FAX CIT; 1450 City Counsellors, Suite 750, Montreal, Quebec H3A 2E6, ✆ (514) 845 4939; *www.cittours.com* or *www.fs-on-line.com*

## Passports and Customs Formalities

To get into Italy you need a valid passport. EU citizens do not need visas in order to enter Italy. US, Canadian and Australian nationals do not need visas if they are staying for less than three months. If you mean to stay longer than three months in Italy you will have to get a *permesso di soggiorno*. For this you will need to state your reason for staying, be able to prove a source of income and have medical insurance. After a couple of exasperating days at some provincial Questura office filling out forms you should walk out with your permit.

According to Italian law, you must register with the police within eight days of your arrival. If you check into a hotel this is done automatically. If you come to grief in the mesh of rules and forms, you can at least get someone to explain it to you in English by calling the Rome Police Office for visitors, ✆ 06 4686, ext. 2928.

EU nationals over the age of 17 can now import a limitless amount of goods for their personal use. Arrivals from non-EU countries have to pass through Italian Customs which are usually benign, although how the frontier police manage to recruit such ugly, mean-looking characters to hold the submachine guns and drug-sniffing dogs from such a good-looking population is a mystery. However, they'll let you be if you don't look suspicious (sadly, not being Caucasian is often 'suspicious' enough) and aren't carrying more than 150 cigarettes or

75 cigars, or not more than a litre of hard drink or three bottles of wine, a couple of cameras, a movie camera, 10 rolls of film for each, a tape-recorder, radio, record-player, one canoe less than 5.5m, sports equipment for personal use, and one TV (though you'll have to pay for a licence for it at Customs). Pets must be accompanied by a bilingual Certificate of Health from your local veterinary inspector.

US citizens may return with $400-worth of merchandise—keep your receipts. There are no limits to how much money you bring into Italy: legally you may not export more than L400,000 in Italian banknotes, though they rarely check.

## Getting Around

The republic has an excellent network of airports, railways, highways and byways, and you'll find getting around fairly easy—unless one union or another goes on strike (to be fair, this rarely happens during the main holiday season). There's plenty of talk about passing a law to regulate strikes, but don't count on it happening soon. Instead learn to recognize the word in Italian: *sciopero* (SHO-per-o) and be prepared to do as the Romans do when you hear it— quiver with resignation. There's always a day or two's notice in advance, and usually strikes last only 12 or 24 hours—but long enough to throw a spanner in the works if you have to catch a plane. Keep your ears open.

### By Train

*Train information from anywhere in Italy, © 1478 88088, open 7am–9pm, www.fs-on-line.com.*

Trains in Umbria are operated by Italy's national railway, the FS (*Ferrovie dello Stato*) or the FCU (*Ferrovia Centrale Umbra*). A major FS line runs from Rome to Ancona, by way of the major junction of Orte, continuing to Narni, Terni, Spoleto and Foligno (where you can pick up a connection to Assisi or Perugia). If you're approaching Umbria from the north, a few of the slower Milan–Bologna–Florence–Rome trains call at Terontola, where you can change for the secondary line to Lake Trasimeno, Perugia, Assisi, Spello and Foligno; Orvieto and Orte are on the Florence–Rome stretch as well. The FCU for its part links Terni, Todi, Perugia, Umbertide, Città di Castello and Sansepolcro. At some of the sleepier stations without information boards, the imminent presence of a train is signalled by a platform bell.

**Train fares** have increased greatly over the last couple of years and only those without extra supplements can still be called cheap, although at roughly L100 per kilometre, they're very reasonable compared to the UK. You may encounter delays and crowding (especially on Friday nights, at weekends and in the summer). **Reserve a seat** in advance (*fare una preno-tazione*). The fee is small and can save you hours of standing. On the upper echelon trains and the *Eurostars*, reservations are mandatory. Tickets are valid for two months from the date of purchase unless you specify otherwise.

**Tickets** may be purchased not only in the stations but at many travel agents, and it's wise to buy them in advance as the queues can be long. Be sure you ask which platform (*binario*) your train arrives at; the big permanent boards posted in the stations are not always correct. Always remember to stamp your ticket (*convalidare*) in the not-very-obvious machine at the head of the platform before boarding the train. Failure to do so will result in a fine. If you get on a train without a ticket you can buy one from the conductor, with an added 20 per cent penalty. You can also pay a conductor to move up to first class if there are places available.

There is a strict **hierarchy of trains**. A *Regionale* travels shortish distances, and tends to stop at all the stations. There are only a few *Espressi* trains left in service, but they are in poor condition, and mostly service the long runs from the south of Italy. No supplement is required. *Intercity* trains link Italian cities, with minimum stops. Some carry an obligatory seat reservation requirement (free in this case), and all have a supplement. The true kings of the rails are the super-swish and super-fast (Rome–Florence in 1½ hours) *Eurostars* (no relation to the London–Paris service). These make very few stops, have both first and second class carriages, and carry a supplement which includes an obligatory seat reservation on Friday, Saturday, Sunday and holidays. So, the faster the train, the more you pay.

The FS offers several **passes**. A flexible option is the *Flexi Card* (also available through CIT, *see* above) which allows unlimited travel for either four days within a month (L278,800), eight days within a month (L391,100) or 12 days within a month (L501,500), plus supplements and seat reservations on *Eurostars* (all prices quoted are second class). Another ticket, the *Kilometrico*, gives you 3,000 kilometres of travel, made on a maximum of 20 journeys, and is valid for two months (2nd class L214,000, 1st class L350,000 plus supplements); one advantage is that it can be used by up to five people at the same time. However, supplements are payable on *Intercity* trains and *Eurostars*. Other discounts, available only once you're in Italy, are 15 per cent on same-day return tickets and three-day returns (depending on the distance involved), and discounts for families of at least four travelling together. Senior citizens (men 65 and over, women 60) can also get a *Carta d'Argento* ('silver card') for L40,000 entitling them to a 20 per cent reduction in fares. A *Carta Verde* bestows a 20 per cent discount on people under 26 and costs L40,000.

**Refreshments** on routes of any great distance are provided by buffet cars or trolleys; you can usually get sandwiches and coffee from vendors along the tracks at intermediary stops. Station bars often have a good variety of take-away travellers' fare; consider at least investing in a plastic bottle of mineral water, since there's no drinking water on the trains.

Besides trains and bars, Italy's stations offer other facilities. All have a *deposito*, where you can leave your bags for hours or days for a fee. The larger ones have porters (who charge around L5,000 per piece) and luggage trolleys; major stations have an *albergo diurno* ('day hotel', where you can take a shower, get a shave and haircut, etc.), information offices, currency exchanges open at weekends (not at the most advantageous rates, however), hotel-finding and reservation services, kiosks with foreign papers, restaurants, etc. You can also arrange to have a rental car awaiting you at your destination—Avis, Hertz and Maggiore are the firms that provide this service.

## By Coach and Bus

Intercity coach travel is often quicker than train travel, but also a bit more expensive. The Italians aren't dumb; you will find regular coach connections only where there is no train to offer competition. Coaches almost always depart from the vicinity of the train station, and tickets usually need to be purchased before you get on. In many regions they are the only means of public transport and are well used, with frequent schedules. If you can't get a ticket before the coach leaves, get on anyway and pretend you can't speak a word of Italian; the worst that can happen is that someone will make you pay for a ticket. Understand clearly that the base for all country bus lines will be the provincial capitals; we've done our best to explain the connections even for the most out-of-the-way routes.

City buses are the traveller's friend. Most cities label routes well; all charge flat fees for rides within the city limits and immediate suburbs, at the time of writing around L1,500. Bus tickets must always be purchased before you get on, either at a tobacconist's, a newspaper kiosk, in many bars, or from ticket machines near the main stops. Once you get on, you must 'obliterate' your ticket in the machines in the front or back of the bus; controllers stage random checks to make sure you've punched your ticket. Fines for cheaters are about L50,000, and the odds are about 12 to 1 against a check, so you may take your chances against how lucky you feel. If you're good-hearted, you'll buy a ticket and help some over-burdened municipal transit line meet its annual deficit.

## By Taxi

Taxi charges vary from place to place but meters start at around L4,500 plus extras, and add about L1,450 per km. There is a minimum charge of around L7,000. Each piece of baggage will cost extra, and there are surcharges for trips outside the city limits, trips between 10pm and 6am, and trips on Sundays and holidays.

## By Car

The advantages of driving in Umbria generally outweigh the disadvantages. If you just want to tour the region's art cities you'd be best off not driving at all: parking is impossible, traffic impossible, deciphering one-way streets, signals and signs impossible. In nearly every other case, however, a car gives you the freedom and possibility of making your way through Italy's lovely countryside.

Be prepared to encounter some of the highest fuel costs in Europe, to spend a very long time looking for a place to park in any town bigger than a peanut, and to face drivers who look at motoring as if it were a video game. The Italians, whether 21-year-old madcaps or elderly nuns, turn into aggressive starfighters once behind the wheel, whose mission is to reach their destination in a certain allotted time (especially around lunch or dinner, if they think the pasta is already on the boil), regardless of minor nuisances such as other cars, road signs, traffic signals, solid no-passing lines, or blind curves on mountain roads. No matter how fast you trip along on the *autostrade* (Italy's toll motorways, official speed limit 130km/80 miles per hour) someone will pass you going twice as fast.

If you aren't intimidated, buy a good road map of Umbria (the Italian Touring Club produces excellent ones). Many petrol stations close for lunch in the afternoon, and few stay open late at night, though you may find a 'self-service' where you feed a machine nice smooth L10,000 or L50,000 notes. *Autostrada* tolls are high—to drive on the A1 from Milan to Rome will cost you around L60,000 at the time of writing. Most exits now accept credit cards. The rest stops and petrol stations along the motorways are open 24 hours. Other roads—*superstrade* on down through the Italian grading system—are free of charge. The Italians are good about signposting, and roads are almost all excellently maintained. Some highways seem to be built of sheer bravura, suspended on cliffs, crossing valleys on enormous piers—feats of engineering that will remind you, more than almost anything else, that this is the land of the ancient Romans. Beware that you may be fined on the spot for speeding, a burnt-out headlamp, etc.; if you're especially unlucky you may be slapped with a *super multa*, a superfine, of L150,000 or more. You may even be fined for not having a portable triangle danger signal (pick one up at the frontier or from an ACI office for L2500).

The **Automobile Club of Italy** (ACI), while no longer offering a free breakdown service, is a good friend to the foreign motorist. Besides having bushels of useful information and tips, they can be reached from anywhere by calling *C* 116—also use this number if you have an accident, need an ambulance, or simply have to find the nearest service station. If you need major repairs, the ACI can make sure the prices charged are according to their guidelines.

**Hiring a car** is fairly simple if not particularly cheap. Italian car rental firms are called *autonoleggi*. There are both large international firms through which you can reserve a car in advance, and local agencies, which often have lower prices. Air or train travellers should check out possible discount packages. It pays to shop around, as prices vary dramatically.

Most companies will require a deposit amounting to the estimated cost of the hire, and there is 19 per cent VAT added to the final cost. At the time of writing, the cheapest Grade B car costs around L70,000 a day. Petrol is 50 per cent more expensive than in the UK. Rates become more advantageous if you take the car for a week with unlimited mileage. If you need a car for more than three weeks, leasing is a more economic alternative. The National Tourist Office has a list of firms in Italy that hire caravans (trailers) and campers.

### By Motorbike and Bicycle

The means of transport of choice for many Italians, motorbikes, mopeds and Vespas can be a delightful way to get between the cities and see the country-side. You should only consider it, however, if you've ridden them before —Italy's hills and aggravating traffic make it no place to learn. Helmets are compulsory. Hire costs for a *motorino* (moped) range from about L40,000 per day; Vespas (scooters) somewhat more, from about L50,000.

Italians are keen cyclists as well, racing drivers up the steepest hills; if you're not training for the Tour de France, consider the region's hills well before planning a bicycling tour—especially in the hot summer months. Bikes can be transported by train in Italy, either with you or within a couple of days—apply at the baggage office (*ufficio bagagli*). Hire prices range from about L20,000 per day; to buy one costs upwards of L250,000, either in a bike shop or through the local classifieds. Alternatively, if you bring your own bike, do check with the airline to see what their policy is on transporting it.

## Disabled Travellers

Recent access-for-all laws in Italy have improved the once dire situation: the number of ramps and stair lifts has increased a hundredfold in the past few years, and nearly every hotel has one or two rooms with facilities for the disabled—although the older ones don't have a lift, or not one large enough for a chair. Although service stations on the *autostrade* have equipped rest rooms, you could get very stuck in the middle of a city. Florence, visited by zillions of tourists, notoriously lacked accessible loos for years although the situation is now improving. Local tourist offices are helpful, and have been known to find a pusher on the spot, while the National Tourist Office can offer suggestions on hill towns that are particularly difficult to get around. Some will tire out the fittest tourist. Italian churches are a problem unto themselves. Long flights of steps in front were designed to impress on the would-be worshipper the feeling of going upwards to God—another raw deal for the disabled.

### some specialist organizations in Italy

**CO.IN** (Consorzio Cooperative Integrate), Via Enrico Giglioli 54a, 00169 Rome, ✆ 06 232 67504, ✉ 06 232 67505, has a tourist information centre (*open Mon–Fri 9–5*) which offers advice and information on accessibility.

**Centro Studi Consulenza Invalidi,** Via Gozzadini 7, 20148 Milan, publishes an annual guide, *Vacanze per Disabili,* with details of suitable accommodation in Italy.

**Vacanze Serene,** ✆ 800 271 027 (toll-free number), gives information on accessibility throughout Italy (*open Mon–Fri 9–5*).

### some specialist organizations in the UK

**Holiday Care Service,** 2nd floor, Imperial Buildings, Victoria Road, Horley, Surrey RH6 9HW, ✆ 01293 774 535, for travel information and details of accessible accommodation and care holidays.

**RADAR** (Royal Association for Disability and Rehabilitation), 12 City Forum, 250 City Road, London EC1V 8AF, ✆ 020 7250 3222, publishes a guide to *European Holidays and Travel* (£5).

**Royal National Institute for the Blind**, 224 Great Portland Street, London W1N 6AA, ✆ 020 7388 1266, can advise on all aspects of travelling abroad; also organizes short trips to the Continent with Travelsphere: for more details call Carol Lambert, the RNIB holiday adviser.

**Tripscope**, Alexandra House, Albany Road, Brentford, Middlesex TW8 0NE, ✆ 0345 585 641, offers limited practical advice and information on every aspect of travel and transport for elderly and disabled travellers. On request, information can be provided by letter or tape.

### some specialist organizations in the USA and Canada

**American Foundation for the Blind**, 11 Penn Plaza, Suite 300, New York, NY 10001, ✆ (212) 502 7600; toll free, ✆ (800) AFB LINE, is the best source of information in the USA for visually impaired travellers.

**Mobility International USA**, PO Box 3551, Eugene, OR 97403, ✆ (541) 343 1284, ✉ (541) 343 6812, *info@niusa.org*, organizes educational and study programmes for disabled travellers abroad; $35 membership fee.

**SATH** (Society for the Advancement of Travel for the Handicapped), 347 5th Avenue, Suite 610, New York, NY 10016, ✆ (212) 725 8253, offers advice on all aspects of travel for the disabled, on an ad hoc basis for a $3 charge, or unlimited to members ($45, concessions $25).

**Travel Information Service**, Moss Rehab Hospital, 1200 West Tabor Road, Philadelphia, PA 19141, ✆ (215) 456 9600, has a telephone information service supplying travel advice to people with disabilities.

The **Italian Institute**, 39 Belgrave Square, London SW1X 8NX, ✆ 020 7235 1461, or 686 Park Avenue, New York, NY 10021, ✆ (212) 889 4057, is the main source of information on courses for foreigners in Italy. Graduate students should also contact their nearest Italian consulate to find out about scholarships—apparently many go unused each year because no one knows about them.

One obvious course to take, especially in this linguistically pure land of Dante, is **Italian language and culture**: there are special summer classes offered by the Università per Stranieri in **Perugia** (Palazzo Gallenga, Piazza Fortebraccio 4, 57461 Perugia, ✆ 075 574 6211, ✉ 075 574 5213), with special classes in August for teachers of Italian.

**Art lovers** can take a course on medieval art in **Spoleto** at the Centro Italiano Studi di Alto Medioevo, in the Palazzo Ancaiani, ✆ 0743 23271, held in April. **Perugia**'s Accademia delle Belle Arti Pietro Vanucci, Piazza San Francesco al Prato 5, ✆ 075 573 0631, ✉ 075 573 0632, has painting and sculpture courses.

### *specialist tour operators in the UK*

A selection of specialist companies are listed below. Not all of them are necesssarily ABTA-bonded; we recommend you check before booking.

**Magic of Italy**, 227 Shepherds Bush Road, London W6 7AS, ✆ 020 8748 2661. Tailor-made breaks in 3–5-star luxury hotels, self-catering villas and converted farmhouses.

**Abercrombie & Kent**, Sloane Square House, Holbein Place, London SW1W 8NS, ✆ 020 7730 9600. Has a range of 4–5-star deluxe hotels.

**Brompton Travel**, Brompton House, 64 Richmond Road, Kingston-upon-Thames, Surrey KT2 5EH, ✆ 020 8549 3334. Reliable travel agents: can organize tailor-made trips and city breaks; also package holidays etc.

**Citalia**, Marco Polo House, 3–5 Lansdowne Road, Croydon CR9 1LL, ✆ 020 8686 5533. Tailor-made breaks in Umbria, self-catering flats etc.

**Kirker**, 3 New Concordia Wharf, Mill Street, London SE1 2BB, ✆ (020) 7231 3333. Short breaks and tailor-made tours; can also arrange internal rail travel and any length of stay.

**Martin Randall Travel**, 10 Barley Mow Passage, Chiswick, London W4 4PH, ✆ 020 8742 3355. 4–10-day tailor-made cultural tours for groups of up to 22: focusing on art, architecture, archaeology, gardens and music, led by expert guides.

**Andante Travels**, The Old Telephone Exchange, Winterborne Dauntsey, Salisbury SP4 6EH, ✆ 01980 610 555. 'Romantic ruins in rural Italy': 5-day tour of Tuscany and Umbria's most important Etruscan archaeological sites, art and architecture.

**Italiatour**, Unit 9, Whyteleafe Business Village, Whyteleafe Hill, Surrey CR3 0AT, ✆ 01883 623 363. All-inclusive tours staying in everything from farmhouses to castles.

**Prospect Music & Art**, 36 Manchester Street, London W1M 5PE, ✆ 020 7486 5705, ✉ 020 7486 5868. 'Hill Towns of Umbria': lavish 8-day guided art, architecture, music and archaeology tour taking in Rome, Orvieto, Perugia, Urbino and flying back from Bologna; 4-star accommodation.

**ATG**, 69–71 Banbury Road, Oxford OX2 6PE, ✆ 01865 310 399. Features two escorted walking tours for groups of 16 or less: 'Unknown Umbria' (over the Piano Grande) and 'Ways to Assisi' taking in Todi and Orvieto. All tours are fully escorted and led by expert guides staying in 3-star hotels.

**Sherpa Expeditions**, 131a Heston Road, Hounslow, Middlesex TWR 0RD, ✆ 020 8577 2717, ✉ 020 8572 9788, *www.sherpa-walking-holidays.co.uk.* 4–7-day walking and cycling holidays throughout Tuscany and Umbria, taking in mountains and coast.

**Arblaster & Clarke Wine Tours**, 104 Church Road, Steep, Petersfield, Hants GU32 2PD, ✆ 01730 893 344, *www.winetours.co.uk.* Organizes a Tuscany and Umbria wine tour in October, visiting the Arnaldo Caprai wine estate and the Lungarotti wine museum in Torgiano.

**British Museum Tours**, 46 Bloomsbury Street, London WC1B 3QQ, ✆ 020 7323 8895. Organizes a 10-day Tuscany and Umbria art history tour in October staying in 3–4-star accommodation: tours led by curators from the museum.

**Special Tours**, 81a Elizabeth Street, London SW1W 9PG, ✆ 020 7730 2297. Escorted cultural tours and private visits to houses and gardens in Umbria. For National Art Collections Fund members only.

### *specialist tour operators in the USA/Canada*

The Italian Tourist Office in New York can provide an extensive list of specialist tour operators. Here is a selection:

**American Express Vacations**, 300 Pinnacle Way, Norcross, GA 30093, ✆ (800) 241 1700. Tailor-made tours to Perugia, etc.

**Archaeological Tours Inc.**, Suite 904, 271 Madison Avenue, New York, NY 11116, ✆ (212) 986 3054. Tours of Etruscan sites in Tuscany and Umbria taking in Orvieto and Perugia, led by Professor Larissa Bonfante from NYU.

**Italiatour**, 666 5th Avenue, New York, NY 10103, ✆ (212) 765 2183. Fly-drive.

**Maupintour**, 1471 Research Park Drive, Suite 300, Lawrence, KS 66047, ✆ (785) 843 1211. Fully escorted 12–18-day tours; deluxe accommodation, meals included.

**Stay and Visit Italy**, 5506 Connecticut Avenue NW, Suite 23, Washington, DC 20015, ✆ (202) 237 5220/✆ (800) 411 3728, ✉ (202) 966 6972. Tailor-made tours throughout Umbria.

| | |
|---|---|
| Climate and When to Go | 14 |
| Festivals | 14 |
| Food and Drink | 17 |
| Embassies and Consulates | 22 |
| Insurance and Health | 22 |
| Lavatories | 22 |
| Money and Banks | 22 |
| Official Holidays | 23 |
| Opening Hours and Museums | 24 |

# Practical A–Z

| | |
|---|---|
| Packing | 24 |
| Photography | 25 |
| Police Business | 25 |
| Post Offices | 25 |
| Purchasing a House | 35 |
| Telephones | 26 |
| Shopping | 26 |
| Sports and Activities | 27 |
| Tourist Information | 28 |
| Where to Stay | 28 |

## Climate and When to Go

The climate in Umbria is temperate, but considerably cooler up in the mountains; the higher Apennines have enough snow to support skis until April. Summers are hot and humid; in August most city dwellers hand their cities over to the tourist (even the good restaurants tend to close) and seek relief by the sea or in the mountains. Spring days, especially in the month of May, when it (usually) rains less, are pleasantly warm, and the fields are brimming with wildflowers. Autumn, too, is a classic time to visit, in October and November; before the winter rains begin and the air is clear, the colours of the countryside are brilliant and rare, with red and yellow highlights. The hills of Umbria are always beautiful, but in October they're extraordinary.

Winter can be an agreeable time to visit the indoor attractions of the cities and avoid crowds; it seldom snows but may rain for several days at a time. Umbria is not called the Green Heart of Italy for its arid climate, and it can be hung over with mists for weeks at a time, which, depending on how one looks at it, can be terribly romantic or a big bore. The mountains also get a considerable amount of rain, with 80–120mm in a year.

### Average temperatures in °C (°F)

|         | January | April   | July    | October |
|---------|---------|---------|---------|---------|
| Perugia | 5 (40)  | 11 (52) | 24 (75) | 13 (55) |
| Terni   | 5 (40)  | 13 (55) | 25 (77) | 15 (59) |

### Average monthly rainfall in millimetres (inches)

|         | January | April  | July    | October |
|---------|---------|--------|---------|---------|
| Perugia | 60 (3)  | 70 (3) | 30 (1)  | 115 (4) |
| Terni   | 68 (3)  | 85 (3) | 43 (2)  | 123 (5) |

## Festivals

Although festivals in Umbria are often more show than spirit (though there are several exceptions to the rule), they can be very lively. Some are great costume affairs, with roots dating back to the Middle Ages, and there are quite a few music festivals, antique fairs, and, most of all, festivals devoted to food and drink. Dates vary, so be sure to ring the local tourist offices to check (*see* relevant chapters for phone numbers). The following is a calendar of the major events.

### January

| 24 | Feast of San Feliciano, with a traditional fair, **Foligno** |
| 27 | Feast of Sant'Emiliano, with a procession of lights, **Trevi** |

### February

| *changeable date* | International gastronomic festival of the black truffle, **Norcia** |
| | Olive and *bruschetta* festival, **Spello**, with a parade of olive-pickers and garlic toast feast, all to traditional music |

| Carnival | Celebrated in private parties nearly everywhere |
| 14 | St Valentine's Day, with a fair, music and fireworks, **Terni** |
| End of month | Truffle and Valnerina food fair, **Norcia** |

## March

| Holy Week | Religious rites, torchlight processions, etc., **Assisi** |
| | Umbria jazz, gospel and soul music festival, **Terni** |
| Holy Thursday | Trial of Jesus and re-enactment of Passion of Christ, **Sigillo** (Perugia) |
| Good Friday | Evening procession and Passion of the Dead Christ, a 13th-century tradition accompanied by ancient penitential chants, **Gubbio** |
| | Procession of the Dead Christ, dating from the 16th century, **Bevagna** |

## April

| First 3 weeks | Huge antiques fair, **Todi** |
| 15 April–15 May | *Cantamaggio*, parade of illuminated floats, **Terni** |
| 30 April–5 May | Feast of San Pellegrino, with the marriage of trees, near **Gualdo Tadino** |
| End of month | *Corso dell'Anello*, medieval ring tournament, **Narni** |
| | National antiques fair, **Bastia Umbra** |
| Late April–mid May | *Cantamaggio*, parade of illuminated floats, **Terni** |

## May

| First week | *Calendimaggio*, May Day celebrations, **Assisi** |
| | Kite festival, even-numbered years only, **Castiglione del Lago** |
| 15 | *Corso dei Ceri*, race of tower shrines, **Gubbio** |
| 17–21 | *Giostro della Quintana*, medieval joust, **Foligno** |
| 21–22 | Feast of Santa Rita, **Cascia** |
| Last Sunday | *Palio della Balestra*, crossbow competition against Sansepolcro, in medieval costume, **Gubbio** |
| Pentecost | *La Palombella*, **Orvieto** (*see* p.181) |
| Late May–early June | Processions, **Orvieto** |
| (1st Sun after Corpus Domini) | Flower carpets in the streets, **Spello** |

## June

| June–July | International ceramics competition, **Gualdo Tadino** |
| 2nd half of June | *Corso del Bove*, **Montefalco**; *Mercato della Gaite*, old-fashioned fair, **Bevagna** |
| June–July | Festival of the Two Worlds, **Spoleto** |
| Sun nearest 21st | *L'Infiorata*, flower festival, **Città della Pieve** |
| End June | Umbria Jazz Festival, **Perugia** and **Terni** |
| End June–early July | *Festa delle Acque*, with fireworks, **Piediluco** |

## July

| | |
|---|---|
| *All month* | **Gubbio** festival, with classical plays and concerts |
| *3rd Sunday* | *Palio delle Barche*, boat race in medieval costume, **Passignano** |

## August

| | |
|---|---|
| *All month* | Folkloric and religious festivals, **Assisi** |
| *First 3 weeks* | **Corciano** festival, with theatres and concerts |
| *Aug–Sept* | **Todi** festival, with music, ballet, film, culture |
| | Experimental opera festival, **Spoleto** |
| *14* | *Palio dei Quartieri*, flag-tossing and crossbow contest, **Gubbio** |
| *15* | *Palio dei Terzieri,* archery contests and costumes, **Città della Pieve** |
| *Late Aug–Sept* | Chamber music festival, **Città di Castello** |
| | Sacred music festival, **Perugia** |

## September

| | |
|---|---|
| *2 weeks* | Festival of Peace, **Assisi** |
| *All month* | Baroque music and theatre festival, **Foligno** |
| *2nd Sunday* | Crossbow contest with Gubbio in **Sansepolcro** |
| *2nd and 3rd Sun* | *Giostra della Quintana*, jousts in **Foligno** |
| *2nd week* | National horse festival, **Città di Castello** |
| *14–15* | San Manno fair, **Foligno** |
| *22–24* | Festival of the Portals, re-enactment in costume of historical events, **Gualdo Tadino** |
| *Late Sept–early Oct* | *Giostra dell'Arme,* jousting and fine dining, **San Gemini** |

## October

| | |
|---|---|
| *All month* | Eurochocolate festival, **Perugia** |
| *1* | *Palio dei terzieri*, historical parade and cart race, **Trevi** |
| *3–4* | Feast of San Francesco, religious and civic rites, **Assisi** |
| *31 Oct–2 Nov* | *Festa del Bosco,* a festival of edibles from the woods, **Montone** |
| *Oct/Nov* | Antiquarian festival, **Perugia** |

## November

| | |
|---|---|
| *First week* | *Fiera dei Morti*, big fair at the Pian di Massiano, **Perugia** |
| *11* | Feast of San Martino, with wine and chestnuts, **Sigillo** |
| *2nd weekend* | Truffle festival, **Città di Castello** |
| *24* | Offering of candles, with processions in 14th-century costume, **Amelia** |

## December

| | |
|---|---|
| *Last 2 weeks* | 'World's largest Christmas tree', **Gubbio** |
| *24* | Christmas cribs and Franciscan rites, **Assisi** |
| *29–early Jan* | Umbria Jazz Winter, with music and bands, **Orvieto** |

In Italy, the three Ms (the Madonna, Mamma and *Mangiare*) are still a force to be reckoned with, and, in a country where millions of otherwise sane people spend much of their waking hours worrying about their digestion, standards at home and in restaurants are understandably high. Everybody is a gourmet, or at least thinks he or she is, and food is not only something to eat but a subject approaching the heights of philosophy—two Umbrian businessmen once overheard on a train heatedly discussed mushrooms for over *four hours*. Although ready-made pasta, tinned minestrone and frozen pizza in the *supermercato* tempt the virtue of the Italian cook, few give in (although many a working mother wishes she could at times).

Regional traditions are strong in Italy, not only in dialect but in the kitchen. Umbrians are no exception and firmly maintain their distinctive cuisine even when you really wish they wouldn't—especially in the case of bread, described by astonished visitors as 'tasty as chewy water' and 'scarcely distinguishable from a cricket bat'. It often comes stamped with the name of the bakery on it, like a brick. First, though, a few general comments on eating in Italy.

### Eating Out

In Italy the various types of restaurants—*ristorante*, *trattoria* or *osteria*—have been confused. A *trattoria* or *osteria* can be just as elaborate as a restaurant, though rarely is a *ristorante* as informal as a traditional *trattoria*. Unfortunately the old habit of posting menus and prices in the windows has fallen from fashion, so it's often difficult to judge variety or prices. Remember that the fancier the fittings, the fancier the bill, though neither of these points has anything at all to do with the quality of the food. If you're uncertain, do as you would at home—look for lots of locals.

### prices

When you eat out, mentally add to the bill (*conto*) the bread and cover charge (*pane e coperto*, usually L1500–3000) and a 10 per cent service charge. This is often included in the bill (*servizio compreso*); if not, it will say *servizio non compreso*, and you'll have to do your own arithmetic. Additional tipping is at your own discretion, but never do it in family-owned and -run places.

Prices quoted for meals in this book are for an average complete meal, Italian-style with wine, for one person.

| | |
|---|---|
| ***very expensive*** | over L90,000 |
| ***expensive*** | L60,000–90,000 |
| ***moderate*** | L40,000–60,000 |
| ***inexpensive*** | below L40,000 |

People who haven't visited Italy for years and have fond memories of eating full meals for under a pound will be amazed at how much prices have risen; though in some respects eating out in Italy is still a bargain, especially when you figure out how much all that wine would have cost you at home. In many places you'll often find restaurants offering a *menu turistico*—full, set meals of usually meagre inspiration for L20–25,000. Good, imaginative chefs often offer a *menu degustazione*—a set-price gourmet meal that allows you to taste their daily specialities and seasonal dishes. Both of these are cheaper than if you ordered the same food à *la carte*. When you leave a restaurant you will be given a receipt (*ricevuto fiscale*) which, according to Italian law, you must take with you out of the door and carry for at least 300 metres. If you aren't given one, it means the restaurant is probably fudging its taxes and thus offering you lower prices. There is a slim chance the tax police may have their eye on you and the restaurant; if you don't have a receipt they could slap you with a heavy fine.

### meals

**Breakfast** (*prima colazione*) in Italy is no lingering affair, but an early morning wake-up shot to the brain: a *cappuccino*, a *caffè latte* (white coffee), or a *caffè lungo* (a generous portion of espresso), accompanied by a croissant-type roll, called a *cornetto* or *briosce*. This can be consumed in nearly any bar, and repeated during the morning as often as necessary, which is why breakfast in most Italian hotels is no big deal and seldom worth the price charged.

**Lunch** or *pranzo*, generally served around 1pm, is the most important meal of the day for the Italians, with a minimum of a first course (*primo*—any kind of pasta dish, broth or soup, or rice dish or pizza), a second course (*secondo*—a meat or fish dish, accompanied by a *contorno* or side dish—usually a vegetable, salad or potatoes), followed by fruit or dessert and coffee. You can, however, begin with a platter of *antipasti*—the appetizers Italians do so brilliantly, ranging from warm seafood delicacies to raw ham (*prosciutto crudo*), salami in a hundred varieties, lovely vegetables, savoury toasts, olives, pâté, and many, many more. There are restaurants that specialize in *antipasti*, and they usually don't take it amiss if you decide to forget the pasta and meat and just nibble on these scrumptious hors d'œuvres (though in the end it will probably cost as much as a full meal). Most Italians accompany their meal with wine and mineral water (*acqua minerale*, with or without bubbles, *con* or *senza gas*, which supposedly aids digestion), and conclude it with a *digestivo* (liqueur).

**Dinner**, *cena*, is usually eaten at around 8pm. This is much the same as *pranzo* although lighter, without the pasta; often a *piatto unico*, a pizza and beer, omelette, or a fish dish. In restaurants, however, Italians often order all the courses, so if you have only a sandwich for lunch you have a full meal in the evening.

### specialities of Umbria

Umbria's cooking is simple, honest, hearty and excellent. It may not officially rank among the great culinary regions of Italy, but it rarely disappoints, either; it is not elaborate but the local ingredients are very good—in the case of truffles, they are transcendent. Although Umbria boasts one of Italy's top gourmet restaurants in Baschi, on the whole the region is gastronomically conservative and not so sure about this new-fangled *cucina nuova*, much less the *cucina* from anywhere else in Italy, and even less anything non-Italian. This devotion to Umbrian food can reach astonishing proportions: Umbrian teenagers on their summer language courses in England who had to be flown home after two days because they were starving to death; adventurous Umbrian diners who dared to enter a Chinese restaurant, but could only eat the rice; our Umbrian landlord who went to Dalmatia on his honeymoon, found the pasta overcooked and returned to Terni, swearing he would never leave again as long as he lived.

Umbria produces excellent olive oil, which it now treats like wine, divided into several growing regions. It grows wheat, which it makes into delicious fresh pasta as well as dried pasta sold nationwide (Buitoni is one of several firms in Perugia). It is known for its game dishes, especially wild boar, its wild mushrooms (best April–June and October–November) and various kinds of cold cuts made from the acorn-fed pigs of Norcia, so renowned that all over Italy a pork butcher is known as a *norcino*. But because of the long centuries of poverty, many specialities were born of thrift; some of these have died out, while others have become trendy.

Dense, heavy, salt-free Umbrian bread, potential murder weapon that it is, has the one great virtue of being made to order for *bruschetta*, a favourite **antipasto** now made familiar by Italian restuarants around the world, although in Umbria it seems to taste best, grilled over an open fire, covered with the region's exquisite olive oil and rubbed with garlic; a fancier version has chopped tomatoes and basil. For any special occasion, out come the *crostini*, thin slices of toast with a piquant pâté spread of chicken livers (or spleen), or anchovies, capers and lemons, or truffles with mayonnaise. The other traditional Umbrian *antipasto* is a platter (*afettati*) of prosciutto, salami, sliced stuffed rabbit and *capocollo* (cured neck of pork, rolled in pepper).

Umbrians are more than fond of their **pasta**, with good reason—*tagliatelle ai funghi* (with wild porcini mushrooms), or *ai tartufi* (with grated truffles); *tortellini con panna* (with cream sauce); *ciriole* or *pici* or *umbricelli or trangozzi* (various names for fat, home-made spaghetti) with various sauces, of which wild asparagus (*asparago salvatico*) holds pride of place in May and June (it's also excellent in omelettes). Other pasta sauces you may see are *sugo alle rigaglie*, made of chicken livers and other innards, with onion and parsley, or *alla Ternana* (a rich tomato sauce with pecorino cheese), or *all'amatriciana*, from nearby Rieti province, made with tomatoes, bacon, black pepper and pecorino, or its close cousin, *spaghetti col rancetto*, from Spoleto. In autumn many restaurants serve *pappardelle al cinghiale*, thick pasta with a rich sauce made from wild boar, red wine, juniper berries, tomatoes and so on. In northern Umbria look for *strascinati*, homemade macaroni served with sausage, eggs, and cheese; Amelia is famous for its *manfricoli all'arrabbiata*, homemade pasta with a spicy hot tomato sauce. The real test of an Umbrian chef is eggs with truffles, a difficult dish to time correctly but superb when successful; risotti with truffles or mushrooms are also delicious.

Menus usually include some kind of **soup**. Spelt (*farro*) was long regarded as a poor man's wheat, but now is specially cultivated organically for its authentic taste in minestrone; the lentils of Castellucio, once regarded as a poor kind of protein, are now in demand (in Umbria they make them into a soup with garlic, celery and olive oil). Another soup, one you're more likely to see in a home than in a restaurant, is *pancotto*, made of stale bread, olive oil, tomatoes, onions and often peppers, served cold in the summer. You may also see *baggiana*, a soup of fava beans, tomatoes and basil (especially in the north) or the archetypal *pasta con ceci*.

The average restaurant in Umbria rarely offers exceptional **secondi**. Most Umbrians are content with grilled chops, salad and fried potatoes. The meats—lamb, pork or veal—are of fine quality, especially the lamb, often served in a pile of small chops with a lemon (*agnello alla scottadito*: 'finger burning lamb'). *Fritto misto* is an interesting alternative, where lamb chops, liver, sweetbreads, artichokes and courgettes (*zucchini*) are dipped in batter and deep-fried. Otherwise look for *arista di maiale* (pork loin with rosemary and garlic), *anatra* (duck, often served with truffles), *piccione* (stuffed wild pigeon), *palombe* (wood pigeon), or *cinghiale* (boar)—either in sausages or *stufato* (stewed) or *alla cacciatora*. Umbrians are rather too fond of their *girarrosto*, a great spit of tiny song birds and pork livers. The one chicken dish the region is famous for is Orvieto's *gallina ubriaca*, 'drunken' in white wine and slowly cooked with raw ham, tomatoes, and garlic.

In landlocked Umbria, **fish** is rare outside the fancy restaurants that have it brought in daily from the coast, although you can usually get trout and occasionally crayfish (*gamberi*) especially in the Valnerina and by Lake Piediluco. A couple of restaurants by Lake Trasimeno specialize in the lake's tench, perch, eel and carp. You'll have to be lucky or persistent, however, to find the classsic *regina alla porchetta* (a big carp, stuffed with garlic, fennel and lard, wrapped in rosemary, tied up with reeds and roasted on a spit or more often baked in the oven). The thick local fish soup, *tegamaccio*, is made with onions, garlic, and lots of tomatoes.

Umbria is not known for its **cheese**, but its best, the fresh ewe's milk *caciotto*, comes from Norcia and is often on sale in the *norcinerie*; another is tangy pecorino, made by the Sard shepherds who immigrated to the region. Although most Umbrians prefer fruit to sweet desserts, they have no lack of **sweets** for other times of the day, and especially for special occasions and holidays. Typical sweets include Perugia's *torciglione*, shaped like a coiled serpent, made of flour and almond paste; Terni's *panpepato* (a rich, spicy, dense cake full of nuts and candied fruit); *frappe* or *cenci* or *strufoli* (deep-fried strips of dough, served with honey, lemon rind or sugar, made for carnival), *castagnaccio* (chestnut cake, with pine nuts, raisins and rosemary), *crostate* (fruit tarts), *torcolo* (ring-shaped cake with pine nuts and candied fruit, or perhaps a *gelato ai Baci* (made with Perugia's famous hazelnut chocolates). In Assisi, the shops sell *rocciata*, a spicy strudel filled with a mixture of almonds, walnuts, prunes, figs, raisins and honey, and *pane di San Francesco*, a hard cake made with pine nuts, currants, honey and aniseed. *Tozzetti*, made with aniseed and almonds, are favourite *vin santo* dunkers.

### picnics, snacks and porchetta

There are several alternatives to sit-down meals. Little shops selling pizza by the slice (*pizza al taglio*) are common in city centres; some, called *gastronomie*, offer other take-out delicacies as well. At any delicatessen (*pizzicheria*), grocer's (*alimentari*) or market (*mercato*) you can buy the materials for picnics; some places in the smaller towns will make the sandwiches for you. Common snacks you'll encounter include *panini* of cheese, tomatoes and prosciutto (or other meats); and *tramezzini*, little sandwiches on plain, square white bread that are always much better than they look. In and around Perugia the favourite snack is *torta al testa*, a pizza-like flat bread cooked on a hot stove, filled with prosciutto or sausage or cheese.

The traditional sandwich of Umbria, however, is nothing so dainty, but a hard roll filled with fat slices of warm *porchetta* (roast whole pig stuffed with fennel and garlic and pepper, complete with all the fat and gristle). Often it is *girarrosto* (cooked on a spit) or roast in the oven. You can often find it in the *norcinerie*, or in roadside vans. The fact that these roadside vans resemble those used by itinerant prostitutes has led at least one near-sighted hungry Umbrian into a comedy of errors, but you really do have to try hard to confuse them.

### Wine in Umbria

Most Italian wines are named after the grape and the district they come from. If the label says DOC (*Denominazione di Origine Controllata*) it means that the wine comes from a specially defined area and was produced according to a certain traditional method; DOCG (the G stands for *Garantita*) means that a high quality is also guaranteed—a badge worn only by the noblest wines. *Classico* means that a wine comes from the oldest part of the zone of production; *Riserva*, or *Superiore*, means a wine has been aged longer.

Umbria has been a wine region ever since the Etruscans planted the first cuttings from the Greeks, but through much of its history the main concern was to produce wine rather than good wine. The naturally fertile soil brought forth luxuriant vines, which were often planted alongside outcrops and simply trained over the trees. The one exception to the generally mediocre plonk was the still-reigning king of Umbrian vines, **Orvieto** and **Orvieto Classico**, a delicate wine, dry with a slightly bitter aftertaste; Orvieto Classico comes from the old *zona* around the Paglia river.

Orvieto, like nearly all of Umbria's wine, is a blend that flies in the face of modern trends towards single varietal wines. The white grapes of Umbria are *grechetto* (according to legend, introduced by the ancient Greeks), *trebbiano toscano* and the great Byzantine *malvasia*; reds, which have radically improved in the last two decades, are predominantly *sangiovese, sagrantino* and *ciliegiolo*. Even the excellent **Sagrantino di Montefalco**, recently elevated to DOCG status, has lots of *sangiovese* in it; it comes as the dry, garnet Sagrantino, with the aroma of blackberries, or the sweet Sagrantino Passito, made from raisins. Adanti, one of the top makers, also produces a dry, velvety *rosso*; other names of repute are Rocca di Fabbri, Decio Fongoli, Arnaldo Caprai, Antonelli, Val di Maggio and Scaccia Diavoli.

Among the finest and most innovative DOC wines are those of **Torgiano**, from a small zone near the village south of Perugia; it produces magnificent dry, full-bodied reds that can take years of ageing, especially its famous Rubesco di Torgiano (*sangiovese, montepulciano, canaiolo* and *ciliegiolo*), and the light and lively Torre di Giano, made of *trebbiano* and *grechetto*.

Umbria's other DOC wines are grown on the western hills of the region; most are very drinkable, and many are economical as well. **Colli del Trasimeno** wines come from the hills around Umbria's largest lake (a garnet, slightly tannic red wine and deep, straw-coloured, dry and mellow whites); **Colli Perugini** from the hills of Perugia (dry ruby red, fruity light white, and a dry, intense rosé); **Colli Amerini**, from the Amelia region (the three primary colours, with very good blended reds, a not terribly exciting Novella or new wine, and Malvasia); the **Colli Martiri** between Montefalco and Todi (light reds and aged *riservas*, and whites based on *grechetto*); and **Colli Altotiberini** from around Umbertide (a pleasant dry white, reds based on *sangiovese* and merlot, and a pale, fresh rosé).

One of the more unusual wines is the dessert wine **Vernaccia di Cannara**; only made in Cannara, it's unlike every other vernaccia in Italy, in that it's red. The most famous dessert wine in the region, however, is **vin santo**, a rich, deep, unctious golden wine made from semi-dried grapes; it's sweet and strong (14 per cent), and holy only because priests are so fond of it. Although some producers make it commercially, the best is still homemade in small quantities; you know you're in with the locals when they serve you a glass from their precious cache, with the traditional hard biscuit or crunchy waffle (*cialde*). It's best to stop there; Umbria's Tartufo, even though made from truffles, tastes even worse than medicine.

## Embassies and Consulates

| | |
|---|---|
| **UK:** | Via XX Settembre 80a, Rome, ✆ 06 482 5441. |
| | Lungarno Corsini 2, Florence, ✆ 055 284 133. |
| **Ireland:** | Largo Nazareno 3, Rome, ✆ 06 697 9121. |
| **USA:** | Via Vittorio Veneto 121a, Rome, ✆ 06 487 0235 or 4788 8629. |
| | Lungarno Amerigo Vespucci 38, Florence, ✆ 055 239 8276. |
| **Canada:** | Via Zara 30, Rome, ✆ 06 440 3028. |
| **Australia:** | Via Alessandria 215, Rome, ✆ 06 85 2721. |
| **New Zealand:** | Via Zara 28, Rome, ✆ 06 440 2928. |

## Insurance and Health

**Emergencies, ✆ 113**

You can insure yourself against almost any mishap—cancelled flight, stolen or lost baggage, and medical bills—for a price. While national health services in the UK and Australia have reciprocal health care agreements with Italy (pack a stamped E-111 form), others should check their current policies to see if they cover you while abroad, and under what circumstances, and judge whether you need a special traveller's insurance policy. Travel agencies sell policies, as well as insurance companies, but they are not cheap.

Minor illnesses and problems that crop up in Italy can usually be handled free of charge in a public hospital clinic or *ambulatorio*. If you need minor aid, Italian pharmacists are highly trained and can probably diagnose your problem; look for a *farmacia* (they all have a list in the window with details of which ones are open during the night and on holidays). Extreme cases should head for the *Pronto Soccorso* (First Aid Service). Italian doctors are not always great linguists; contact your embassy or consulate for a list of English-speaking doctors.

## Lavatories

Frequent travellers have noted a steady improvement over the years in the cleanliness of Italy's public conveniences; there are fewer holes in the ground, and loo paper is more generally on offer, although as ever you will only find them in places like train and bus stations and bars. If you can't find a public loo, go into the nearest bar; they are legally obliged to let you use their *bagno*. In stations, motorway rest stops and the smarter cafés there are washroom attendants who expect a few hundred lire. Don't confuse the Italian plurals: *signori* (gents), *signore* (ladies).

## Money and Banks

It's a good idea to bring some Italian lire with you; unforeseen delays and unexpected public holidays may foul up your plans to find a bank open when you arrive. **Traveller's cheques** or Eurocheques remain the most secure way of financing your holiday in Italy; they are easy to change and an insurance against unpleasant surprises. **Credit cards** (American Express,

Diner's Club, Mastercard, Access, Eurocard, Barclaycard, Visa) are accepted in most hotels, restaurants, shops and petrol stations (possibly not in single pump operations in the middle of the country), but do not be surprised if you are asked to show identification. If you have a PIN number you can use the many **cashpoint machines**.

There's been a lot of loose talk about knocking three noughts off the Italian lira, but Italy will go on to the Euro before that happens; until then, everybody can be a 'millionaire'. It can, however, be confusing to visitors unaccustomed to dealing with rows of zeros, and more than once you'll think you're getting a great deal until you re-count the zeros on the price tag. Some unscrupulous operators may try to take advantage when you're changing money, so do be careful. **Notes** come in denominations of L500,000, L100,000, L50,000, L10,000, L5,000, L2,000 and L1,000; coins are in L500, L200, L100, L50. Money can be sent to Italy through Thomas Cook travel agents, Western Union and American Express or by having someone at home telex the amount to an Italian bank for you to go and pick up. Technically, it shouldn't take more than a couple of days to arrive (but it always does). Make sure the telex includes the number of your passport, ID card or driver's licence, or the Italians may not hand over the cash.

### *banking hours*

Banks are usually open 8.30am–1.20pm, and for one hour in the afternoon (3–4 or 4–5pm). They are closed on Saturdays, Sundays and national holidays. Some are worth visiting for their space-capsule doors alone.

## Official Holidays

The Italians have cut down somewhat on their official national holidays, but note that every town has one or two local holidays of its own—usually the feast day of its patron saint. Official holidays, shown on transport timetables and museum opening hours, etc., are treated the same as Sundays.

| | |
|---|---|
| **1 January** | New Year's Day—*Capodanno.* |
| **6 January** | Epiphany, better known to Italians as the day of *La Befana*—a kindly witch who brings the *bambini* the toys Santa Claus or *Babbo Natale* somehow forgot. |
| **Easter Monday** | Usually pretty dull. |
| **25 April** | Liberation Day—even duller. |
| **1 May** | Labour Day—lots of parades, speeches, picnics, music and drinking. |
| **15 August** | Assumption, or *Ferragosto*—the biggest of them all—woe to the innocent traveller on the road or train! |
| **1 November** | All Saints, or *Ognissanti*—liveliest at the cemeteries. |
| **8 December** | Immaculate Conception of the Virgin Mary—a dull one. |
| **25 December** | Christmas Day. |
| **Boxing Day** | *Santo Stefano.* |

## Opening Hours and Museums

Most of Umbria closes down at 1pm until 3 or 4pm, to eat and properly digest the main meal of the day, although things are now beginning to change in the cities. Many more shops in the centre of town now stay open during lunch. Afternoon working hours are from 4 to 7, often from 5 to 8 in the hot summer months.

**Food shops** shut on Wednesday afternoons in the winter. They close on Saturday afternoons only from the end of June to the beginning of September. Sunday opening is becoming more usual, particularly for shops in the centre of town. Bars are often the only places open during the early afternoon and sometimes on a Sunday. (For **bank** opening hours, *see* p.23).

**Churches** have always been a prime target for art thieves and as a consequence are usually locked when there isn't a sacristan or caretaker to keep an eye on things. All churches, except for the really important cathedrals and basilicas, close in the afternoon at the same hours as the shops, and the little ones tend to stay closed. Always have a pocketful of L100, L200 and L500 coins to batten the light machines in churches, or what you came to see is bound to be hidden in ecclesiastical shadows. Some churches now have light machines that accept only L1,000 notes, but the light-up time rarely lasts more than a minute. Don't do your visiting during services, and don't come to see paintings and statues in churches the week preceding Easter—you will probably find them covered with mourning shrouds.

Most **museums** are now open all day from 9am to 7pm and tend to close on a Monday and often Sunday afternoons as well. Many are magnificent, many are run with shameful neglect, and many have been closed for years for 'restoration'. Expect to pay between L4,000 and L8,000 for museum entrance. The good new is that state-run museums and monuments are free if you're under 18 or over 60 (bring ID). With an estimated one work of art per inhabitant, Italy has a hard time financing the preservation of its national heritage, and if there's something you really want to see, you would do well to enquire at the tourist office whether it's open or 'temporarily' closed before setting out.

## Packing

You simply cannot overdress in Italy. Whether or not you want to try to keep up with the natives, however, is your own affair and your own heavy suitcase—you may do well to compromise and just bring a couple of smart outfits for big nights out. It's not that the Italians are very formal; they simply like to dress up with a gorgeousness that adorns their cities just as much as those old Renaissance churches and palaces. The few places with dress codes are the major churches and basilicas (no shorts or sleeveless shirts), and the smarter restaurants.

After agonizing over fashion, remember to pack small and light: transatlantic airlines limit baggage by size (two pieces are free, up to 1.5m, in height and width; in second class you're allowed one of 1.5m and another up to 110cm). Within Europe limits are by weight: 20 kilos (44lbs) in second class, 30 kilos (66lbs) in first. You may well be penalized for anything bigger. If you're travelling mainly by train, you'll especially want to keep bags to a minimum: jamming big suitcases in overhead racks isn't much fun.

Never take more than you can carry, but do bring the following: any prescription medicine you need, an extra pair of glasses or contact lenses, a pocket knife and corkscrew (for picnics), a torch (for dark frescoed churches and hotel corridors), a travel alarm (for those early trains) and a pocket Italian–English dictionary (for flirting and other emergencies). You may want to invest in earplugs. Your European electric appliances will work in Italy; just change your plug to the two-prong variety or buy a travel plug; American appliances need transformers as well.

## Photography

Film and developing are much more expensive than they are in the USA or UK. You are not allowed to take pictures in most museums and in some churches. Most cities now offer one-hour processing if you need your pics in a hurry.

## Police Business

### Police/Emergency, ✆ 113

There is a fair amount of petty crime in the cities—purse snatchings, pickpocketing, minor thievery of the white-collar kind (always check your change) and car break-ins and theft—but violent crime is rare. Nearly all mishaps can be avoided with adequate precautions. Scooter-borne purse-snatchers can be foiled if you stay on the inside of the pavement and keep a firm hold on your property; pickpockets most often strike in crowded buses and gatherings; don't carry too much cash, or keep some of it in another place. Be extra careful in train stations; don't leave valuables in hotel rooms; and park your car in garages, guarded car parks, or on well-lit streets, with temptations like radios, cassettes, etc., out of sight. Purchasing small quantities of cannabis is legal although what a small quantity might be exactly is unspecified, so if the police don't like you to begin with it will probably be enough to get you into big trouble.

Once the scourge of Italy, political terrorism has declined drastically in recent years, mainly thanks to special squads of the *Carabinieri*, the black-uniformed national police, technically part of the Italian army. Local matters are usually in the hands of the *Polizia Urbana*; the nattily dressed *Vigili Urbani* concern themselves with directing traffic and handing out parking fines. You will be unlikely to have anything to do with the *Guardia di Finanza*, the financial police, who spend their time chasing corrupt politicians and their friends (unless they catch you leaving a bar or restaurant without a receipt!).

## Post Offices

The postal service in Italy is both the least efficient and the most expensive in Europe, and disgracefully slow; if you're sending postcards back home you often arrive there before they do. If it's important that it arrives in less than a week, send your letter *Espresso* (Swift Air Mail) for a L3,600 supplement, or *Raccomandata* (registered delivery) for a L4,000 supplement. Stamps (*francobolli*) may also be purchased at tobacconists (look for a big black T on the sign), but you're bound to get differing opinions on your exact postage. Mail to the UK goes at the same rate as domestic Italian mail, but it's still twice as much to send a letter from Italy to Britain as vice versa (L800). Airmail letters to and from North America can quite often take up to two weeks. This can be a nightmare if you're making hotel reservations and are sending a deposit—faxing or telephoning ahead is far more secure if time is short.

Ask for mail to be sent to you in Italy either care of your hotel or addressed *Fermo Posta* (poste restante: general delivery) to a post office, or, if you're a card-holder, to an American Express Office. When you pick up your mail at the *Fermo Posta* window, bring your passport for identification. Make sure that your mail is sent to the proper post office; the **Posta Centrale** is often the easiest option.

The Italian post achieves genuine Gormenghastian levels of inscrutability if you try to send a package overseas. Packages have to be of a certain size, under a certain weight, sent in certain ways, and must have a flap open for inspection or be sealed with string and lead. You're best off taking it to a stationer's shop (*cartoleria*) and paying them to wrap it—they usually know what the postal demons are going to require.

## Telephones

> *To call Italy from abroad, dial* © *00 39 followed by the area prefix—including the first 0.*

Like many things in Italy, telephoning can be unduly complicated and usually costs over the odds to boot. Public phones will accept L100, L200 and L500 coins, as well as phone cards. These are the best option for long-distance phoning; they cost L5000, L10,000 and L15,000 and are available in tobacconists, stationers (*cartolerie*), bars and news stands. A digital display will indicate the money you have put in or how much credit is left on your card. When you hear the beep it is usually too late to put any more money in, so keep an eye on the display. If your credit on the phone card runs out, insert another one when you hear a beep. Hotels and bars sometimes have metered telephones. If you want to reverse charges (call collect) you can call from a phone box; dial © 172 followed by the country code and you will be connected to an international operator.

## Shopping

'Made in Italy' has long been a byword for style and quality, especially in fashion and leather, but also in home design, ceramics, kitchenware, jewellery, lace and linens, glassware and crystal, chocolates, hats, straw-work, art books, engravings, handmade stationery, gold and silverware, a hundred kinds of liqueurs, wine, aperitifs, gastronomic specialities, antique reproductions, as well as the antiques themselves. If you are looking for the latter and are spending a lot of money, be sure to demand a certificate of authenticity—reproductions can be very, very good. Non-EU nationals should save their receipts for Customs on the way home.

There is a large **antiques market** at Assisi in late April and early May, and a smaller one held in Perugia on the last Sunday of each month. Ceramics are an old tradition in Gubbio, Deruta, Ficulle, Gualdo Tadino and Città di Castello. Wine and olive oil, bags of porcini mushrooms, jars of truffles and other 'gastronomic' specialities are available everywhere.

Most shops close from 1pm to 3 or 4pm.

### gliding

**Gliding** and **hang-gliding** are big in Umbria, where the hills provide the proper updraughts; Monte Subasio by Assisi and Castelluccio are centres for the sport, but the Parco Naturale di Monte Cucco is the best organized—there's a club, the Centro di Volo Libero, at Sigillo, © 075 530 8703. The little airports at Foligno, © 0742 670201, and Perugia, S. Egidio, © 075 692 9445 also offer gliding.

### golf

There is a golf course near Lake Trasimeno (Perugia-Circolo Golf Perugia, Loc. Santa Sabina, Ellera Umbra, © 075 5172204); another north of Perugia at Antognola, currently being transformed by Robert Trent Jones into an 18-hole course; and a third at Panicale, south of Lake Trasimeno, the Golf Club Lamborghini, Loc. Soderi, © 075 837582.

### hunting

The most controversial sport in Italy is hunting, pitting avid enthusiasts against a burgeoning number of environmentalists who stage protests. The Apennines, especially in Umbria, are boar territory, and in autumn the woods are full of hunters. Pathetically tiny birds, as well as ducks and pigeons, are the other principal game.

### medieval sports

Some ancient sports are still popular, and not entirely as a tourist attraction—the rivalries between neighbourhoods and cities are intense. Sansepolcro and Gubbio stage two crossbow matches a year against each other. Narni and Foligno have annual jousts.

### potholing

Monte Cucco near Gualdo Tadino has the most important of the 865 caves in Umbria; the Centro Nazionale di Speleologia Monte Cucco is in Costacciaro, © 075 917 0236. For information on other subterranean excursions in the region, contact the Gruppo Speleologico CAI Perugia, Via Santini 8, © 075 584 7070, *speleopg@edistons.it*

### riding

Horse riding is increasingly popular, and Agriturist has a number of villa and riding holidays on offer (for more information, write directly to the local Agriturist office—*see* 'Where to Stay', *below*). There are riding centres at Assisi (Centro Ippica Malvarina, Via Malvarina 32, © 075 8064280), Bettona (Agriturismo Torre Burchio, © 075 9885017), Ficulle (Centro Ippica Le Casella, Strada Casella 4, © 0763 86075) and Spoleto (Associazione Ippica Camporoppolo, Loc. Camporoppolo 68, © 0743 56237).

### rowing/rafting/canoeing

Rowing is the big sport at Umbria's Lake Piediluco, site of the Federazione Italiana di Canottaggio and an international championship, while the upper Tiber and river Nera, below the Cascata delle Marmore, are the place to hire a raft or canoe.

### skiing

In Umbria there's downhill skiing in the Monti Sibillini, at Forca Canapine (1541m) on the border of the Marche; many people also head south of the border into Lazio to the big ski complex at Terminillo, east of Rieti. Cross-country skiers head up to Castelluccio above Norcia, or Monte Cucco, or Monte Serra above Gualdo Tadino.

Tennis courts are nearly everywhere; each *comune* has at least one or two that you can hire by the hour.

*walking*

There are a number of marked paths in the mountains, especially in the natural parks; the local Club Alpino Italiano offices can suggest routes: in Perugia, at Via della Gabbia 9; in Spoleto, at Via Pianciani 4; in Terni, at Via Fratelli Cervi 31.

## Tourist Information

For more information before you go, write to the Italian National Tourist Office:

**UK:**      1 Princes Street, London, W1R 8AY, ✆ (020) 7408 1254.

**USA:**      630 Fifth Ave, Suite 1565, New York, NY 10111, ✆ (212) 245 4822.

        12400 Wilshire Blvd, Suite 550, Los Angeles, CA 90025, ✆ (310) 820 1959.

        500 N. Michigan Ave, Suite 2240, Chicago, IL 60611, ✆ (312) 644 0996.

**Australia:** c/o Italian Embassy, 1 Macquarie St, Sydney 2000, NSW, ✆ (02) 9392 7900.

**Canada:**   1 Place Ville Marie, Suite 1914, Montreal, Quebec, H3B 3M9, ✆ (418) 529 9801.

Tourist and travel information is also available at the **Italian Travel Centre**, at Thomas Cook, 30 St James' Street, London, SW1A 1HB, ✆ (020) 7853 6464.

You can pick up more detailed information by writing directly to any of the city or provincial tourist offices (addresses are in the text). These are usually helpful in sending out lists of flats, villas or farmhouses to hire, or at least lists of agents who handle the properties.

The head **regional tourism office** in Umbria is the Azienda di Promozione Turistica (APT), Via Mazzini 21, Perugia, ✆ 075 575 951, ✉ 075 573 6828, *www.regione.umbria.it/ www.umbria2000.it*, e-mail *ente@regione.umbria*.it

## Where to Stay

*Hotels*

Umbria is endowed with hotels (*alberghi*) of every description, from the spectacular to the humble. These are rated by the government's tourism bureaucracy, from five stars at the luxurious top to one star at the bottom. The ratings take into account such things as a restaurant on the premises, plumbing, air-conditioning, etc., but not character, style or charm. Use the stars, which we include in this book, as a quick reference only. Another thing to remember about government ratings is that a hotel can stay at a lower rating than it has earned, so you may find a three-star hotel as comfortable as a four.

There's no inflation in Italy, if you believe the government; the prices just go up by themselves. This curious paradox is well expressed in hotel prices; every year costs rise by 6–8 per cent across the board, and are often more expensive than hotels in northern Europe. The prices listed in this book are for double rooms only. For a single, count on paying two-thirds of a double; to add an extra bed in a double will add 35 per cent to the bill. Taxes and service charges are included in the given rate. Some establishments charge L10–25,000 for air-conditioning. Also note that if rooms are listed without bath, it simply means the shower and lavatory are in the corridor. Prices are by law listed on the door of each room and will be printed in the hotel lists available from the local tourist office; any discrepancies should be reported to the tourist office. Most rooms have two or three different rates, depending on the season. Costs are sometimes a third less if you travel in the district's low season. Some hotels, especially in resorts, close down altogether for several months of the year.

Breakfast is optional only in some hotels, and in *pensions* it is mandatory. And you may as well expect to face half- (breakfast and lunch or dinner) or full-board requirements in the hotels that can get away with it—seaside, lake or mountain resorts in season, spas and country villa hotels. Otherwise, meal arrangements are optional. Although eating in the hotel restaurant can be a genuine gourmet experience, in the majority of cases hotel food is bland, just as it is in any other country.

**Throughout this book, prices listed are for a double room in high season; unless otherwise stated, including a private bath.** Here is the range of prices you are likely to encounter for hotels in the various classifications in 2000:

| Category | | Double with bath |
|---|---|---|
| *luxury* | ★★★★ | over L500,000 |
| *very expensive*, Class I | ★★★★ | L350–500,000 |
| *expensive*, Class II | ★★★ | L240–350,000 |
| *moderate*, Class III | ★★ | L120–240,000 |
| *inexpensive*, Class IV | ★ | up to L120,000 |

For rooms without bath, subtract 20–30 per cent. A *camera matrimoniale* is a room with a double bed, a *camera doppia* has twin beds, a single is a *camera singola*. For the summer, book in advance, preferably by fax or internet. A booking is valid once a deposit has been paid. If you have to cancel your reservation, the hotel will keep the deposit unless another agreement has been reached. If you come in the summer without reservations, start calling around for a place in the morning or put yourself at the mercy of one of the tourist office hotel finding services.

Besides classic hotels, there are an increasing number of alternatives, nearly always in historic buildings, and nearly always on the pricey side. In Umbria these are classified as **residenza d'epoca** or *country house*. Accommodation can be in a castle, villa, hamlet, or so on, with period furnishings and lots of character. Usually there are only a few rooms, and occasionally some of these are self-catering.

### Rural Bed and Breakfast

For a breath of country living, the gregarious Italians head for a spell on a working farm or estate, an experience known in Italian as **agriturismo**. This is an increasingly popular form of accommodation—at the end of 1999, there were some 4700 *agriturismo* beds available in Umbria. Accommodation is either self-catering or more often bed and breakfast; it varies from the rustic to the positively luxurious, but is generally a more economical alternative to hotels, particularly for families (in the summer you often have to stay at least three days or a week). Many places now have swimming pools and riding stables; sometimes fishing, boating and other activities are available as well. Often the real pull of the place is a restaurant in which you can sample some home-grown produce.

The APT publishes an annual listing, or contact:

**Agriturist Umbria**, Via San Bartolomeo 79, Ponte San Giovanni, Perugia, ✆ 075 599 7289 and Corso del Popolo 37, Terni, ✆ 0744 421848; publishes an annual guide 'Agriturist', available for L30,000 in bookshops in Italy.

**Turismo Verde Umbria**, Via Campo di Marte 14, Perugia, ✆ 075 500 2954.

**Terranostra Umbria**, Via Campo di Marte 10, Perugia, ✆ 075 500 9559; their publication 'Vacanze e Natura' is also available in bookshops in Italy for L30,000.

**Umbria in Campagna**, Strada San Cristoforo 16, Amelia, ✆ 0744 988 249 (a farmers' cooperative).

---

### Youth and Student Hostels

You'll find youth hostels in Perugia, Assisi, Gubbio, Magione, Trevi, Sigillo, and Poggiodomo. The head regional office in Umbria is the Ostello della Pace, Via di Valecchia, Assisi, ✆ 075 816 767. It's best to pick up an IYHF card before you leave: in the UK, contact the Youth Hostels Association, Trevelyan House, 8 St Stephen's Hill, St Albans, Herts, AL1 2DY; in the USA, American Youth Hostels Inc, PO Box 37613, Washington DC 20013-7613. There are no age limits, and senior citizens are often given added discounts. Accommodation— a bunk bed in single-sex room and breakfast—costs around L16,000 per day. There is often a curfew, and you usually can't check in before 5 or 6pm. You can book in advance by sending your arrival and departure dates along with the number of guests (by sex) to the individual hostel, including international postal coupons for the return reply. The worst time to use the hostels is the spring, when noisy Italian school groups use them for field trips.

---

### Self-catering Holidays: Villas, Farmhouses and Flats

Renting a villa, farmhouse, cottage or flat has always been the choice way to visit Umbria. If you're travelling with a family it is the most economic alternative—there are simple, inexpensive cottages as well as the fabulous Renaissance villas furnished with antiques, gourmet meals and swimming pools.

One place to look for holiday villas is in the Sunday paper; or, if you have your heart set on a particular area, write to its tourist office for a list of local rental agencies. These ought to provide photos of the accommodation to give you an idea of what to expect, and you should make sure all pertinent details are written down in your rental agreement to avoid misunderstandings later. In general, minimum lets are for two weeks; rental prices usually include insurance, water and electricity, and sometimes linen and maid service.

Don't be surprised if upon arrival the owner 'denounces' (*denunziare*) you to the police; according to Italian law, all visitors must be registered upon arrival. Common problems are water shortages, unruly insects and low kilowatts (often you can't have your hot-water heater and oven on at the same time). Many of the companies listed below offer, in addition to homes, savings on charter flights and ferry crossings, or fly-drive schemes to sweeten the deal. Try to book as far in advance as possible for the summer season.

### holiday rental companies in the UK

**International Chapters**, 47–51 St John's Wood High Street, London, NW8 7NJ, ✆ (020) 7722 9560, has the fullest listings and handles bookings for the major Italian holiday home companies, the largest of which is **Cuendet** which publishes an extensive illustrated catalogue of holiday villas, flats and farmhouses in Umbria; their headquarters are at Il Cerreto, 53030 Strove, Siena.

Other firms specializing in holiday rentals in the region include:

**Citalia**, Marco Polo House 3–5, Lansdowne Road, Croydon, CR9 9EQ, ✆ (020) 8686 5533.

**Interhome**, 383 Richmond Road, Twickenham, TW1 2EF, ✆ (020) 8891 1294. Villas and apartments for 2–16 people.

**Magic of Italy**, 227 Shepherds Bush Road, London, W6 7AS, ✆ (020) 8748 7575.

**Sovereign Villas**, Astral Towers, Betts Way, Crawley, West Sussex, RH10 2GX, ✆ (0161) 742 2233.

### holiday rental companies in the USA

**At Home Abroad**, 405 East 56th St, New York, NY 10022, ✆ (212) 421 9165.

**RentVillas.com**, Suzanne T. Pidduck, 1742 Calle Corva, Camarillo, CA 93010, ✆ (805) 987 5278.

**Hideaways International**, 767 Islington Street, Portsmouth, New Hampshire 03801, ✆ (603) 430 4433.

**Overseas Connection**, 70 West 71st Street, Suite 1C, New York, NY 10023, ✆ (212) 769 1170.

**The Parker Company**, 152 The Lynnway, Lynn, MA 01902, ✆ 800 280 2811.

**RAVE** (Rent-a-Vacation-Everywhere), 383 Park Avenue, Rochester, NY 14607, ✆ (716) 256 0760.

**Italian Rentals**, 3801 Ingomar Street NW, Washington DC 20015, ✆ (202) 244 5345, ✆ (202) 362 0520. Specialist in Italian villa rentals.

### holiday rental companies in Italy

**The Best in Italy**, Via Ugo Foscolo 72, Firenze, ✆ 055 223 064, which specializes in posh villas with domestic staff.

### farm holidays

*See* 'Rural Bed and Breakfast', *above*.

---

### Camping

Umbria has a few campsites in the mountains and near the lakes, and usually one within commuting distance of major tourist centres. A complete list with full details for all of Italy is published annually in the Italian Touring Club's *Campeggi e Villaggi Turistici*, available in Italian bookshops, or you can obtain an abbreviated list free from the Centro Internazionale Prenotazioni Federcampeggio, Casella Postale 23, 50042, Calenzano (Firenze), ✆ 055 882

381, ✆ 055 882 3918; request their booking forms as well to reserve a place—essential in the summer months. Camping fees vary according to facilities on offer: L6,000–15,000 per adult, L4,000–12,000 per child, L11,000–30,000 per tent or caravan. Camping outside official sites is kosher if you ask the landowner's permission first. Caravans are expensive to hire: the National Tourist Office and local tourist offices have lists of firms.

| | |
|---|---|
| History | 34 |
| Art in Umbria | 45 |

# History and Art

Umbrian history is not a nice thread with events hanging on it like beads, but rather a ball of yarn that a naughty kitten has pounced on. Most of the time, of course, the naughty kitten was Rome. Being just upriver from the Big Noise on the Tiber has proved a mixed blessing.

## Early Days

Umbria has always been green, but long ago it was very wet, too, drowned under the prehistoric 'Lago Tiberino' that submerged all but the highest hills, which were covered with lush vegetation and giant sequoias. Some of these, fossilized in the mud, were uncovered by chance in a quarry near Todi in the 1980s, and now form the petrified forest of Dunarobba. As sediment filled in the shores and the water receded, the first people moved in, although no one is sure where they came from: a cave on Monte Peglia, northeast of Orvieto, was inhabited in the Lower Palaeolithic (c. 500,000 BC), by people of the Pebble Culture who managed to bag deer, porcupines and sabre-toothed tigers. Finds from the Middle Palaeolithic (Abeto, near Norcia, Mousterian site, from c. 70,000–35,000 BC) and Upper Palaeolithic (the Tane del Diavolo, near Parrano, c. 30,000 BC) show that the first residents of Umbria kept up with the Stone Age Joneses across Europe and beyond. They also kept up with the first artistic trends, and produced at least one tiny but buxom female fertility figure, the 'Venus of Trasimeno', discovered at Castiglione del Lago and now at the archaeology museum in Florence.

No one knows much about Mesolithic Umbria, but the wide variety of Neolithic artefacts from various cultures show that this central, landlocked region was already something of a cultural sponge at an important crossroads. These Late Stone Age inhabitants were shepherds, and eventually farmers, but it seems that they hadn't settled down for long when the new metal cultures were introduced from the coasts; bronze made better tools, but also better weapons, and in general people took to the hills for defence, and there they would stay for thousands of years, safe from invaders and from the malarial vapours that would plague the region until the end of the Second World War.

It was in the Bronze Age (1600–1000 BC) that the first Indo-Europeans appeared, who by the Iron Age can be defined as the **Umbrii** who occupied a good portion of central Italy. According to Pliny the Elder these sober, serious-minded folk were the most ancient of all inhabitants in Italy (the modern Umbrians agree) and they spoke an Italic language similar to Latin. They founded many of Umbria's towns, including Città di Castello, Todi, Spoleto, Terni, Assisi and Amelia; in Amelia they left an astonishing set of travertine cyclopean walls from the 5th century BC, similar to those built by the Latins and other central Italian peoples.

Beginning in the 9th century BC, the **Villanovan culture** prevailed on the western edge of the region. The Villanovans were peaceful farmers who lived in huts (they made their funerary urns in the same shape as their homes, so we know what they looked like) and were the first in the area to cremate their dead; they were also fairly arty potters and metalworkers, as can be seen in Perugia's archaeology museum. Near the end of the 8th century BC, they came in contact with the first Greek colonists down by the Bay of Naples, who introduced more advanced metal and ceramic techniques, writing, and a taste for luxury goods.

When or how or why the Villanovans evolved into **Etruscans** is a mystery: according to Herodotus, writing in the 5th century BC, they came out of Lydia in Asia Minor in the 13th century BC, during a famine, and after sailing about for a while 'came to Umbria, where they settled, building the cities in which they all lived. Because they wanted to change their name they assumed the name of *Tirreni*, deriving it from the prince who led them there.' This is close to the Etruscans' own version of events, and goes some way towards explaining their non-Indo-European language (the only inscriptions similar to Etruscan have been found on the far northeastern Greek island of Limnos) and also coincides with the tales of the 'Sea Peoples' who wandered over the Mediterranean during Mycenaean times and the Dark Age that followed (1500–1000 BC). In the oldest Egyptian records they are the *Tursha,* who once invaded the Nile Delta along with the Achaeans, the Shardana of Sardinia and the Sicans of Sicily.

By historical times in the western Mediterranean, however, the Greeks regarded them as pirates, the *Tyrennoi*, who gave their name to the Tyrrhenian sea. Their maritime empire got in the way of the ambitions of their rival thalassocrats, the Greeks, to exploit the mines of Elba and the Tuscan coast. In the 7th century BC the Etruscans emerge as the most powerful people of Italy. According to inscriptions, their own name for themselves was *Rasena.* The Latins called them *Tuscii* (hence Tuscany). Their city states controlled that region, parts of Emilia-Romagna, northern Lazio, and parts of what is now western Umbria, including Orvieto (*Volsinii Veteres*), one of their most important cities and the guardian of the great federal religious sanctuary called the *Fanum Voltumnae*. By the 6th century they had pushed the native Umbrians east over the Tiber. A desire to control the fertile plain around Trasimeno led to the founding of Perugia by the Etruscans of Chiusi (*Camars*).

In spite of their violent rivalry, the Greeks and Etruscans traded like crazy. The luxury-loving Etruscans adored Greek vases, and imported them in great numbers from the 7th century on. Later they learned to imitate them. When the Greeks started building temples in the 8th century BC, so did the Etruscans, although theirs were of wood, with projecting rafters and beams in a style that seems a curious cross between the Classical Greek and something Japanese. They were very religious and superstitious, obsessed with divination and death; nearly all their surviving architectural works are tombs, and most of their surviving art was found there too, although no one is sure how the dead were supposed to use these things in the afterlife. The Etruscans borrowed the Greek alphabet, but as far we know they never produced an imaginative literature. They excelled in sculpture and portraiture, and intricate gold and metal work in the 'minor arts'; they learned fresco from the Greeks and decorated their tombs, usually with joyful and life-filled scenes. The classic funerary urn shows a man and wife reclining at the banquet; compared to the women in ancient Greece, Etruscan women seemed to have enjoyed a much higher status in society.

The less sophisticated Umbrii never liked the nouveau riche Etruscans much, but they learned to live with them. Towns on the frontier like *Tuder* (Todi) and Perugia were bi-lingual, and the Etruscans exerted a powerful cultural and economic influence. Nevertheless, the Umbrii retained their own ethnic identity especially in the more easterly towns of Assisi and Spello. The most important inscription ever found in the Umbrian language, the so-called **Eugubine tablets** (in Gubbio, *see* p.124) date from the 3rd and 1st century BC. The earliest, significantly, are written in the Etruscan alphabet, later ones in the Latin script, a clear sign of the power shift of the times. Mostly devoted to religious practices, the tablets also ask that the gods protect the locals (the *Ikuvini*) from three groups of troublesome people, the *Narharkum nomen*, the *Japuzkem nomen* and the *Turskem nomen*, who are believed to be, respectively, the people from the Nera valley, the people from the coast of Croatia, and the Etruscans. The astonishing thing is that the tablets offer instructions on how to sacrifice any one of the above peoples (or anyone from nearby Gualdo Tadino) if the Ikuvini should happen to nab them. Umbria does seem to have been an exceptionally conservative hillbilly backwater—but then, the early Romans practised human sacrifice too.

In ancient Umbria it may have been very much every city state for itself, as in the case of Etruria. Another inscription, found in Spello and known as the **Constantine Rescript**, dates from the 330s AD and records the emperor's acquiescence to Spello's request to hold their own religious ceremonies and gladiatorial games rather than send the usual priest to the federal Etruscan sanctuary at *Fanum Voltumnae*. So if the Ikuvini in Gubbio were ready to sacrifice any Etruscan they met, the Umbrians in Spello worshipped side by side with the Etruscans, centuries after both people had been subjugated by the Romans.

## Roman Umbria

The Romans had one talent and one delight: making war. Almost everything else we associate with them they got from the Etruscans: their religious practices and art, togas, concrete, sewers, road building, rectilinear town planning, races and gladiators. But the Etruscans were hardly conquered overnight. Things began to go wrong for them in 550 BC when the Greeks of Cumae defeated their attempts to expand in Campania. Etruscan kings were booted out of Rome a few years later, and the next century saw the Romans take the upper hand in the slow battle to the death with Veii, the first of the many Etruscan cities they gobbled up. In 299 BC the Romans destroyed the strategic Umbrian town of *Nequinum* (Narni) and replaced it with a Roman colony. This drove the Umbrians to ally themselves with the Etruscans, the Gauls and the Samnites to fight the intruders. It was all too little, too late, and the Romans soundly defeated them in 295 BC at the Battle of Sentinum.

One reason why the Etruscans fell to their protégés may have been the fact that they were an elite, and that the plebeians and slaves weren't especially interested in fighting for their cause. *Volsinii Veteres* (Orvieto) was conquered in 280 BC, which led to social upheaval and strife between the old aristocratic leadership and the plebeians who took power. Eventually the aristocrats appealed to the Roman Senate for assistance; the Senate responded, but, as an added and probably unwanted bonus, razed the town and resettled everyone in the new foundation of *Volsinii Noves* (Bolsena, in Lazio). Etruscan Perugia took note, and never challenged the rising power. In 241 BC the Romans consolidated their power to the east by founding a colony at the ancient Umbrian town of *Spoletium* (Spoleto).

One of the first and most important acts of the Romans in Umbria was the construction in 222 BC, financed by the wealthy Roman politician Gaius Flaminius, of the **Via Flaminia** from Rome to Rimini, passing through the heart of the region; this link between east and west and north and south grew more and more important as time went on, and to this day it remains a busy route. In 217 BC, during the Second Punic War, the same Gaius Flaminius would return to Umbria in an attempt to head off Hannibal at Lake Trasimeno, only to ignore the omens and his Etruscan diviners (*haruspices*) and walk into a terrible Carthaginian trap (see pp.85–6). It was one of the greatest defeats ever suffered by Rome, but none of the Etruscan or Umbrian towns in the neighbourhood took advantage of the opportunity to revolt. Perugia in particular went out of its way to take in the Roman survivors from the battle. Spoleto and Spello likewise shut their gates to Hannibal.

Rome rewarded Umbria's loyalty with peace and prosperity; drainage schemes opened up new lands to the farmers, some of whom were smallholders and former slaves under the Etruscans. In 90 BC, under the *lex Julia*, all Umbrians were made Roman citizens. Many towns, especially along the two branches of the Via Flaminia (it splits at Narni into easterly and westerly routes) were built up by the Romans, and to this day they retain important remains of antiquity's master engineers. But it wasn't all roses: in 40 BC the Perugians and Norcians made the mistake of siding with Mark Antony, and were attacked by Octavian for their error; after Perugia went up in flames, however, the now-emperor Augustus took pains to restore Perugia as *Perusia Augusta* and it continued to prosper.

When Augustus divided Italy into administrative districts, he based his divisions on ethnic lines, and made Umbria the Sixth Region, which included the modern region east of the Tiber, but also much of the Marche, and parts of Lazio (but excluding Perugia and Orvieto, which were in Etruria, and Norcia which was in Samnium). The Romans were fond of Umbria, where they built many villas and loved the fresh beauty of the landscapes. Virgil and Propertius (the poet of Assisi), Ovid and Pliny the Younger wrote lovingly of the idyllic springs of Clitumnus, where white oxen were purified for sacrifice by a temple to the river god.

Thanks to its proximity to Rome, Umbria carried on blithely over the next pair of centuries. By the end of the 3rd century AD it had started its conversion to Christianity, showing an early propensity for producing saints. Most of these were martyrs in the persecutions of the time—the most famous, outside of Umbria at any rate, was St Valentine, a bishop of Terni. At the same time, echoes of troubles on the empire's frontier began to resound at home. When Diocletian split the empire into more manageable eastern and western sections, he reordered the boundaries, dividing Umbria between the new province of *Flaminia et Picenum* east of the Tiber, and *Tuscia et Umbria* west of the Tiber. Soon the name 'Umbria' was simply dropped, and would remain forgotten until the 17th century, when it was revived by classical scholars (who would spend centuries arguing over its borders).

Diocletian's splitting of the empire had, for Umbria, the slow but same inexorable effect of splitting the atom, especially once **Constantine**, emperor of the west, defeated his co-emperor of the east, and became the single emperor of the Roman Empire, only to move its capital east to Constantinople. No longer at the centre of the world, Rome and Umbria and the west went into a tailspin. And to add insult to injury, when it was decided that the west needed a capital after all, Ravenna was chosen (404). Four years later Alaric and the Visigoths marched down the Via Flaminia to besiege and later plunder Rome. The Vandals followed suit (455) and in 476 the Roman empire was given its *coup de grâce* when the last feeble emperor was packed off and replaced by the first Ostrogothic King of Italy, Odoacer.

Four years later, **St Benedict** was born in Norcia. In hindsight it seems that the man who would one day be proclaimed the Patron Saint of Europe was born just in the nick of time to establish his Rule for western monasticism, creating an efficient model of order, labour, spirituality, authority and learning in a world turned upside down. Another, rather original contribution to Umbria's mystical reputation was the hundreds of Syrian ascetics who arrived in 514, fleeing the persecutions of the Arian Byzantine emperor Anastasius to live in small communities and caves around the Valnerina.

## The Greeks and Goths, and Especially the Lombards

In the early Middle Ages, Umbria's once cosy position near Rome on the Via Flaminia became its great misfortune. Although Italy revived a little under Odoacer's successor, King Theodoric, after he died the Byzantine emperor Justinian saw his chance to reclaim the west, and sent his general Belisarius to Italy to start the ruinous **Greek-Gothic wars** in 535. Caught between Rome and Ravenna, Umbria became a doormat for armies marching back and forth, armies that often destroyed the towns along the way; famine and plague forced many inhabitants to take refuge in the mountains to survive. Perugia endured a seven-year siege by the Gothic king Totila, but the behaviour of the imperial side was little better: important towns such as Carsulae were abandoned forever. The Byzantines finally prevailed in 552, when Narses decisively defeated Totila and the Ostrogoths near Gualdo Tadino.

The wars left Italy on its knees, making it easy prey for the next invaders, the **Lombards**, (*Longobardi*, the 'people of the long axe'), a Germanic tribe that made its Gothic and Frankish cousins look like choirboys. The Lombards kept the rain off by coating themselves in bear grease, and they drank their wine out of their enemies' skulls. They easily captured most of northern Italy, made Pavia their capital, and set up various feudal states elsewhere, as in Tuscany, Campania and Umbria (571). The Umbrian Duchy of Spoleto proved to be the longest lasting of all these, enduring until 1250: it encompassed all of eastern Umbria from Gualdo Tadino to Terni as well as parts of Abruzzo, Lazio and the Marche. Fortunately for Spoleto, the Lombards soon mellowed, and gave up their Arian heresy to become pious Catholics; among their contributions to the cultural life of the area were the endowments of the powerful Benedictine abbeys of San Pietro in Valle in the Valnerina and Sant'Eutizio near Preci.

With the exception of Orvieto (which was in the Lombard duchy of Tuscany) the rest of Umbria remained Byzantine, a province of the Exarchate of Ravenna, with Perugia as its administrative seat. The delicate political balance between the Byzantines and Lombards ended in 751, when the Lombards conquered Ravenna and threatened Rome; the pope, in alarm, summoned in the **Franks** and Pepin the Short, who kicked the Lombards out and gave Ravenna to the popes. A similar appeal in 774 to Pepin's son **Charlemagne** was met with an equally enthusiastic response; Charlemagne married the daughter of the Lombard King Desiderius, and then forced him to abdicate. He crowned himself King of Italy, then repudiated his new wife.

It was around this time that one of the popes pulled an underhand stunt that would effect Umbria for centuries, by forging a document called the **Donation of Constantine**, which was presented as a 4th-century testament from the emperor written before he went east, willing the popes perpetual control over Rome and Italy as a token for his conversion to Christianity (the document was often challenged by lawyers, and in the 1450s, humanist Lorenzo Valla categorically proved it a fake). When Pepin gave the Exarchate of Ravenna to the popes, they used the 'Donation' to justify their temporal control of the former Byzantine territories, as well as their ambition to control central Italy, as a buffer around Rome but also a buffer rich with farms and taxes. In the hopes of gaining Frankish support for this policy, Pope Leo III confirmed Charlemagne's hold over much of Europe by crowning him Holy Roman Emperor in 800, reviving a title that would be a bugbear in Italy for a thousand years, especially as later popes came to think of themselves as the true heirs of the Roman emperors. For the next six centuries the pope and the German emperor would usually be at one another's throats.

After Charlemagne's death, however, any kind of central control fell apart under the pressure of raiding **Saracens** from Sicily, who came right up the Valnerina in the 800s, and then from the **Magyars**, who marched down the Via Flaminia in the 900s. Places would nominally belong to pope or emperor, or be claimed by both, while in practice it was every town, castle or monastery for itself. The Duchy of Spoleto held on under the auspices of the emperors, although the dukes were now more Frankish than Lombard.

## *Comuni,* Guelphs and Ghibellines

> *In the republics there is greater life, greater hatred, and more desire for vengeance.*
>
> Machiavelli

When the curtain rises again, around the year 1000, the towns of Umbria, as in the rest of Italy, while nominally pledging their allegiance to either pope (eventually to be known as the **Guelph party***, see* pp.51–2) or emperor (the **Ghibellines**), emerged as little city states that spent much of their energy clobbering one another. Yet as rough and tumble as it was, the 11th to mid-14th century was a golden age for Umbria, the period when its towns and landscapes formed their character, when it built its greatest monuments, and when **St Francis of Assisi** started the religious revival that would sweep across Italy and Europe in the 1200s. Even Francis as a young man fought in the wars, and was captured by Perugia and spent time in its prison.

As the threat of outside invasion lessened, people returned to the old Umbrian-Etruscan-Roman towns; the population began to grow, agriculture revived, and trade took off. Although the papacy gained a new militancy and prestige on a European scale, it was still too weak to assert itself at home. Umbria, like all the papal possessions, was plagued by problems of succession, schisms, and challenges to its authority by various Church councils, heresies, and secular rulers. In the vacuum of any central authority from Rome, local abbots and bishops organized councils of men from the established families to attend to each town's defence, its militia, land drainage and other communal improvements.

These informal associations led, throughout northern Italy in the 11th century, to the formation of the secular **comune** (plural *comuni* ). Similar to the city states of ancient Greece, the *comuni* were at first dominated by town-dwelling nobles, though each citizen was directly involved in the affairs of the day. The piazza became the *agora* or forum, and the patron saint was a *comune*'s tutelary divinity.

The first battles were over land, as each *comune* fought to increase its control of the surrounding land, the *contado*, at the expense of smaller towns, feudal lords, and monasteries. The garden-like appearance of Umbrian landscapes in frescoes dates from the age of the *comuni* (also the bare brown hills you often see—massive deforestation took place, before problems of erosion led the *comuni* to initiate re-forestation programmes). The majority of the population were farmers, and they lived in a city or village and worked in the surrounding fields. During the rare interludes of peace, good health and good crops, it was a small but perfectly manageable world. As agriculture remained the economic backbone in Umbria, the *comuni* were more self-sufficient but also more conservative and inward-looking than, say, in neighbouring Tuscany, and feelings of loyalty to the *comune*, or *campanilismo* (the attachment to one's own bell tower) as it was known, were intense. While people certainly travelled, they rarely married or moved outside their *comune*; to be exiled, like Dante, was a dreaded fate.

Although each *comune*'s Grand Council kept the peace at first, trouble began as more and more feudal lords moved into the towns, bringing into the streets the battles they once fought in the countryside, now with Guelph and Ghibelline labels attached; each family had its band of faithful clients and dependants ready to spring into action. The new men, the *popolo*, who owed their wealth to trade, opposed the nobles' endless quarrels and demanded a greater say in running the towns. Eventually the *comuni* came up with an ingenious solution to the rising factionalism: they would elect a **podestà** (formerly an appointive imperial office), a respected and impartial umpire, nearly always someone from another town. He would serve for an appointed period, usually from six months to a year, and with his entourage of judges and notaries would set up housekeeping in the Palazzo del Comune. Many men made a career of being *podestà*, travelling from town to town, bringing to all of Umbria's *comuni* the same institutions: the council, a *Capitano del popolo* (in charge of the citizen militia) and the council of *Anziani* or Priors, of leading guild members, who were especially powerful in Perugia. What they lacked was a police force, and most disputes were still settled with vendettas.

Occasionally players from the First Division burst in on Umbria's parochial cocoon and made a nuisance of themselves. Emperor Frederick Barbarossa came down and wrecked havoc in the 1150s. The powerful **Pope Innocent III** toured Umbria in an attempt to assert his temporal authority before the Perugians poisoned him (1216). A few decades later, Barbarossa's grandson, **Frederick II 'Stupor Mundi'** promised to give the Church the Duchy of Spoleto, but then fell out with the pope; when the pope excommunicated him, Frederick responded by seizing much of Umbria, and took up residence in Foligno, where he held a grand parliament in the cathedral. The Ghibellines of Umbria were in their ascendancy, but after his death in 1250, the Guelphs clawed their way back.

By 1300, Umbria's *comuni* had reached their peak in wealth and population. Streets and squares were paved, fountains and sewers brought water to the hill towns and took it away again, wooden houses were replaced with stone, markets were established, cathedrals and Franciscan churches were built, and people began to dress in fine linens, wool tunics and furs, and light their houses with candles. Perugia, far and away the richest and most populous city in Umbria with *c.* 28,000 in 1300 (down from 40,000 in Etruscan times) had a university reputed for law. Yet at the same time the system was becoming untenable. The nobles and high churchmen and bourgeois had become so partisan that they couldn't agree on a candidate for *podestà*; on occasion they would even elect two.

# The Signoria

A combination of internal factionalism and external events tolled the death knell for the *comuni*. The papacy's leave of absence in Avignon (1305–76) at first limited meddling from that quarter, but in 1313 the announced arrival in Orvieto of German emperor Henry VII, who died in Siena before he even reached Umbria, sparked off a battle that involved Guelphs and Ghibellines from all over the region, ending in a horrific massacre at Orvieto (*see* p.178).

The real troubles began in 1347. The crops failed, leading to a famine, which was followed by something even worse: the Black Death. In 1348 the plague took with it some 100,000 Umbrians, striking the towns especially hard: Spoleto lost two-thirds of its population. The same area was subject to a devastating earthquake. Umbria was a mess, and in 1353 Pope Innocent VI in Avignon made the most determined attempt yet to take the papal dominions under his wing when he appointed the Spanish **Cardinal Gil Albornoz** to assert his authority. A nobleman who had fought the Moors in Spain, Albornoz came with an army to crush any who opposed him, notably Spoleto, which still thought of itself as an Imperial city, and Perugia, which was loath to give up its independence and was besieged by the famous White Company led by the English *condottiere* (mercenary captain) Sir John Hawkwood. Although Perugia never surrendered, it was weakened enough for Albornoz to subdue the towns of its territory. The Cardinal built mighty fortresses in Spoleto, Narni, Assisi and elsewhere, to keep them in line; he also divided the Papal States into administrative provinces, and wrote the so-called **Egidian Constitutions**, a law code that would remain in place until 1816.

Once Albornoz was dead, the *comuni* tried to go back to their old ways, but things had changed, and in the social turmoil and confusion strong men took advantage of the situation to seize power. Sometimes a noblemen or the leader of the *popolo* took power, or a *podestà* became the *signore* or lord of a town. It happened first in Orvieto in 1334, when the first Monaldeschi seized power in the confusion after the massacre; in Perugia it came in 1416 when the *condottiere* **Braccio Fortebraccio** captured the city. The *condottieri* and their companies generally thrived in the confusion of the day, and Fortebraccio was one of the more successful, in spite of being excommunicated twice by Pope Martin V for horning in on his territory; he ruled all of Umbria and part of southern Tuscany until he died in battle in 1424.

After Fortebraccio, the popes and the *signori* gradually worked out an arrangement: the Church defended the lords' right to rule their turf, and the lords acknowledged the Church as their overlord; as an added sweetener, the pope exempted Umbria from the papal salt tax, although henceforth the region had to get its supply from the papal pans. Pope Alexander VI sent his son Cesare Borgia with an army through the region to remind the *signori* who was boss, and he briefly installed his teenage daughter Lucrezia as governor of Spoleto while looking about for a suitable third husband for the unfortunate girl. In Perugia, however, the gangster noble families, the Baglioni and Oddi, made papal authority a distant rumour; the mayhem and violence and vendettas in the city became legendary, and the Baglioni ultimately outdid even the Medici in the body count in their day. In 1540, **Pope Paul III** finally got rid of the Baglioni by provocatively levying the hated salt tax on Perugia; refusing to negotiate, he sent his son at the head of an army to crush them once and for all in the **Salt War**.

# The Papal States

*They seem to stay alive only because the earth refuses to swallow them.*

Goethe

Goethe saw Umbria in the 1780s, but the poverty, bad roads, backward agricultural practices and bigoted ignorance he and many other travellers found in that century did not happen to Umbria all at once. Nor did the curse of papal rule happen to all parts of the region at the same time and to the same degree. While Perugia was clobbered into submission, Città di Castello, for instance, managed to maintain much of its autonomy under the Vitelli family for a long time in respect for their long support of the popes, while Gubbio escaped by belonging to the Montefeltro Dukes of Urbino, at least until 1624.

Once all the potential rival *signori* had been crushed and replaced with papal supporters, the Egidian constitution of Cardinal Albornoz was dusted off and clerical administrators were installed. The bottom line is that the popes, whose political activities soon gave them much bigger fish to fry, simply lost interest in Umbria, except as a tax cow to be milked to fund their beautification projects in Rome and as the occasional escape hatch when events in the Urbs became too hot to handle—most notably, Clement VII's retreat to Orvieto in 1527, during the sack of Rome by Emperor Charles V. Taxes doubled, then doubled again. The wars inside and outside of the towns of Umbria ceased, but **brigandage** increased by leaps and bounds, many of the culprits coming from the noble families on the outs with the pope. When the popes in the late 1500s took action, they executed on average a thousand bandits each year.

Except for a few churches, building ground to a halt, and investment in agriculture or trade dried up; outside of the shameless greed and nepotism most popes practised for their families, their policies were so shortsighted and incompetent that those with any money invested only in land, taking advantage of every drought and misfortune to buy up the small landowners. Farmers were forced into sharecropping or *mezzadria*, which, although on the surface it seemed fairer, was little better than feudal serfdom; although the farmer split the harvest fifty-fifty with the landowner, he bore all the other costs, from seed to transport, and in many cases could not marry without the landowner's consent, or even leave the countryside once the lease was over. The towns were still very much dependent on their immediate surrounding territory, or *contado*, for food, and the peasants who tried to escape were often compelled to return to the land (while their lives were made ever more insecure with shorter and shorter leases). On the other hand, there were increasingly fewer mouths to feed as populations dwindled—by 1800 Perugia's had shrunk to 13,000, while Orvieto could barely muster 5000 souls.

Anyone with talent or ambition took orders or simply left the region. Trade and contacts with the outside world dried up, and the Church's war on thought in the Counter-reformation confirmed the Umbrians in their provincialism and *campanilismo*. The 17th and 18th centuries were not good ones for Italy; in Umbria they brought such stagnation that the whole region seemed locked in a degraded sort of suspended animation. At the same time the very first **Grand Tourists** began to trickle into Umbria, usually only because they were on the way to somewhere else (most travelled from Venice and Ravenna to Rome on the Via Flaminia); if they came from the well-run Grand Duchy of Tuscany they were invariably appalled at conditions just over the border in Umbria. In 1766 Tobias Smollett found that 'the inns are dismal and dirty beyond all description; the bedclothes filthy enough to turn the stomach of a muleteer; the victuals cooked in such a manner that even a Hottentot could not have beheld them without loathing.' Goethe, twenty years later, discovered that the Umbrians were 'all bitter rivals: they indulge in the oddest provincialism and local patriotism, and cannot stand one another.' The Irish writer Lady Morgan (Sydney Owenson) came in the 1820s and found desolation: 'Something like population was visible, in the swollen, squalid, hollow figures, who steal from straw sheds, or appear at work in the pestilential marshes; many of them were ghastly spectres, with nothing of humanity but its sensibility to suffering.'

This, of course, was after **Napoleon** burst into the somnolent province in 1798 and made it part of the 'Republic of Rome'; he divided it into two provinces, and sent in French administrators to undo centuries of papal misgovernment. While some cheered, pious peasants joined Catholic guerrilla bands who attacked the Jacobins and began a reign of terror in the countryside. The clergy returned when Napoleon signed his concordat with Pius VII, but then left again when Napoleon declared himself Emperor in 1808 and imprisoned the Pope. There was another flurry of activity, including an attempt to refound the University of Perugia, before Napoleon was overthrown in 1814. Umbria returned to the status quo, and two years later suffered one of its periodic famines and epidemics.

But even here, in this embalmed, browbeaten backwater, there was no going back. Reactionary popes such as Gregory XVI (1831–46) and Pius IX (1846–78) pushed some Umbrians to join in the general European revolutions, and to fight with Garibaldi and Mazzini to defend the short-lived Roman Republic in 1848–9. Pius had begun his papacy as a promising moderate reformer, but the revolution gave him an obsessive horror of anything connected with the modern world; typically, he refused to allow railways in Umbria for fear that the passengers might snog in the tunnels. When it became increasingly apparent that there was no use in waiting for Rome to reform, the Perugini rose in 1859 in support of the Risorgimento and the Piemontese king Vittorio Emanuele II. Pius sent in the Swiss Guards to quell the revolt, which they did with such brutality that all of Europe was shocked. But the Pope could hardly find anyone else to support his dying state. Two years later, Umbria along with the rest of the Papal States was joined to the new kingdom of Italy. The monasteries were dissolved, and the Perugini took the greatest pleasure imaginable in seizing the Rocca Paolina, the huge fortress that had become the ultimate symbol of papal oppression, and turning it into rubble.

## The Green Heart of Italy

Unfortunately, joining the new kingdom of Italy did not improve things for many Umbrians. For decades, it made things even worse. The majority were trying to scrape a living from the land, but the reactionary Piemontese kings were the last ones to rock the boat when it came to property and privilege. There were new taxes, and *mezzadria* would continue for another whole century, while even worse off were the day labourers, the *braccianti*, who survived hand to mouth. Many were so overworked and so malnourished that they became easy prey to pellagra and other diseases. Over the next few decades, tens of thousands emigrated to survive, mostly to France and Germany.

But, at the same time, major investments by the state worked to end Umbria's isolation, both physical and economic. Railways were finally built, and Terni, with its cheap hydroelectric power, was chosen to be the first centre of heavy industry in Italy: armaments, steel, jute and chemical factories were established here, and other centres, such as Narni, followed. Terni boomed to the position it holds today, as Umbria's second city.

Side by side with this modernization was a general awakening (by outsiders, mostly) to the region's special beauty that had begun with the early 18th-century Romantics. In 1870, the name Umbria was revived for the first time since Roman days as an administrative region, and only a few years later the poet Giosuè Carducci became the first to call it *Umbria Verde!* (Green Umbria) in one of his poems. As the Industrial Revolution chugged ahead, there was a revival of interest throughout Europe in St Francis, the nature-loving saint: parallels were drawn with his life and Christ's, and Umbria was proclaimed the Galilee of Italy; in the early 20th century, Umbrian politican Guido Pompili called it *verde e mistica*.

But this green Umbria was also rapidly taking on a new colour: red. In 1919 the first post-war elections in Umbria gave the Partito Socialista Italiano an absolute majority of votes, as the long oppressed farm and newly exploited industrial workers united. Reaction was not long in coming, in January 1920, when landowners formed the first Fascist group in Perugia, and immediately began to clash with the Socialists. A decade later the only Socialists were in Terni, although they had to remain clandestine as Mussolini went about busting up their union. For Terni was important to the Fascists, especially once Italy entered the war. The industry earned it unwanted attention from the Allied bombers; in the raids 2,000 were killed and medieval Terni was all but wiped off the map. Northern Umbria, where partisans harried the Germans, suffered severe reprisals.

After the war, 72 per cent of Umbrians voted for a republic over a monarchy and on the whole it has done well by them. The ancient curse of malaria was eradicated with DDT. New opportunities in industry and immigration proved to be the death knell at last for *mezzadria*, especially after a freak frost in 1956 killed nearly all of the region's olive trees. Small
industrial zones now surround most towns, some of them processing the foods Umbria is famous for, from Buitoni pasta to sausages, wine and Perugina chocolates. Perugia's university with its well-known school for foreigners has recaptured much of its old glory. Natural parks have been set up to preserve Umbria's remarkable natural beauty. And the region that was for hundreds of years a cultural desert has become a cultural dessert, serving up delights such as the Spoleto and Umbria Jazz Festivals to go with Umbria's innumerable art treasures and the spiritual lure of its saints. In the past two decades tourism has grown by leaps and bounds, and an average of two million visitors pass through every year.

Umbria has long suffered from earthquakes, and the one in September 1997 was a serious setback, especially as the region was preparing for the Jubilee Year 2000. Assisi managed to get the Basilica of St Francis open on time for the celebrations, but it will be another decade before everything is put to rights (*see* p.50).

# Art in Umbria

Umbria is full of treasures from the Middle Ages and Renaissance, and many of them can still be found in the church or convent or palazzo they were designed for. Much of this remarkable heritage was contributed by non-Umbrians, especially by painters and sculptors from the neighbouring art powerhouses of Florence, Siena and Rome, who worked on the prestigious projects at the Basilica of San Francesco in Assisi and the Cathedral of Orvieto. Native Umbrian artists learned from the works they left behind.

Reading the accounts of the Grand Tourists of the 18th century, it comes as a shock to realize that they sniffed at and disdained the frescoes we travel thousands of miles to see. Even Goethe 'turned away in distaste' from the trecento treasurehouse of the Basilica of San Francesco. After centuries of neglect, the first to take up the cause of Umbrian art, especially of Perugino and his school, were the German Nazarenes in the early 19th century. In the 1820s, the French painter Valéry made illustrations of the frescoes in Assisi, the Pinturicchios in Spello and the Peruginos in Città della Pieve and Panicale, and awakened a new interest in Umbrian art just as the Romantic poets were awakening a new interest in the landscapes. In the mid 19th century, the Pre-Raphaelites led a revival of interest in Perugino and the Umbrian school, the 'holy painters' who by some geo-psycho process of osmosis were influenced by the landscape and the mysticism of the region's saints to create a more spiritual art.

## The Pre-Peruginos

The first frescoes of note in Umbria are in the abbey of San Pietro in Valle, in the Valnerina, dated at around 1190 and among the most important in Italy for the time: not only because they've survived, but because they show the first inklings of a whole new western or Latin sensibility in art as opposed to the Greek Byzantine styles that had dominated the early ages in Ravenna and Rome. The anonymous **Master of the St Francis Cycle**, who worked in the great basilica in Assisi, is believed to have been an Umbrian; he worked in the mid 1200s, with the Florentine **Cimabue** (*c.* 1240–1302), who took the art of San Pietro in Valle a giant step further along the western road. The frescoes of the Master of St Francis and Cimabue in the basilica were only the first of many by great artists who would inspire generations of Umbrian painters. The most important of these was **Giotto** (*c.* 1266–1337), Cimabue's student, whose contribution to the basilica was as powerful as its exact nature is controversial. He and/or his disciples led the way, in the great *Life of St Francis* cycle in the upper church, in exploring new ideas in composition and expressing psychological meaning and humanity in his subjects. Through his intuitive grasp of perspective, Giotto was able to go further than any previous artist in representing his subjects as actual figures in space. In a sense Giotto actually invented space; it was this, despite his often awkward draughtsmanship, that so astounded his contemporaries. The recognizable Assisi settings were the precursors of the Umbrian fondness for localizing settings that would become a trademark of Perugino.

Along with the revolutionary Florentines, the other major contribution to Umbria's heritage and to its own trecento style came from Siena. In the 13th and 14th centuries, Siena's artists, while less innovative, rivalled and often surpassed those of Florence. The pivotal figure was **Duccio di Buoninsegna** (d. 1319), the catalyst who founded the essentials of Sienese art by uniting the beauty of Byzantine line and colour with the sweet finesse of western Gothic art.

Two of Duccio's greatest followers, **Pietro Lorenzetti** (d. 1348) and **Simone Martini** (d. 1344), worked in Assisi. The elegant and rarefied Martini was the great exponent of the International Gothic style—flowery and ornate, with all the bright tones of May—while Lorenzetti, known for his emotional expressiveness, left his most powerful works in Assisi. His talented brother-in-law and assistant, **Lippo Memmi** (d. 1347), contributed his masterpiece to Orvieto cathedral.

Their Umbrian followers were usually just as colourful if less sophisticated. In the next generation, the itinerant painters **Giovanni di Corraduccio** of Foligno and **Cola Petruccioli** introduced the International Gothic style around the region. Its greatest master, **Gentile da Fabriano** (c. 1360–1427) came from just over the border in the Marche, but left Perugia a fine altarpiece now in the Galleria Nazionale and a pretty fresco in Orvieto cathedral; his near contemporary, **Ottaviano Nelli** (c. 1375–c. 1440), had a delicate sense of colour and harmony, and left most of his work in his home town of Gubbio. Another Umbrian painter active in this period was the Dominican **Bartolomeo di Tommaso** of Foligno, more workmanlike and less original but still worth a look—one of his best works is based on the *Divine Comedy*, in Terni's church of San Francesco. The greatest of the native Umbrian painters of the time was **Masolino da Panicale** (c. 1383–1447), who worked alongside the revolutionary Masaccio in the famous Brancacci Chapel in Florence, but was otherwise known for his lyrical decorative work; in Umbria he left only one mediocre fresco, in San Fortunato in Todi.

Fresh influences came from Tuscany in the 15th century. The spiritual **Beato Angelico** (1400–55) worked in Orvieto and Perugia in the last decade of his life and left a major altarpiece now in Perugia's Galleria Nazionale, but most of all he left Umbria his student **Benozzo Gozzoli** (c. 1421–97), who learned much of his master's grace and sweetness if little of his spirituality. Gozzoli left a number of works in Umbria, but none of them equal to the splendid, worldly fairy-tale pageant he created for the Medici palace in Florence; his fresco cycle on the *Life of St Francis* at Montefalco seems soft, sweet and sentimental, but would exert a slippery influence on many Umbrian artists. One was the prolific and polished **L'Alunno** (Nicolò di Liberatore, c. 1430–1502) of Foligno; although his later works show more drama, they still rarely challenge the imagination.

Along with the spirituality of Angelico, another powerful inspiration for the region's artists was the work of **Piero della Francesca** (c. 1415–92), who is often considered an honorary Umbrian. Piero explored the limits of perspective and geometrical forms to create some of the most compelling, haunting images of the quattrocento, fusing geometry, light, colour, and landscapes (many of his native Upper Tiber) to create a mystical total atmosphere. His subjects are often archetypes of immense psychological depth, not to be fully explained now or ever. His altarpiece in the Galleria Nazionale in Perugia is his only work in Umbria proper, but some of his masterpieces are just over the border in Borgo Sansepolcro and Monterchi.

Perugia in particular produced a group of fine painters in the generation before Perugino. There's the meticulous **Benedetto Bonfigli** (c. 1420–96), known for his painted banners in Perugia churches; his best works, the Cappella dei Priori frescoes, show the spatial influence of Piero. The elegant and colourful **Bartolomeo Caporali** (1420–1503) was closer to Gozzoli, and a great lover of natural detail; many of his paintings still decorate the churches in and around Perugia. A third Perugian, **Fiorenzo di Lorenzo** (c. 1440–1525), changed his style so often that attributions are often a problem; one of his best frescoes is now in the Pinacoteca of Deruta. Outside of Perugia, two painters who worked mainly around their home towns were **Pierantonio Mezzastris** (*c.* 1430–1506) of Foligno and **Matteo da Gualdo** of Gualdo Tadino (*c.* 1430–1503), who created conventional, colourful, stylized works and had probably never heard of Florence.

## Perugino and the Umbrian School

When most art historians talk of an 'Umbrian School of art', they start with Pietro Vannucci, better known as **Perugino**, *c.* 1450–1523, of Città della Pieve near Lake Trasimeno. Like Leonardo da Vinci, Perugino was a student of Andrea Verrocchio, who instilled a love of nature and landscapes in both of his students. They would both make their landscapes a very integral part of their paintings—Leonardo preferring the dramatic scenery of the Italian lakes, Perugino opting for the more idyllic soothing countryside around Trasimeno. Another tradition has it that Perugino studied under Piero della Francesca; true or not, he certainly absorbed Piero's lessons of space and clarity, and developed a distinctive idealized type of figure. He was one of the most famous painters of his time, with commissions from all over Italy; the Pope summoned him to Rome with Botticelli and Ghirlandaio to paint the walls of the Sistine Chapel. Although he was adept at fresco and portraiture, most of his commissions were for devotional paintings, which his patrons couldn't get enough of. At his best he created works of genius, along with countless idyllic nativity scenes, each with its impeccably sweet Madonna and characteristic blue-green tinted landscape, filled with the stillness of Umbria. His art—classic, Virgilian, eulogic, serene, beautiful—turned its back on the individualist, restless, innovative spirits of Leonardo and Michelangelo. When not at his best, Perugino walks a fine tightrope over the Umbrian tendency to tumble into sweetness. Some of his later works are so awful they make you want to brush your teeth, although in most cases he wasn't completely at fault: in his cynical old age he let his workshop sign his name to anything.

Perugino is perhaps best known for his precocious pupil **Raphael** (1483–1520). Raphael's painter-humanist father, Giovanni di Santi, was a great admirer of Perugino, and during his son's earliest phase as an independent artist, working around Umbria and Tuscany, Perugino's influence is overwhelming even as Raphael quickly surpassed him. He left quite a few works in Umbria, but unfortunately his reputation as the greatest painter who ever lived saw most of them looted by Napoleon's troops, and none were ever returned: the superb *Betrothal of the Virgin*, painted for the Franciscans in Città di Castello, was carried off to the Brera in Milan; the *Madonna di Foligno* is now in the Vatican museum; the *Crucifixion* from San Domenico in Perugia is now in the National Gallery in London. The only Raphaels in Umbria today are Città di Castello's standard and some frescoes he painted as a teenager in the Collegio del Cambio and San Severo in Perugia.

Another student or rather collegue of Perugino was **Pinturicchio** (Bernardino di Betto, 1454–1513) of Perugia, who earned his name for his use of gold and rich colours. Pinturicchio was never an innovator, but as a virtuoso in colour, style and charming decorative effects few could beat him; he followed the Gozzoli of the Medici frescoes rather than the Gozzoli of Montefalco. He was another establishment artist, especially favoured by the popes, and, like Perugino, he was slandered most vilely by Vasari; in Umbria his best works are in Spello's Santa Maria Maggiore and in Perugia's Galleria Nazionale.

The most exceptional works in Umbria from this period, however, are the frescoes in Orvieto cathedral by **Luca Signorelli** (*c.* 1441–1523), a pupil of Piero della Francesca from Cortona, just north of Lake Trasimeno. Signorelli never painted anything else like these six great scenes of the end of the world; his imaginative, forceful compositions, combining geometrical rigour with a touch of unreality, owe something to Piero, while his vigorous, expressive male nudes were derived from a study of the Florentine Antonio Pollaiolo. Michelangelo took a good long look at them on his way to painting his own *Last Judgement* in the Sistine Chapel.

Other Umbrian artists of the 16th century followed the leaders: **Lo Spagna** (Giovanni di Pietro, *c.* 1450–1528) at his best incorporates the more delicate aspects of Perugino's sweetness with some of the compositional mastery of Raphael. Others who followed Perugino to a degree were **Tiberio d'Assisi** (*c.* 1470–1524), **Giannicola di Paolo** (*c.* 1460–1544) and **Pier Matteo d'Amelia** (d. 1508); the latter is best known for his work with Fra Lippi in Spoleto cathedral. Another, **Eusebio da San Giorgio** (*c.* 1470–1540) was a follower of Raphael, while **Dono Doni** of Assisi (d. 1575) and **Domenico di Paride Alfani** of Perugia (d. 1554) looked towards Michelangelo. Non-Umbrians such as the Pisan painter **Niccolò Pomarancio** and his son Antonio worked extensively in the region, and there's an excellent **Rosso Fiorentino** in Città di Castello, along with a couple of **Guercinos**. Afterwards Rome sucked in all the money and talent, leaving almost nothing of note in or from Umbria until the 20th century and **Alberto Burri** of Città di Castello (1915–95), whose visceral reaction to the horrors of the Second World War was to seek a more honest and moral art in the detritus of modern civilization.

## Topics

After the Earthquakes: Art versus People     50

Guelphs and Ghibellines     51

St Francis of Assisi     52

Landscapes and Nature     55

Umbria's Totem Tubers     57

The Ultimate Umbrian Accessory     58

## After the Earthquakes: Art versus People

According to geologists, the earthquakes that violently jolted Umbria and the Marche twice on 26 September 1997, killing 11 and wounding many more, and the aftershocks that continued throughout 1998, when over 10,000 minor and not so minor tremors were registered, were merely part of a million-year-old trend as the Apennines yawn and stretch and adjust to fit their crust. The 100,000 people in Umbria and the Marche whose homes were rendered uninhabitable by the tremors obviously didn't find much comfort in their scientific long-range perspective, but in the immediate aftermath of the disaster things could have been worse. The government, both on a local and national level, responded quickly, so that by Christmas 1997 everyone was housed as close to their villages as possible, in rental accommodation, in prefab housing or, as a last resort, in shipping containers (fitted with doors, windows, room dividers, and soon with electricity and plumbing). People got on with their lives relatively quickly, nor was it long before the famous skylines of the hill towns were dominated by cranes and scaffolding. After all, there's a certainly familiarity with earthquakes in the area; a serious one rocked the eastern Valnerina and parts of the Valle Umbra in 1979.

This one, however, grabbed the world's attention because it gravely damaged one of Italy's most precious and best loved treasures, the Basilica di San Francesco in Assisi, just as the town was gearing up for the Holy Year 2000 celebrations. For most of the world, the earthquakes became the 'Assisi earthquakes'. Billions of lire poured in from the state, charities and other sources to restore the art, and a regional office of the Commissione dei Beni Culturali opened in Foligno to direct the flow. Priority was given to a 'Jubilee list' of art and monuments on the official pilgrimage route, but even so, nearly a third of the entire budget in 1998 went to the big basilica; in Assisi everyone vowed it would reopen by Christmas 1999 and it did—an impressive feat, especially in Italy where projects on that scale usually take decades to complete.

Yet even in mid 2000, some people in Assisi are still living in a 'container village' on the outskirts of town. Less famous towns sometimes have two or three container villages. The worst hit places (Colfiorito, for instance, which was one of the epicentres in September 1997) are all but abandoned except for the occasional stalwarts who refuse to leave, living amid the rubble and ruined houses, where fallen walls still reveal bright wallpaper or other poignant vignettes of the residents' former lives. Some of the smaller villages may never be rebuilt. But elsewhere there has been no lack of polemics over the way the government has handled the rehousing. Plenty of money was available for restoration, but a huge amount of it (in some cases, as much as half of a town's allotted sum) has gone into other pockets—not those of corrupt politicians and organized crime, as happened in Naples after its big earthquake in 1983—but to pay for the countless permits, licences, and opinions by various state experts required even before the real work could begin. In the opinion of many residents, the bureaucrats were battening on Umbria's misfortune.

Another controversy is the decision to take temporary measures. Since the rebuilding of houses in some cases will take several years to complete, there are plans, such as in Foligno, to move people out of the containers and put them into wooden chalet-style buildings. Many feel these are a ridiculous waste of time and money, when the resources could be poured into the final result. There's also the fear that people will get used to living in prefab housing and their villages may never be the same; or the question of just who will live in the wooden chalets once people are rehoused, with dark hints that they will be taken over by the numerous but not universally popular Albanians and Kosovans now living in the area. It also brings to the surface some often bitter soul-searching on the question of just whom Umbria really belongs to: the descendants of people who have lived there for generations, many just working their way out of real poverty, or the owners of second homes, who want the region to remain quaint and old and beautiful, and complain about the newish unattractive suburbs and small factories where the year-round Umbrians work for a living, those who have managed to stay and not leave for Rome or Florence or even France and Germany to find decent jobs.

So has art been given precedence over people in Umbria? In many cases the answer is yes, although the result isn't quite as cold and heartless as it may sound. For a year or so after the earthquakes, tourists shied away from the region, partly because they were afraid of more tremors, but mostly because the key sights were closed. Tourism is a major source of income in Umbria and 1998 was an economic disaster for the area. So, by repairing and reopening the major attractions (and bringing visitors back in a big way), many argue that the overall result benefits everybody, and will even trickle down to the unfortunate souls still living in the containers—for the most part the unemployed, the poor and the old-age pensioners.

All kinds of restoration projects on buildings not directly damaged by the earthquakes have been undertaken, on buildings and art that otherwise would have been left to crumble slowly. In these cases, local authorities benefited from the influx of expert restorers and of money, and from a heightened focus of attention on 'Art' in Umbria. Once work has been completed, visitors will find things in a much better state than they would have been had the earthquake never happened. Assisi is a particular example. The damage was extensive, but the restoration has been so spectacular that those buildings will be in better condition than they have been for hundreds of years once the scaffolding comes down. Even the priceless frescoes inside the Basilica of San Francesco may shine again. Some twenty restorers are employed full-time working their way through trays of rubble, trying to piece together the world's most intricate jigsaw puzzle. Apparently they can, at a glance, distinguish fragments of colours enough to know which artist the minute pieces belong to. On that note, at least in the long-range view of things, the disaster may have been a blessing in disguise.

## Guelphs and Ghibellines

One medieval Italian writer claimed that the great age of factional strife in his nation began with two brothers of Pistoia, named Guelf and Gibel. Like Cain and Abel, or Romulus and Remus, one murdered the other, starting the seemingly endless troubles that to many seemed a God-sent plague, meant to punish the proud and wealthy Italians for their sins. Medieval Italy may in fact have been guilty of every sort of jealousy, greed and wrath— Perugia was near the top of the list on all three counts—but most historians trace the beginnings of this party conflict to two great German houses, *Welf* and *Waiblingen*.

To the Italians, what those barbarians did across the Alps meant little; the chroniclers pinpoint the outbreak of the troubles to the year 1215, when a politically prominent Florentine noble named Buondelmonte dei Buondelmonti was assassinated by his enemies while crossing the Ponte Vecchio. It was the tinder that ignited a smouldering quarrel all over Italy, and explains the often pathological behaviour of medieval Umbria. The atmosphere of contentious city-states, each with its own internal struggles between nobles, rich merchant class and commoners, crystallized rapidly into parties. In the beginning, at least, they stood for something. The Guelphs, largely a creation of the newly wealthy bourgeois, were all for free trade and the rights of the free cities; the Ghibellines from the start were the party of the German emperors, nominal overlords of Italy who had been trying to assert their control ever since the days of Charlemagne. Naturally, the Guelphs found their protector in the emperors' bitter temporal rivals, the popes. This brought a religious angle into the story, especially with the advent of the ex-communicated Emperor Frederick II, who destroyed and rebuilt a number of villages in Umbria and set up court in Foligno in defiance of the tirades from Rome.

Everything about this convoluted history tends to confirm the worst suspicions of modern behavioural scientists. Before long, the labels Guelph and Ghibelline ceased to have any meaning at all. In the 13th and 14th centuries, the emperors and their Ghibelline allies helped the Church root out heretical movements like the Patarenes, while the popes schemed to destroy the liberty of good Guelph cities, especially in Umbria, and incorporate them into the Papal States. Black was the Ghibelline colour, white the Guelph, and cities arranged themselves like squares on a chessboard. When one suffered a revolution and changed from Guelph to Ghibelline, or vice versa, of course its nearest enemies would soon change the other way.

The English, like many uninvolved European nations, looked on all this with bewilderment. Edmund Spenser, in glosses to his *Shepheards' Calendar* (1579), wrote this fanciful etymology:

> *When all Italy was distraicte into the Factions of the Guelfes and the Gibelins, being two famous houses in Florence, the name began through their great mischiefes and many outrages, to be so odious or rather dreadfull in the peoples eares, that if theyr children at any time were frowarde and wanton, they would say to them the Guelfe or the Gibeline came. Which words nowe from them (as may thinge els) be come into our vsage, and for Guelfes and Gibelines, we say Elfes and Goblins.*

## St Francis of Assisi

Francesco Bernardone was one of most remarkable men who ever lived, and although he's now the patron saint of all Italy, he always remained closely attached to his native Umbria, in life as well as death; nearly every town in the region seems to have a legend about him, or at least a Franciscan church founded in the early days of his movement. He lived in what the Chinese call interesting times. His gentle spiritual revolution occurred amidst the sound and the fury that fills the chronicles of the 13th century. While the Guelphs and Ghibellines were going at it tooth and nail and the Church was becoming increasingly worldly, wealthy and ambitious, Francis taught that the natural world was a beautiful place, and that there was tremendous joy in living an ordinary humble life in it in the imitation of Christ.

Francis was born in 1182 to a merchant, Pietro Bernardone, and his Provençal wife, Madonna Pica. Some say Pietro was the richest man in Assisi; he travelled often through the south of France, buying and selling fine cloth, and although he named his son Giovanni at the baptismal font he always called him Francesco after the country he loved. At one point Francis accompanied his father on his annual journey through Provence and up the Rhône to Bruges and Ghent, but most of all he used his father's wealth to finance a merry and dissipated youth; according to his first biographer, Tommaso da Celano, he was 'the first instigator of every evil, and behind none in foolishness'. He was also a poet in the troubadour tradition. His Francophile upbringing gave him an early taste for the cult of chivalry and mystic love, imported from Provence and by 1200 all the rage among young Italians.

His conversion to saintliness did not happen overnight. In 1202, Francis joined the cavalry of Assisi in one of its many wars against Perugia, but was captured and spent a dismal year in a Perugian prison. He also suffered a long, severe illness. The two events that made him stop and think; he yearned for something more than the carefree life he had been living. At first he thought it might be chivalry, so he joined with a band riding to join the Fourth Crusade. He got as far as Spoleto when he fell ill again. He took this as a warning that he was on the wrong track, and changed his allegiance from a temporal lord to a spiritual one.

Francis began to spend his time alone in the woods and meadows around Assisi, reflecting on the world's vanity. A revelation came to him while attending Mass one Sunday in 1205, as the priest read the words of the Gospel: '... and as ye go, preach, saying, the kingdom of Heaven is at hand. Heal the sick, cleanse the lepers, raise the dead, cast out devils: freely have ye received, freely give.' Francis took this message literally: he would live like Christ, in poverty and humility. The story goes that he took his final decision before the Crucifix in the little church of San Damiano outside Assisi, which spoke to him, saying 'Repair my house, which you see is in ruins.' Francis sold his father's pack horse and merchandise in Foligno to do just that; when his angry father hauled him before the bishop of Assisi and reproached him, Francis stripped off his rich clothes and declared that henceforth his only father was his father in heaven.

It has been commented that much of Franciscan legend comes in too tidy exemplary packages to be taken as literal truth, but there is no doubt that this merchant's son who called himself 'God's Fool' and lived in total poverty, kissing lepers and preaching to the outcasts of the world, struck a chord in the hearts of many thirsting for something beyond the carrot and stick fare offered by the medieval Church. Although at first he was chased and stoned by the boys of Assisi as he begged for alms, Francis soon attracted a band of followers who lived with him in the Porziuncola, a chapel on the plain below Assisi, and wandered about the area preaching, doing odd jobs to support themselves or begging their bread.

His visit in 1210 to Pope Innocent III is part of Franciscan legend. Innocent was the man perhaps most responsible for the new worldly and militant direction of the Church, and he had little truck with reformers or anyone critical of its ambitions and corruption (in the previous year, he had declared the Albigensian Crusade against the other-worldly Cathars in southern France). His proud and wealthy court scoffed at the shabby Umbrian holy man, but that night Innocent dreamt that his church of St John Lateran—then the seat of the popes—was collapsing, and that this same Francis came along to hold up its walls.

Dream or not, it did occur to the pope that he might be able to harness the spiritual renewal that Francis preached within the institutions of the Church; unlike the Cathars and other heretics, Francis never attacked the papal hierarchy, explicitly at any rate, although his beliefs that a person could live by the Gospel in the 13th century and that the love of money was the root of all evil were harder to fit in the current scheme. Innocent nevertheless confirmed his First Rule for a simple lay order based on poverty, which Francis called the *Frati Minori*. As the movement quickly grew and the roads filled with begging friars, the Church tried to convince Francis to impose on it the discipline of a monastic rule. Francis resisted this, having no interest in organization; he never even took holy orders.

In the meantime, Francis spent his time travelling and preaching, mostly in Umbria, where many villages can show a humble stone in a cave where the saint rested his head or tell a legend of his sway over the birds and beasts. In 1219, he went further afield, as far as Spain in an unsuccessful attempt to reach Morocco, and then to the Holy Land and Egypt, accompanying the Crusaders. At Damietta, on the Nile, he preached to Sultan Malik el Kamil and was warmly received. The story goes that Francis was on an apostolic mission to convert the infidels, but it's just as likely he went to learn from them, especially from the Sufi mystics, not too surprising for a former troubadour, immersed in ideas of divine love that had come originally from the East during the first Crusades. One of the more intriguing parallels was a Sufi brotherhood very similar to the Friars Minor, founded some sixty years before Francis's birth by a holy man named Najmuddin Kubra, a wandering preacher with an uncanny influence over birds and animals.

Drawing on his troubadour days, Francis composed some of the first and finest vernacular verse in Italy, including the famous *Canticle of the Sun*, a poem in his native Umbrian dialect on the unity of all creation. His poetry became the foundation of a literary movement, based on Christian devotion: Tommaso da Celano, one of Francis's first followers and his autobiographer, composed the powerful *Dies Irae*, followed a few decades later by Jacopone da Todi (*see* pp.170–72), after Dante the greatest poet of his century.

By 1221 Francis's extraordinary character and sanctity had inspired a movement of spiritual renewal that had spread across Italy and beyond. Unwilling to manage the growing organization, he turned the vicarship of the Friars Minor to Pietro Catani, who soon died, and then to Brother Elias. 'Henceforth I am dead to you,' he declared to the friars, and went to live in retreat with his early followers. But he wasn't quite dead; realizing that the movement was already slipping away from his intentions, he wrote a second Rule (1223) under Pope Honorius III that created the Franciscan order based on poverty as a supreme good, and confirmed it in his testament, urging his friars to remain 'wayfarers and pilgrims in this world'. It was at Christmas in the same year that he reconstructed a manger scene in Greccio (a village just south of Umbria), to emphasize the humble, human, child side of Christ as opposed to the stern arbitrator of the Last Judgement. The Italians were charmed and have been making their Christmas *presepi* ever since.

During the last three years of his life, Francis spent most of his time at the sanctuary of La Verna in Tuscany, where in 1225 he received the stigmata that seemed to confirm his life as an imitation of Christ. Increasingly frail, he returned to Assisi a year later to meet his good Sister Death at age 44. In less than two years he was canonized by Gregory IX, who as Cardinal Ugolino had been his friend and one of the Order's first protectors. At the same time, Gregory also did much to defuse Francis's dangerous legacy by declaring that his testament was not binding, and by directing the Franciscans down the path of the other new preaching order of the 13th century, the Dominicans. Huge churches, urban convents, university education, rich donations to be 'used' by the property-less friars soon came into being, explained away as being necessary for the times. The order split into the 'Conventuals', who agreed, and the 'Spirituals', who wanted to hold on to their founders' prescription of poverty, the more extreme going off on paths of esoteric mysticism that would have probably appalled Francis as much as his order's prosperity.

But for the average Italian in the streets these intermural disputes took nothing away from the humane Christianity of love and charity exemplified by Francis and preached by his friars. His native Assisi quickly became a place of pilgrimage, and his native land was well on its way to becoming *Umbria mistica*.

## Landscapes and Nature

Other regions in Italy have taller mountains and more fertile valleys, others support a far greater variety of flora and enjoy a more temperate climate. Yet when all is said and done, it is the landscapes of Umbria that exert the most lasting charm of the region. Would St Francis now be the patron saint of the Green Party if he had been born in the sun-baked prairies of Oklahoma? In the paintings of the Renaissance, the backgrounds of rolling hills and rocky peaked mountains, orderly cypresses, poplars and parasol pines, blue-green Lake Trasimeno and multi-towered towns in the distance are often more beautiful than the nominally religious subject in the foreground. Very early on, beginning with Giotto and his followers, Umbrian artists took special care to relate the figures in their composition to the architecture and the landscape around them, to the extent that for many art lovers, at any rate, the expression 'Holy Land' conjures lush scenes of Umbria rather than the decidedly more arid countryside around Jerusalem.

The beauty of the countryside may be natural, but it's no accident. Every Italian is born with an obsessive instinct to put in order, or *sistemare* things; with a history of wars, earthquakes, foreign rulers, and an age-old tendency to extremes of all descriptions, the race has had a bellyful of disorder and unpredictability. The tidy, ordered geometry and clipped hedges of an Italian garden are a perfect example of the urge to *sistemare* nature; the Tuscans, in the vanguard of Italy in so many ways, were the first to *sistemare* their entire territory. The vicious medieval wars between cities and the Guelphs and Ghibellines devastated the countryside and much of the forests; the Black Death in the 1300s depopulated the cultivated areas, offering a unique opportunity to arrange things just so.

The Valle Umbra has an air of exquisite civilization not unlike Tuscany, but in general Umbria is more dramatic than its Tuscan neighbour; hills here tend to be steeper, the precious valleys narrower, its forests denser, just the sort of countryside sought by hermits and saints. Since the 19th century it has been celebrated for its greenness, the most mystical of colours, which suits its mystical nature. One feature of the Umbrian landscape, however, is as artful as Tuscany—its hill towns of pinkish-grey stone. From some vantage points you can see several at a time, like an archipelago of islands crowned with villages, one behind the other, vanishing into the bluish haze of the horizon, in autumn swirled in mists.

Close up, the flora and fauna that populate Umbria's hills are close cousins to those seen in northern Europe and America, only somehow they seem more splendid, like the saints in Perugino's paintings, for their lovely settings. There are a million varieties of buttercup, usually tiny ones like the *ranuncolo* and *bottoncini d'oro*, and of bluebell, called *campanella* or *campanellina*. Many of the common five-petalled pink blossoms in spring fields are really small wild geraniums (*geranio*), with pointed leaves like the anemone, and you'll see quite a few varieties of violets (*violette*) with round or spade-shaped leaves (a few species are yellow). A daisy, in Italian, is a *margherita*, and they come in all sizes. Tiniest of all are the wild pink and blue forget-me-nots (*non ti scordar di me*); you'll have to look closely to see them in overgrown fields.

The real star of the fields is the poppy, bright red and thriving everywhere in the spring as if the whole landscape was kissed with a dashing shade of lipstick. Dandelions and wild mustard are plentiful, along with white, umbrella-like bunches of florets called *tragosellino* or *podragraria*, similar to what Americans call Queen Anne's Lace. More exotic flowers include wild orchids, some with small florets growing in spiky shoots, and rhododendrons (in mountainous areas). The best wildflowers are up in the Sibillini mountains; the Piano Grande blooming in early summer is an unforgettable sight.

There are other plants to look for. A dozen kinds of wild greens that go into somewhat bitter salads, anise, fennel, mint, rosemary and sage are common. The Umbrians beat the bushes with fervour every spring looking for wild asparagus and repeat the performance in autumn searching for truffles and mushrooms.

As for the animals, you can start with those two regional totems, the viper and the boar. The bad old viper, the only really unpleasant thing you may encounter in Umbria, proliferates especially where farmlands have been abandoned; he's brownish-grey, about a foot and half long (never more than a yard), and has a vaguely diamond-shaped head. In spite of his retiring, shy nature, the viper is a nuisance only because he is so numerous, and because he objects to being stepped on. If one bites you, you've got half an hour to find someone with the serum—or you can buy your own in any pharmacy and keep it in the fridge. The boar, an equally shy creature, flourishes everywhere despite the Umbrian hunters' best efforts to turn him into salami or prosciutto. In summer, you may hear him nosing around the villages at night looking for water.

Beyond these, there are plenty of hares and rabbits, foxes and weasels, also polecats, badgers and porcupine (the latter a local delicacy in the more remote corners of Umbria). Wolves, lynxes and deer were once common, and a few of each survive in the higher reaches of the Apennines; in the 1990s wolves were spotted again near Assisi and Nocera, and brown bears apparently have migrated from the Abruzzo into the Sibylline mountains.

Many writers on Umbria comment on the silence of the country and the absence of birdsong. They're exaggerating, although it is true the Umbria has more hunters per capita and they do shoot anything that flies, but there are still quite a few thrushes, starlings, wrens and such, along with the white doves, ubiquitous in Umbria, that always make you think of Assisi and St Francis. Cuckoos unfailingly announce the spring, pheasants lie low during the hunting season, and an occasional owl can be heard in the country. Nightingales are rare; in the evening you're far more likely to see bats.

The insect world is well represented, and if you spend time in the country you'll meet many (perhaps too many) of them: lovely butterflies and moths and delicate white feather-winged creatures; rather forbidding black bullet bees and wasps that resemble vintage fighter planes. Beetles especially reach disproportionate sizes, especially the *diavolo*, a large black or red beetle with long, gracefully curving antlers that sing when you trap it; Leonardo drew one in his notebooks, and rumour has it that they mate for life. On summer nights in the country, if you're lucky, the fireflies put on a magical kinetic display worthy of Times Square. There are enough mosquitoes, midges and little biting flies to be a nuisance, and, perhaps most alarming at first sight, the shiny black scorpion, who may crawl inside through the window or up drains—you may want to keep the plugs in—or come in with the firewood. Once inside they head for dark places like beds or shoes. One thwack with a shoe means curtains for a scorpion (they're actually quite soft), but you may start feeling sorry for the little critters. Most people we know have devised cunning scorpion traps and take their captives back to the woods. If you happen to be stung, it may be painful but not deadly; the Italians recommend a trip to the doctor for treatment against an infection or allergic reaction.

## Umbria's Totem Tubers

Umbria's most valuable cash crop has neither seeds nor a planting season, and adamantly refuses to grow in straight rows. An aura of mystery surrounds their very nature; according to legend they are spawned by lightning bolts flickering among the oaks. Truffles they are, *tartufi*, and although they look a lot like granulated mud on your pasta, these earthy, aromatic and aphrodisiac tubers that are actually a weird type of fungi are the most prized gourmet delicacy in Italy. Even in their natural state they aren't much to look at, bulbous lumps from the size of a pea to a baby's fist, and they're very picky about where they grow. Umbria is one of their favourite spots—here are the proper calcareous soils, oak and beech forests and exposures, especially around Spoleto, Norcia, and most especially in the Valnerina around Scheggino. This is the realm of the highest quality black truffle (*tuber melangosporum Vittadini*), which in Europe grow here, and in Perigord in France, and almost nowhere else. The even rarer white truffle (*tuber magnatum Pico*), mostly found in Piemonte, deigns to grow around Gubbio, and is avidly sought from October to December. The black truffle season is considerably longer, extending into March. Out of season you can find them bottled in oil (never buy fresh except in season—they just won't be good) but they are absolutely heavenly when fresh from the ground and offer a perfectly legitimate reason for visiting Umbria in the off season (serious eaters might want to aim for the February gastronomic fair in Norcia).

Except for saffron, gram for gram truffles are the most expensive comestible in the world. Prices for a good white truffle can easily top a staggering L4,500,000 a kilo, while the more common black truffles are half as much, but still make a dent in the pocketbook. Not only are they resistant to cultivation, but they're fiendishly hard to track down. The vast majority are still brought to market by secretive truffle hunters and their keen-nosed, specially trained hounds, who learn to love the smell as tiny pups, because of the truffle juice rubbed around their mother's teats. They are gathered during the night, when the truffles smell the strongest, or perhaps because the best truffles are always on someone else's land. Beware: truffle-hunting requires not only a dog and a special digging implement called a *vanghetta*, but also a licence. And competition can be deadly—the 1997 season was marred in Umbria by a psycho truffle-dog poisoner. Fortunately, a little *tartufo* goes a long way, and Italians will travel far to look, dreamy-eyed, at glass jars of them at Umbria's truffle fairs.

Profits are such that imitations have made considerable headway in recent years. Beware synthesized truffle aromas, which are nothing like the real thing, or cheap low-grade black truffles imported from China that lack the pungent, aromatic intensity of the Umbrian-grown. Also you'd do well to steer clear of one local truffle product—the nubby black bottles of Tartufo liqueur, which tastes as vile as it looks.

If you want to make a good impression in rural Umbria, there is one accessory, one essential item that will open every door and heart to you. It may not be the fashionable sort of thing you'd want in Milan or Florence, nor can you buy it in any shop, but if you aren't already blessed you may want to consider borrowing one from a relative or friend for the duration of your stay. This useful accessory is, of course, a small child.

All the stereotypes you've ever heard about Italians and *bambini* are two hundred per cent true, but in the lovely hill towns of Umbria there's a distinct shortage of little people—a shortage even more acute than Italy's negative birth rate would suggest. The economics, not at all improved by the earthquakes, are such that many Umbrian villagers are elderly, and when they die their houses tend to become second homes for their heirs or sold on a hungry market—these days an Umbrian villa or farmhouse, exquisitely restored to a luxurious level of medieval authenticity is the ultimate fashion statement for wealthy Milanese and Romans, not to mention foreigners. But unfortunately, from their greying neighbours' point of view, they rarely bring along any children to tear down the lanes of the hill town. The famous silence of Umbria is not only from a lack of traffic and birdsong.

If you have young children, however, there is a distinct danger that you may forget what they look like. An Umbrian village, especially a small one, will absorb them the way a thirsty plant sucks up water. You also may as well give up any thought of having an identity of your own; you will be *la mamma di Johnny* or *il pappa di Suzy*, nothing more or nothing less. But it's almost as good as being minor royalty.

Unlike children, however, you as a parent can do wrong in the eyes of the villagers, sometimes in unexpected ways: letting them go outside with wet hair, or drink something directly from the fridge, or work up a sweat, or giving them sandwiches for lunch. You may be forgiven for being a non-Umbrian, but the village will make up for your shortcomings by stuffing your child with prosciutto, homemade tortellini and wild pigeon as a supplement to all the cakes and sweets and sodas that simply go without saying. The sheer pleasure many Umbrians get from simply watching a child eat is extraordinary, and many women go about armed with a pound of sweets in their bags, ready to pop one into any little mouth they see. Our three-year-old caused a sensation in the local nursery, the *asilo*, by asking for more: '*più pasta asciutta*' in her baby accent. Unlike the case of Dickens' Oliver, however, this request was regarded as immensely clever and wonderful and within weeks the entire Valnerina, with only slight exaggeration, was singing her praises.

In many ways, if you have the luxury to pick and choose, an Umbrian village is an ideal place to bring up a child. Few places in western Europe have such a close-knit sense of community. Everyone looks out for everyone else, and the natural kindness of the Umbrians is simply overwhelming. But try to find one with a few children already on location, or yours may be a bit lonesome for their peers. The reason why the birth rate is so low is certainly not from any lack of love for children, but oddly from too much: the Italian desire to give them absolutely everything (this includes not only the finest designer clothes, but eventually a car and a furnished apartment) is so strong that the idea of dividing it by having more than one child just seems unfair.

| | |
|---|---|
| Perugia | 60 |
| Around Perugia: Torgiano, Deruta and Corciano | 80 |
| Lake Trasimeno | 82 |
| South of Lake Trasimeno | 88 |
| Città della Pieve | 88 |
| Panicale and Around | 90 |
| Assisi | 91 |
| West of Assisi | 109 |

## Perugia, Lake Trasimeno, and Assisi

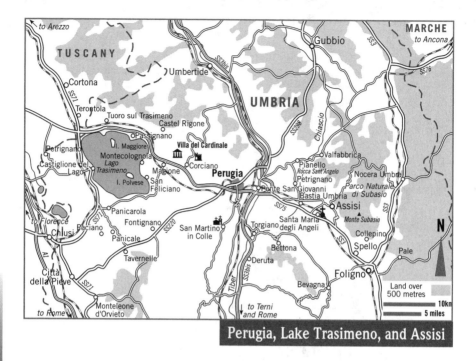

Perugia, Lake Trasimeno, and Assisi

Umbria's capital Perugia is one of Italy's greatest art cities, an intensely atmospheric place with some of the most medieval streets in Europe. The Perugians have their own 'riviera' just a hop and skip to the west, on the gentle shores of Lake Trasimeno, with its bijou islands and mighty castles; Perugino was born just to the south of the lake in Città della Pieve and made these bluish-green landscapes his own. To the east, in view from Perugia's balconies, there's lovely cream- and pink-coloured Assisi, the home of St Francis, and Italy's finest collection of trecento painting.

## Perugia

*What a town for assassinations!*

H. V. Morton

Balanced on a commanding hill high over the Tiber, Perugia (pop. 155,000) is a fascinating medieval acrobat able to juggle adroitly several roles at the same time: that of an ancient hill town, a magnificent *città d'arte*, a bustling university centre and a slick cosmopolitan city, famous above all for chocolates. It is a fit capital for Umbria, with splendid monuments from the Etruscan era to the Late Renaissance stacked next to one another; its gallery contains the region's finest art, but in the alleyways cats sleep undisturbed.

Yet its sun-filled present is haunted by sinister shadows from the past. Four medieval popes died in Perugia. One did himself in—stuffing his gut with Lake Trasimeno eels—but for the other three the verdict was poison. And then there were the Baglioni, the powerful family that ruled this city for a time; they were so dangerous they nearly exterminated themselves. Blissful Assisi, perfumed with the odour of sanctity, may be only over the next hill, but Perugia in the old days was as full of trouble as a town could be. As so often in medieval and Renaissance Italy, creativity and feistiness went hand-in-hand, and the Umbrian capital has contributed more than its share to Italian culture and art. Their biggest annual event is a jazz festival. Just as remarkable as the people is the stage they act on: the oldest, most romantically medieval streets and squares in Italy.

A strange thing happened to Perugia in the middle of its rough-house career. The great cities of Tuscany also suffered in the political changes of the 1500s, but to Perugia fell the singular privilege of becoming a part of the Papal States. Art, scholarship, trade and civic life quickly withered, and the town's traditional penchant for violence was rocked to sleep under a warm blanket of Hail Marys. Look at Perugia now, a little over a hundred years after liberation—its people famed for their politeness, urbanity and good taste; Perugians dress more sharply than the Florentines for half the money and effort. They make their living from chocolates and ladies' shoes, and teaching Italian language and culture to foreigners. Maybe a few centuries under the pope was just what they needed.

## History

Gubbio, Perugia's longtime rival, liked to claim it was one of the first cities founded by Noah's sons after the flood. Naturally the Perugians had to top that, and one of the city's medieval chroniclers records that Noah himself, at the age of 500 or so, pitched his tents on Perugia's mountain. That would probably have been news to the Etruscans, who had settled *Pieresa* by the 5th century BC and probably much earlier. *Pieresa* was the easternmost city of the Dodecapolis, and maintained its freedom until the Roman conquest of 309 BC.

Never entirely happy under Roman rule, the city staged several revolts in the republican era. In the years after Caesar's assassination it chose the wrong side with catastrophic results: Octavian's troops besieged it for seven months, and after the capitulation an Etruscan diehard decided to commit suicide rather than surrender—unfortunately his funeral pyre started a conflagration that took the rest of the city with him. Some years later Octavian, by then **Emperor Augustus**, decided to rebuild the city and rename it after himself—*Augusta Perusia*. Almost nothing is known of the city's passage through the Dark Ages. Totila the Goth took it from the Byzantines around 545, after a (probably apocryphal) siege of seven years, but the Exarchs of Ravenna were still, with the Lombards, contending for it 50 years later.

Among the constantly changing alliances of medieval Italian states, Perugia found itself in a fortunate position: out of the turbulent mainstream, with no large and dangerous neighbours, and a potential ally (when it suited Perugia) of pope, emperor, or any of the contentious cities over in Tuscany. As a result, the Perugians, although they never established a republic like Florence or Siena, were almost always able to manage their own affairs. Mostly, they spent their time subjugating neighbours: Lake Trasimeno towns in 1130, Città di Castello not long after, then Assisi and Spello. Foligno, another bitter enemy, fell in 1282.

Almost always a Guelph city, Perugia maintained a special relationship with Florence and the popes—it had allies, certainly, but friends, never. Even fierce factional cities like Florence and Siena were careful to walk wide of this wildcat which was constantly molesting its neighbours when not itself convulsed in civil wars. One contemporary 13th-century account mentions that it was common for everyday Perugians to walk around with gaff hooks to snare muggers. Siena had its annual festive punch-up, the *Gioco del Pugno*, but the Perugians enjoyed spending their holidays at the **Battaglia de' Sassi**, the 'battle of stones' in the Piazza del Duomo, pitting different quarters of the city against one another; the object was to disable the other side, and there were usually a dozen or so fatalities each year. The local authorities thought it was a splendid way to toughen men up for real warfare.

Not even in religion could Perugia behave itself; besides being a graveyard for popes, Perugia gave the cold shoulder to most of the early revivalists and reformers. Even St Francis, who before he became a preacher spent a year in a Perugian dungeon, couldn't make the city mend its ways. One product of Perugian piety cannot be denied, but characteristically of the city it involved blood: the medieval mass-psychosis of the Flagellants or **Disciplinati** began here in 1259 with the hallucinations of a Franciscan hermit Ranieri Fasani, who after years of private devotions was told by the saints and the Virgin to take the idea to the bishop of Perugia, who was impressed and ordered a two-week city-wide flagellation. This mode of penitence seemed right for the time: the Calabrian prophet Joachim da Fiore had pinpointed 1260 as the end of the second age of the world, which everyone interpreted as the apocalypse. Soon bands of Disciplinati were wandering from town to town in Umbria, singing *laude* or simple hymns to the tunes of the popular ballads of the day. Thousands joined in, and the movement spread to Tuscany and across Europe, meeting only occasional pockets of resistance: the king of Poland, for instance, turned the Disciplinati aside at his frontiers. After the initial fervour, the movement would survive in the 20th century, organized into lay confraternities by the Franciscans; you can often see them in paintings, in their specially designed hoods with bare backs.

In principle, Perugia was part of the papal dominions, the 'Patrimony of St Peter', since the days of Charlemagne. Few popes, though, were able to exercise much control over such a volatile city. After 1303 the Priors of the ten major guilds established their rule, although noble families like the **Oddi** and the **Baglioni** remained extremely influential. In 1304, Pope Benedict XI came to Perugia while mediating a dispute in Florence, only to be slipped some poisoned figs by a nun. In 1305, one of the five papal conclaves that took place in Perugia selected the Gascon Bertrand de Got as Pope Clement V. Perhaps not surprisingly, he wanted to get out of Perugia as soon as possible. But instead of Rome he took refuge in Avignon.

In the 1360s and 70s, when **Cardinal Albornoz** was raising armies and building castles to reassert papal authority over central Italy, Perugia revolted. Pope Urban VI paid a visit in 1387 to make up—a wild dove perched on his shoulder as he passed through the city gate, which the Perugians took as a good omen. At least he managed to get out of Perugia alive.

Unfortunately, the rebellion only took the lid off a cauldron of conflicting ambitions that had long been ready to boil over, and Perugia's three big factions—the nobles, the commoners, and the *raspanti* (the 'scratchers' or the wealthy merchant class)—leapt at each other's throats. In 1393, with the connivance of the pope, a *raspanto* named **Biondo Michelotti** seized power by liquidating two Baglioni pretenders. Five years later (again the pope was involved) Michelotti was murdered on his wedding day by the Abbot of San Pietro. In the resulting confusion, Giangaleazzo Visconti of Milan was able to grab the city for a time (1400–2), followed by a period under the rule of King Ladislas of Naples (1402–14).

After Ladislas, celebrated Perugian *condottiere* **Braccio Fortebraccio** ('Arm Strongarm', the Popeye of the Renaissance, whose coat of arms pictures a bouquet of spinach and a helmet), won the city by defeating another *condottiere*, Carlo Malatesta of Rimini, at the Battle of Sant'Egidio. Fortebraccio, soon master of all Umbria and 'Prince of Capua', had king-sized ambitions and potent friends—according to contemporary gossip he owned a crystal with a genie imprisoned inside who gave him good advice. After conquering most of the Marche, Fortebraccio had dreams of ruling a united Italy, but his luck ran out in 1424, when he died at the hands of another Perugian with a grudge during the siege of L'Aquila, in Abruzzo.

In the aftermath, Pope Martin V took control of Perugia, although he could do nothing to stop the increasingly bloody feud between the noble clans of the **Oddi** and the **Baglioni**; the latter, with their legendary good looks, pet lions and tendency towards fratricide, blazed meteorically through Perugia's history like the House of Atreus and along the way spon-sored some of the city's great Renaissance art. The first to take power, Malatesta I Baglioni, married the niece of Fortebraccio and manoeuvred to put Perugia under the Pope's suzerainty, and as a reward received the lordship of Perugia, Spello, Bettona, Torgiano, Cannara, Bastia and Collemancio. His eldest son, Braccio I, only killed a couple of cousins, but when his second son Guido came to power, the fight with the Oddi reached such a point that there was a pitched battle in Piazza IV Novembre that left 130 dead. After losing a second battle in 1488, the Oddi were expelled from the city, but only went as far as Lake Trasimeno where they plotted and stirred up more trouble, twice trying to capture Perugia; scores of their bodies and those of their supporters were left dangling from the windows of the Palazzo dei Priori.

In 1500, on the occasion of the great wedding of Guido's son and heir Astorre I, a group of Baglioni enemies plotted to kill the whole family in a single night. They managed to get seven out of eight; the eighth, **Giampaolo Baglioni**, escaped and spent the next few years killing all the conspirators, and the last surviving Oddi for good measure. After having elimi-nated all his enemies, he became the family's most successful ruler, fought for Julius II against Bologna, and later became a *condottiere* for Venice; but in 1520 an even bigger shark, the Medici pope Leo X, tricked him into coming to Rome, where he was imprisoned, tortured and beheaded.

His death set off a new round of bloody fighting for Perugia between his sons and nephew. The one who survived the demolition derby, Malatesta II Baglioni, distinguished himself by betraying Florence to the Medici and Charles V in the siege of 1530. Another, Rodolfo, murdered a papal legate in revenge for the death of his uncle Giampaolo, giving **Pope Paul III** the perfect excuse to visit Perugia. Over the centuries it had become customary for popes reasserting their authority to make a formal visit to Perugia; contemporaries record Paul, father of the Inquisition and one of the kinkiest and most corrupt of all popes, requiring all the nuns of the city to queue up and kiss his feet, an experience which left him 'very greatly edified'.

To put an end to Perugia's independence for ever, Paul needed yet one more provocation; he found it in 1539, by initiating the salt tax a year after promising not to. The Perugians sent delegates to talk it over, but the pope refused to see them, and instead initiated the **Salt War** by sending his son Pierluigi Farnese to Perugia at the head of a huge papal force of mercenaries and Spaniards. They took care to devastate the lands of Perugia's *contado*, and handed government over to officials entitled Preservers of Ecclesiastical Obedience; its trade ruined and its streets full of monks, nuns and Jesuits, Perugia began a precipitous economic decline that would not be reversed until the Risorgimento. To this day, the Perugini, and indeed all Umbrians, eat bread made without salt, an unappetizing hangover from the Salt War (although Umbrians will stubbornly swear that it tastes better).

Until then, the only event in the conquered city was to be the Napoleonic occupation: the emperor's troops sent the hordes of monks and nuns packing, but also packed much of Perugia's art—some of the best Peruginos included—back to the Louvre. In 1859, during the disturbances of the Risorgimento, Perugia rebelled once more against the pope. Pius IX sent his **Swiss Guard** to quell them—some 2,000 Switzers forced the city, burning, sacking the monastery of San Pietro, looting and butchering innocent citizens in the streets. All of Europe heard, and although the Swiss succeeded in crushing the revolt, it backfired into a major propaganda weapon against the papacy. After that, the city's final liberation a year later was greeted with delirium. King Vittorio Emanuele II's army had to protect the retiring Swiss Guards from massacre at the hands of the Perugini.

### Getting There and Around
#### by air

Perugia's **airport**, Sant'Egidio-Perugia, is 12km west of the city towards Assisi and has connections only with Milan (Linate) and, from June to September, with Olbia in Sardinia; for information call ✆ 075 692 9447. Alitalia: Via Fani 14, ✆ 1478 65641.

#### by train

Because Perugia is up on a hill, its two train stations are both some distance from the centre. Regular city buses (nos.6, 7, 8 and 9) connect the FS station with Piazza G. Matteotti or Piazza Italia in the centre; the more convenient FCU station is a short walk from Piazza dei Partigiani and the escalators up to the centre.

The main **FS station**, on Piazza V. Veneto, lies about 3km from the centre in the lower suburb of Fontevegge; it has connections for Florence (154km/2½hrs) and Arezzo (78km/1½hrs) all via Terontola junction on the northern shore of Lake Trasimeno; for Siena (147km/3½hrs) another change is required, at Chiusi (a big pain—the FS has replaced several of these routes with direct buses).

Another line passes through Assisi (26km/25mins), Spoleto (47km/70mins), Foligno and Terni on the way to Rome (3hrs), while the route to Ancona (3hrs) via Foligno stops at Nocera Umbra, Gualdo Tadino, Gubbio, Genga and Fabriano. For other destinations in Umbria, you'll find the narrow-gauge Ferrovia Centrale Umbria or **FCU** handy, ✆ 075 575401. Its main station in Perugia is Stazione Sant'Anna, halfway up the hill, just off Piazza dei Partigiani. The FCU goes north to Città di Castello (45km/1hr) and Sansepolcro (60km/1½hrs) and south to Todi (41km/1hr) and Terni.

Perugia's **bus depot** is near the FCU station in Piazza dei Partigiani, linked to Piazza Italia by a system of steps and escalators (*scala mobile*). APM buses, ✆ 075 573 1707, serve the villages in Perugia province (roughly the northern two-thirds of Umbria). There are about a dozen a day to Santa Maria degli Angeli (for Assisi), with five continuing on to Spello and Foligno; others to Deruta and Todi; Torgiano and Bettona; Gubbio; Gualdo Tadino; the towns of Lake Trasimeno; one to Orvieto; and five a day to Città della Pieve and Chiusi, that important rail stop on the Florence–Rome line.

SSIT (same phone) has one bus a day to Nocera Umbra, Spoleto, and Norcia and Cascia. SULGA coaches (✆ 075 500 9641) provide direct links to Florence and Rome (and its airports), SENA (✆ 075 500 4888) go to Siena, CONTRAM (✆ 0737 2402) to Civitanova Marche and Macerata, and Freccia dell'Appennino (✆ 075 572 1266) down the coast of the Marche to San Benedetto del Tronto and Porto Ascoli.

Radio taxi: ✆ 075 500 4888.

Parking in Perugia can be a headache; most of the city is closed to traffic, and peripheral garages and **car parks** are few and usually charge by the hour. Car parks nearest the centre are at Piazza Italia, Piazza Pellini, the Mercato Coperto and Piazza dei Partigiani, all connected to the centre by elevator or escalator. You can **hire a car** from AVIS at the airport, ✆ 075 692 9346, or at the train station, ✆ 075 500 0395; from Hertz at the railway station, Piazza V. Veneto 4, ✆ 075 500 2439; from Maggiore, at the airport, ✆ 075 692 9276/075 500 7499; or from Europcar, at Via Ruggero d'Andreotto 7, ✆ 075 573 1704.

Walking in Perugia is a delight, though you'll often find yourself out of breath. In the oldest parts, densely packed and half-covered with arches and passageways, Perugia often seems like one big building. Its difficult topography has been mastered with some cleverness—there always seem to be stairs, elevators or escalators to carry you from one part to another. Many of these are on the edges, where some truly beautiful parks have been strung along the cliffs to take advantage of unusable land—Perugia has one of the highest densities of green areas per capita in Italy. Enjoy the street names: Via Curiosa, *Curious* Street; Via Perduta, *Lost* Street; Via Piacevole, *Pleasant* Street; Via Pericolosa, *Dangerous* Street, among many others. And look for medieval details—carved symbols and coats-of-arms. One local peculiarity is the narrow little *Porta del Morte*, 'Death's Door', used only to carry out the dead, and bricked up the rest of the time—where death has once passed, the superstition went, he might pass again. Or so the story goes; in most houses these little doors were the only access to the upper floors, with ladders just inside that could be pulled up in case of emergency.

*See city plan on inside back cover.*

Piazza IV Novembre, ✆ 075 573 6458, 🖷 075 573 9386, or Via Mazzini 21, ✆ 575951. Check out the website *www.umbria2000.it*, or there's the *Digiplan* computer, which (on the rare occasions when it's working) is always right. Look for it on the *scala mobile*, just up from the Piazza dei Partigiani; it will print out details on almost any hotel, restaurant or sight in town.

**Post office**: Piazza Matteotti, ✆ 075 573 6977.

**Churches**: Unless otherwise noted, all churches in Perugia are open 8–12 noon and from 4 till sunset.

## Piazza IV Novembre

Magnificent, time-worn Piazza IV Novembre, once the setting for the 'War of the Stones' and countless riots and street battles, remains the heart and soul of Perugia, as well as the central node of its meandering streets. As in many Umbrian cities, the old town hall, symbol of the *comune*, entirely upstages the cathedral, but here, the two stare at each other over Italy's most beautiful medieval fountain, the 25-sided polygonal pink and white **Fontana Maggiore**, designed in the 1270s by Fra Bevignate. The occasion was the construction of Perugia's first aqueduct since Roman times, and the Priors commissioned Nicola Pisano and his son Giovanni to sculpt the 48 double relief-panels around the lower basin. Twelve of these portray that favourite medieval conceit, the *Labours of the Months*, each accompanied by its zodiacal sign; in between are scenes from Roman legend, Aesop's fables, and saints' lives, personifications of the sciences and arts—altogether a complete, circular image of the medieval world. Above them, the twelve-sided upper basin has concave panels filled with 24 saints and figures from Perugia's history, most of them by Giovanni Pisano, with three water nymphs to keep them all company. The more you look at it, the more you realize the subtlety and dynamism of Fra Bevignate's design, especially in how the panels of the lower basin are never congruent, but pull the eye along.

Surveying the piazza, high up on the wall of the **Palazzo dei Priori**, perch a Guelph lion and Perugia's totem, the famous brass griffin, an emblem you will see at least once on every street in town. The scrap iron dangling beneath it is said to be chains and bolts from the gates of Siena, captured after a famous victory at Torrita in 1358 (this isn't true—the real war trophies, whatever they were, disappeared two centuries ago; these chains simply held them up). This stern, Gothic, asymmetrical complex, crowned with toothsome crenellations and pierced by beautiful, narrowly spaced windows, has been cleaned to look as sharp and new as when it was begun in 1297. Two later building phases left an elegant, slightly curved, elongated building, housing Perugia's finest art (*see* pp.68–9).

The whole first floor of the Piazza IV Novembre section is occupied by the **Sala dei Notari** (*open 9–1 and 3–7, closed Mon*), a remarkable room divided into bays by huge round arches, with interesting early 13th-century frescoes of Old Testament scenes along the top, by a student of Pietro Cavallini. The other frescoes, painted in the 19th century, are the coats of arms of all the *podestà* and *capitani del popolo* who served Perugia from 1293 to 1443.

# The Cathedral of San Lorenzo

For all the attention they lavished on their Palazzo dei Priori, the Perugians never seemed much interested in the fate of their cathedral. After laying the cornerstone in 1345, they didn't add another stone for a decade. A century later, when the building was substantially completed, a papal legate tore part of it down to use the stone for his own palace. For the façade, they once stole half a marble facing destined for the cathedral at Arezzo, but not long after, the Aretini whipped them in battle and made them give it back. The cathedral's finest hour, perhaps, came during a fit of civic strife in 1488, when the Baglioni, fighting the Oddi, seized the building and turned it into a fortress, complete with cannon pointing out of its Gothic windows. So much blood was spilled that the cathedral had to be washed out with wine and reconsecrated.

Despite its lack of a proper façade, this prim old dear of a building seems just right for its post on lovely Piazza IV Novembre. The side facing the Fontana Maggiore has a geometrical pattern, employing the warm pink marble quarried near Assisi that you'll see everywhere in Umbria. Next to it a bronze statue commemorates the pleasure-loving Julius III, the only pope the Perugians ever liked. The unfinished pulpit on the façade was especially built for the great charismatic revivalist San Bernardino of Siena, who preached to vast crowds in the piazza, finally persuading them to stop at least the *Battaglia de' Sassi* in 1425; Perugia, he claimed, was his favourite town, and judging by the church the Perugians gave him (*see* p.72), he was their favourite saint. The best feature of the façade, however, is the elegant travertine **Loggia di Braccio Fortebraccio**, added by the *condottiere* in 1423.

The Duomo's Baroqued interior is determinedly unimpressive, supported by columns badly painted to simulate marble. But there are a few things worth picking out. In the first chapel on the right, the tomb of Bishop Baglioni (d. 1451) by Urbano da Cortona, stands across from a saccharine *Descent from the Cross* by the 16th-century painter Federico Barocci of Urbino. In the **Cappella del Sacramento**, designed by Galeazzo Alessi, Perugia's top 16th-century architect, hangs Luca Signorelli's luminous and recently restored *Pala di Sant'Onofrio* (1484), one of his earliest and best works, showing the Madonna enthroned with saints and a pot-bellied angel tuning a lute. The presbytery has beautiful intarsia choir stalls by Gianiano da Mairano and Domenico del Taso (1486–91).

On the left side, near a pair of reliefs of the *Eternal Father* and *Pietà* by Agostino di Duccio, the Perugians keep their most prized relic in the **Cappella del Santo Anello**. This is nothing less than the wedding ring of the Virgin Mary. Many stories have grown up around this prodigy, a big onyx stone that, like a 1970s mood-ring, changes colour according to the moral character of the person wearing it. A Perugian woman stole the ring from Chiusi back in the Middle Ages, and the townspeople have never stopped worrying that the Chiusini might try to get it back: they keep it in 15 nested cases under 15 locks, and spread the keys out among 15 notable and trustworthy citizens, and only take it out of the box on 29–30 July. The relic indirectly inspired Raphael's famous *Betrothal of the Virgin*; Raphael picked up the idea from a painting by Perugino that hung in this chapel before Napoleon spirited it off to France (it's now in the museum in Caen)—the emperor always had a weakness for doe-eyed Virgins and Perugino was one of his favourite painters.

Behind the cathedral, the cloister of the **Canonica** witnessed five conclaves of cardinals between 1124 and 1305. Among the popes elected here was Frenchman Clement V, who began the 'Babylonian Captivity' by moving the papacy to Avignon. The cloister contains the **Museo dell'Opera del Duomo** (*there is no clear idea of when or if it will ever re-open*), with a small collection of art and a supporting cast of reliquaries and hymnals. If it's noon, the bells in the campanile, right over your head, will make sure you know it.

## Galleria Nazionale

> *Lift up to the third floor, open daily 9–7; closed first Mon of each month; adm exp. Call Ⓒ 075 574 1247.*

The elaborate **main door** (1326) of the Palazzo dei Priori is around the corner in Corso Vannucci, its lunette featuring statues of Perugia's patron saints, Louis of Toulouse, Lawrence and Ercolanus. Through this and up the lift, the Galleria Nazionale dell'Umbria has the finest and largest collection of Umbrian (and many other) paintings anywhere, now displayed in beautifully renovated and well-lit halls, with explanations in English. Although the mezzanine floor was left unsound by the earthquake, the museum has made sure that its masterpieces are accessible, although the usual chronological order may be temporarily changed. The first rooms contain some striking early works, among them sculptures for a public fountain by **Arnolfo di Cambio** (1281), and others from the Fontana Maggiore by **Giovanni Pisano**, which were replaced by copies. There's a pre-Giotto *Crucifixion* and other works of the **Maestro di San Francesco** from the 1270s. Nor are all the best works Umbrian—the Sienese in particular are well represented, with a fine polyptych by Vigoroso da Siena (*c.* 1290), and a sweet *Madonna* by **Duccio di Buoninsegna**.

Mesmerizing rooms of trecento and early quattrocento gold-ground fairy-tale *Madonnas* and *Annunciations* (by Ambrogia Maitani, Meo di Guido da Siena, Ottaviano Nelli, Peccio Capanna) culminate in **Beato Angelico**'s triptych of the *Dominicans* and the *Madonna with Angels and Saints* (restored in 1999) and **Piero della Francesca**'s *Polyptych di Sant'Antonio* (1465–70), painted for a Franciscan convent. Piero himself was responsible for the assembly of works from two distinct periods to fulfil the wishes of the buyers, who thought the project was dragging on a bit. The *Annunciation* on the top shows the painter at the height of his powers, creating an eerie stillness out of mathematical purity—on either side of Gabriel and the Virgin rows of arches recede into a blank wall. From the International Gothic wizards of the Marche come two fine paintings, **Gentile da Fabriano**'s *Virgin and Child* (1408), painted for Perugia's San Domenico—note how the wood of the Virgin's throne is alive and budding—and a detailed *Madonna dell'Orchestra* (1445) by **Giovanni Boccati da Camerino**, master of angelic choirs, putti, flowers and perspective tricks.

The best Perugians of the same period, **Benedetto Bonfigli** and **Bartolomeo Caporali**, show perhaps less spirituality, but fancier clothes and a lilting lyricism. Bonfigli also contributes the sharp and meticulously drawn **Cappella dei Priori** frescoes (1454–80). These are dedicated to two of Perugia's three patrons: the older frescoes, late Gothic in style, are on the life of St Louis of Toulouse, while the unfinished later frescoes on the life of St Ercolanus show a more mature, Renaissance handling of space. They also feature the best portraits of Perugia itself, bristling with towers—at the time it had around 500, an astonishing number even for such a belligerent city. Another beautiful work here is a bronze relief of the *Scourging of Christ*, by **Francesco di Giorgio Martini**, as well as terracotta reliefs by **Agostino di Duccio**.

In the next section two Perugian painters of the next generation, **Pinturicchio** and **Perugino**, also take pride of place. Both, when young, worked on the *Miracles of San Bernardino of Siena* (1473), a series of eight small panels with charming imaginary town settings that act as stages for the deeds of the famous preacher. Although he stubbornly refused to participate in the High Renaissance (Umbrians are a notoriously conservative lot) Pinturicchio rarely fails to charm; his nickname, 'rich painter', is derived from his use of gold and gorgeous colours, in evidence here in his *Pala di Santa Maria dei Fossi*. Perugino was equally conservative in his own way, always maintaining an ideal classical vision, touched with the 'sweetness' that Raphael mastered and which tends to give sugar-shock to people who cut their teeth on Michelangelo. At his worst Perugino can be painfully unconvincing ('I'll give them their Virgin and Saints,' you can imagine him grumbling as he dabbed on another rolling eyeball). The gallery has about a dozen of these, many of them almost entirely by his assistants; there's also an *Adorazione* featuring the most disdainful Magi ever, as well as Perugino at his finest, in the *Polyptych of Sant'Agostino*.

When the mezzanine floor has been repaired, you'll have long galleries of numb, gigantic canvases to wade through from the 16th to 18th centuries (a particularly good one is by **Pietro da Cortona**, the ultimate idealized *Nativity*). The handsome wooden horse was a model for an equestrian monument to Orazio Baglioni. At the end, though, there's a surprise; an interesting collection of 19th-century views of the city by a local artist, Giuseppe Rossi, showing the Rocca Paolina and the old market square, along with some of the 19th-century engineers' plans for shoring up Perugia and keeping it from sliding into the valley.

Down on the first floor, you can look through the glass door into the **Sala del Malconsiglio** ('bad counsel'), so called because it was here in the 1360s that the Priors decided to release some prisoners—almost the entire English mercenary company of Sir John Hawkwood. The very next year Hawkwood's men defeated Perugia at the Battle of Ponte San Giovanni. The Perugians learned their lesson; they were never nice to anyone again. It contains the original bronze lion and griffin from the façade of the palace; over the door (on the inside) there's an early lunette by Pinturicchio.

## Corso Vannucci and the Collegio del Cambio

To complement the excellent Piazza IV Novembre, Perugia has a truly noble main street. The **Corso Vannucci** is named after Pietro Vannucci, who, after all, was named Perugino after Perugia; it is always closed to traffic, and the citizens stroll along it every evening in central Italy's liveliest *passeggiata*.

At Corso Vannucci 25, in the confines of the third and final annexe to the enormous Palazzo dei Priori (1443), Perugino received a commission in 1499 to decorate the **Collegio del Cambio**, headquarters of Perugia's moneychangers' guild. He and his assistants did it in style, according to a humanistic programme devised by the Perugian scholar Francesco Maturanzio, with an array of Christian and Classical allegorical figures, prophets and sibyls, all fashionably clothed in Renaissance *haute couture*; the result is one of the finest pure Renaissance rooms in all Italy. Among these beautiful figures, Perugino painted an unflattering self-portrait in the middle of the left wall, tight-lipped and stern and sceptical; his pupil Raphael, then a mere pup of 17, contributed the figure of *Fortitude* and is said to have served as the model for the figure of the *Prophet Daniel*. The ceiling was later decorated with grotesques and pagan gods, not long after Raphael set the fashion for them in Rome with the discovery of Nero's Golden House; the magnificent woodwork is by Domenico del Tasso and Antonio Bencivenni da Mercatello (1493–1508), and the gilded terracotta statue of *Justice* (the moneychangers' guild arbitrated in financial disputes) is by Benedetto da Maiano.

The frescoes on the *Life of St John the Baptist* in the Bankers' chapel, the **Cappella di San Giovanni Battista**, are by another of Perugino's students, Giannicola di Paolo (*open 1 Mar–31 Oct and 20 Dec–6 Jan, Mon–Sat 9–12.30 and 2.30–5.30, Sun 9–12.30; 1 Nov–19 Dec and 7 Jan–28 Feb, Tues–Sat 8–2, Sun 9–12.30; Nov–Feb, closed Mon; adm*). Nor is that all; the adjacent **Collegio della Mercanzia**, at No.15bis, was the seat of the merchants' guild, one of the oldest and most important in Perugia; the Sala di Udienza is richly decorated with 15th-century carvings, panelling and inlays, perhaps by craftsmen from northern Europe.

## A Vanished Fortress and Underground Perugia

Continuing down the Corso Vannucci, past the hotels and formidable Perugian pastry shops, you pass from the Middle Ages to 19th-century neoclassical in the twinkling of an eye at **Piazza Italia**, dominated by the bulky, 1870s **Prefettura**, emblazoned with another griffin; behind it, the balustrades of the **Giardini Carducci** offer a splendid view over the Perugian suburbs and the distant countryside.

To find out why there are no old buildings on this piazza, take the down escalator, unobtrusively hidden under the colonnades of the Prefettura, into a Perugia that for over 300 years was lost to view and almost forgotten. Only days after the end of the Salt War, Paul III found a way to intimidate the Perugians into obedience until Judgement Day while obliterating the Baglioni family at the same stroke. The quarter of town he demolished for his famous **Rocca Paolina** was the stronghold of the Baglioni, and it included all of their palaces, 138 houses that they owned and seven churches. Most of the buildings were not completely razed, however, because Paul's architect, Antonio da Sangallo the Younger, needed them to give the new fortress a level foundation.

The 16th century may have been the age of the Renaissance, but in Italy it was also the era of grudges; Paul III came to Perugia seven times over the next three years to make sure the fortress was sufficiently repressive, and to crown it off he had the Rocca inscribed with large letters: *Ad repellandam Perusinorum audaciam* (To curb the audacity of the Perugians). From the beginning the Perugians looked upon it as a loathsome symbol of oppression, of the grisly terror that came to Italy in the 1500s. No enemy ever attacked it, and throughout the centuries of papal rule its only real use was as a prison—a prison from which few ever found their way out again. In the general revolutionary year of 1848, when the Pope's back was turned, a pick was ceremoniously handed to Count Benedetto Baglioni to begin its longed-for demolition. This was far from complete when the papal forces returned, but as soon as Perugia was liberated from the murderous Swiss Guard in 1860, the Piemontese General Pepoli signed a decree giving the Rocca to the Perugians, and they gleefully tore the rest with the same enthusiasm that the Parisians went after the Bastille; the workmen, with their dynamite, found themselves joined by the entire populace, including women and children, some with pickaxes, some with their bare hands.

In a way it's a pity the Rocca Paolina no longer stands. The old paintings and prints in the Palazzo dei Priori show it as a startlingly modern building, beautiful in a way, designed by one of the best Renaissance architects. After demolishing it, the Perugians built the neoclassical ensemble of the Piazza Italia and the Carducci Gardens to replace it; few even knew about the medieval streets underneath, until the city made use of them to create a quick pedestrian passage down to Piazza dei Partigiani—convenient, and also one of the most fascinating things to visit in Perugia. At the bottom of the first escalator, you'll be at the medieval street level, among the brick palaces of the Baglioni and their unfortunate neighbours, all roofed over by the arches and vaults of Sangallo. There are many interesting corners to explore, including parts of the Rocca Paolina bastions (*open 8am–7pm*) where you can peek out through the pope's gun slits over peaceful Viale Indipendenza below.

The entrance to the bastions from the outside is on Via Marzia, where you can also see the **Porta Marzia**, the best surviving piece of Etruscan architecture anywhere that isn't a tomb. Antonio da Sangallo was so impressed with it that he carefully reassembled it here after destroying Perugia's original walls. The five sculpted panels, now almost completely eroded away, probably represented five gods, although the Perugians have a strange old story that they are a Roman family that died from eating poisonous mushrooms.

## Perugia's West End: Down Via dei Priori

On the Corso Vannucci side of the Palazzo dei Priori, a little archway, easy to overlook, leads into Via dei Priori and Perugia's west end, a quiet and lovely part of the city. The first sight you'll encounter along this street is the church of **San Filippo Neri**, rebuilt by Roman architect Paolo Marucelli from an earlier church in the 1630s, with façade awkwardly squeezed and only visible in its entirety from across the small square. Perugians still call this impressive pile, the showiest Baroque building in Umbria, the *Chiesa Nuova*; its interior, full of florid paintings, seems to be made of dirty ice-cream, an echo of Rome out in the provinces. Currently being repaired after earthquake damage, you can still step in to see its high altarpiece, of the *Immaculate Conception*, completed by Pietro da Cortona. The very medieval Via della Cupa descends from here under a series of arches to the Etruscan walls and the old Etruscan gate, the **Porta della Mandorla**.

Further down Via dei Priori, stop for a look at the charming **Santi Stefano e Valentino**, a vaulted medieval church almost hidden among the surrounding houses: the altarpiece is a fine *Madonna* by the 16th-century Perugian artist Domenico Alfani. Next, in the shadow of the 150ft **Torre degli Sciri** (13th century), Perugia's tallest surviving tower-fortress, the huge **Santa Teresa degli Scalzi** (*always locked*) was an ambitious Baroque project that was never finished. In the charming little piazza by the **Porta Trasimena**, built in the Middle Ages on Etruscan foundations, the church of the **Madonna della Luce** has a good Renaissance façade and a round fresco of *God the Father* by Giovanni Battista Caporali and another of the *Madonna and Saints* by Tiberio d'Assisi. The church commemorates a miracle: a barber, playing cards in front of his shop, cussed so hard after losing a hand that a wooden Madonna in a nearby street-corner shrine shut her eyes and didn't open them for four whole days.

## Piazza San Francesco

Turning right at the Madonna della Luce, the street opens into the green lawn of Piazza San Francesco. This was originally outside the walls, and since 1230 it has been the site of **San Francesco al Prato**. Once the finest and most richly decorated church in Perugia, it suffered a partial collapse in a mud-slide in 1737 and a thorough looting by Napoleon's soldiers; the elegant façade remains, in patterns of pink and white stone; part of it is now open to the elements.

Next door, the **Oratorio di San Bernardino** commemorates the 15th-century Franciscan from Siena who made such an impression on the Perugians. 'Little St Bernard' must certainly have been a crafty preacher to affect this nest of pirates. Just coincidentally, his celebrated powers of persuasion, and in particular his famous dictum: 'Make it clear, make it short and keep to the point', have earned him a difficult posthumous responsibility—a recent pope has declared him Patron Saint of Advertising. The oratory was begun in 1461, the year after the saint's canonization, and placed on this site because Bernardino always stayed at the convent of San Francesco during his visits.

Agostino di Duccio (1418–81), that rare Florentine sculptor who decorated the Malatesta Temple of Rimini, was commissioned to do the façade, and he turned the little chapel into Umbria's greatest temple of pure Renaissance art. Framed in rich pink and green marbles, Agostino's reliefs are exquisite: beatific angel musicians, scenes of miracles from the life of the saint, and allegorical virtues: Mercy, Holiness and Purity on the left; Religion, Mortification and Penance on the right. One of the panels on the lower frieze portrays the original Bonfire of Vanities, held in front of the cathedral after a particularly stirring sermon from Bernardino (the chronicles record seven bales of women's hair going up in smoke)— which may have given Savonarola in Florence the idea.

Inside, the chapel's altar is a late Roman sarcophagus, perhaps that of a Christian; it seems to tell the story of Jonah and the whale and was the tomb of the Beato Egidio of Assisi (d. 1262), the third person to follow St Francis. The Oratory also has two works from the church of San Francesco: one of Benedetto Bonfigli's gonfalons, depicting the Madonna sheltering Perugia from the plague (1464), and a copy of Raphael's *Deposition,* now in Rome's Galleria Borghese.

Just behind, the convent of San Francesco holds the **Museo dell'Accademia di Belle Arti** (*closed since the earthquake, © 075 572 6562*) displaying a huge collection of plaster models, starring Canova's *Three Graces*; there are also prints, and typically academic 18th- and 19th-century paintings.

## Old Streets Around the Cathedral

Quite a few old tales start with a child going around a church widdershins (counter-clockwise) and ending up in fairyland. Try it with Perugia's cathedral, and you'll find yourself transported immediately back to the Middle Ages, a half-vertical cityscape of dark, grim buildings and overhanging arches, some incorporating bits of Gothic palaces and Etruscan walls, a set no movie director could possibly improve upon. And they are as old as they look. Many of the arches originally supported buildings over the street; medieval Perugia must have seemed like one continuous building, all linked by arches and passageways.

## An Etruscan Well and the Arch of Augustus

At Piazza Dante 18, right behind the cathedral, you can marvel at an example of ancient engineering, the 3rd-century BC **Pozzo Etrusco** (*open in summer daily, 10–1.30 and 2.30–6.30; in winter, Mon–Fri, 10.30–1.30 and 2.30–4.30, Sat and Sun, 10.30–1.30 and 2.30–5.30; adm*), a monumental 116ft-deep well and cistern; if the debris at the bottom is ever excavated it may prove considerably deeper. According to estimates it held 95,000 gallons of water, enough to supply all of Etruscan *Perusia*. Via Ulisse Rocchi, leading down steeply to the old northern gate, used to be called Via Vecchia, traditionally the oldest street in town; Perugians have been walking it for at least 2500 years.

The old north gate along Via Ulisse Rocchi just happens to be formed of another fabulous relic of the city's past, the **Arco di Augusto**. The huge stones of the lower levels are Etruscan; above them rises a perfectly preserved Roman arch built during the emperor's refounding of *Augusta Perusia*. The city's new name is inscribed with typical Imperial modesty: 'Augusta' in very large letters, 'Perusia' in tiny ones. The portico atop the Roman bastion, an addition that makes this gate one of the most beautiful in Italy, was added in the 16th century. The arch faces Piazza Fortebraccio and the 18th-century Palazzo Gallenga Stuart, now home of the **University for Foreigners**, founded in 1921 as a centre for studies in Italian language and culture and attended by students from all over the world.

Another little walk, beginning back in Piazza IV Novembre, is down **Via Maestà delle Volte**, one of the most picturesque medieval streets in Perugia, covered with arches that once supported a large Gothic hall. It leads down to **Piazza Cavallotti**, where Roman houses and a road have been discovered just under the pavement.

## The University and Borgo Sant'Angelo

Another itinerary through this ancient district would begin west from behind the cathedral down into a jumble of interwoven medieval arches and asymmetrical vaults that lead down to Via Battisti. Near Via Battisti, a long stairway descends through the Roman-Etruscan walls into the **Borgo Sant'Angelo**, Perugia's medieval suburb that was once a proletarian quarter, the centre of popular resistance to the Baglioni and the popes, and now is the seat of the city's famous university. Walk over the **Acquedotto**, which in the Middle Ages supplied water from Monte Pacciano to the Fontana Maggiore; in the last century it was converted into a long stone footbridge carried over the housetops on graceful arches to the precincts of the **university**, founded in 1307 and still one of the most prestigious in Italy. The central university buildings are now on Via Ariodante Fabretti, in an Olivetan monastery liquidated by Napoleon in 1801. In the Institute of Chemistry, on Via Sant'Elisabetta (*open Mon–Fri 8am–8pm, Sat 8–1; closed Sun and public holidays*), you can see a **Roman mosaic** of the 2nd century, discovered during recent construction. The scene represents Orpheus charming the wild animals with his lyre—one of the key religious images of the late Classical world.

Beyond the university quarters, Corso Garibaldi runs northwards through the old working neighbourhood of Borgo Sant'Angelo, passing the bulky pink and white checked church of **Sant'Agostino**; here the main attraction is the set of extravagantly carved choir-stalls by Baccio d'Agnolo, from designs by Perugino. The fresco over the altar is by Giannicola di Paolo, a student of Perugino, but the real prize, a five-part altarpiece by the master himself, was looted by Napoleon. Its panels are now scattered across France, except for the Madonna herself, who took a cannonball on the nose in Strasbourg during the Franco-Prussian war. Further up Corso Garibaldi, you will see a plaque commemorating the meeting of St Francis and St Dominic, founders of the two greatest preaching orders of the Middle Ages, both in Perugia to visit Pope Honorius III; contemporary accounts have the two saints embracing and going their separate ways, without more than a word or two.

One of the many convents in this area is **Santa Colomba** at Corso Garibaldi 191 (*ring the bell*) whose most famous nun, the Blessed Colomba of Rieti (1467–1501) was so wise that the magistrates of Perugia often consulted her; her cell has a lovely painting of *Christ Carrying the Cross*, by Lo Spagno, and mementoes of her life. At the end of Corso Garibaldi, one of the highest points in the city was graced in ancient times by a circular temple, dedicated to either Venus or Vulcan. Christians converted it into a church of **Sant'Angelo** in the 5th century, replacing the outer circle of columns with a plain stone wall. Many legends grew up around this singular church in the Middle Ages—some writers referred to it as the 'pavilion of Roland'. Today, with tons of Baroque frippery cleared away in a recent remodelling, the church has returned to something like its original appearance. Some scholars doubt there really was a temple here: the 16 beautiful Corinthian columns do come in a wild variety of styles and heights and some were undoubtedly brought from other buildings. Still, this oldest church in Umbria casts its quiet spell, especially in the early hours when the sunlight streams through the little window in the apse.

The tall **Porta Sant'Angelo** behind the church, a key point in Perugia's medieval defences, was built by Lorenzo Maitani in 1326 next to a castle tower added by Braccio Fortebraccio. Outside of it, enjoy a rare piece of countryside that has remained unchanged over the centuries; here the church of **San Matteo degli Armeni** has good, recently restored 13th-century frescoes.

## On *Perusia*'s Acropolis

Yet another excursion from the cathedral and Piazza Danti would be up Via del Sole, through another ancient part of the city to **Piazza Michelotti**, an attractive spot and the highest point in Perugia. Long before the Rocca Paolina, the popes built their fortress here; and. like the work of Paul III, this castle was also destroyed by the Perugians. In the rebellion of 1375, the people besieged it; after bribing off Sir John Hawkwood, the paid protector of the papal legate, they knocked down the walls with the aid of a fearsome home-made catapult called the *cacciaprete* (priest-chaser). Today it is surrounded by peaceful 17th-century houses.

From here, an arched lane leads to **San Severo** (*open April–Sept, 10–1.30 and 2.30–6.30; Oct–March, 10.30–1.30 and 2.30–4.30; adm*), founded in 1007 by Camaldolese monks; the story goes that this high ground was ancient *Augusta Perusia*'s acropolis, and that the monks built their church over the ruins of a Temple of the Sun. One chapel survives the Baroque remodelling of the 1750s, and it contains a celebrated fresco of the *Holy Trinity and Saints*, one of Raphael's very first solo efforts; underneath are more saints by his master Perugino, ironically painted a couple of year after Raphael's premature death when Perugino was in a noticeable artistic decline.

Via Bontempi leads around to another Etruscan gate, the **Porta del Sole**. Two churches near here, **San Fiorenzo** in Via Alessi and the 14th-century **Santa Maria Nuova** on Via Pinturicchio (at the bottom of Via Roscetto), both have one of Benedetto Bonfigli's bizarre gonfalons; these painted banners were intended to be carried during mournful *misericordia* processions in the streets, invoking God's mercy during plagues, famines, or the frequent attacks of communal guilt to which the Perugians were always subject. The one in Santa Maria Nuova (1472) is badly damaged but shows a vengeful Christ raining down thunderbolts of plague on sinful Perugia, while the Virgin, SS. Benedict and Scholastica, and the Blessed Paolo Bigazzini try to placate his wrath.

East of Santa Maria Nuova, Corso Bersaglieri continues out to the gate of Porta Sant'Antonio, where the church of **Sant'Antonio** has a frescoed *Crucifixion* recently attributed to Raphael

## To San Domenico

The streets to the southeast of the cathedral, while not quite as dramatic, are just as ancient and intractable as those to the north and west. If you care to climb a bit, a tour of this area will take you to such sights as the **Via delle Volte della Pace**, an ancient vaulted tunnel of a street just east of the cathedral, where the Perugians signed their peace treaties (with their fingers crossed behind their backs). One of the few breathing spaces in the whole crowded district is the elongated **Piazza Matteotti**, the former marketplace and field for burning witches, parallel and below Corso Vannucci. In the old days it was called Piazza Sopramura, being actually built on top of a section of the Etruscan-Roman walls. The west side of the piazza is shared by the post office and an old Perugian institution, a brightly decorated kiosk with an eccentric owner who sells nothing but bananas. Opposite them stand the 17th-century Gesù church, and two splendid 15th-century buildings: the **Palazzo del Capitano del Popolo** and, next to it, the **Palazzo dell'Università Vecchia**, built between 1453 and 1515 and used as the quarters of the university until 1811.

From Piazza Matteotti, Via Oberdan descends to Perugia's oddest church, **Sant'Ercolano** (1326), a tall octagon built on the old walls with a gigantic pointed arch in each facet, a double Baroque stair, a train station clock and lace curtains in the upstairs window; the interior, in good if rotting Baroque, has a Roman sarcophagus for its altar. From here, the city extends itself along a narrow ridge, following Corso Cavour to another colossal, ambitious, woefully unfinished church, **San Domenico**, designed by Giovanni Pisano and rebuilt in 1632 by Carlo Maderno when the vaulting caved in, although one wall and the apse are original; the latter has the second largest stained glass window in Italy after Milan cathedral, dated 1411. The light streaming through this colourful luminous glass is the main feature of the interior, but there is also the fine *Tomb of Pope Benedict XI*, by a student of Arnolfo di Cambio. Poisoned figs did Benedict in a year after his election, during a visit in 1304, but surprisingly this time the Perugians had nothing to do with it; prime suspects behind the nun who served them to the pope included the Florentines and King Philip the Fair of France. The fourth chapel on the right holds a beautiful marble and terracotta *dossale* (1459) by Agostino di Duccio.

## The Museo Archeologico Nazionale dell'Umbria

*Open Mon–Sat 9–7, Sun 9–1; adm.*

This is housed around the back of San Domenico, in an equally grandiose yet unfinished convent. It has an excellent collection of material from prehistoric and Etruscan Umbria. The prehistoric collection will get you in touch with Palaeolithic, Neolithic and Bronze Age

Umbria, while a large part of the historic collection comes from the Etruscan cemeteries around Perugia: a lovely incised bronze mirror (an Etruscan speciality, 3rd century BC); intricate gold-filigree jewellery; sarcophagi; a famous stone marker called the *Cippus Perusinus*, with one of the longest Etruscan inscriptions ever found (151 words); and bronzes, armour and weapons. Among the funeral vases and urns there is one portraying a hero who looks like a dentist about to examine a monster's teeth; another shows a procession, perhaps of a victor. One of the most impressive Roman pieces is a bronze statue of Germanicus, father of Caligula, found in Amelia in 1963. Other Roman finds include inscriptions in honour of Augustus, the re-builder of Perugia, and a beautiful sarcophagus sculpted with the myth of Meleager.

## San Pietro

From San Domenico, Corso Cavour leaves the city at the elegant **Porta San Pietro** (1473), designed by Agostino di Duccio with help from Polidoro di Stefano. Changing its name to Borgo XX Giugno, the street continues to the end of the ridge, past the university's **Orto Medievale** at No.74, a botanical garden where each plant has a symbolic meaning (*open Mon–Fri 9–6, Sat 9–1, closed Sun*) to an 18th-century park, the **Giardino del Frontone**, main venue of the Umbria Jazz Festival.

Facing it is the Benedictine church of **San Pietro**, founded in the 10th century and still retaining substantial parts of its original structure. This is the most gloriously decorated church in Perugia, nearly every square inch inside covered with frescoes and canvases, and the Perugians have always taken good care of it—especially since 1859, when, during the sack by the Swiss Guards, the monks of San Pietro shielded the leaders of the revolt from the papal bloodhounds. The story goes that they cut down their bell-ropes by night, and used them to lower the fugitives down the cliffs to safety. The twelve-sided bell tower is one of the landmarks of Perugia. On the façade there's a rare fresco of the Trinity, which is a feminine word in Italian and here represented by a three-headed woman.

The basilican interior (*closed 12–3*) dates from the early 1500s and has a carved, gilded ceiling. Among the acres of painting are the large canvases in the nave by a Greek student of Veronese called L'Alisense. Two paintings in the right aisle are attributed to Perugino's pupil Eusebio da San Giorgio, a *Madonna and two Saints* and a *St Benedict*. The Cappella di San Giuseppe has fine 16th-century works, while the sacristy has paintings of *Five Saints* by Perugino, all that remains of yet another altarpiece looted by Napoleon, as well as a *Portrait of Christ* by Dosso Dossi, and a bronze *Crucifix* by Algardi. The best works in the whole church, however, are the extraordinary **choir stalls** from the 1520s, sculpted and inlaid by Benardino Antonibi of Perugia, Nicola di Stefano of Bologna and Stefano Zambelli of Bergamo. A pretty door in the choir gives on to a little balcony with a memorable view over Assisi and Spello.

And there's more. The left aisle has a *Pietà* by Fiorenzo di Lorenzo. There's a tabernacle attributed to Mino da Fiesole in the Cappella Vibi; the nearby Cappella Ranieri has a *Christ on the Mount* by Guido Reni, *SS Peter and Paul* attributed to Guercino, and a *Judith* by Sassoferrato, who was also responsible for the several Raphael and Perugino copies in the church. Beyond the Cappella del Sacramento, with paintings by Vasari, is an *Adoration of the Magi* in the nave by Eusebio da San Giorgio, and a *Pietà* by Perugino.

## Santa Giuliana

Leaving Perugia, Via XX Settembre, the twisting boulevard down to the train station, passes the 13th-century church of Santa Giuliana, with a delicate pink and white façade and beautiful campanile, one of Perugia's landmarks. Attributed to Gattapone, it is one of the few medieval churches in Perugia to survive essentially intact, with frescoes from the 1200s and 1300s and a cloister from 1375 now used as a military hospital. A new business centre is growing up in the flatlands around the station; one of the new developments has a post-Modernist office block with a small piazza, one of the slickest new buildings in Italy.

## Ipogeo dei Volumni

*Open daily 9.30–12.30 and 3–5, Sun 9.30–12.30, July–Aug 9.30–12.30 and 4.30–6.30; adm; visits are limited to a maximum of five people at a time and for a maximum of 5 minutes.*

Near Ponte San Giovanni, just east of Perugia, signs lead to one of the best preserved Etruscan tombs anywhere, sheltered by a modern yellow building next to a gritty bypass and train tracks; the way can be confusing and is most painlessly done from Perugia by taxi. Dating from the 2nd century BC, the hypogeum is characerically shaped like an Etruscan house, with an underground 'atrium' under a high gabled roof carved in the rock, surrounded by small rooms, the main one holding the travertine urns containing the ashes of four generations of the family. The oldest one, that of a man named Arnth, is a typical Etruscan tomb with a representation of the deceased on the lid, while that of his descendant, the 1st-century AD Pulius Voluminius, demonstrates Perugia's rapid Romanization. Unlike most Etruscan tombs, the Volumni has unusual high reliefs in stucco, rather than paintings.

### *Shopping, Activities and Entertainment*

The monthly *Viva Perugia What Where When* (L1,000) lists all the exhibitions and events happening in the city. Nonetheless, the principal Perugian occupation in the evening remains the *passeggiata* down Corso Vannucci, with a stop for a tantalizing bite at the **Bar Ferrari** (No.43), full of Perugia's famous chocolate *Baci* and other confections, or perhaps an ice-cream at the **Gelateria Veneta** (No.20) before loitering in Piazza IV Novembre.

The city holds a market with a view, the **Mercato della Terrazza**, with clothes and shoes, near the Kennedy escalator, off Piazza Matteotti, as well as a Saturday morning food market in Pian di Massiano.

Year-round courses in Italian are offered for some 4,000 students a year at the **Università per Stranieri**; write in advance for details (Palazzo Gallenga, Piazza Fortebraccio 4, ✉ 57461, ✆ 075 574 6211, ✉ 075 574 5213, *relstu@unistrapg.it*).

In July, the excellent **Umbria Jazz Festival** (*www.umbriajazz.com*) has drawn such luminaries as the late Stan Getz and Wynton Marsalis to Perugia; pick up tickets at the booth in Piazza della Repubblica. There are performances in the city's cloisters and squares in the *Teatro in Piazza* festival in July and August. The first week of November sees the *Fiera dei Morti*, the oldest surviving fair in Central Italy, at Pian di Massiano. In September the *Sagra Musicale Umbra* features sacred music in

Perugia's churches. At other times the large student population brings in numerous concerts, films and other performances: music, usually live and in every possible shade from jazz to traditional Turkish and tango, is on tap every Tuesday, Thursday and Saturday at **Il Contrappunto**, Via Scortici 4/A, near the University for Foreigners and Piazza Grimana, ℗ 075 573 3667.

If you're travelling with children, Perugia has a large brightly lit funfair and Umbria's modest but sincerely meant answer to Disneyland, the **Città della Domenica**, ℗ 075 *500 4865*, (*open daily April–Sept, weekends only Oct–Mar*), just west of the city, with a miniature Africa, a serpentarium, bumper cars and more.

---

*Perugia* ✉ *06100*

## Where to Stay
### very expensive

★★★★★**Brufani**, Piazza Italia 12, ℗ 075 573 2541, ✆ 075 572 0210, is a renovated, traditional 19th-century hotel which has recently doubled in size to provide some 80 rooms. There are fine views over the countryside, luxurious fittings, air-conditioning, an attractive central courtyard and a private garage downstairs.

### expensive

Set in greenery at the foot of the city, the prestigious ★★★★**Perugia Plaza**, Via Palermo 88, ℗ 075 34643, ✆ 075 30863, is big and comfortable, with a pool and sauna, and an excellent restaurant, the **Fortebraccio,** with fixed-price menus under L40,000. *Closed Mon.* ★★★★**La Rosetta**, Piazza Italia 19, ℗/✆ 075 572 0841, is another older hotel, deservedly popular, with a wide variety of rooms from various periods and remodellings. The hotel has a celebrated restaurant, and dining in the garden in the summer; the rooms, either modern or furnished with antiques, are cosy and quiet. Goethe slept at ★★★★**Locanda della Posta** on Corso Vannucci 97, ℗ 075 572 8925, ✆ 075 572 2413, the oldest hotel in town, with an ornate exterior and pleasant, renovated rooms and private garage. Out of the centre, but worth the extra few minutes' drive, is the memorable ★★★★**Giò Arte e Vini**, Via Ruggero d'Andreotto 19, ℗/✆ 075 573 1100, a hotel dedicated to the noble art of wine-drinking. Each room is furnished with rustic Umbrian furniture, including a display case filled with bottles of wine. Guests are encouraged to taste them and buy from the amply stocked cellars on departure. The restaurant is another treat: every evening, the *sommelier* chooses three different wines and, for a surprisingly modest fee, diners can quaff to their heart's content.

### moderate

In a good location just off Corso Vannucci, ★★★**Fortuna**, Via Bonazzi 19, ℗ 075 572 2845, ✆ 075 573 5040, has more comfort than charm; all rooms have bath and TV, and there's a garage. The recently refurbished ★★**Priori**, Via Vermiglioli 3, ℗ 075 572 3378, ✆ 075 572 3213, occupies a historic building in the historic centre; some of the more elaborate rooms fall into the *expensive* category. The friendly and convenient ★★**Aurora**, Viale Indipendenza 21, ℗/✆ 075 572 4819, is only a minute's walk from Piazza Italia, on the main road up from the station. Rooms are rather spartan, but comfortable enough for a short stay, and priced at the bottom of this category.

**★Etruria**, Via della Luna 21, ✆ 075 572 3730, is a simple place just off Corso Vannucci (only a few en suite rooms). Similar and just as central are **★Piccolo**, Via Bonazzi 25, ✆ 075 572 2987, and **★Paola**, Via della Canapina 5, ✆ 075 572 3816. Even without a youth hostel card, you can check in at the **Centro Internazionale Accoglienza per la Gioventù**, by the Duomo on Via Bontempi 13, ✆ 075 572 2880, ✆ 075 573 9449, with bunk beds. The tourist office has a list of rooms to rent.

## Outside Perugia

There are a number of comfortable hotels in Perugia's environs for motorists, including two special choices: the neo-Renaissance **★★★★Castello dell'Oscano**, in a large park at Cenerente, ✉ 06070, 9km northwest of Perugia, ✆ 075 690125, ✆ 075 690666 (*expensive*), with 20 lovely, antique-furnished rooms, satellite TV, and pool; and at Bosco, ✉ 06080, 10km east on the road to Gubbio, the larger **★★★★Relais San Clemente**, ✆ 075 591 5100, ✆ 075 591 5001, occupying a 14th-century Benedictine abbey, has a pool and tennis on its lovely grounds, luxurious, stylish rooms and a choice restaurant.

## Eating Out

Note that some of Perugia's best restaurants are in the aforementioned hotels, especially the Perugia Plaza, La Rosetta, and Giò Arte e Vini.

### expensive–moderate

For a taste of old Umbria, try the **Osteria del Bartolo**, Via Bartolo 30, ✆ 075 573 1561, where inventive and beautifully prepared dishes are created from ancient recipes you won't see anywhere else. *Closed Sun.* Just north of the Duomo, **Aladino**, Via delle Prome 11 (the extension of Via del Sole), ✆ 075 572 0938, is one of the most popular restaurants in the city, specializing in sunny Sardinian and other fresh Mediterranean dishes to go with its fine choice of wines. *Evenings only, closed Mon.* Near the cathedral, **Falchetto**, Via Bartolo 20, ✆ 075 573 1775, reeks of medieval atmosphere and serves Umbrian specialities— *salumeria, crostini* (pâté on toast), tagliatelle with truffles, *pasta e fagioli* (pasta with beans), grilled lamb and trout, all well prepared and followed by tasty desserts. *Closed Mon.* In the same area, in a quattrocento palazzo, the chef at **Ubu Re**, Via Baldeschi 17, ✆ 075 573 5461, has a lighter touch, but here too there are good variations on the usual Umbrian theme, including an excellent *coscio di agnello alle olive* (leg of lamb cooked with olives) and a well-stocked wine cellar. *Evenings only, closed Mon, and part of July and Aug.* **Il Cantinone**, Via Ritorto 6, just to the left of the cathedral, ✆ 075 573 4430, offers mostly simple things: *spaghetti all'amatriciana*, beans and sausage, also *filetto tartufato*—fillet of steak smothered with a black truffle sauce. *Closed Tues.* Some of the best seafood in town is served near the Etruscan Arch at **La Bocca Mia**, Via Rocchi 36, ✆ 075 572 2873; they also have a good reputation for desserts, not usually an Umbrian forte. *Closed Sun.* Near the cathedral, just behind Piazza IV Novembre at Via Baldeschi 17, ✆ 075 573 5461, **Osteria del Gambero** is a pleasant place with a long menu of both local and not-so-local dishes: *strangozzi* with aubergine and porcini mushrooms, *zuppa di farro* with courgettes, and monkfish with yellow peppers. *Evenings only, closed Mon.* Old favourite **Da Cesarino**, also near Piazza IV Novembre at Via della Gabbia 15, ✆ 075 572 8974, serves reliable homemade pasta and quality traditional meat dishes. *Closed Wed.*

### *inexpensive*

In a Renaissance palazzo, **Paiolo**, Via Augusta 11, ✆ 075 572 5611, has good value good food, as well as delicious pizzas. *Closed Wed, and part of Aug.* If you watch the prices, you can dine very well very cheaply at **Osteria Il Gufo**, Via della Viola 18 (by San Fiorenzo), ✆ 075 573 4126, which serves seasonal dishes with a flair. *Evenings only, closed Sun and Mon.* **Cambio**, Corso Vannucci 29, ✆ 075 572 4165, serves reasonable meals and simple lunches. *Closed Wed.* If you want to make a picnic, Perugia's best bread is baked in some 30 different ways at **Ceccarani**, Piazza Matteotti 16. **Sandri**, on Corso Vannucci, is one of the prettiest pastry shops in Italy, with a frescoed ceiling and divinely artistic confections; their window has even more colours than the Pinacoteca across the street.

## Around Perugia: Torgiano, Deruta and Corciano

### *Tourist Information*

**Deruta**: Piazza dei Consoli 4, ✆ 075 971 1559. Open April–October.

## Torgiano

Traditionally in Perugia's sphere of influence, Torgiano lies 15km south of the capital. These days it is practically synonymous with wine and the Lungarotti family, proprietors of one of Umbria's best-known vineyards; beginning in the late 1970s, Dr Giorgio Lungarotti has, through hard work and innovative techniques, made this minute DOC growing area internationally famous. If Orvieto still rules the roost in Umbria's white wine league, Rubesco di Torgiano wins in the reds. The Lungarotti foundation runs an excellent **wine museum**, with an enormous press, housed in the cellars of the 17th-century Palazzo Baglioni in Corso Vittorio Emanuele (*open daily, 9–1 and 3–6 in winter, 3–7 in summer; adm*). Displays, labelled in English, trace the history of wine, techniques, rules and regulations; it also has a history of wine jars and vessels, a beautiful display of majolica, from Deruta, Faenza and Montelupo, and a wine library, with books going back to the Renaissance.

## Deruta

If there's room in your suitcase, give in to the roadside blandishments and buy a plate in the tiny hill town of Deruta (pop. 7500), 5km south of Torgiano. Along with Gubbio, Deruta has been Umbria's centre for ceramics and majolica since the 13th century, and, with 200 ceramic workshops maintaining the old tradition, nearly every other building in the lower part of town is devoted to the craft. Deruta's location, on the fringe of Perugia's *contado*, brought it some hard knocks from Perugia's enemies over the centuries. During the height of its fame in the 1500s, Deruta was sacked twice, by Cesare Borgia and Braccio Baglioni, but it picked itself up and carried on making colourful ceramics.

There are dozens of ceramics shops, particularly in the lower part of the town. One of the biggest—and it has an awe-inspiring and rather chaotic display of everything from egg cups to vast vases and dishes—is Maioliche Sberna, © 075 971206, where you can also watch the ceramics being made and hand-painted in the basement workshop. They will ship their wares anywhere in the world.

You can admire works of past artisans in the **Museo Regionale della Ceramica** (*open Oct–Mar daily exc Tues, 10.30–1 and 2.30–5; April–June, daily, 10.30–1 and 3–6; July–Sept daily, 10–1 and 3.30–7; adm*), housed in a former convent on Largo San Francesco. There are examples from Deruta's golden age in the early 1500s, lovely floor tiles from the church of San Francesco, devotional plaques and a majolica baptismal font. In Piazza dei Consoli (note the miniature copy of Perugia's Fontana Maggiore, minus the reliefs), the 14th-century church of **San Francesco** has patches of Sienese and Umbrian frescoes, while the medieval Palazzo Comunale holds a **Pinacoteca** (*open April–Oct, same hours as ceramics museum*) featuring paintings and a gonfalon by Nicolò Alunno, painted on both sides. There's also a fine detached fresco by Fiorenzo di Lorenzo, one of his best works, of the *Plague Saints Rocco and Romano standing over Deruta* (1478).

Another church in Deruta, **Sant'Antonio Abate**, has a fresco by Bartolomeo Caporali of the *All-Protecting Virgin*, a figure who plays the lead role in the decorations in the country church of the **Madonna del Bagno**, 3km south of Deruta along SS3bis. This is full of hundreds of quaint ceramic votive plaques made in the 17th and 18th centuries, showing various pratfalls, sinking ships and exorcisms, all with happy endings thanks to the Madonna (*visits by request, © 075 973455*).

Closer to Perugia, on the west bank of the Tiber, a country chapel outside of **San Martino in Colle** has a fresco of the *Madonna and Child*, recently restored and attributed to Pinturicchio.

## Corciano

On its hill midway to Lake Trasimeno, pretty Corciano is protected by nearly intact 13th-century walls and castle. Controlled by Perugia into the 15th century, it has small scale versions of all the essential buildings of a *comune*, all neatly labelled with a ceramic plaque, which gives it a slight museumish air, but Corciano doesn't care. There's a convenient car park outside the walls near the pink and white striped church of **San Francesco**; this was founded after St Francis' visit in 1211 (the Corcianese had no doubt that he was going to be canonized, so they got a headstart on his church). The **municipio** was the 16th-century summer palace of the Della Corgna dukes of Città di Castello, who ran Corciano for a while after the Salt War; enquire here about visiting the little **Museo della Casa Contadina** with a collection of agricultural implements. Perugino left one of his finest late works, the *Assumption* altarpiece (1513) in the 13th-century church of **Santa Maria**; the church also has one of Bonfigli's strange gonfalons, dedicated to the *Madonna della Misericordia,* here defending Corciano from outrageous fortune.

The big castle just north of Corciano at **Pieve del Vescovo** was restored in the late 1500s by Galeazzo Alessi as a residence, but there's an even more impressive work by the same architect just north off the main road, the **Villa del Cardinale**, built for Cardinal Fulvio Della Corgna. Now owned by the state, plans are to open it to the public; it has a very imposing gate and a lovely Renaissance garden.

**★★★★★Le Tre Vaselle**, Via Garibaldi 48, ✆ 075 988 0447, 🖷 075 988 0214, *www.3vaselle.it* (*very expensive*), a luxurious hotel situated in an old palazzo and adjoining houses on the edge of the village, surrounded by Lungarotti vineyards and olive groves and offering air-conditioning, minibars, baby-sitting service, swimming pool, whirlpool, sauna, fitness suite, etc. It is often used for conferences, but these are run in a separate part of the building. The expensive restaurant is ranked among the top in Umbria, although standards are not always consistent.

# Lake Trasimeno

The fourth largest lake in Italy, Trasimeno (45km in circumference) has a subtle charm, sleepy, placid and shallow, almost marshy in places; large enough to create its own soft micro-climate, it shimmers like a mirror embedded in gentle rolling hills covered with olives and vineyards. The Etruscans of Camars (Chiusi) coveted the lake for its fish and the fertility of its shores, and around the time of their famous king Lars Porsena, the bad guy in Macaulay's *Horatio at the Bridge,* they founded Perugia to control it. In the 12th and 13th century wars were fought for its eels. Napoleon took one look at it and wondered how to drain it.

Hans Christian Andersen, drawing on his own travels, put Trasimeno in one of his fairy-tales, *The Galoshes of Fortune*—how beautiful it was, but how poor the people were (in the 1830s), and how wretched their lives among the swarms of biting flies and mosquitoes and malaria. A postwar dose of American DDT wiped out the latter, and since then the lake has become a modest resort—the Umbrian Riviera. Never one to fully cooperate with human wishes, Trasimeno, once prone to flooding, is now doing its best to become a peat bog. A few fishermen in special flat-bottomed boats skim over its waters, fishing for eels, tench, shad and carp. Ducks, cormorants and kingfishers love it, waterlilies float among the reeds, and, as the lake's tourist offices remind visitors, some 20 per cent of the world's artistic heritage listed by UNESCO lies within two hours of its quiet shores.

### Getting Around

Lake Trasimeno lies 37km south of Arezzo, 13km south of Cortona, 69km east of Siena, and 30km west of Perugia. By **car**, approach by the A1 from the north, take the Val di Chiana exit for the spur of the *autostrada* that skirts the north shore en route to Perugia; from the south, the Chiusi exit will bring you near the SS71 to Castiglione del Lago. **Train** travel can be awkward: Castiglione del Lago is a stop on the main Florence–Rome line, but not on fast trains (*Intercity* and *Eurostar*), so check before setting out. Also on the main Florence–Rome line, change at Terontola for Perugia and the north-shore towns of Tuoro sul Trasimeno and Passignano; from Siena, change at Chiusi for Castiglione. Perugia is the main **bus** terminus for the area; connections from Cortona and Siena are less frequent.

A fairly frequent bus service runs round the north shore (Tuoro–Passignano–Magione–San Feliciano–San Savino–Perugia) and around the southern shore (Perugia–Magione–S. Arcangelo–Panicarola–Macchie–Castiglione del Lago). Contact tourist offices for timetables. Or get there on your own two wheels: you can hire **bicycles** in Castiglione from Marinelli, Via B. Buozzi, ✆ 075 953126 or in Passignano from Ragnoni, Via 2 Giugno 32, ✆ 075 829 6064.

Lake ports Castiglione, Tuoro and Passignano are linked by **boat** to one another and to Isola Maggiore and Isola Polvese. Connections are frequent in the summer, but diminish to only one or two a day in winter; for sailing times, call ✆ 075 827157.

### Tourist Information

**Passignano sul Trasimeno**: Via Roma 25, ✆ 075 965 2484.

**Castiglione del Lago**: Piazza Mazzini 10, ✆ 075 965 8210, *www.comune.passignano-sul-trasimeno.perugia.it*

### market day

**Castiglione del Lago**: Wednesday.

## Magione and Trasimeno's East Shore

From Perugia it's 30km to Trasimeno; if you snub the fast company of the *autostrada* you can visit the hilltown of **Magione**, a little industrial centre known for its copper and brass ware. Like any place within Perugia's radius, it spent much of the Middle Ages fighting: there's a ruined 13th-century **Torre dei Lombardi** on top of town, and on the edge stands a striking **Castello dei Cavalieri di Malta** of 1420, built by the Bolognese architect Fieravante Fieravanti, and still owned by the Knights of Malta, now headquartered in Rome (and open in summer for guided tours, ✆ 075 847 9261). The knights had inherited a 11th-century Templar hospital here, of which a few traces remain. Their church, **San Giovanni,** was damaged in the last war, and was rebuilt and frescoed in a traditional manner by the Perugian futurist Gherardo Dottori in 1947. On the main road, the little 13th-century church of the **Madonna delle Grazie** has a lovely fresco of the *Madonna Enthroned* by Andrea di Giovanni da Orvieto.

Long before the knights, this was the birthplace of the early missionary, Fra Giovanni di Pian di Carpine ('of the hornbeam plain' as the area under Magione was known), who was sent in 1245 by Innocent IV to convert the Mongols; although his preaching failed to make much of an impact, he returned from Karakorum after twenty years and wrote the *Historia Mongolorum*, the first eye-witness account of China and the Far East, a book much studied by later missionaries and Marco Polo. (Some scholars even suspect the Venetian merchant never visited Kubla Khan at all but actually cribbed much of his *Travels* from Fra Giovanni. Needless to say, this doesn't go down too well in Venice.)

Three of Trasimeno's prettiest beaches are spread between Magione's lakeside *frazioni*. One of these *frazioni*, **Montecolognola**, high on a hill blanketed with olives, has another castle built in the late 13th century by the beleaugered residents of Magione and has lovely views over the lake. Montecolognola's parish church has 14th- to 16th-century frescoes, another one of 1947 by Gherardo Dottori, and a pretty majolica altarpiece made in Deruta. Further south are picturesque **Monte del Lago**, near the impressive but ruined **Castello di Zocco** (1400) with its five towers, and **San Feliciano**. The latter village has a fascinating little **Museo della Pesca** dedicated to the lake's fishermen, and enjoys magical sunsets over the water and Isola Polvese.

**Isola Polvese**, the largest of Trasimeno's three islands, is linked in the summer by boats from San Feliciano. The large village that once stood here was abandoned in the 17th century because of malaria; today only the 14th-century castle and an older monastery still stand. Now owned by the province, Polvese has olive groves and lush vegetation, and hundreds of birds who nest on its shores; a path encircles it and takes about an hour to walk, and there's a little beach and summer snack bar.

South of San Feliciano, the **Oasi delle Valle** run by the environmental group Legambiente is the most important bird-watching area on Trasimeno (*© 075 847 6007, open Tues–Sun 10–1 and 3–6; adm*), hosting an impressive number of migratory visitors, especially in the spring. It is here that the Romans dug a 7km underground emissary to drain the lake when water levels reached the flood stage, diverting the water through several streams and into the Tiber; a second emissary was built in 1423 by Braccio Fortebraccio. Leonardo da Vinci, who visited these shores in 1503, suggested diverting its flow into the Tiber, Arno and Chiana rivers. As the shore grew swampier over the next few centuries, Leonardo's proposal was seriously considered, until yet another emissary was dug here in 1896. You can walk along it, and visit a museum on the site which tells the whole soggy story.

## The North Shore: Castel Rigone, Passignano and Isola Maggiore

North of Magione, a road ascends to **Castel Rigone**, a dramatically poised fortress hilltown founded in 543 by Rigone, lieutenant of Totila the Goth. It has spectacular views over the lake and a delightful Renaissance church, the recently restored **Madonna dei Miracoli**, built in 1494 by Perugia as a votive for the Virgin who spared the city from a plague. Built in the form of a Latin cross, it has a doorway with a relief by a student of Michelangelo, Domenico Bertini da Settignano (who, like most Renaissance artists, had a nickname—Topolino, or 'Mousey'—the same as Italian for Mickey Mouse). The church has a fine interior and a beautiful gilded high altar by Bernardino di Lazzaro, a chapel with ex votos dedicated to the miraculous Madonna, and a sweet statue of St Anthony Abbot and his pet pig.

The lake's busiest resort, **Passignano sul Trasimeno** (from the Roman *Passum Jani*) enjoys a favoured position on its own promontory, lying midway between Perugia and Cortona. In the 1930s this was the headquarters of the Società Aeronautica Italiana, which made zippy sea planes and boats, until it was bombed in the war. Within Passignano's walls is an attractive old quarter around the 14th-century castle; below lies a beach hiring out windsurfers. The art is outside the centre: near the cemetery, the **Pieve di San Cristoforo** dates from the 11th century and has recently restored frescoes from the 1300s, while, 1.5km northeast, the **Madonna dell'Olivo** is an elegant Renaissance church with a beautiful high altar and a fresco attributed to Bartolomeo Caporali. The town is at its liveliest for the *Palio delle Barche* on the third Sunday of July, when strapping young Passignanesi dressed in medieval costume carry their boats shoulder-high through the streets and launch them on to the lake for a race.

Passignano is the nearest port to lovely **Isola Maggiore** (20mins), Trasimeno's second-largest and only inhabited island, with a charming 15th-century village inhabited by fishermen and women famous for their lace-making. In 1211, St Francis came to the then-deserted island to spend Lent alone. He made a lasting impression by throwing back a pike a fisherman had given him, only to be followed doggedly across the lake by his grateful 'Brother Fish' until the saint blessed him. Francis took only two loaves of bread to sustain himself, and when the fisherman returned to the island to pick him up, he was amazed to see that only one loaf had been half eaten in forty days.

A footpath encircles the island, passing by the Franciscan convent, built to commemorate the saint's visit and converted in the late 19th century into a neo-Gothic folly by Senator Giacinto Guglielmi from Rome, the whole now crumbling into a romantic ruin (shown by a village cústodian). Nearby, the 13th-century church of **San Michele Arcangelo** has frescoes and an excellent painted *Crucifixion* by Bartolomeo Caporali (*c.* 1460).

## Tuoro sul Trasimeno

West of Passignano, **Tuoro sul Trasimeno** grew up in the late Middle Ages near the **Castello di Montegualandro**, a safe haven for the citizens while their town was attacked and sacked by every army crossing the Italian peninsula or heading south to Rome.

## The Battle of Trasimeno

Tuoro's first battle was the worst. Two years into the Second Punic War, Hannibal was on a winning streak, having defeated the Romans twice, on the rivers Ticino and Trebbia, victories that had rallied the local Gaulish and Ligurian tribes to his banner. As it made its way south towards Rome, this swollen army got bogged down in the disease-ridden marshland of the Arno, at the cost of thousands of troops and all of the exasperated elephants who had survived the march over the Pyrenees and Alps. Meanwhile, the Roman Senate sent Consul Gaius Flaminius, a bold populist politician (builder of the Via Flaminia), and an army of 25,000 to destroy the Carthaginians once and for all. With Flaminius in pursuit through the Valdichiana, Hannibal led his army, now reduced to 40,000, to Trasimeno. Finding a perfect place for an ambush just west of Tuoro, in a natural amphitheatre closed off by the lake (the water level was considerably higher back then) he arranged his troops in the hills, determined to risk all to defeat the Romans and convince the restive Etruscan cities to join him.

Believing that Hannibal was at least a day's march in front, Flaminius failed to send scouts ahead; the morning of 24 June 217 BC was foggy, and, according to the chroniclers, he ignored a number of auguries pointed out by his Etruscan soothsayers (he fell off his horse and the sacred chickens were off their feed). He marched his columns straight into Hannibal's trap, along the narrow shore passage at Malpasso. In a panic, unable to get into battle formations, 15–16,000 legionaries (including Flaminius) were drowned or slaughtered within a few hours, while those who got away found a safe haven in Perugia. The blood of the dead, that legend says ran in a river for three days, is recalled in the name of the hamlet Sanguineto, their whitened bones in the hamlet of Ossaia (from *ossa*, bones). Although Hannibal slew all of the Roman prisoners, he freed all members of the various Italic tribes, hoping to gather support.

After Trasimeno the Roman military machine grimly threw even more legions to their death against Hannibal at Cannae, before changing strategy and giving the Carthaginians the run of the southern Italy for 15 years, harassing Hannibal while refusing to fight him before ultimately defeating him in Africa. The long-term effects of the war are felt in Italy to this day: as small farmers fled before the ravaging armies, they lost their source of income, and were forced to sell their land to pay their debts. Snapped up cheap by a few rich men, it marked the beginning of the feudal *latifondo* system that condemned the once-prosperous south of Italy to grinding poverty.

You can visit the battlefield by car or foot, along the signposted **Percorso Storico Archeologico della Battaglia**, dotted with viewing platforms; explanatory notes along the way and maps help to bring the Roman disaster to life. Near the first platform, note the pretty portal of the Romanesque **Pieve di Confini**. Recently, Tuoro has decorated its lake shore with something unexpected: Pietro Cascella's **Campo del Sole** (1985–89), a contemporary 'solar temple' garden of 27 pillars in locally quarried sandstone, each about 12ft high and sculpted by a different artist, arranged in a wide spiral like a forest of idols to a preposterous god. **La Dogana** near here was the Customs House between the Papal States and the Grand Duchy of Tuscany, and has plaques to the many famous folks who passed this way.

## Castiglione ndel Lago

Among the olive groves that soften the west shore of Trasimeno juts the picturesque promontory of **Castiglione del Lago** (pop. 13,500), the setting for the lake's biggest town, a cheerful and mostly modern place that goes back to the Etruscans. Emperor Frederick II destroyed Castiglione for being an ally of Guelph Perugia, then ordered Fra Elia Coppi to lay out a new Castiglione, neatly in six streets, served by three gates and three squares. Afterwards, the town kept siding with Cortona, causing no end of friction with Perugia until 1490, when it came once and for all under the Baglioni family, who during their brief period of glory hosted here such luminaries as Machiavelli and Leonardo da Vinci.

Eventually the town was recovered by the popes, one of whom, Julius III, gave it to his sister. In 1550, her son, the celebrated *condottiere* Ascanio della Corgna and husband of Giovanna Baglioni, became the first in a series of dukes who ruled the lake as an independent duchy; this lasted until 1648, when it passed into the Grand Duchy of Tuscany before returning to the popes the next century. During Castiglione's ruritanian interlude, the great architect Vignola designed the ducal **Palazzo della Corgna**, or Palazzo Ducale (*closed for restoration; new opening hours not yet know; call ℂ 075 965 8210 for information*). Many of the rooms retain fetching late Renaissance frescoes by Niccolò Pomarancio and the Roman school; one scene shows the *Battle of Trasimeno*, and another the *Battle of Lepanto*, in which Ascanio distinguished himself; like the great *condottiere* Federico da Montefeltro (*see* 'Gubbio'), Ascanio was something of a humanist and had his study decorated with frescoes on the *Life of Caesar*. From the palace, a covered walkway, fortified in case of surprise attack, allowed direct access to the mightiest of all the castles on the lake, the pentagonal **Rocca del Leone** designed in 1247 by Friar Elia Coppi with a sturdy triangular keep and four outer towers. Also to see in Castiglione, in the 19th-century church of the **Maddalena**, is a lovely painting of the *Madonna and Child with SS Anthony Abbot and Mary Magdalene* (1500), by Eusebio da San Giorgio.

## The South Shore

Vines producing Colli del Trasimeno DOC cover much of the south shore of the lake. In **Panicarola**, the most famous producer was Ferruccio Lamborghini, who declared his intention to make wines as fine as his sports cars—his father had been a farmer, and the first motors young Ferruccio built were tractors. He died in 1993, before quite succeeding, but you can still buy a Lamborghini to call your own.

### Activities

Lake Trasimeno's beautiful shoreline is dotted with little ports, which make it a popular place for sailing and water skiing. For **sailing**, contact the Club Velistico in Castiglione del Lago (Viale Brigata Garibaldi 3a, ✆ 075 953035) or in Passignano (Loc. Darsena, ✆ 075 8296021). For **water skiing**, try the Scuola Federale Sci Nautica at Tuoro sul Trasimeno (Punta Navaccia, Via Navaccia 4, ✆ 075 826357), or the Sci Club Trasimeno at Castiglione del Lago (✆ 075 965 2836).

### Where to Stay and Eating Out

Not many Italians think of Trasimeno as a beach resort, but the shallow water is warm and clean. There are modest holiday hotels around Castiglione, Passignano and Magione, and plenty of *agriturismo* (the local tourist offices can send complete lists of local farmhouses), but perhaps the most unusual possibility is out on **Isola Maggiore**— the best place in Umbria to really get away from it all; the island's only hotel is called ★★★**Da Sauro**, Via Guglielmi, ✆ 075 826168, ✪ 075 825130 (*moderate–inexpensive*), gracious and uncomplicated with just 12 rooms. It has a brilliant restaurant that naturally specializes in fish from the lake: eels, carp and such, along with more traditional Umbrian dishes; a good bargain altogether.

### San Feliciano ✉ 06060

In this lakeside hamlet, 7km south of Magione, ★**Da Settimio**, Via Lunga Lago 1, ✆/✪ 075 849104 (*moderate*) is a small charmer, with peaceful rooms and a simple but good restaurant. Watch the sunsets from the tables at **Rosso di Sera**, a new *osteria* at Via Fratelli Papini 91, ✆ 075 847 6277 (*moderate*), where the lake fish, especially in the classic *tegamaccio*, is delicious; they serve land dishes, too. *Open evenings only. Sat and Sun all day. Closed Tues.*

### Castel Rigone ✉ 06060

★★★★**Relais La Fattoria**, Via Rigone 1, ✆ 075 845322, ✪ 075 845197 (*expensive–moderate*) is a pretty hotel, converted from a cluster of 17th-century farm buildings, with a pool, 30 luxuriously furnished rooms and a good restaurant, **La Corte**, serving specialities such as *filetto di persico* (perch) and *spaghetti al sugo di Trasimeno* (with a sauce of mixed lake fish). *Closed Wed.*

### Passignano sul Trasimeno ✉ 06065

★★★**Villa Paradiso**, Via Fratelli Rosselli 5, ✆ 075 829191, ✪ 075 828118 (*moderate*) is a large but comfortable hotel with a rustic feel and a pool. For a few notes less, ★★★**Lido**, Via Roma 1, ✆ 075 827219,✪ 075 827251, is right on the water, with well-equipped rooms and a garden to sit and watch the ferries sailing to and fro. *Open April–Nov)*. A good *inexpensive* choice, **★Florida**, Via 2 Giugno 2, ✆ 075 827228, ✆ 075 827834, has simple rooms and a welcoming atmosphere. There are also basic rooms at **★Del Pescatore**, Via San Bernadino 5, ✆ 075 829 6063, ✆ 075 829201 (*moderate*) but the main business is food, especially lake fish, in the attractive trattoria. *Closed Tues*. The **Fischio del Merlo**, Via A. Gramsci 14, ✆ 075 829283, is similar. *Closed Tues*. **Cacciatori**, Via Nazionale 14, ✆ 075 827210 (*expensive*) is a lakeside restaurant with slightly higher pretensions and excellent fish, but the prices tend to be a bit steep. *Closed Wed.*

## Castiglione del Lago ✉ 06061

In a quiet wooded setting, **★★★Duca della Corgna**, Via Buozzi 143, ✆ 075 953238, ✆ 075 965 2446 (*moderate*) is comfortable and relaxing, but the restaurant only opens in the summer. Little **★★★Miralago**, Piazza Mazzini 6, ✆ 075 951157, ✆ 075 951924 (*moderate*) has pretty lake views. *Closed Jan and Feb.* **★★★Trasimeno**, Via Roma 174, ✆ 075 965 2494, ✆ 075 952 5258 (*moderate*) has a pool to make up for the lake's indifferent waters, but is only open in July and August. Medieval Perugians were so fond of fish from Trasimeno that Nicola Pisano jokingly sculpted some on his famous fountain in front of the cathedral in their city. Today the catch isn't really big enough to send far outside the lake area, but you can try some at the little restaurants around the lake, most of them unpretentious places with reasonable prices. A reliable one is **L'Acquario**, in the historic centre at Via Vittorio Emanuele 69, ✆ 075 965 2463 (*moderate*). Try delicately smoked eel fillets, risotto of lake fish, or carp wrapped in *porchetta* (a typical Trasimeno dish). *Closed Wed, and Tues in winter.*

## South of Lake Trasimeno

These hills and their towns are known for two things: their magical views over the lake and their souvenirs of Perugino who made this loveliness part of his artistic vocabulary. Italian writers have often commented that Città della Pieve looks more like a Sienese town than an Umbrian one; the Tuscan border and interesting towns like Chiusi and Montepulciano are only a few miles away.

### *Tourist Information*

**Città della Pieve**: Piazza del Plebiscito 1, ✆ 0578 299375 (*open 10.30–12.30 and 4–7)*.

**Panicale**: Piazza Umberto I, ✆ 075 837 581. Contact them for their visits to San Sebastiano and the Teatro Cesare Caporali.

### *market day*

Città della Pieve: Saturday.

## Città della Pieve

From Castiglione del Lago it's 27km to the handsome red brick town of Città della Pieve (pop. 6500). The Etruscans and Romans were here, and in the Middle Ages it became *Castrum Plebis*, then *Castel della Pieve*. Perugia considered it as within the western borders of its turf, and in the 1320s built the imposing square fortress to defend it. In 1503, Cesare

Borgia sacked the town and then, in typical Borgia fashion, had two of his colleagues, the Duke of Gavina and Piero Orsini, strangled for conspiring against him. Later the town was ruled by Ascanio della Corgna and his heirs, until 1601, when the Church picked it up and Clement VIII made it a bishopric, and changed its name to Città della Pieve.

But Città della Pieve is best known as the birthplace of **Perugino** (Pietro Vannucci, *c.* 1446–1523). To Giorgio Vasari, he committed the unpardonable sin of not being born in Tuscany; if there is anything to the nasty biography in Vasari's *Lives of the Artists*, Perugino was perhaps the most bitter artist of the Renaissance. Born into a desperately poor family, success made him an untrusting miser: 'he would have gone to any lengths for money' and he would ride out from job to job with saddle-bags full of the money he was afraid to leave anywhere else. About midpoint in his career, he became an atheist; even so, he cranked out two more decades of richly rewarded, if often vacuous, Madonnas and religious scenes with lyrical soft-tinted Trasimeno backgrounds, before dying, stubbornly unconfessed and unab-solved on his deathbed—an extremely rare event in the 16th century—rejecting any future with the sweet angels he depicted for others.

Perugino did leave several paintings in his home town; greatest among these is a lovely fresco of *The Adoration of the Magi* (1504) painted for a charitable confraternity in the **Oratorio di Santa Maria dei Bianchi**, just within the city walls (*open June–Sept daily, 10.30–12.30 and 4–7; Oct–May, Fri–Sun, 10–12.30 and 3.30–6*). It portrays the birth of the Saviour in an Arcadian springtime, with the view from Città della Pieve towards Lake Trasimeno in the background and members of an elegant Renaissance garden party in attendance—a world that seems hardly to need a redeemer at all. The two letters from Perugino on display show that although he demanded 200 florins for his work here, he settled for much less, partly because he was painting for his fellow citizens.

Via Vannucci leads uphill to the town's cluster of monuments in Piazza Plebiscito. The rather undistinguished **Duomo** (*open daily 9.30–5*), was built in the 17th century to replace the far older church of SS Gervasio e Protasio, the *pieve* (parish church) that gave the town its name; pieces of its 9th-century sculptural work are embedded in the façade. There are more works by Perugino (the *Baptism of Christ* in the Cappella del Rosario and the *Madonna in Glory* in the apse), as well a *Crucifix* in the first chapel on the right, attributed to Pietro Tacca. The second chapel has one of Domenico Alfani's finest works, the *Madonna and Child and Saints*.

Next to the Duomo is the lofty **Torre del Pubblico**, built in the 12th century and height-ened in 1471; in the same piazza, stand the trecento **Palazzo dei Priori** and the **Palazzo della Corgna** (*open in summer daily 10.30–12.30 and 5–7*), designed in 1551 by the Perugian architect Galeazzo Alessi for Ascanio della Corgna; inside there are some good 16th-century frescoes by Pomarancio and Salvio Savini and a little sandstone obelisk, brought here from the convent of San Francesco. Near the piazza is what the locals claim is the narrowest lane in Italy (although there are several contenders), **Vicolo Bacciadonne**—'Kiss-the-Women Lane'—which is what one is compelled to do, just to get past.

Just off the Piazza Pretorio in Via Roma stands the brick **Palazzo Bandini**, remodelled in the 16th century by Galeazzo Alessi; if you carry on, you'll come to the Porta Romana and **Santa Maria dei Servi**, frescoed by Perugino with a famous *Deposition* of 1517, although it was sadly damaged when the monks erected a *cantoria* in front of it (the church is often locked;

the custodian at Santa Maria dei Bianchi has the key). The Porta Romana is linked by walls to the Perugian **Rocca**, built by Ambrogio and Lorenzo Maitani in 1326. Opposite the Rocca, the 13th-century church of **San Francesco** was completely redone in the 18th century and is now a popular shrine of Fatima. It has two good paintings, Domenico Alfani's *Virgin and Saints* and a *Pentecost* by Niccolò Pomarancio. Next door to the right, the **Oratorio di San Bartolomeo** (*open 10–12 and 4–7*) has a large fresco of the *Crucifixion* (1342) by the Sienese painter Jacopo di Mino del Pellicciaio, surrounded by weeping angels, hence its nickname, the *Pianto degli Angeli.*

## Panicale and Around

Panicale is famous for its enchanting, and strategic, view over Lake Trasimeno, which in the Middle Ages made it a prize sought by Chiusi and Perugia; even so, in 1037, Panicale became an independent *comune*, one of the first in Italy. In the 14th century it produced the sweet early Renaissance master Tommaso Fini, otherwise known as Masolino da Panicale, who painted with Masaccio in Florence; it also produced Giacomo Paneri, a fierce and brutal *condottiere* known as Boldrino di Panicale, who was briefly lord of the town. Another native, who tips the balance on the side of art, was the poet Cesare Caporali, born in 1530.

An old walled town built on a natural terrace *a chiocciola*, 'in a spiral', Panicale has several pretty squares, beginning with the asymmetrical Piazza Umberto I, home to a charming fountain of 1473 and the 14th-century **Palazzo Pretorio**, decorated with some peculiar carvings and coats of arms. Near here is endearingly stuccoed **Teatro Cesare Caporali**, from the late 18th century and restored in 1991. Further up, the handsome semi-fortified Baroque **Collegiata di San Michele** contains an *Adoration of the Shepherds* by Gian Battista Caporali (1519).

Panicale's most important treasure is in the church of **San Sebastiano**, located just outside the walls. Here Perugino left one of his finest frescoes: a formal, dream-like *Martyrdom of St Sebastian* (1505), a geometrical composition laden with antique ornamentation, where four superbly costumed and cod-pieced archers stand powerfully poised to shoot the saint, while in the background is Panicale's beautiful view over Lake Trasimeno. The same church also contains Perugino's *Madonna*, a detached fresco from the church of Sant'Agostino.

Just to the west of Panicale, **Paciano** is a well preserved medieval village on a spur of Monte Petrarvella, wrapped in its 14th-century walls, towers and gates. The **Confraternità del Santissimo Sacramento**, now a museum (✆ *075 830120*), has a fresco of the *Crucifixion* (1425) by the first reputed teacher of Perugino, Francesco di Castel della Pieve. Another church, **San Giuseppe**, keeps the communal gonfalon from the workshop of Benedetto Bonfigli (*c.* 1480). Outside the walls, the **Madonna della Stella** (1574) is a simple Renaissance church with frescoes by Scilla Pecennini.

The lignite-mining village of **Tavernelle**, just off the SS220, has a pretty main piazza. Near here, the tiny *frazione* of **Mongiovino Vecchio** has a well-preserved castle overlooking a stately domed Renaissance temple, the **Sanctuario di Mongiovino**. This was begun in 1513, an early but characteristic shrine to Mary (encouraged by the Marian preaching of San Bernardino of Siena, the Virgin began to make frequent apparitions in Umbria and Tuscany, and it became the fashion to mark each one with a centrally planned church; the best one in Umbria is in Todi). This one, with its fine octagonal cupola, has been dubiously attributed to

Michelangelo or Bramante, but a more likely candidate is Rocco di Tommaso from Vicenza, who made the two finely sculpted doorways. Inside are cinquecento frescoes by Niccolò Pomarancio and the Flemish painter Heinrich van den Broek (aka Arrigo Fiammingo).

Perugino died of the plague in nearby **Fontignano** in 1523; his tomb, and the fresco he was working on when he died, an almost primitive *Madonna and Child*, can be seen in the parish church, the **Annunziata** (*open 10–12 and 4.30–6.30; Oct–May, Sat and Sun only*). There's a photo of another fresco he made for the church, of the *Adoration of the Shepherds*, now in the National Gallery in London.

### *Where to Stay and Eating Out*

#### Città della Pieve ✉ 06062

Nothing fancy here: **★★Vanucci**, Via Icilio Vanni 1, ✆ 0578 299572, ✉ 0578 298063 (*moderate*) is adequate for a night or two. **Da Bruno**, Via Pietro Vannucci 90, ✆ 0578 298108, serves unpretentious home cooking (*moderate–inexpensive*), as does the **Trattoria Serenella**, Via Fiorenzuola 28, ✆ 0578 299683 (*moderate*).

#### Panicale ✉ 06064

You can sleep sweetly in **★★★Le Grotte di Boldrino**, Via V. Ceppari 43, ✆ 075 837 161, ✉ 075 837 166 (*inexpensive*), a little hotel with 19th-century furniture and Panicale's best restaurant.

# Assisi

Less than half an hour east of Perugia, and visible for miles around, Assisi (pop. 26,000) sweeps the flanks of Monte Subasio in a broad curve, like a pink ship sailing over the green sea of a valley below. This is Umbria's most famous town, and one of its loveliest, but there's more to it than St Francis. Occupied from the Iron Age, Assisi emerged as an ancient Umbrian town in the 6th century BC, one that maintained its cultural distinction into the 1st century BC. As wealthy Roman *Asisium*, it produced the poet Sextus Propertius, and first heard of Christianity from St Rufino in 238. Part of the Lombard Duchy of Spoleto, the city came into prominence again in the Middle Ages as another of Umbria's battling *comuni*, one firmly on the side of the Ghibellines, although in 1198 it rebelled against the Duke of Spoleto and defied its nominal lord, Emperor Frederick Barbarossa.

But Assisi saved most of its bile for incessant wars with arch-rival Perugia; St Francis in his chivalry-obsessed youth had joined in the fighting. The 13th century, which saw his great religious revival, was also the time of Assisi's greatest power and prosperity, leaving behind a collection of beautiful buildings any Italian city could be proud of, as well as one of Europe's greatest hordes of 13th- and 14th-century frescoes in the Basilica di San Francesco. Although Cardinal Albornoz nominally put Assisi under the Church's thumb and rebuilt the Rocca Maggiore to keep it there, the city was controlled by various *signori* until the early 16th century when the papal pall descended like a curtain at the end of a play. Even pilgrimages declined dramatically after the Council of Trent began the Counter-reformation. Another pall that fell over Assisi was taste. In 1786, Goethe, on his way to view the Temple of Minerva, walked past the Basilica of St Francis, dismissing it as 'a Babylonian tower'.

Nevertheless, it was Francis who in the long term would make all the difference to Assisi (*see* pp.52–5). Pilgrimages began again in the 19th century with the revival of interest both in the saint and in the artists who decorated his shrine—Ruskin, who went into ecstatic overdrive at the medieval purity of the frescoes and used to dream that he was a Franciscan friar, was the locomotive drawing the first train of English speakers. Five million pilgrims and tourists crowded Assisi's narrow streets for Francis's 800th birthday year in 1982, and although now passed up by the new shrine of the miracle-working Padre Pio in Puglia, Assisi remains the third most visited pilgrimage site in Italy; on any given summer day you'll see coachloads of tourists and stands peddling ceramic friars and plastic medieval torture instruments intermingled with flocks of serene Franciscans and enthusiastic, almost bouncy

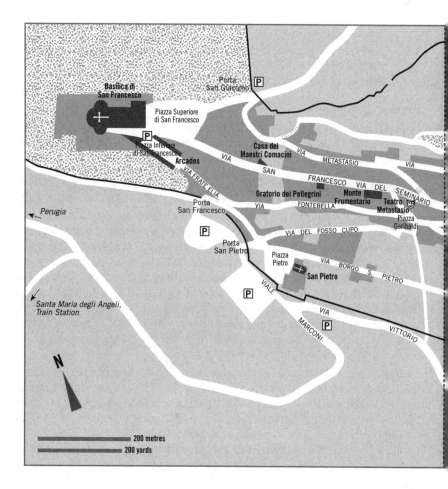

nuns from Africa or Missouri or Bavaria, having the time of their lives visiting a place that, much more than Rome, is the symbol of a living faith. And it's true that something simple and good and joyful has survived in Assisi in spite of the odds.

In recent years, the city has hosted unusual demonstrations, that could never have happened in Rome, or anywhere else—in 1986, when Pope John Paul II hosted his inter-faith World Day of Prayer, complete with Tibetan lamas, Zoroastrians and American Indian medicine-men, and in the 1988 Umbria Jazz Festival, when gospel choirs from New Orleans sang in the upper church of San Francesco. The friars would only let them sing for 15 minutes at a time, fearing that the rhythm might bring down the roof and Giotto's frescoes along with it.

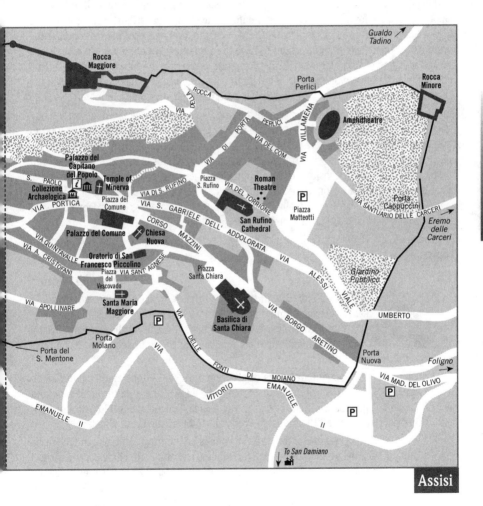

Assisi

Providence saw that the building came to no harm, and by the end the Franciscans were clapping and stomping along with everyone else.

Tragically, as everyone knows, where gospel singing failed, the earthquakes succeeded in September 1997, bringing the roof down and killing two friars and two journalists who were examining the damage caused by the first shock of the day. The original medieval builders, knowing the seismic nature of the land, had given the basilica the flexibility to withstand earthquakes, but the restorers over the centuries had been too lazy to haul out all the rubble they had created, and it accumulated, tons and tons of it, in the essential breathing space between the pricelessly frescoed ceiling vaults and the walls, and the weight brought it down.

The upper church re-opened in November 1999 after extensive restoration and structural reinforcements. To ensure (can you ever be sure of such things?) that a similar disaster never happens again, the foundations have been reinforced to withstand earth tremors of 12 on the Richter Scale. The two arches which collapsed (over the nave and over the main door—the former killed the people standing under it) have been repaired, but are blank; 16 technicians are still working on the incredibly painstaking task of piecing the frescoes back together; much of what they are working with is little more than fine rubble. The other frescoes in the nave were virtually unscathed. The façade has been beautifully restored.

The palazzi on the east side of Piazza del Comune were all badly damaged, as were many other buildings around the town, but the scaffolding is due to come down by Easter 2000 to reveal pristine façades in time for the big jubilee celebrations. Santa Chiara and San Rufino are still closed—both suffered severe structural damage—but even these are expected to be open by summer 2000. In fact, visitors to Assisi in the next few years will see the city, and to a lesser extent the whole region, in better condition than ever before. As a result of the quake, even buildings which were not actually damaged have been restored, as it was deemed a good time to do the work and the funds were there. It's an ill wind...?

The social effects of the quake have not been addressed with such vigour, however, *see* **Topics**, p.50.

---

### Getting Around

 Assisi is a 23km/30min **train** ride from Perugia or Foligno, where you'll have to change from Rome (177km/2½hrs) or Terni. The station is down on the plain, only a block from the suburban Basilica of Santa Maria degli Angeli, and there are regular connecting **buses** every 20 minutes to Piazza Unità d'Italia.

There are also convenient **buses** direct from Perugia, Bettona and Gualdo Tadino (APM, ✆ 573 1707); Rome and Florence (SULGA); one a day from Norcia and Cascia (SIT); and a few from Bevagna, Montefalco, Foligno and Spello (APM or SIT). Stops are in Piazza Matteotti, Largo Properzio and Piazzale Unità d'Italia.

If you're driving, use one of the three **car parks** on the fringes of town: in the Piazza Unità d'Italia below the Basilica of San Francesco, at the Porta Nuova at the eastern end of town, and in a vast underground lot in the walls at Piazza Matteotti, by the Duomo. A series of little buses, the A and B, run between Piazza del Comune and Piazza Matteotti every 20 minutes or so (tickets available from news stands, bars and tobacconists); Assisi isn't really that big, but it's steep in places.

Piazza del Comune 12, ✆ 075 812534, ✉ 075 813727, *info@iat.
assisi.pg.it, www.umbria2000.it*; also a seasonal office (Easter–Oct) at
Largo Properzio. **Hotel booking service**: Via Cristofani, ✆ 075 816566,
✉ 075 812315, *caa@krenet.it*

**Post office**: Piazza del Comune, ✆ 075 812355.

**Churches**: Unless otherwise stated, all churches are open daily 7am–12 noon and
2pm–sunset.

*market day*

Saturday, in Piazza Matteotti.

## The Basilica of San Francesco

*I would give all the churches in Rome for this cave.*

Hippolyte Taine (19th-century French critic)

Although the medieval popes were mistrustful of the spontaneous, personal approach to faith
preached by Francis and his followers, they soon realized that this powerful movement
would be better off within the Church than outside it. In transforming the Franciscans into a
respectable, doctrinally safe arm of Catholicism they had the invaluable aid of Francis's
successor, Brother Elias, Vicar-General of the Order, a worldly, businesslike, organization
man, something of an epicurean and a friend of Emperor Frederick II. Elias's methods caused
the first split within the Franciscans, between those who enjoyed the growing opulence of
the new dispensation and those who tried to keep to the poverty preached by their founder.
This monumental building complex, begun the day after Francis's canonization in 1228
when Pope Gregory IX laid the cornerstone, was one of the biggest causes of contention.
Nothing could have been further removed from the philosophy and intentions of Francis
himself; on the other hand, nothing could have been more successful in perpetuating the
memory of Francis and his teaching than this great treasurehouse of art.

From the beginning, the popes were entirely behind the effort. They paid for it by promoting
a great sale of special indulgences across Europe, and to this day the basilica belongs to the
Vatican (although thanks to a clause in the Lateran Treaty of 1929, signed by Mussolini and
renewed in 1989 by the late Socialist prime minister Bettino Craxi, the Italian State is responsible for the upkeep—including all the earthquake repairs). There's a story that Brother Elias
himself supplied the design—the lower basilica, one of the less successful attempts to trans-
plant the Gothic style on Italian soil, does have an amateurish, clumsy form. The beautiful
**campanile** dates from 1239; the completed basilica was consecrated by Innocent IV in
1253. Behind it, visible for miles around, propped up on huge buttressed vaults, is the enormous **convent** built by Sixtus IV in the 15th century. Now a missionary college, it was
damaged by the earthquake as well, although a part of it is being used as a fresco hospital.

### The Lower Church

*Open daily 6.30am–7pm summer, 6.30am–6pm winter. No shorts or bare shoulders.*

The usual approach to the basilica is by way of the Lower Church from the **Piazza Inferiore
di San Francesco**, lined with arcades where medieval pilgrims bought their souvenirs
before returning home. Because of its partially underground location on a hill, the Lower

Church has no façade, but it does have a rather grand Renaissance portico of 1487, which protects a fine Gothic portal. Brother Elias, or whoever was responsible, designed the church to hold the saint's body, and with its low dark vaults, dimly illuminated through stained glass, it certainly resembles a crypt (it's a good idea to bring a torch). It is confusing at first in its overwhelming detail, and perhaps even a bit claustrophobic if it's crowded, yet tucked in here are some of Italy's finest 13th- and 14th-century frescoes. Those in the **narthex**, as you enter, are 17th-century works by Girolamo Martelli and Cesare Sermei.

The large polygonal **Cappella di Santa Caterina** at the far end of the narthex was designed for Cardinal Albornoz by Matteo Gattapone and frescoed by Andrea de' Bartoli. The Cardinal's nephew, appointed governor of Spoleto, and his nephew's son were buried here after they were murdered by the Spoletines. The Cardinal (d. 1367) was entombed here as well, before his body was removed to safer keeping in Toledo; you can see him on the left wall of the chapel, kneeling before three saints.

The **nave**, with its original pavement, gently slopes down to the high altar. The frescoes on the walls are the oldest in the basilica, dating back to 1253 and are by the so-called Master of St Francis, who may have been an Umbrian painter. Note how their iconography already

## Lower Church key

1    Cerchi Tomb with big porphyry vase (13th century)
2    Cappella di San Sebastiano, frescoes by Girolamo Martelli (1646) and the *Madonna della Salute*, the only known work by the 15th-century painter Ceccolo di Giovanni
3    *Madonna with Saints*, by Ottaviano Nelli (1422)
4    Tomb of John of Brienne, Latin Emperor of Constantinople (and friend of St Francis)
5    Cappella del Sacramento, with two 14th-century tombs
6    Cemetery cloister
7    Cappella di Santa Caterina, frescoes by Andrea de' Bartoli of Bologna (1360s)
8    Cappella di Santo Stefano, frescoes by Dono Doni (1574)
9    Cappella di San Martino by Simone Martini (c. 1320)
10   Cappella di San Lorenzo, frescoes by Andrea de' Bartoli (1360s)
11   Stairs to the crypt
12   Cappella di Sant'Antonio da Padova, frescoes by Cesare Sermei (1610), early 14th-century stained glass
13   Cappella di San Valentino, with a pavement tomb of Friar Ugo of Hartlepool, one of the first English Franciscans (d. 1302)
14   Cappella della Maddalena, frescoes by Giotto and assistants (c. 1309)
15   *Coronation of the Virgin*, by Puccio Capanna (1337), over a Cosmati work pulpit
16   The *Quattro Vele* (*Poverty, Chastity, Obedience* and the *Glory of St Francis*)
17   *The Last Judgement*, by Cesare Sermei (1623)
18   Frescoes of the Passion, by Pietro Lorenzetti (c. 1320)
19   Cappella di San Giovanni Battista, triptych by Lorenzetti (c. 1320–30)
20   Frescoes by Cimabue, Giotto, Martini and Lorenzetti
21   Cappella di San Nicola, frescoes by Giotto and assistants
22   Steps to the chapterhouse
23   Stairs to terrace and treasury

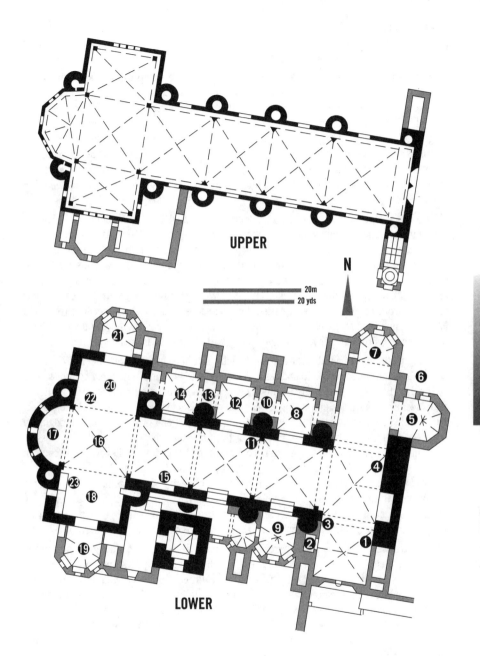

UPPER

20m
20 yds

N

LOWER

The Basilica of San Francesco

identifies Francis as a Christ figure: on the right wall are scenes of the *Passion of Christ*, on the left wall the *Life of St Francis*. Both were unfortunately damaged as new chapels were opened up, but as compensation, some of these contain masterpieces.

One of these is the first chapel to the left of the nave, the **Cappella di San Martino**, a unique example of a total Gothic decorative scheme, where the frescoes, stained glass, and even the inlaid floor were designed by the great Sienese master Simone Martini (*c.* 1315–20). Martini's courtly International Gothic-style poses are a serious artistic challenge to Giotto and the other great precursors of the Renaissance. This master of line and colour, whom Berenson called the 'most lovable painter of the pre-Renaissance', creates here a wonderful, elegant narrative on the *Life of St Martin*, the 4th-century Gaulish soldier and wastrel who ended up as a bishop and friend of the poor, and whose life foreshadowed that of Francis.

Next to the chapel is the stair down to the **crypt**, built in 1925 for the bones of St Francis and four of his closest followers. These were discovered only in 1818. At first Francis had been buried in the church of San Giorgio (now incorporated into the church of Santa Chiara), but Brother Elias, worried that the Perugians would come to steal the saint's body, made off with it himself during the canonization ceremonies and then hid it here with exceeding care behind tons of stone. His fears were not unfounded; when Francis was returning from La Verna to die in Assisi, the wicked Perugians (who never listened when Francis came to preach) were lying in wait to kidnap him along the road, and would have succeeded had Brother Elias not had the foresight to direct Francis on a longer route.

The **Cappella della Maddalena** on the right contains frescoes on the *Life of Mary Magdalene*, attributed to Giotto and his assistants (*c.* 1309). The scenes were commissioned by the then Bishop of Assisi, who is shown being crowned with a mitre by St Rufino. There's also a scene of the Magdalene sailing to Marseille, not a subject you often see outside France. The barrel-vaulted transept on the west end (the usual east end of a church, but topography forced Brother Elias to lay it out backwards) is even more lavishly decorated. In the crossing over the high altar, known as the **Quattro Vele**, are four beautiful allegorical frescoes, of *Poverty, Chastity, Obedience* (the three Virtues of St Francis) and the *Glory of St Francis*. The *Marriage of St Francis with Lady Poverty* is one of the most striking images ever to come out of the 13th-century religious revival; Obedience has her finger to her lips, extolling silence. Long attributed to Giotto, these are now attributed to two of his students, one from Tuscany and one an Umbrian now known as the Maestro della Vele.

The **left transept** has a remarkable fresco cycle on the *Life of Christ*, among the best in the basilica, by Pietro Lorenzetti of Siena (*c.* 1320–30). Lorenzetti, a contemporary of Martini, could be just as decorative and elegant, as in the *Entrance in Jerusalem*, but he could also achieve a powerful degree of drama and emotion, as in his *Crucifixion* and the immensely sombre and harrowing *Descent from the Cross*. These frescoes are his masterpieces; it may be that working among the likes of Cimabue and Giotto inspired Lorenzetti to make the imaginative breakthrough in composition and meaning, here leaving all the typical Sienese decoration behind to convey the depths of tragedy and despair.

In the **right transept**, Giotto's assistants frescoed the *Childhood of Christ* and the *Posthumous Miracles of St Francis* (1315–20), while the *Crucifixion* here is believed to be by Giotto himself. Cimabue's famous *Madonna and Child, with Angels and St Francis*

(1280), is one of the most famous images of the saint, and believed to be an accurate likeness. This is a sole survivor of the frescoes that Cimabue and the Master of St Francis painted in the transepts, before they were redone in the 1300s. A serious-looking female saint nearby, by Simone Martini, is believed to be St Clare. Martini also painted the *Madonna and Child and Two of the Wise Men*. This transept also has Pietro Lorenzetti's first contribution to the church, the graceful *Madonna della Tramontana* ('of the sunset') *with St Francis and St John*, a fresco in a painted frame. The polygonal **Cappella di San Nicola** has frescoes on the *Life of St Nicholas* by Giotto and his assistants.

In 1995, the contents of the 'secret sacristy' were put on display in the **chapterhouse**: Pope Honorius III's Bull approving the Order's Rule (1223), the saint's tunic, cowl, girdle and sandals, an ivory horn given to Francis by the Sultan of Egypt which he would blow to assemble his followers, the *Laud to the Creator* and *Benediction of Brother Leone* on parchment, in the saint's own hand, and a chalice and paten used by Francis and his followers. The *Crucifixion* fresco on the wall here is by Puccio Capanna (1340).

From the transepts, stairs lead up to a terrace and the Sala Gotica, home of the **Museo-Tesoro della Basilica**, which went on tour when the building was damaged by the quake, but reopen for Easter 2000. This contains many beautiful things that somehow escaped being pillaged or pinched through the centuries: a Venetian cross in rock crystal, a French ivory Madonna from the 13th century; a 15th-century Flemish tapestry with St Francis and an altar frontal with a scene by Antonio del Pollaiolo (both presented to the basilica by Sixtus V), the ornate Chalice of Nicholas IV (1290), and much more. Since 1986, the treasury has also contained the **Mason Perkins Collection**, donated by the art historian, who gathered together works by Pietro Lorenzetti, Lorenzo Monaco, Taddeo di Bartolo, Bartolo di Fredi and other trecento masters.

### The Upper Church

*Open 8am–7pm daily; until 6pm in winter.*

In complete contrast to the Lower Church, the Upper Church with its big rose window and false front gable (beautifully restored after the earthquake) is strikingly bright and airy and vibrant, and filled with frescoes that emphasize its perfectly balanced proportions. Architecturally, this is Gothic reduced to its basics. The medieval Italians, who never took to the style imported from the north and regarded all the flamboyant vaults and spires and buttresses as barbaric, nevertheless did appreciate the possibilities that the style offered over Romanesque, especially the opportunity the new techniques offered in creating a single open space. The Upper Church, whoever designed it, became the great prototype of Italian Gothic, the model for countless Franciscan and Dominican churches: here all the features emphasized by northern architects are minimalized to provide a perfect framework for the frescoes in a revolutionary synthesis of art and architecture. The space, the simplicity, and the easy to 'read' illustrations were just what a popular preaching order required. Although the frescoes tend to steal all the thunder, give a few minutes to the beautiful 13th-century **stained glass**, considered the finest in medieval Italy.

Two bands of frescoes run in narrative bands along the nave. The **lower register**, on the *Life of St Francis* (*c.* 1290–95), constitutes perhaps the longest-raging controversy in the history of art. Vasari in the 16th century attributed them to Giotto, and the Italian faction is convinced that they are the climax of his early career, painted some two decades before his work in the Lower Church, while most foreign scholars, faced with the stylistic differences between these and Giotto's uncontroversial surviving fresco cycle in the Arena chapel in Padua (1305) believe that Giotto didn't paint them at all, but that they are the work of three or four of his followers. What convinces most Italian scholars that the San Francesco frescoes were at least partially by Giotto is the artist's mastery of composition; Giotto amazed his contemporaries with his ability to illustrate the physical and spiritual essentials of a scene with simplicity and drama, cutting to the core of the matter. Although the controversy may never be resolved to everyone's satisfaction, one thing is certainly true: even if the man recogonized in his own lifetime as the greatest painter since antiquity didn't actually apply brush to wall, his guiding spirit is certainly here, not least in the frescoes' humane qualities that have made them posterity's image of Francis.

The scenes are perfectly integrated in the four bays of the nave, all knit together with a *trompe l'œil* cornice. They begin in the fourth bay on the right, with *Francis honoured by the simple man*, who lays down his cloak and foretells the saint's destiny (note Assisi's Temple of Minerva in the background), followed by 2. *Francis gives his cloak to a poor knight* (with Assisi in the background). 3. *He dreams of a palace full of arms.* 4. *The voice in San Damiano tells Francis to 'Rebuild my Church'.* 5. *He renounces the world before the bishop of Assisi and his father*, who in his anger and disappointment has to be restrained. 6. *The Dream of Innocent III*, a memorable scene, in which Francis supports the falling Church. 7. *Innocent III approves Francis's Rule.* 8. *The Fiery Chariot*, from a vision of one of the saint's followers. 9. *Fra Leone dreams of the throne reserved for Francis in heaven.* 10. *The demons are expelled from Arezzo by Fra Silvestro.* 11. *Francis meets the Sultan of Egypt and offers to undergo the Ordeal by Fire.* 12. *Francis in Ecstasy.* 13. *The creation of the first Christmas crib at Greccio.*

On the inner wall of the façade: 14. *Francis brings forth a spring for a thirsty man.* 15. *Francis preaches to the birds.*

Then around on the left wall of the nave: 16. *The knight of Celano dies, as foretold by the saint.* 17. *Francis preaches to Pope Honorius III.* 18. *He appears in two places at the same time.* 19. *He receives the stigmata*, from a six-winged cherub. 20. *The death of Francis.* 21. *The saint appears to the Bishop of Assisi and Fra Augustine.* 22. *Girolamo of Assisi accepts the truth of the stigmata.* 23. *Francis mourned by the Poor Clares.* 24. *Coronation of Francis.* 25. *He appears to Gregory IX in a dream.* 26. *He heals a wounded man.* 27. *He revives a devout woman.* 28. *He releases Pietro d'Alife from prison.* The last three scenes are generally ascribed to the Master of Santa Cecilia, who was famous for his lively figures, warm colours and very meticulous architectural scenes.

The **upper register** of frescoes, of *Old Testament and New Testament Scenes*, were commissioned in 1288 to celebrate the election of Nicholas IV, the first Franciscan pope. Badly damaged in places and much harder to see, they are usually attributed to the Roman painters Pietro Cavallini and Jacopo Torriti, and to Cimabue's followers (including, some say, the young Giotto, who may have painted those with the most striking architectural compositions, *Isaac blessing Jacob* and *Esau before Isaac*). Giotto is also generally credited with the *Four Doctors of the Church*, in the vault of the first bay, part of which collapsed in the earthquake, along with the arch. Some of the frescoes have been reconstructed.

The transepts were painted with a famous cycle of frescoes by Giotto's master, Cimabue, though the works have been much damaged over the centuries and oxidized into mere shadows, or negatives of their former selves. In the left transept are scenes of the *Apocalypse* and the famous *Crucifixion*, a faded masterpiece of 1277 that still radiates some of its original drama and feeling. The earthquake shattered two bays of the vault and arch, and took Cimabue's *St Matthew* from the Four Evangelists in the crossing. The bays have since been reconstructed, and the hundreds of thousands of coloured pieces of the Cimabue and other frescoes wait in trays to be put back together again. Restorers hope that a hyper-colour-sensitive computer programme will work with their own skills to make the impossible feasible.

## To the Piazza del Comune

On entering Assisi, along the main road from the car park, you may have noticed the excellent Romanesque-Gothic façade of **San Pietro** with three rose windows, just inside the gate of the same name (down Via Frate Elia from the piazza of the Lower Church). This Benedictine church was built in the 1200s, although Assisi's chroniclers date the original building back to Palaeochristian times. It was restored before the earthquake, but now it's closed again.

From the tidy lawn of the Upper Church, Via San Francesco, the main street of Assisi, leads into the *centro storico*, passing some fine medieval houses and a rather unexpected **Museo degli Indios dell'Amazzonia,** with ethnographic items collected by Capuchin missionaries in the Amazon (*open 10–12 and 3–6; free*), while in the same building Amazonian fish and plants are on show as the **Mostra Etnologica.** At No.14 stands the Masons' Guild, or **Casa dei Maestri Comacini** (most of the basilica builders came from the Lake Como area, medieval Italy's cradle of masons). **Palazzo Vallemani**, on the left, may soon be the new location of the **Pinacoteca**, with detached frescoes, including a scene of 13th-century knights from the Palazzo del Capitano del Popolo that probably caught the fancy of the young Francis, and others by Tiberio d'Assisi; there's also a rather sleepy collection of Umbrian paintings, including a *Madonna della Misericordia* by L'Alunno.

At No.11, the **Oratorio dei Pellegrini** is a 15th-century gem, all that survives from a pilgrims' hospice, frescoed on the façade and altar wall by Matteo da Gualdo. The frescoes on the walls are by another Umbrian, Pierantonio Mezzastris (1477), with scenes of miracles that happened on the road to Compostela and the life of St Anthony Abbot (with the friendly camels). At No.3, the portico belonged to **Monte Frumentario**, which was built in the 13th-century as a hospital, one of the first in Italy, and was later converted into a granary. Next to it, a 16th-century **fountain** still bears the warning that the penalty for washing clothes here is one *scudo* and confiscation of laundry. Via San Francesco then passes through an archway from the city's Roman walls, and continues as the Via del Arco del Seminario, named for the former missionary college on the left. Further up is the 19th-century **Teatro Comunale Metastasio**, now used as a cinema.

Near here, at Via Portica 1, is the **Collezione Archeologica** (*open daily exc Mon 10–1 and 3–7; Oct–Mar 10–1 and 2–5; adm*), located in the crypt of the now-vanished church of San Niccolò (1097); it has a small collection of urns, statues, and bits of Roman fresco. The collection was founded in 1793 by the local Accademia Properziano del Subasio and hasn't changed much since. A passage from the museum leads into the ancient **Roman forum** (or the sacred area of *Asisium*), excavated in the 19th century, directly under the modern Piazza del Comune. Here you can see bases of statues, a platform that may have been an altar, an inscription to the Dioscuri, steps to the temple of Minerva, and remains of a fountain.

## Piazza del Comune

The long, attractive Piazza del Comune, the medieval centre of Assisi, is embellished with 13th-century buildings of the old *comune*: the lofty **Torre del Popolo** and the **Palazzo del Capitano del Popolo**, the **Palazzo del Podestà** (now the **Palazzo del Comune**), and what at first looks like a decrepit bank building but is in reality a genuine Roman **Temple of Minerva** from around the 1st century BC, with Corinthian columns and travertine steps. When Goethe, a muddle-headed classicist who felt a national embarrassment whenever he heard the word 'Gothic', came to Assisi it was to see this—and nothing else. It has the best surviving Roman temple front on the Italian peninsula, as good as any ruin in Rome for helping your imagination conjure up the classical world. But only the pronaos and façade remain; inside you'll be treated to some eccentric Baroque belonging to the church of Santa Maria della Minerva.

To the left of the palazzo, the **Chiesa Nuova** (being restored) was built in 1615 by Philip III of Spain on property owned by St Francis's father. In an adjacent alley, the **Oratorio di San Francesco Piccolino** is believed to mark the saint's birthplace.

## Upper Assisi: the Cathedral, the Castle and Around

Most visitors labour under the impression that the Basilica of St Francis is Assisi's cathedral, and never find their way up Via di San Rufino from Piazza del Comune to the real **Cattedrale di San Rufino**. This, set over a piazza (another candidate for the Roman forum), has a huge campanile and a beautiful Romanesque façade restored since the quake, the finest in Assisi, designed by Giovanni da Gubbio in 1140 and adorned with fine rose windows and the kind of robust medieval carvings of animals and saints that Goethe so disdained.

Inside (under restoration after the earthquake) it houses the porphyry font where Saints Francis and Clare were baptized, as well as Emperor Frederick II, who was born nearby in Jesi, in the Marche. It is an amazing coincidence that these two leading protagonists of the 13th century should have been baptized in the same place; the holy water must have had a special essence in it, as both Francis and Frederick were profoundly influenced by the East and were among the very first poets to write in vernacular Italian, rather than Latin.

San Rufino's interior was restored in the 16th century, when the beautiful carved wooden choir was added. Off the right nave, there's a small **Museo Capitolare** (*open daily 10–12 and 3–6; Aug 10–6; closed Christmas; adm*) with Romanesque capitals, codices, detached frescoes, paintings by Matteo da Gualdo and a beautiful triptych by L'Alunno (1470). When the church reopens you can explore the ancient **crypt**, dating from an earlier, 11th-century church, with a few frescoes and a 3rd-century Roman sarcophagus decorated with fine reliefs of the myth of Endymion, where St Rufino was buried (*open April–Oct 10–12.30 and 3–6; Aug 10–6; adm; combined ticket available*). Don't miss the barrel-vaulted Roman cistern directly under the cathedral's campanile, with an inscription in the Umbrian language. The Umbrii worshipped springs, and this is believed to have been a sacred fountain. The inscription names the *marones*, or officials who were in charge of building projects, not unlike the Roman *aediles*.

From the cathedral, it's a bracing walk up to the **Rocca Maggiore** (*open 10–sunset; adm*), Assisi's well-preserved castle, built in 1174 and used by Conrad von Luetzen (who cared for the little orphan Emperor Frederick II). It was then destroyed and rebuilt on several occasions, once by Cardinal Albornoz; it offers excellent views of Assisi, the Valle Umbra, a second, inaccessible fortress built by Albornoz called the Rocciciola, and the surrounding countryside.

East of the cathedral you can visit more of Roman *Asisium*—the **theatre** in Via del Torrione, flanking the cathedral, and the remains of the **amphitheatre**, off Piazza Matteotti and Via Villamena. The **Porta Perlici** near the amphitheatre dates from 1199, and there are some well-preserved 13th-century houses on the Via del Comune Vecchio. The **Giardino Pubblico**, with its pavilions and goldfish ponds, is a pretty city park, a fine place to have a picnic after a hard day's sightseeing. *Asisium* had up-to-date plumbing; you might be able to pick out the Roman drain between the amphitheatre and the Giardino Pubblico, built to carry off water after the amphitheatre was flooded for mock sea battles.

## Basilica di Santa Chiara

Born in 1194, Chiara Offreduccio was 17 when she ran away from her wealthy and noble family to become a disciple of St Francis at the Porziuncola, and by 1215 she was the abbess of a Franciscan Second Order, the Poor Clares or Clarisse, based on the primitive rule of St Francis. Whatever the later church mythology, gratifying rumours were never lacking that there was more to her relationship with Francis than practical piety. Gentle and humble, she once had a vision of a Christmas service in the Basilica of St Francis while at San Damiano, over a kilometre away, a feat that led Pope Pius XII in 1958 to declare her the Patron Saint of Television. (Unfortunately, the plastic, reception-guaranteeing statues of St Clare, with two holes in the back for your TV antenna, are now impossible to find in Assisi's souvenir shops). Like Francis, she lived on alms, and is reputed to have twice saved Assisi from the army of Frederick II. Her rule of poverty was only confirmed by Pope Innocent IV while she lay on her deathbed, two days before she died in 1253. She was canonized two years later, but, as in the case of Francis, her desire for her followers to live in absolute poverty was denied when Pope Urban IV approved a new Rule for her Order (1264). Still, it did offer something of an alternative for women in an age where many were forced into arranged marriages or convents if there wasn't enough dowry to go around; two Umbrian women who followed in Clare's footsteps were the great 13th-century mystics, the Blessed Angela of Foligno and St Clare of Montefalco.

Her **basilica**, built in 1265 below the Piazza del Comune by way of Corso Mazzini, is a pink and white striped beauty with a lovely rose window, supported by huge flying buttresses added a century later that not only keep it from falling over but create a memorable architectural space below. The church stands on the site of the old church of San Giorgio, where Francis attended school and where his body lay for two years awaiting the completion of his own basilica.

Badly damaged by the earthquake, it may be a while before the basilica reopens. The shadowy **interior** has frescoes in the transepts by followers of Giotto, although they are damaged and hard to see; by the altar are scenes from her life by the late 13th-century Maestro di Santa Chiara. On the right, the **Oratorio del Crocifisso** contains the famous

*Crucifix of San Damiano* (*see* below), a 13th-century triptych by Rinaldo di Ranuccio and reliquaries of St Clare, containing some of her garments and golden curls. The adjacent **Cappella del Sacramento** has fine Sienese frescoes; these two chapels were part of San Giorgio. Clare's body, rediscovered in 1850 under the high altar, shrivelled and darkened with age, lies like a never-kissed Snow White in a crystal coffin down in the neo-Gothic crypt.

## Piazza Vescovado and Around

From Santa Chiara, Via Sant'Agnese leads down to the delightful Piazza Vescovado and the simple church of **Santa Maria Maggiore** (1163), with a pink and white checked façade. This was Assisi's first cathedral, built on the site of the Roman Temple of Apollo, traces of which are still visible in the 9th-century crypt. Near here the reputed **house of Sextus Propertius**, the Roman poet of love (46 BC–AD 14), was discovered, complete with wall paintings, awaiting funds to have it kitted out for public access (until then you'll need permission from the Soprintendenza Archeologica in Perugia to visit). Between here and Piazza Unità d'Italia are Via Cristofani and Via Fontebella, the latter adorned with wrought-iron dragons and another pretty fountain.

## Around Assisi

### San Damiano

*Open daily, 10–12.30 and 2–6; until 4.30 in winter.*

Many of the key events of Francis's life took place in the countryside around Assisi. San Damiano is a short drive or a pleasant 2km walk down from Santa Chiara on Via Borgo Aretino, through the Porta Nuova and down along the signposted route. It was here in this simple, asymmetrical Benedictine priory (1030) surrounded by olives and cypress trees that the Crucifix bowed and spoke to Francis in 1205, commanding him to 'rebuild my church'. Francis took the injunction literally, and sold his father's horse and cloth to raise the money—which the priest at San Damiano refused to take, so Francis threw it out of the window and returned to restore the church with his own hands. He brought Clare to San Damiano in 1212, when the restoration was complete, and here she and her followers passed their frugal, contemplative lives (forbidden to beg, they nearly starved). While sitting in the garden during one of his visits, Francis composed his superb *Cantico della creature*, the 'Canticle of All Things Created', in 1224.

The church is entered through the Cappella di San Girolamo, with a fine fresco by Tiberio d'Assisi of the *Madonna and Child, with SS. Francis, Clare, Bernardino and Jerome* (1517); the next chapel contains a large wooden *Crucifix* of 1637 by Fra Innocenzo da Palermo. Frescoes in the church record the events that happened here (one shows the saint's father chasing him with a stick when he found out that he had sold his property). The crucifix over the altar is a copy of the original one, now in Santa Chiara. In the convent there's a fresco of the *Crucifixion* by Mezzastris, the room where St Clare died in 1253, and the tiny cloister with frescoes by Eusebio da San Giorgio (1507) of the *Annunciation* and *St Francis Receiving the Stigmata.*

San Damiano owes its preservation to the foresight of an English traveller. In 1870, when the Papal States were united to the new Kingdom of Italy, Lord Ripon, who had converted to

Catholicism, bought San Damiano to keep it from becoming state property—the fate of all the state's monastic institutions—and he let it to the friars on the sole condition that they did nothing to restore it. Lord Lothian, who inherited it, returned it to the Franciscans in 1983.

## The Eremo delle Carceri and Monte Subasio

Another Franciscan shrine more true to the spirit of the saint than the great art-filled basilicas is the peaceful **Eremo delle Carceri**, located in a beautiful setting on the edge of a ravine, deep in the woods along the road up Monte Subasio, a spectacular walk or drive 4km east of Assisi (leave by way of the Porta dei Cappuccini; *open 6.30am–5, summer till 7.30*). This 'Hermitage of the Prison' was Francis's retreat, where he and his followers strove to live like the first Umbrian saints, walking through the woods and meditating. Bernardino of Siena founded the small convent here in 1426, where a handful of friars still live a traditional Franciscan existence on the alms they receive. By the little triangular courtyard there are two small chapels to visit, the **Cappella di San Bernardino**, with tiny stained glass windows, and the **Cappella di Santa Maria delle Carceri**, with a fresco of the *Madonna and Child and St Francis* by Tiberio d'Assisi. A steep stair leads down to the **Grotto di San Francesco**, with one of the saint's beds hollowed from the rock, and the very old ilex down in the ravine, where the birds are said to have flocked to hear him preach, as a faded fresco on the cave recounts.

From the Eremo delle Carceri, it's 7.5km up the Collepino road to the distinctive bald summit of **Monte Subasio** (4229ft), now the centre of a regional park, with superb views over the high Apennines to the east and marked walking paths. In the summer you can continue another spectacular 10km over the mountains on an unpaved road to **Collepino**, above Spello (*see* p.137).

## Santa Maria degli Angeli

The real centre of early Franciscanism, however, was down on the plain, at the little 11th-century oratory called the Porziuncola ('the little portion'), where angels were wont to appear. Francis, in return for the use of the oratory, owed a yearly basket of carp from the river Tescio to the Benedictines, still faithfully paid by the Franciscans. The saint and his followers stayed in rustic huts around the oratory; here Clare took her vows of poverty as the spiritual daughter of St Francis, and it was here that Francis asked to be brought to die. It quickly became a pilgrimage site, and in 1569 a monumental domed basilica, designed by Galeazzo Alessi, was begun to shelter the Porziuncola. Not completed until 1684, it is, in its way, an excellent piece of nostalgic Baroque, although most of it was rebuilt after an 1832 earthquake (the dome managed somehow to survive from the original church). The grandiose façade was only added in 1927. You certainly can't miss it—you could probably see it from the moon with a good telescope, rising over a modern suburb and Assisi's train station: Santa Maria degli Angeli is the eighth largest church in the world. On its flank it is graced by a suitably enormous **fountain**, donated by the Medici in 1610 and designed for pilgrims to wash away the dust from the road.

The side chapels, some of which are still being restored after the earthquake, are mostly decorated with early Baroque works. Beneath the dome, the **Cappella della Porziuncola** has an entrance dolled up with frescoes from the 19th century on the *Pardon of St Francis*. The rugged stone oratory can be seen inside, with a superb altarpiece on the *Life of*

*St Francis* (1393) by Ilario da Viterbo, this artist's only known work (but undergroing restoration). One of the very few benefits of the 1997 earthquake was the revealing of the decoration on the oratory's roof. The chapel also has the stone marking the tomb of Pietro Cattani (d. 1221), who was appointed first Vicar of the Order when the pope encouraged Francis, who had no interest in organization or discipline, to step down, or rather sideways, since he considered the position as only the first among equals. On the back wall there's a fine 15th-century fresco of the *Crucifixion*.

St Francis died in the infirmary cell, which is now the tiny **Cappella del Transito**. His last concerns was for 'his lady Poverty'; he insisted on being laid out on the bare earth, and would have died naked had not the bishop of Assisi insisted that as the tunic he wore was borrowed, he could truly leave the world with no possessions. Through the gate you can see some unusual frescoes by Lo Spagna of the saint's oldest companions, along with a statue of St Francis by Andrea della Robbia. The rope the saint used to belt his habit is displayed in a case. There are more early Baroque chapels in the transept, and in the south transept, off a corridor, the entrance to the **crypt**, part of the excavations in 1968 that revealed the foundations and some of the walls of the first Franciscan convent. It also has a very beautiful altarpiece by Andrea della Robbia (you may have to find the sacristan to unlock it).

The garden contains the roses that Francis is said to have thrown himself on while wrestling with severe temptation, staining their leaves red with blood, only to find that they lost their thorns on contact with his body. Still thornless, they bloom every May. Francis's own cell at the Porziuncola was covered by St Bonaventura with the frescoed **Cappella del Roseto**, which has some of Tiberio d'Assisi's finest frescoes, one showing the famous scene in the garden. There's an old pharmacy and, in the refectory of the convent, a **museum** (*closed at present*) with a portrait of St Francis by an unknown 13th-century master, another attributed to Cimabue, and a *Crucifix* (1236) by Giunta Pisano; there's also a **Museo Etnografico Universale** with fascinating items relating to Franciscan missionary work (*open Mon–Fri 9–12 and 3–6, Sat 9–12, closed Sun; free*).

A 14km **Via di San Francesco** is being built from the Porziuncola to the Basilica di San Francesco, linking the sites associated with the saint along the way. It is paved with bricks inscribed with the name and city of any benefactor who contributes L85,000.

### *Activities*

Assisi is both Umbria's spiritual and souvenir shopping centre, overflowing with little ceramic friars, crossbows, local ceramics and glass, textiles and serious art galleries. Annual festivals in Assisi include the medieval May Day celebrations of *Calendimaggio*, on the first Thursday, Friday and Saturday in May, commemorating Francis's troubadour past with song, dance, torchlit parades, beautiful costumes and competitions between Lower and Upper Assisi. Easter week is busy with activities— on Holy Thursday there's a mystery play on the Deposition from the Cross, followed by processions on Good Friday and Easter Sunday; 1–2 August sees the *Festa del Perdono* ('Feast of Pardon') at the Porziuncola, initiated by St Francis, who once had a vision of Christ asking him what would be most helpful for the soul. Francis replied forgiveness for anyone who crossed the threshold of the chapel; indulgences are given out on the day.

Tourists have been coming to Assisi for longer than to any town in Umbria, and it does its best to please. There are plenty of rooms, but still not enough for *Calendimaggio*, Easter, and July and August, when you should strive to book in advance.

### expensive

Long Assisi's top hotel, the traditional, formal ★★★★**Subasio**, Via Frate Elia 2, ✆ 075 812206, ✉ 075 816691, is linked to the Basilica of St Francis by a portico. Many of the rooms have views over the famous mystical countryside from vine-shaded terraces, and it has a private garage and an attractive medieval-vaulted restaurant. St Francis never slept here, but the King of Belgium and Charlie Chaplin did. ★★★**Fontebella**, Via Fontebella 25, ✆ 075 812883, ✉ 075 812941, is a bit nearer the centre, housed in a 17th-century palazzo. Rooms are comfortable, public rooms elegant and a garden and garage are added attractions. ★★★**Giotto**, Via Fontebella 41, ✆ 075 812209, ✉ 075 816479, has very pleasant modern rooms near the basilica, as well as a garage and garden terraces for relaxing. At Armenzano, 10km from the centre on Monte Subasio, the 10th-century hostel ★★★★**Le Silve,** ✆ 075 801 9000, ✉ 075 801 9005, has been prettily fixed up for 20th-century guests, with antique furnishings and a pool and sauna. *Open Mar–Oct*. For longer stays, a 16th-century farmhouse on a working farm has recently been converted into the three self-catering **Brigolante Guest Apartments**, 6km from the centre of Assisi at the foot of Mount Subasio at Via Costa di Trex 31, ✆ 075 802250; each houses 4–6 people and has fine views over Subasio, as well as a chance to experience rural life and purchase fresh meat, vegetables, eggs and cheese from the premises.

### moderate

★★★**Umbra**, near Piazza del Comune at the end of a narrow alley, Via degli Archi 6, ✆ 075 812240, ✉ 075 813653, is a real charmer, a little family-run inn; quiet, sunny and friendly with a little walled garden in front. Rooms can be a bit small but serendipitous, and many have balconies overlooking the countryside (some of these are in the *expensive* range). The Umbra's restaurant is one of the most attractive in Assisi, with the best of regional cuisine like risotto with white truffles from Gubbio and a cellar full of excellent wine; in good weather meals are served in the garden. Parking can be a minor problem, however—the nearest car park is by Santa Chiara.

★★★**Hotel dei Priori**, Corso Mazzini 15, ✆ 075 812237, ✉ 075 816804, is housed in a gracious 18th-century palazzo, well restored and very conveniently placed, just off Assisi's main piazza (again, some rooms are up in the *expensive* category). ★★★**Hermitage**, Via G. Degli Aromatari 1, ✆ 075 812764, ✉ 075 816691, is a comfortable, reasonably priced hotel in a good central position, a short walk from the basilica. In the historic centre, ★★**San Giacomo**, Via S. Giacomo 6, ✆ 075 816778, ✉ 075 816779, is reliable and welcoming. Near the amphitheatre, at Piazza Matteotti 1, ★★**Ideale per Turisti**, ✆ 075 813570, ✉ 075 813020, has a name that says it all: a fine, small hotel with a garden and views. ★★**Il Palazzo**, Via San Francesco 8, ✆ 075 816841, ✉ 075 812370, *hotel.ilpalazzo@edisons.it*, occupies a

13th-century building right in the centre of town, halfway between San Francesco and Piazza del Comune. Its 12 rooms are simply but tastefully furnished with antiques.

Nearly 1km away and a bit hard to find—a 10min walk to the west gate of Assisi—in a pretty country setting, the old stone **★★Country House**, S. Pietro Campagna 168, ✆/✉ 075 816363, has lovely rooms, furnished with items from the owner's antique shop on the ground floor (no restaurant, but the *signora* prepares a substantial, reasonably priced evening meal for guests in her kitchen; ask in the morning). 12km northwest of Assisi at San Gregorio (✉ 06086), **★★★Castel San Gregorio**, Via S. Gregorio 16, ✆ 075 803 8009, ✉ 075 803 8904, offers only 12 rooms in a romantic, restored 13th-century castle, set in a pretty garden.

### inexpensive

**★Anfiteatro Romano**, Via Anfiteatro 4, ✆ 075 813025, ✉ 075 815110, is a good quiet choice near Piazza Matteotti, with only seven rooms, some with private bath. Other good central choices include **★Italia**, Vicolo della Fortezza, ✆ 075 812625, ✉ 075 804 3749, near Piazza del Comune; **★★Sole**, Corso Mazzini 35, ✆ 075 812373, ✉ 075 813706, a large place with a good restaurant, the Ceppo della Catena; or the much smaller **★★Pallotta**, Via S. Rufina 4, ✆/✉ 075 812307, also attatched to a good, traditional eatery.

If everything is full, try the large pilgrimage houses in Santa Maria degli Angeli, especially the **★★Cenacolo Francescano**, Via Piazza d'Italia 70, ✆ 075 804 1083, ✉ 075 804 0552, with 130 basic rooms, all with private bath, a short walk from the train station; or go to the tourist office for a list of smaller religious houses and rooms in private houses, of which there are dozens in Assisi. American sisters run one of the nicest, **Sant'Antonio's Guest House**, Via G. Alessi 10, ✆ 075 812542, ✉ 075 813723, in a 12th-century villa, with pleasant rooms. Guests who sign can also have a good cheap lunch here, but no dinner; beware the early curfew. There are three **youth hostels**, all outside the centre: **Victor**, Via Sacro Tuturio 116, at Rivotorto, 3km south of Assisi, ✆ 075 806 5562; the new dormitory **Della Pace**, at Via di Valecchie 177, ✆/✉ 075 816767, 1km out of Porta San Pietro, and **Fontemaggio**, 3km east on Via Eremo delle Carceri, ✆ 075 813636.

---

### Eating Out

#### moderate

Besides the Umbra, mentioned above, Assisi has the well-known **Buca di San Francesco**, Via Brizi 1, ✆ 075 812204, below street level in a cavernous medieval cellar. Try the delicious cannelloni, homemade pasta with meat and porcini mushrooms, pigeon cooked Assisi-style, or *filet al Rubesco* (fillet of steak cooked in red Umbrian wine), accompanied by good wines from Umbria and other regions. *Closed Mon, Jan, Feb and most of July*. Another venerable choice, **Il Medio Evo**, Via dell'Arco dei Priori 4, ✆ 075 813068, has an elegant medieval atmosphere and tasty *antipasti* with Umbrian prosciutto, pasta with truffles, and *faraone all'uva* (guinea fowl cooked with grapes). *Closed Wed, Sun eve, most of Jan and the mid two weeks of July*.

San Francesco, with a veranda beautifully overlooking the basilica on Via S. Francesco 52, ✆ 075 812329, defies the old Italian rule that places with views serve food for dogs: good Umbrian cuisine here combines with an *enoteca* wine list. *Closed Wed and some of Aug.* La Fortezza, Via della Fortezza (near the Piazza del Comune), ✆ 075 812418, has delicious *cappelletti al tartufo nero o funghi* (truffle- or mushroom-filled pasta caps), roast guinea hen (*faraona alla Fortezza*), or rabbit in asparagus sauce. *Closed Thurs and Feb.*

*inexpensive*

Near the Temple of Minerva, Piazzetta dell'Erba, Via S. Gabriele dell'Addolorata 15b, ✆ 075 815352, features delicious daily specials at kind prices. *Closed Mon.* A lovely stop on the road up to the breathtaking sanctuary of Eremo delle Carceri is La Stalla, Via Eremo delle Carceri, at Fontemaggio, ✆ 075 812317, a typical country trattoria, converted from an old barn. Good hearty fare is served here at very reasonable prices, washed down with flagons of local wine. *Closed Mon.* Don't neglect one of the rich strudels or chocolate and nut breads in the speciality bakery in Piazza del Comune, near the Temple of Minerva, or at La Bottega del Pasticcera, Via Portica 9. You can sample and buy a vast selection of local cheeses, wines, biscuits, honeys, jams, sauces and spreads at Enoteca Hispellum, Corso Cavour 35, ✆ 0742 651766.

## West of Assisi

### Bastia Umbria and Around

APM buses from Assisi descend to Bastia Umbria, which has several hotels that may come in handy when Assisi is all filled up. A prosperous industrial centre, Bastia began as an island, the *Insula Romana*, before the valley was drained. Surrounded by walls in the Middle Ages, it was a hot potato contested by Perugia and Assisi. Although its unattractive environs fend off most visitors, the *centro storico* has a pretty pink and white 14th-century church of Santa Croce has a large triptych by L'Alunno and frescoes by Tiberio d'Assisi and students of Bartolomeo Caporali. North of Bastia and the village of Petrignano (famous at Christmas time for its animated *presepio*), the valley of the Chiascio is guarded by the splendidly sited Rocca Sant'Angelo; near it, the Convento di Santa Maria della Rocchicciola has frescoes by Bartolomeo Caporali and Lo Spagna, and a *Crucifix* by Matteo da Gualdo.

### Bettona

Southwest of Assisi, Bettona is a compact, nearly elliptical hill town wrapped in olive groves. It was big enough to have a long history as *Vettona*, an Etruscan city—interestingly, it is the only town in Umbria east of the Tiber to have Etruscan origins—and later as a Roman *municipium*. At the northern end of the walls you can still see the huge 4th-century BC golden stones of the original Etruscan fortifications, and 1km west there's a simple, barrel-vaulted Ipogeo Etrusco from the 2nd century BC, with funerary urns in situ (*to visit, collect the key from the Vigili Urbani at the Municipio in Piazza Cavour*).

Up inside Bettona, central Piazza Cavour has a fountain and the 14th-century Palazzo del Podestà. Housed within this and an adjoining palazzo is the Museo Civico (*open Mar–Oct* daily, *10.30–1 and 2–6, and later in July and Aug; Nov–Feb, daily exc Mon, 10.30–1 and 2.30–5; adm*) with two minor paintings by Perugino, detached frescoes by Fiorenzo di Lorenzo and Tiberio d'Assisi, Dono Doni (*Adoration of the Shepherds* with a predella on the *Life of San Crispolto*, the first Bishop of Bettona), ceramics from Deruta and wooden chests. In 1987, the most important works were stolen and found their way to Jamaica where they were recovered; they came back to Bettona in 1990. A small archaeological museum containing local finds (Etruscan and on) is due to open in the same building in June 2000. At the museum, ask to visit the **Oratorio di Sant'Andrea** in the same piazza, decorated with a recently discovered fresco of the *Passion*, by Giotto's school; opposite, the church of **Santa Maria Maggiore** has a gonfalon by Perugino and works by L'Alunno (*currently in the museum while the church is being restored*).

---

Bettona ✉ 06084                                   ***Where to Stay and Eating Out***

The brand new **Hotel S. Andrea**, Via Caterina 2, ✆ 075 987114, ✉ 075 986 9130 (*expensive–moderate*) adds a totally unexpected corner of contemporary style to sleepy Bettona. Situated in an old stone building which has been in turn a hospital, an *oratorio* and an oil press, the 19 rooms are beautifully furnished in simple good taste. There is a good restaurant, **Opera Prima** (*moderate*), which serves Umbrian dishes with the odd twist.

| | |
|---|---|
| Umbertide and Around | 112 |
| Montone | 114 |
| Morra | 114 |
| Città di Castello | 115 |
| Gubbio | 121 |
| Down the Via Flaminia | 130 |
| Gualdo Tadino | 131 |
| Nocera Umbra | 132 |

# Northern Umbria

Route SS3bis and Umbria's lumbering private railway, the FCU, follow the Upper Tiber Valley into a green landscape of tobacco farms, olive groves and rolling hills, enclosed by large stretches of forest and mountains— some of the emptiest and most underpopulated countryside in Italy. To the west near Tuscany, arty Città di Castello is full of surprises, both ancient and modern, while to the east is stern, grey Gubbio, a drop of pure distilled Umbrian essence up in the rugged mountains. In between you'll find a host of lesser known attractions: frescoes by Signorelli at Morra, a garden maze at Castello Bufalini in San Giustino, and beautiful hill towns such as Monte Santa Maria Tiberina, Citerna and Montone. The mountains along the border of the Marche form one of Umbria's beautiful natural parks, although the main towns here, Gualdo Tadino and Nocera Umbra, were the worst hit by the 1997 earthquake.

## Umbertide and Around

Approaching Umbertide from Perugia, the SS3bis is fairly straight and fairly dull, but there are a couple of possible detours along the way, in the nest of little villages between the SS3bis and the road to Gubbio. The most important town is **Montelabate,** where the large church of Santa Maria (1325) has an 11th-century crypt and some good frescoes, a *Madonna and Saints* by Bartolomeo Caporali and a *Crucifixion* by Fiorenzo di Lorenzo. It also has a pretty cloister from an earlier church. The other village to aim for is **Civitella Benazzone,** where the medieval Abbazia Celestina has been restored, and where the parish church has paintings by Benedetto Bonfigli and Domenico Alfani.

Midway between Perugia and Città di Castello, **Umbertide** (pop. 14,000) is right on the Tiber and started out as a trading post for the Etruscans and Umbrians. It was known as *Pitulum* by the Romans, and then as Fratta until 1863, when in its enthusiasm for the new Kingdom of Italy it changed its name to honour Umberto, the son of Vittorio Emanuele II. Today Umbertide is a sprawling industrial town with a small *centro storico* that somehow survived the allied bombs that blew the rest of town to smithereens.

The main landmark, the **Rocca**, a castle with fat round crenellated towers, was built by the Perugians in the 1300s and is now the **Centro per l'Arte Contemporanea**, with temporary exhibitions (*open daily exc Mon, winter 10.30–12.30 and 4–7; summer 10.30–12.30 and 4.30–7.30; adm*). There are three churches in Piazza San Francesco, near the train tracks. One, **Santa Croce**, is now a small museum, containing an excellent *Deposition* (1515) by Luca Signorelli, returned to its original setting and glory in 1999 after a 15-year restoration job, as well as Niccolò Pomarancio's *Madonna and Child and Angels* (1577). Its neighbour, **San Francesco**, has good if damaged 17th-century frescoes. And, like so many Umbrian towns, Umbertide has a geometrical Renaissance temple dedicated to Mary outside the walls, the octagonal **Santa Maria della Reggia**, begun in 1559.

Just east of Umbertide, the magnificent 15th-century castle **Civitella Ranieri** lords it high over a wooded park, and although it is privately owned it is occasionally open in the summer. Three km south of town, at the foot of 2273ft Monte Corona, the **Badia di San Salvatore** was founded by the wandering hermit saint Romualdo in 1008 for his

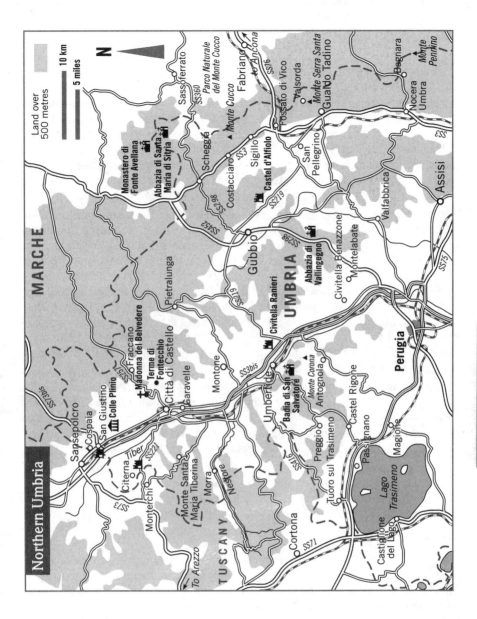

Camaldolesian monks. Remodelled in the 18th century, and partly unremodelled recently, it has an unusual campanile that doubled as a defensive tower. The bare stone interior has traces of 14th-century frescoes, and the nave is supported by an interesting hotchpotch of capitals and columns. The 8th-century stone ciborium was brought here from another church. The scenery from here towards Lake Trasimeno is lovely, especially around the medieval village of **Preggio**.

## Montone

Northeast of Umbertide, the prettiest village is fortified hilltop **Montone**, on the road to Pietralunga. Founded in the 9th century, its strategic position high over the Tiber valley made it a prize fought over by Perugia, Città di Castello and Gubbio. It was the birthplace of Andrea Braccio, better known as Braccio Fortebraccio (1368–1424), who grew up in Perugia only to be exiled from there with other members of the nobility in 1393. It became his life-long ambition to return, and over the next 23 years he made himself one of the most feared *condottieri* in Italy, serving Ladislas King of Naples and the anti-pope John XXIII, at times taking Rome and the Romagna, but in 1416 finally realizing his goal of returning to Perugia as its lord and master. It's worth making the trudge up to the top of the town, where one of the towers of Fortebraccio's citadel is used as a fantastic belvedere over the region.

Today Montone is a quiet and evocative medieval village. The Gothic church of **San Francesco** (1305) and its convent have recently been arranged as a **Museo Comunale** (*© 075 930 6535, open April–Sept, Fri–Sun, 10.30–1 and 3–5.30; Oct–Mar, Sat and Sun only, same hours*). The church has fine frescoes, including a *St Anthony Abbot* by Bartolomeo Caporali and a damaged cycle on the *Life of St Francis*. Among the paintings in the convent there's Caporali's standard for the confraternity of the *Madonna del Soccorso*, with a charming scene of Montone, and paintings by local 16th-century artist Vittorio Cirelli, who let his imagination run wild in a fantastical *Immaculate Conception*, and a remarkable life-sized wooden sculptural group of the *Deposition of the Cross* from the 1200s. As a change of pace, the ground floor has a fascinating **Museo Etnografico**, not of Umbrian farm tools, but of artefacts from East Africa collected by a local resident.

Montone's most sacred relic, a thorn from the crown of thorns that was donated by the *condottiere*'s son Carlo, is carefully kept in the **Collegiata di Santa Maria** and shown on Easter Monday, an excuse for a pageant in medieval finery. The church also has a *Last Supper* by Denis Calvaert of Antwerp. Another church, **San Fedele**, has a weird relief of a pair of flagellants over the door, as a memory of Perugia's contribution to medieval religion.

Further up the valley, Fortebraccio's castle, the magnificent **Rocca d'Aries**, was recently restored by its owner, the Region of Umbria. Further up the narrow road to the northeast is **Pietralunga**, a remote medieval village and a good base for exploring the mountains and forests, and for communing with the boars, foxes, and other wildlife.

## Morra

Tobacco is king west of the Tiber, where **Morra**, on the banks of the torrential Nestore, is the one village in particular to aim for. The story goes that Luca Signorelli, a native of nearby Cortona, happened to be passing through in 1508 when he fell in love with a pretty girl and decided to stay awhile. He picked up the commission to fresco the 15th-century **Oratorio di San Crescentino**, located on a hill outside Morra (usually locked, but the custodian lives in the modern house nearby). Signorelli worked with his assistants, but the master's hand is easily identifiable in the *Flagellation, Crucifixion* and *Christ between two Angels*. Unfortunately most of the other frescoes aren't as well preserved (they were restored in the 1970s) but they are beautiful; don't miss the older Gothic frescoes in the 13th-century sacristy.

There are a pair of comfortable choices (*moderate*) along the SS3bis: ★★★**Rio**, ✆ 075 941 5033, 🖅 075 941 7029, and the slightly cheaper. ★★**Moderno**, ✆/🖅 075 941 3759.

Or there's a simple central hotel with an equally simple restaurant, ★★**Capponi**, Piazza 25 Aprile 19, ✆ 075 941 2662, 🖅 075 941 3803 (*inexpensive*).

## Città di Castello

Set on a plateau overlooking the Tiber valley, Città di Castello (pop. 38,000) is the most important city in northern Umbria, and one that has a marked Tuscan air.

It started as the ancient Umbrian *Tifernum*, and prospered under the early Roman Empire, when it had the rolling name of *Tifernum Tiberinum* and controlled much of the trade in the upper Tiber valley. Totila and his Goths knocked it flat, and the early Christian bishops rebuilt it into a fortress town and called it, perhaps euphemistically, *Castrum Felicitatis* (Happy Castle). In the 1400s and 1500s, under the enlightened tyranny of the Vitelli family, the city hired some of the best Renaissance artists (Raphael among them) to help in its decoration.

In the 20th century it was the birthplace of one of Italy's best known postwar artists, Alberto Burri, who has left the city an impressive collection of his works. Although bombed in war, Città di Castello has recovered well, and today the Tifernati, as they are still known, make their living from textiles, printing and tobacco, but recall their love of culture in Umbria's second most important art museum.

### Getting Around

Città di Castello has a station on the FCU **train**. Parking within the city walls can be a nightmare; there are **car parks** outside the walls—the free one to the north on Viale Nazario Sauro (Parcheggio Enrico Ferri) is close to an escalator taking you up into the town.

### Tourist Information

**Città di Castello**: Via Sant'Antonio 1, ✆ 075 855 4817, 🖅 075 855 2100, or Piazza Fanti, ✆ 075 855 4922, 🖅 075 855 2100.

### market days

The food market is on Thursdays and Saturdays, in Piazza Gabriotti.

There is also a huge 'retro' flea market on the third Saturday and Sunday of each month in Piazza Matteotti and surrounding streets.

## The Duomo and its Museum

Within its Renaissance walls, Città di Castello is a neat rectangle, still roughly following the street plan of ancient *Tifernum*. It offers the surprises of any little town in central Italy—the **Duomo**, for instance, with exactly one half of a harmonious Baroque façade, looks a bit screwy, despite its venerable age; it was *rebuilt* in 580. After several other rebuildings, much of what you see comes from the 1400s, although parts of the original Romanesque cathedral remain—especially the intriguing round campanile from the 11th century, inspired by the ancient towers of Ravenna (and just as tilted as any of them). Two handsome Gothic reliefs decorate the north portal. Inside, the single nave has a panelled wooden ceiling: the best painting is a mystical, dramatically charged altarpiece of the *Transfiguration* in the fourth chapel by the great Florentine mannerist Rosso Fiorentino, who took refuge here with the Vitelli family when he fled the sack of Rome in 1527. Much of the rest of the decoration is by local artists: one, the 17th-century Giovanni Battista Pacetti (but better known as Lo Sguazzino or 'Splashy') painted a view of his hometown in the third chapel. The lower church was the ancient crypt, and contains the bodies of Città's patrons, SS Florido and Amanzio.

The adjacent and excellent **Museo del Duomo** is newly opened after six months of restoration work (*open daily exc Mon, April–Sept 10–1 and 3–6; Oct–Mar, 10.30–1 and 3–5.30; adm*). It has a chronological layout, beginning with its rarest prize: the **Treasure of Canoscio**—beautiful 6th-century liturgical silver, probably hidden in a safe place by the priest when Totila and the Goths came thundering into town and found again 1400 years later, in 1932. The lovely enamelled and gilded 12th-century altar frontal, showing Christ, the Evangelists and scenes from the Life of Christ, is said to have been donated to the cathedral by Pope Celestine II. There's a beautifully worked 14th-century crozier, and 15th-century paintings, including a *Madonna* by a follower of Signorelli; a rich collection of liturgical items, two angels attributed to Giulio Romano, a small but refined *Madonna and Child and St John the Baptist* by Pinturicchio.

## Near the Duomo

The triangular Piazza Gabriotti by the Duomo faces a small park where the papal fortress once stood; here too is the trecento **Palazzo dei Priori** (or Comunale) designed by Angelo da Orvieto, a handsome but unfinished building in sandstone. Opposite, the **Torre Civico** from the same century once held the city's medieval prisons, and has magnificent views over the valley from the top of its rickety old stair (*open daily exc Mon, 10–12.30 and 2–5.30; adm*).

From a 14th-century **loggia**, Corso Cavour leads past the covered market with an 18th-century print shop on top and a pretty 1890s Art Nouveau bank. Civic life was concentrated in nearby Piazza Matteotti, with a very austere **Palazzo del Podestà** with double clocks on the façade, also by Angelo da Orvieto, although the short side of this was given a fey Baroque treatment. In the next little square, Piazza Costa, you can watch Umbrian cloth being woven on big old traditional looms at the **Laboratorio Tela Umbra** (*open daily 9–12 and 3–5.30; adm*), founded in 1908 by Baron Leopoldo Franchetti. The adjacent museum recounts the history of weaving.

# The Collezione Burri

Rather than nod off with all its art under its belt, 20th-century Città di Castello produced one of Italy's best known contemporary artists, Alberto Burri (1915–95). Burri was a doctor by profession, and ended up a prisoner of war in Texas in 1943, where he turned to art to express the carnage he witnessed, using whatever he could find at hand. After his return to Italy, he continued to explore the evocative power of discarded materials and junk, most famously his sacking soaked in red paint that resembled giant bandages and his carefully composed pieces of twisted metal and charred wood. Burri was one of the great precursors of Abstract Expression and Junk Art in the USA, and of Italian Arte Povera; in later years he explored colour and other materials. Burri donated numerous works from 1943 to 1983 to his home town, which displays them in the **Collezione Burri,** in a quattrocento Palazzo Albizzini, just up from Piazza Costa at the top of Via Mazzini (*open Mar–Oct, Tue–Sat 9–12.30 and 2.30–6, Sun 9–1; Nov–Feb, 10.30–12.30 and 2.30–4.30; closed Mon; adm*). His large-scale works are exhibited in the renovated tobacco-drying shed he used as a studio, the **Seccatoi Tabacchi**, south of town in Via Francesco Pierucci (*same hours*).

# The North End of Town

The ruling Vitelli family simply could not have enough palaces; the Collezione Burri is near their largest spread, the elegant **Palazzo Vitelli a Porta Sant'Egidio** built in 1540 by Giorgio Vasari, the writer and workmanlike painter from nearby Arezzo. It has a beautiful façade facing a huge garden, and an interior lavishly frescoed by Cristoforo Gherardi (Il Doceno) and Prospero Fontana; it's now owned by a bank, and used for concerts. Also here, along Via Albizzini, is the 13th-century church of **San Francesco** with a better than average 18th-century interior. Vasari designed the elaborate Cappella Vitelli and painted the altarpiece, although both are outdone by the fancy wrought iron grille made by a local craftsman, Pietro di Ercolano. There's a majolica of *St Francis receiving the Stigmata* by the Della Robbia workshop, and a German-made wooden polychrome *Pietà* from the 1400s. The *Betrothal of the Virgin* (1504), the masterpiece of Raphael's early years, was painted for this church. Napoleon put it in the Brera, and the Brera won't give it back; Città di Castello still hasn't got over it, and grudgingly shows a copy, a bittersweet consolation prize. In the adjacent piazza is a monument of 1860 celebrating the end of the Papal States.

Via San Bartolomeo heads north of here, passing another but smaller Palazzo Vitelli on the way to the **Museo Civico**, which shares space with the Biblioteca Comunale (*open 9–1 and 3–7, closed Sat afternoon and Sun*). This contains fossils from the Pleistocene era, the time when the Tiber was a lake, and a small archaeological collection. In this part of town, around Via XI Settembre, there are no fewer than three convents of closed orders of the Clarisse; at No.21, the nuns at **Santa Veronica** will show on request their pretty cloister and a small museum dedicated to their order and to St Veronica Giuliani (d. 1727), who lived here for 50 years in a state of almost continuous mystical experience and vision. Near here is the big non-conventual church of **Santa Maria delle Grazie,** which has a fresco of the *Transition of the Virgin* by Ottavino Nelli and a precious and highly venerated painting of the *Madonna della Grazie*, by Giovanni di Piemonte, a collaborator of Piero della Francesca; unfortunately it's kept locked up in its cupboard and only shown on two days of the year, 2 February and 26 August.

## The Pinacoteca Comunale

*From behind the Duomo, take Via di Modello/Via C. Battisti south to Via della Canoniera 22. Open daily exc Mon, April–Oct 10–1 and 2.30–6.30; Nov–Mar 10–12.30 and 3–5.30; adm.*

This contains Città di Castello's only surviving Raphael, a half-ruined, processional standard of 1503 that would never have been noticed without the famous name. Don't let that discourage you; there are plenty of other attractions, beginning with the building itself. The Palazzo Vitelli alla Cannoniera (one of five Vitelli palazzi in town) was built in the 1520s by Antonio da Sangallo the Younger and Pier Francesco da Viterbo, decorated with *sgraffito* by Giorgio Vasari—a very nice façade, facing the inner gardens, suggesting that Vasari could do a good job of things he didn't take too seriously. The 16th-century frescoes inside are the work of Cola dell'Amatrice (on the stairs, celebrating the glory of the Vitelli family) and Doceno.

The star of the early paintings is a beautiful and recently restored 13th-century *Maestà*, by an anonymous painter known as the Master of Città di Castello. Nearby hangs a fine *Madonna and Child* by Spinello Aretino. The next room has another *Madonna* by the Sienese Andrea di Bartolo and early choir stalls, while next there's a residual Gothic Venetian view of the same subject by Antonio Vivarini. Lorenzo Ghiberti, master of Florence's famous baptistry doors, puts in a rare guest appearance with an equally Gothic golden reliquary of St Andrew (1420). The *Head of Christ* is usually attributed to Giusto di Gand, a Flemish painter who worked in Urbino. Other highlights in this room are by Florentines: a *Madonna and Two Angels* by Neri di Bicci, and a *Coronation of the Virgin* from the workshop of Domenico Ghirlandaio.

The next room has the Raphael standard, followed by altarpieces by a local boy, Francesco Tifernate. Many of these rooms have frescoes by Doceno. The most powerful painting in the museum is a *San Sebastiano* by Luca Signorelli and his workshop—a fascinating work with fantasy Roman ruins and a truly surreal treatment of space (or were Signorelli's students just practising random backgrounds?). There's also a good comical kitsch piece, an anonymous *Quo Vadis?*, a strange Virgin by an unknown follower of Pontormo, and a room of works by Raffaellino del Colle.

The sculpture collection includes some fine early medieval woodcarving, or mixtures of painting and wooden sculpture; especially an altarpiece of the *Crucifixion with the Virgin Mary and the Magdalene*, the sun and moon—the wooden crucifix has disappeared, but the work is strangely suggestive without it. Here too is a fine 14th-century Sienese relief on the Baptism of Christ, and works by Della Robbia.

## San Domenico

The first street to the left of the museum, Largo Mons. Muzi, leads to the enormous preaching church of San Domenico, finished in 1424. The façade was never finished but it has a handsome door on the left side; the gloomy interior has good 15th-century frescoes and choir stalls. Signorelli's *San Sebastiano* used to hang in the Renaissance chapels by the altar, along with Raphael's *Crucifixion*, which is now in the National Gallery in London and replaced here by a copy.

## Around Città di Castello

Just 2km south of Città di Castello, in the Villa Cappelletti at **Garavelle**, the **Centro Tradizioni Popolari** (*open daily exc Mon, winter 8.30–12.30 and 2–6, summer 8.30–12.30 and 3–7; adm*) is a fascinating folk museum in an Umbrian farmhouse, furnished as it would have been a century ago, complete with blacksmith's forge, oil press, wine cellars and farm instruments.

Just to the east, Città di Castello has its own little spa, the **Terme di Fontecchio**, where Pliny the Younger used to come to take the alkaline sulphurous waters. The current spa dates from the 19th century, and is open for business from March to December. There's fine scenery along the SS257, especially 5km east of Città di Castello at the hill of **Belvedere**, site of the **Santuario della Madonna del Belvedere**, an octagonal domed Baroque church with a quirky façade and a venerated terracotta *Madonna and Child.*

West of Città di Castello, **Monte Santa Maria Tiberina** is a lovely medieval hill town in a lofty sublime setting. Once inhabited by the Etruscans, in 1355 the emperor Charles IV made this village an independent marquisate for the Del Monte family. A favour to the French earned them the right to call themselves the Bourbon Del Monte, and they ruled their little Ruritania until 1798 when Napoleon, who had no patience for anachronisms, especially with the name Bourbon on them, snatched it away. Today fewer than 150 souls live here, but you can see what remains of the Del Monte family's medieval castle and some of their tombs in the parish church.

---

*Città di Castello* ✉ *06012*     ***Where to Stay and Eating Out***

The central ★★★★**Tiferno**, Piazza R. Sanzio 13, ✆ 075 855 0331, ✉ 075 852 1196 (*rooms expensive–moderate*) is the best place to stay and dine in Città di Castello, a 17th-century palace with good comfortable rooms, a private garage, and one of the best restaurants in the area, with dishes like ravioli with shrimp in orange sauce, or pigeon with white grapes—not perhaps for everyone. Large ★★★**Hotel delle Terme**, ✆ 075 852 0614, ✉ 075 855 7236 (*inexpensive*) at Fontecchio, is a pleasant place to stay, even if you don't take advantage of the thermal treatments on offer and can make do with the fine open-air pool. Cheaper choices inside town, all good, clean, if uninspiring hotels, include ★★**Europa**, Via V.E. Orlando 2, ✆ 075 855 0551, ✉ 075 852 0765 and ★★**Umbria**, Via dei Galanti, ✆ 075 855 4925, ✉ 075 852 0911.

Città di Castello is one place in Umbria where you can find good bread, especially the *pane nociato*, with walnuts. **Il Bersaglio**, Via V.E. Orlando 14, ✆ 075 855 5534 (*moderate*), just outside the city walls, offers a wealth of pasta dishes, well-prepared meat and game and especially good truffles and wild mushrooms, many of them gathered by the restaurant owner himself, Luigi Manfroni; try the local Colli Altotiberini wines. *Closed Wed.* A 10km drive to the village of Fraccano on the SS257 east of Città di Castello will take you to a small trattoria, ✆ 075 855 3870, of the kind fast disappearing in Italy. You choose from a limited but excellent menu of the day—usually a good pasta dish followed by meat grilled over the fire in front of you—and have a pleasant surprise when it comes to the bill.

**Amici Miei**, Via del Monte 2, ✆ 075 855 9904 (*inexpensive*) offers incredible value for wonderful home cooking using fresh, seasonal ingredients: *strangozzi* with goose sauce, calves' kidneys, roast lamb and duck. *Closed Wed.*

## Citerna

To the west of Città di Castello, on the SS221 towards Arezzo, Citerna is a gem of a hill town that has aged like fine wine. Located on the border of Tuscany, peacefully set over the Tiber Valley on a densely wooded hill, Citerna was a Roman town, then rebuilt by the Lombards, fought over by its neighbours and restored after an earthquake in 1917. One unusual feature is the partially vaulted medieval passageway that circles much of the lower part of town. Further up, the church of **San Francesco**, rebuilt in 1508, is the village's chief repository of art, with a late and rather worn fresco by Luca Signorelli and helpers, of the *Madonna and Child, SS Francis and Michael.* The altars are decorated with Della Robbia ceramics that seeped over the Tuscan border, and there are two fine altarpieces by Raffaellino del Colle, the *Christ in Glory* and the *Madonna and St John the Evangelist*, as well as a *Deposition* by Pomarancio. Ask a local for the location of the key to the nearby **Casa Prosperi**, to see its extraordinary carved 16th-century fireplace. Up past the pretty Piazza Scipioni, the dark 18th-century church of **San Michele Arcangelo** contains more colourful Della Robbia work, a *Crucifixion* by Pomarancio and a bell from a church destroyed in the earthquake, signed and dated 1267. In the last war, Citerna's castle on top of the town was blown up by the Germans, leaving the walls and brick tower which offer a spectacular view as far as La Verna in Tuscany, where St Francis received the stigmata. A fountain by the walls commemorates the saint, who visited here in 1224.

## Monterchi

Just 2km from Citerna in Monterchi, stop at the cemetery chapel to see Piero della Francesca's magnificent and recently restored *Madonna del Parto*, a rare portrayal of a weary, pregnant Virgin, painted in the tomb of a nobleman and forgotten for centuries. The rareness of the scene is emphasized by the fact that the Mother of God stands in an exotic tent, the flaps held open by two solemn angels to allow a glimpse of the sacred mystery; it is not only great art, but also a popular icon for expectant mothers in the vicinity.

## Colle Plinio

If you take the old road from Città di Castello, follow the signs east towards Pitigliano, continue over the bridge and take the first road left, you'll come to **Colle Plinio**, where in the 1970s excavations revealed the remains of the 1st-century AD villa of Pliny the Younger. He left a loving description of the countryside around his estate in his Letters:

> The meadows are bright with flowers, covered with trefoil and other delicate plants which always seem soft and fresh, for everything is fed by streams which never run dry... It is a great pleasure to look down on the countryside from the mountain, for the view seems to be a painted scene of unusual beauty rather than a real landscape, and the harmony to be found in this variety refreshes the eye wherever it turns.

Although not open to the public, you can look through the fence at the baths and wine cellar.

## San Giustino

Further up the Tiber valley, San Giustino has the beautiful **Castello Bufalini,** begun in the 1200s as a fortress by the comune of Città di Castello, which gave it in 1487 to the noble Bufalini family to complete (and pay for) the impressive walls and star-shaped moat that surrounded it. A century later, when war seemed unlikely, Giulio Bufalini converted it into an elegant seigneurial villa, on plans by Vasari, complete with a loggia and courtyard. He also planted one of the most beautiful Italian gardens in Umbria inside the moat, with a maze and geometric hedges, fountains and parterres. In 1989, the Bufalini donated the castle to the state; the gardens and the ground floor of the castle with rooms of antiques, frescoed by the 16th-century painter Cristofano Gherardi, have so far been restored but at the time of writing are closed to the public (*call © 075 852 2655 for more information*).

## Borgo Sansepolcro and Cospaia

Over the border in Tuscany, at the terminus of the FCU rail line, Borgo Sansepolcro was part of Umbria until 1441, when Pope Eugenius IV gave it to Cosimo dei Medici to pay back the 25,000 gold florins he owed him for the expenses of the Council of Basle. Which is why the art books so often classify its favourite son, Piero della Francesca, as a member of the Umbrian school. Two of his paintings are in the town hall's **Museo Civico** (*open daily 9.30–1 and 2.30–6; until 7.30 in summer; adm exp. The building suffered some damage in the 1997 earthquake, but most rooms are still open while they determine what restoration work is needed*). The *Resurrection*, an intense, almost eerie depiction of the triumphant Christ rising from his tomb over sleeping soldiers and a dead landscape, shares pride of place with the *Misericordia Polyptych*, a gold-ground altarpiece dominated by a giant-sized Madonna, sheltering under her cloak members of the confraternity who commissioned the picture. Other works present are from Luca Signorelli, Pontormo and Matteo di Giovanni; more Renaissance painting, by both Sienese and Florentine artists, can be seen in Sansepolcro's Romanesque **Duomo.**

**Cospaia**, off the road to Borgo Sansepolcro, has a few houses and a church. It doesn't amount to much, but for nearly four centuries it was nothing less than an independent republic, thanks to a mistake made when the papal and Florentine surveyors unknowingly used two different tributaries of the Tiber to mark the boundaries after Borgo Sansepolcro passed to Tuscany. Between these two little rivers, the Goraccia and the Ascone, in a space only a half kilometre wide, was Cospaia. It became a haven for smugglers, bandits and tax outlaws, and the jealousies between the two big powers insured that it would remain in business until 1826. Its other claim to fame is that it was the first place in Italy to plant tobacco, in 1575, before anyone even thought of a state monopoly.

## Gubbio

In a way, Gubbio (pop. 33,000) is what Umbria has always wanted to be: stony, taciturn and mystical, a tough mountain town that fought its own battles until destiny and the popes caught up with it—also a town of culture, one with its own school of painters. For a city over 2,500 years old it still seems like a frontier town, an elemental place that sticks in the memory: the green mountainside, a rushing stream, straight rows of rugged grey stone houses. On Gubbio's windy slopes, the hard-edged brilliance of the Italian Middle Ages is clear and tangible.

Gubbio is also one of the few Italian hill towns that a stick-in-the-mud geologist might recognize. Everyone has heard of the theory that the dinosaurs became extinct after a large meteor struck the earth 65 million years ago and raised so much dust that it blocked out the sun, making it too cool for the reptiles to survive. Some of the strongest evidence for the theory was discovered just outside Gubbio, in the Camignano valley towards Scheggia, where there's a layer of sedimentary rock, dense with the rare minerals of meteorites. It's thin, but it's chronologically correct and thick enough to have done the dirty deed.

## History

Gubbio was a city of the ancient Umbrii, perhaps even their political and religious centre. In Roman times it flourished under the name *Iguvium*, and, according to Umbrian scuttlebutt, it was far enough away yet close enough for Rome to export its lunatics there, which has left a lingering influence on the populace today. Mad or not, the Eugubini, as the natives are known, certainly weren't stupid; when unsolicited visits by the Goths, Huns and Avars left the place a mess, the survivors moved their town to a more defensible site on the nearby hillside.

As soon as the wall was up, they began annoying their neighbours; the chronicles paint a picture of medieval Gubbio as a tough, querulous *comune*, a fitting rival for Perugia. At one point, in the 1150s, no less than 12 Umbrian cities under Frederick Barbarossa combined to put an end to its pretensions; the city was saved from destruction by its bishop, later San Ubaldo, who persuaded the emperor to leave it in peace and grant it its independence. The chroniclers also claimed for Gubbio a population of 50,000—probably double the real figure but still quite large for a medieval town. As in every other city, there was continuous conflict between the *comune* and ambitious nobles. One of them, Giovanni Gabrielli, became *signore* of the town in 1350, but only four years later Cardinal Albornoz and his papal army snatched it away from him. In 1387, it fell to Urbino's Dukes of Montefeltro, who ruled it well until their line became extinct in 1508. Gubbio remained part of the Duchy of Urbino until 1624, when it became part of the Papal States.

One famous visitor in 1206–7 was St Francis, who found the city plagued by wolves, one of which in particular was ravaging the countryside and terrorizing the populace. Ignoring the townspeople's pleas and fears for his safety, Francis went out and had a word with the wolf, brought it to town, and promised that it would stop terrorizing Gubbio in exchange for regular meals—an agreement sealed with a shake of the paw. The wolf kept its part of the bargain, and is immortalized in a bas relief over the door of a little church on Via Mastro Giorgio. A few years ago, while workmen were repairing another church, the skeleton of a giant wolf was discovered buried under a slab. Recently some of its descendants have been sighted, after a long, long absence, in the remote forests of northern Umbria.

Gubbio saw some terrible fighting in the Second World War. In 1943, after the Italians had surrendered, Umbria was occupied by the Germans, who were harried by partisans, many of them based in the mountains above Gubbio. Although most of Umbria fell relatively quickly to the British and Commonwealth forces as they advanced north after the liberation of Rome on 4 June, the fighting was intense and progress slow in the north. Meanwhile, a number of vicious reprisals on innocent villagers took place around Gubbio, while the Germans took positions and pounded the allies; the battle for Gubbio took three weeks, only ending on 25 July.

Some of Gubbio's churches remain closed after the earthquake. Damage here was relatively minor compared to the 1982 earthquake, which left some 1,500 people homeless.

There are no trains, but around 10 APM **coaches** follow the beautiful SS298 to Perugia (40km/1hr) from the central Piazza Quaranta Martiri where schedules are posted. There are also **buses** to the closest **train** station, 20km southeast at Fossato di Vico on the Foligno–Ancona line, to Rome, and a line to Città di Castello–Arezzo–Florence. There is a bus and train information office for all of the above at Via della Repubblica 13, ✆ 075 922 0066.

*Tourist Information*

Piazza Oderisi, ✆ 075 922 0693, 🖷 075 927 3409.

**Post office**: Via Cairoli 11, ✆ 075 927 3925.

*market day*

Tuesday, in Piazza Quaranta Martiri.

## Gubbio, from the Bottom Up

Most people approach Gubbio from the west, passing acres of open pastureland—once the centre of Roman *Iguvium*. In the middle stands a large, well-preserved 1st-century AD **Roman theatre** (*open 9–1, free*) now used as such for summer performances of classical Greek and Roman drama and Shakespeare. The view of Gubbio from here is better than the one from up on Monte Ingino (*see* p.127); stone houses climb the slope in neat parallel rows, with the tall Palazzo dei Consoli on its massive platform dominating the centre.

Gubbio proper is entered by way of big green **Piazza Quaranta Martiri**, named for the 40 citizens gunned down on this spot by the Nazis in reprisals for partisan activities. On the west end of the square, behind its unfinished façade, the mid 13th-century church of **San Francesco** has an octagonal campanile and a distinctive Gothic design with a triple apse; it is the work of the Perugian architect Fra Bevignate. Some good frescoes are inside, especially the damaged series on the *Life of the Virgin* in the left apse, painted in 1408–13 and one of the greatest works by Gubbio's greatest painter, the International Gothic master Ottaviano Nelli. Other works include a copy of Daniele da Volterra's *Deposition* on the third altar; to the right of the altar are 14th-century frescoes on the *Life of St Francis*. The oldest frescoes from the 1200s are high up in the main apse. In the cloister are bits of polychrome Roman mosaics found in Gubbio, and more frescoes.

On the other side of the piazza is the **Loggia dei Tiratoio**, or Weaver's Loggia, an arcade of 1603 under which newly woven textiles could be stretched to shrink evenly—one of the few such loggias to survive. The nearby church, **Santa Maria dei Laici**, dates from the 14th century and is usually locked; it contains an *Annunciation*, the last painting of Baroque master Federico Barocci.

## Piazza Grande and the Palazzo dei Consoli

From Piazza dei Quaranta Martiri, Via Piccardi ascends past picturesque medieval lanes on the banks of the Camignano, a rushing torrent in the spring and winter. Many of the houses and modest palazzi date back to the 13th century, here and there adorned with carved doors or windows, or 'Death's doors' as in Perugia. At the top is the magnificent **Piazza Grande** (or Piazza della Signoria), occupying a ledge of the hill, a balcony hovering over a steep drop and a stunning view of the town below. The king of the piazza is the beautiful, enormous **Palazzo dei Consoli**, one of the most remarkable public buildings in Italy, begun in 1332 by Gubbio's master architect Gattapone, with a bit of help from Angelo da Orvieto (*consolo*, a word derived from the Roman *consul*, was a common title for an officer of a free medieval *comune*). Supported on the hill by a remarkable substructure of arches, the palazzo is graced with an elegant loggia, a slender campanile, square Guelph crenellations and asymmetrically arranged windows and arches. It faces the **Palazzo Pretorio** (now the *municipio*) designed by the same Gattapone to make the piazza a set piece.

The Palazzo dei Consoli is now the **Museo Civico** (*open daily April–Sept, 10–1 and 3–6; Oct–Mar, 10–1 and 2–5; closed 14–15 May, 25 Dec and 1 Jan; adm*). On the first floor, the enormous barrel-vaulted Sala dell'Arengo, where assemblies were held, is a cluttered, fascinating place that resembles an indoor flea-market, with archaeological odds and ends, tombstones, sarcophagi and crossbows deposited every which way. There is a Roman inscription—Governor Gnaeus Satirus Rufus bragging how much he spent to embellish the town—and a collection of seals and coins from the days when Gubbio minted its own. One unique treasure, the bronze **Eugubine Tablets**, have far and away the most important inscriptions ever found in the Umbrian language and were discovered in the 15th century near the Roman theatre. Partly written in the Etruscan alphabet and partly in the Latin, these codes of religious observances and rituals for Gubbio's priests are also a rare survival of a religious how-to textbook, with details on sacrifices (including human enemies) and how to read the future in a liver or in the flight of birds.

Medieval Gubbio made its living from ceramics, and in the 16th century this tradition produced a real artist, **Mastro Giorgio Andreoli**. Born in 1498, he discovered a beautiful ruby and golden glaze for majolica plates (you'll notice the absence of red in most painted ceramics; it's very hard to do). Mastro Giorgio's secret died with him, and it was long one of Gubbio's deepest regrets that it had not a single example of their magician's work to show. When it became known that Sotheby's had a plate by Mastro Giorgio to auction in 1991, the townspeople purchased it by public subscription, and the Eugubini did it again in 1996. They are displayed up in the loggia and show the *Fall of Phaeton* and *Circe*, and keep company with ceramic works made over the centuries. There are also fine views over Gubbio.

The **Pinacoteca**, up the stairs, is just as quirky and charming, although there are few first-rate pictures: a 13th-century diptych in a Byzantine portable altar; some fine painted crucifixes; a detached 17th-century fresco on the legend of *St Francis and the Wolf*; a *Tree of Jesse* by a cinquecento Gubbio artist; the quattrocento *Madonna del Melograno* by Pier Francesco Florentini; a *Flight into Egypt* by Rutilio Manetti; and an anonymous work of the 1600s called the *Last Night of Babylon*—one of the best crazy paintings in Italy, and deserves a good cleaning. The rooms of the Pinacoteca are an attraction in themselves; some haven't been remodelled since the 1500s. A door leads out on the main **loggia**, with its bird's eye view over Gubbio.

The lower floor of the Palazzo dei Consoli houses the recently arranged **Museo Archeologico** (*same ticket*) with an Umbrian and Roman collection of bronzes and ceramics and architectural odds and ends, and a Byzantine sarcophagus.

## To the Duomo and Palazzo Ducale

From Piazza Grande, stepped **Via Galeotti**, one of the city's most resolutely medieval lanes, leads up to the winding Via Ducale and Gubbio's Duomo; on the way, note the old cellar under the cathedral housing a wine-bibber's impossible dream: the **Botte dei Canonici**, a house-sized barrel from the 1500s that once held some 40,000 litres of wine, a masterpiece of the cooper's art (it was made without nails). The building on top, the 14th-century **Palazzo dei Canonici**, will some day house the Museo Dioceano (with a damaged 14th-century fresco of the *Crucifixion* and a beautiful 16th-century Flemish cope, magnificently embroidered and presented to the cathedral by Pope Marcellus II, a native of Gubbio).

The 13th-century **Duomo**, refitted with a simple, new front in the 1400s, is remarkable for the unusual pointed wagon stone vaulting of the nave, a Eugubine speciality, and for its stained-glass windows. Local talent is well represented in the side chapels, and in the presbytery there's a *Nativity* attributed to Pinturicchio's talented student Eusebio di San Giorgio. The high altar is a Roman sarcophagus. Note the 16th-century choir stalls, painted to resemble intarsia by Benedetto Nucci, and the 1556 carved throne (real) by Girolamo Maffei. From the Duomo you can walk up and up and up to the Sanctuary of San Ubaldo, following the route run in the race of the *Ceri* (*see* p.127), but it's much easier to take the funivia.

Opposite the cathedral, the **Palazzo Ducale** (*open Mon–Sat, 9–7, Sun and holidays, 9–1; closed 1st Mon of each month; adm*) was designed in the 1470s for that great patron of artists and humanists, the *condottiere* Federico da Montefeltro, Duke of Urbino, by the Sienese architect Francesco di Giorgio Martini. The gentlemanly Federico was a paragon among Renaissance rulers (he received the Order of the Garter from Edward IV), and he took a paternalistic interest in the welfare of his subjects and frequently travelled to keep an eye on things. He also liked to be lodged in style, and built at least a dozen palaces in the northern Marche as homes away from home. His Gubbio address was one of the most stylish, a compact version of his famous palace in Urbino: the elegant and serene little courtyard in particular evokes its great model, with *pietra serena* details and the initials F.D. (Federico Duca). The palace was stripped of its furnishings before it was purchased by the state in 1957, but some fireplaces remain, along with the fine stairways, windows and original terracotta floor, one wooden ceiling, a few 15th-century intarsia doors and photos of the beautiful intarsia work of the little Studiolo or ducal study, made by Giuliano da Maiano, and now on display in the Metropolitan Museum in New York. Some rooms have detached fresoces and paintings. Downstairs you can examine the plumbing and old kitchen, the foundations of a Lombard palace from the 10th century. Upstairs, the loggia has a handsome frieze in *pietra serena* and lovely views down on the Palazzo dei Consoli.

## Gubbio's West End

From Piazza Grande, Gubbio's main street, Via dei Consoli, leads past a number of ceramic shops to the very medieval and picturesque western quarter of town. Near Piazza Giordano Bruno, the **Bargello** (1302), the first public building in Gubbio, was a combined police station and governor's office; its round 16th-century **Fontana dei Matti** ('fountain of the mad') used to be Gubbio's main water source, and has the power to make you *loco* if you run around it three times. Here too is **San Domenico** (closed for earthquake repairs), an earlier Romanesque church taken over by the Dominicans in the 1300s. After an 18th-century remodelling only bits of the trecento frescoes remain, along with an exceptional Renaissance *intarsia* reading stand. Vias Vantaggi and Gabrielli lead from here to the 13th-century **Palazzo del Capitano del Popolo**, a no-nonsense Romanesque structure, containing something every medieval town in Europe seems to have: a privately run museum of torture instruments. Nearby is one of the equally austere city gates, **Porta Metauro**, and a medieval tower-fortress belonging to the Palazzo Gabrielli. The church just outside the gate, **Santa Croce della Foce**, is the site of the medieval Good Friday representation of the Passion.

Just inside the Porta Metauro is the entrance to the **Parco Ranghiasci-Brancaleoni**, which sweeps all the way up under the town walls to the Palazzo Ducale. Laid out as an English garden in 1841 by Francesco Ranghiasci (who married an Englishwoman), it was recently purchased and restored by the *comune* and offers the greatest possible contrast to the grey stone streets of the city. It has a pretty little covered bridge, neoclassical pavilions, big shady trees, and a café.

## The East End

At the east end of town, the 13th-century gatehouse of the **Porta Romana** is now a private museum (*open daily 9–1 and 3.30–7; adm*) devoted to medieval gates, with a collection of old keys and a drawbridge mechanism, as well as a collection of Gubbio ceramics which includes some from the workshop of Mastro Giorgio. Near the gate, two 13th-century churches contain works by Ottaviano Nelli. The now deconsecrated **Santa Maria Nuova** has his joyous, worldly *Madonna del Belvedere* and frescoes by his followers (*to visit, enquire at the Palazzo Ducale, © 075 927 5872*), while, just outside the gate, **Sant'Agostino** has more frescoes by Nelli and his pupils: the *Life of St Augustine* in the triumphal arch and apse, and on the fifth altar on the right, *San Umbaldo and two Saints*. The funivia here ascends to Monte Ingino (*see* opposite).

Back within the Porta Romana, the arch to the right, the **Arco di San Marziale**, marks the site of the ancient Umbrian gate. Via Dante leads down to a giant 18th-century tabernacle of San Ubaldo at the crossroads with Corso Garibaldi. Near here, the **Palazzo Accoromboni** was the birthplace in 1557 of famous Vittoria Accoromboni. By age 16 she was not only married but having an affair with the powerful Duke Paolo Giordano Orsini, who killed her husband to marry her (twice), before she was killed, a 28-year-old widow, by Orsini ruffians. Additional papal involvement and other sordid details made it juicy enough for the London stage—John Webster's play on Vittoria's life, *The White Devil*, appeared in 1608.

From Corso Garibaldi, Via Vicenzo Armanni descends to the big church of **San Pietro**, with four Corinthian columns on the façade and a Renaissance interior. The first altar has a *Martyrdom of St Bartholomew* by one of the last great Sienese painters, Rutilio Manetti, while the fourth has a *Visitation* by Giannicola di Paolo, and the fifth was decorated by Raffaellino del Colle. In the left transept there's a 13th-century wooden statue of the *Deposition.*

Below San Pietro is the **Porta Vittoria**: if you follow Via della Piaggiola from here you'll pass **Santa Maria della Piaggiola**, with an ornate Baroque interior, now used for concerts; there's a *Madonna and Child* by Ottaviano Nelli on the altar, although it's been repainted. Another Baroque church, **Santa Maria del Prato** (1662), is a copy of Borromini's San Carlino alla Quattro Fontane in Rome, just over the bridge to the right; it has recently been restored. If you continue along Via della Piaggiola, it's about a mile to the spot where Francis had his meeting with the wolf, on Via Frate Lupo: the isolated **Chiesa della Vittorina** was built in the 13th century and the charming interior (*under restoration*) has another odd nave with pointed Gothic vaulting and some early frescoes undisturbed by the remodelling in the 1500s. A bronze statue (1973) of the saint and wolf marks the famous encounter.

## Monte Ingino

From the cathedral you can make the stiff climb up Monte Ingino to the **Sanctuary of San Ubaldo**, but it's much easier to take the **funivia** which operates year round from the Porta Romana (*open winter 10–1 and 2.30–5, summer 8.30am–7.30pm*). On display in the church, besides the ashes of the patron saint who saved Gubbio from the emperor, are the three *Ceri*. There's a café and restaurant where you can while away the afternoon, or you can walk a bit further up for even more spectacular views from the **Rocca** (2913ft). At Christmas time, the entire slope of Monte Ingino is illuminated to form 'the world's largest Christmas tree.'

## The Corsa dei Ceri

Gubbio has retained some exceedingly medieval festivals that fill its solemn streets with colour and exuberance. On the last Sunday in May, crossbow-men from Sansepolcro come to compete in the *Palio della Balestra*, a fiercely fought contest dating back to 1461, with a procession, flag-throwing and music to warm things up. An even older custom is the Good Friday procession and a representation of the Passion at the little church of Santa Croce della Foce just outside the walls, with medieval chants and music played on wooden instruments called *battistrangoli*. Oldest of them all, however, is the *Corsa dei Ceri*, held every 15 May, the day before the feast of San Ubaldo, the town's patron saint. Although first documented a couple of years after Ubaldo saved the city from Emperor Frederick and his Umbrian allies, the festival over the centuries has taken on the uninhibited trappings of a pagan celebration that may well have predated the good bishop's heroism. The *ceri* ('candles') are three tall, wooden, octagonal towers some 13ft high, each topped by a wax saint who represents one of the three guilds of Gubbio—San Ubaldo (the builders), San Giorgio (the artisans) and Sant'Antonio Abate (the farmers).

The *ceri* are brought down from the sanctuary into Gubbio on 1 May. On May 15, following a mass, the three wax saints are brought out of the church of the Muratori and taken in a procession to the *ceri* in Piazza Grande, where they are afixed to the top of the 'candles'. A second procession then begins at Porta Castello and heads up to Piazza Grande, where the *ceri* are taken around town by their colourfully costumed teams. This is followed by a big fish banquet for participants and officials in the Palazzo dei Consoli. At 4.30 in the afternoon, there's another procession led by the bishop, in which the *ceri* are baptized with a jug of water. The race begins at 6, starting in Piazza Grande; ten bearers hoist the supports of their respective *cero* on their shoulders and race pell-mell through the crowds up the streets (Via XX Settembre, Via Colomboni, Via Appennino to Porta del Monte, where they rest before continuing to the mountain-top church of San Ubaldo). At intervals the teams are replaced by fresh men—a neat trick done without slowing the remarkably quick pace. Ubaldo invariably wins (and what could be more Italian than a fixed race?). In the evening the wax saints are returned to their home in the Muratori with the last procession of the day, by candlelight.

In 1943, during the German occupation, all-women teams carried the *ceri* (each weighs around 450 lbs) and successfully made it all the way up to San Ubaldo, for pride and to spite the Nazis—an experiment that hasn't been repeated since. Since the war, the *ceri* have become the symbol of Umbria, represented by the three red stripes on the region's coat of arms.

### Shopping

Gubbio's artist-craftsmen still turn out some of the most beautiful ceramic ware in Italy, carefully hand-painted in colourful, original floral designs. Some of their best work is too big to fit in your suitcase—majolica lamps and telephone stands, for example—but there are simple plates in every size for a souvenir. Perhaps the most artistic work is done at the **Fabbrica Ranimi** and at the **Fabbrica Mastro Giorgio**, both on Via dei Consoli. The shop down the street at No.44 has some less extravagant work: beautiful plaques and plates at lower prices. Gubbio also has a longstanding tradition in wrought iron work, perhaps even more difficult to carry home, but worth a look.

*Gubbio* ✉ *06024*                                                 ### Where to Stay

Though not yet in the same league as Assisi, Gubbio gets its share of visitors; day-trippers from Perugia looking for the essential Umbria make reservations in July and August essential, otherwise you're bound to be disappointed.

### expensive

In the heart of medieval Gubbio, the recently opened ★★★★**Relais Ducale**, Via Galeotti, ✆ 075 922 0157, ✍ 075 922 0159, occupies three historic buildings, linked by a lift; all are sumptuously furnished with antiques and mod cons, while a shuttle provides transport to the garage on the edge of town. The award-winning ★★★★**Park Hotel ai Cappuccini**, Via Tifernate, ✆ 075 9234, ✍ 075 922 0323, is a beautifully restored Franciscan monastery, 3km out of town, set in its own grounds with a cloister and chapel, and, inside, a pool, sauna and fitness centre.

### moderate

The 18th-century ★★★**Villa Montegranelli**, 4km away at Monteluiano, ✆ 075 922 0185, ✍ 075 927 3372, overlooks Gubbio and has kept many of its original features, especially the *piano nobile* and private chapel; the rooms are comfortable, and the restaurant, serving dishes from Umbria and Apulia, is as exquisite; for a real feast, order the *menu degustazione* (around L70,000). ★★★**Bosone**, Via XX Settembre 22, ✆ 075 922 0688, ✍ 075 922 0552, is located in a picturesque old palazzo just off

Piazza Grande. Rooms are comfortable (the most lavish run up to the *expensive* category), though not brilliant, and there's a garage. In a former convent, ★★★**San Marco**, Via Perugina 5, ✆ 075 922 0234, ✆ 075 927 3716, has modern comforts and a pretty garden terrace at the back. All rooms have bath and there's parking nearby. ★★★**Gattapone**, Via G. Ansidei 6, ✆ 075 927 2489, ✆ 075 927 1269, another pleasant locale in the medieval centre, has just been given a facelift. The recently upscaled ★★★**Beniamino Ubaldi**, Via Perugina 74, ✆ 075 927 7773, ✆ 075 927 6604, occupies a seminarians' college just outside the city walls, and yes, there is a bar (and restaurant, too).

### inexpensive

★★**Dei Consoli**, Via dei Consoli 59, ✆ 075 927 3335, near Piazza Grande, is small and simple, but enjoys an excellent location. It has a good restaurant in a medieval cellar, with tasty *spiedini* (meat on a spit). ★★**Oderisi-Balestrieri**, Via Mazzatinti 2, ✆ 075 922 0662, ✆ 075 922 0663, has good well-furnished rooms (some *moderate*), in a building that has been an inn for ages. ★**Galletti**, Via Ambrogio Piccardi 1, overlooking the river, ✆ 075 927 7753, has simple rooms, some with private bath. The restaurant, which serves roast duck and lamb, has outdoor tables in a pretty setting. **Ostello dell'Aquilone**, Loc. Ghigiano, ✆ 075 929 1144, ✆ 075 922 0197, is Gubbio's youth hostel.

---

### Eating Out

Gubbio has no good wines, but there are local herbal poisons like Amaro Iguvium and Liquore Ingeno to top off a meal.

The name recalls the legend of St Francis: **Taverna del Lupo**, Via Ansidei 21a, ✆ 075 927 4368 (*expensive*), in an atmospheric medieval place, serves excellent, traditional fare such as boar sausage, game in the autumn, and *risotto dei tartufi* (Gubbio, like Piedmont, is a land of white truffles, which are even more expensive than the black truffles of the Valnerina in southern Umbria), as well as delicious pasta dishes like lasagne with *prosciutto* and truffles and *frico*, a local speciality of mixed meats with cress. *Closed Mon.* Another local classic is the **Fornace di Mastro Giorgio**, in the workshop where the master ceramicist once created his famous ruby glaze, Via della Fornace di Mastro Giorgio, ✆ 075 922 1836 (*expensive–moderate*). The new management seems determined to continue the fine work of their predecessors, including some of Umbria's more esoteric specialities on the menu. *Closed Tues.* In the same price range, the family-run **Federico da Montefeltro**, Via della Repubblica 35, ✆ 075 927 3949, prepares memorable mushroom and truffle dishes with a deft hand, with outdoor tables in the summer. *Closed Thurs.*

On a clear day, the restaurant **Funivia**, on Monte Ingino, ✆ 075 922 1259 (*moderate*), is an exceptional dining experience, offering fabulous views as well as delicious pasta with truffles or *porcini* mushrooms, and tasty *secondi* like grilled lamb or stuffed pigeon. Good desserts and local wines. *Closed Wed.* **La Balestra**, Via della Repubblica 41, ✆ 075 927 3810 (*moderate*) features unusual *antipasti* (*aringa*) and dishes like *fondutina con tartufo*, home-made pasta and a good selection of meats. *Closed Tues.* **S. Francesco e Il Lupo**, Via Cairoli 24, ✆ 075 927 2344 (*moderate*) features local products, *porcini* mushrooms, and truffles, or you can just order the cheaper pizza. *Closed Tues.* **Bargello**, Via dei Consoli 37, at Largo Bargello, ✆ 075 927 3724, (*moderate*) also offers pizza as well as polenta (quite popular in this corner of Umbria), *agnolotti*, *agnello scottadito* ('burn-your-fingers lamb') and other grilled meats. *Closed Mon.*

## Excursions from Gubbio

The area around Gubbio is not densely populated: expect long stretches of empty space punctuated by an occasional half-ruined castle or monastery, and with the very plainest of mountain villages. **Castel d'Alfiolo**, 6km south of Gubbio on SS219, was converted from a family fortress to a Benedictine abbey in the 1100s; most of the buildings were redone in the 16th century, but the chapel and the main building conserve some good stone-carving from the 1200s. Another abbey, the 13th-century **Abbazia di Vallignegno**, halfway down the road to Perugia, has been converted into an *agriturismo*, but you can still visit the church with its Roman sarcophagus.

East of Gubbio, the SS298 passes through a lovely gorge with old water mills, on the way to the **Parco Naturale del Monte Cucco** on the border of the Marche. This is a popular spot with the Eugubini on summer weekends, with pretty mountain meadows and beech forests around Pian di Ranco; it's also one of the best places in Umbria for hang-gliding, and in winter people head up for the cross-country skiing. Descendants of Francis's Brother Wolf still roam in **Monte Cucco** itself. At 5137ft, Cucco is one of Umbria's highest peaks, and has, in its flank, one of the world's deepest (3025ft) subterranean systems, the 20km-long **Grotte di Monte Cucco**, reached by a long iron stair, but accessible only with a guide from the park's main base at **Costacciaro** (CENS, ✆ 075 917 0400). Remains of giant prehistoric cave bears were found here, and the innermost, darkest chambers are inhabited by a singular race of blind brown flies.

This mountainous region had a special pull on the holy men of the 10th and 11th centuries. San Romualdo, the nobleman turned monk and founder of the Order of the Camaldolese Benedictines, had a mystical vision of his vocation on Monte Sitria; the site is marked by handsome Romanesque church of the **Abbazia di Santa Maria di Sitria**, located above **Scheggia**, the last Umbrian town on the Via Flaminia. Romualdo, although a great wanderer who founded abbeys as far as the Pyrenees, was also the moving spirit behind the **Monasterio della Fonte Avellana** (off SS360), just over the border in the Marche in an isolated mountain setting. Founded in 979, this was an important centre of learning in the Middle Ages (Dante was one of many famous visitors), and almost nothing has changed here since the 12th century. Perhaps unique in Italy, it preserves the *scriptorium* where codices and manuscripts were copied (*visits 9–11.30, 3–5, Sun 3–4*).

## Down the Via Flaminia

The Via Flaminia (SS3) was a Roman road of conquest; even in the Dark Ages the Goths and Lombards kept it in repair, an important highway linking Ravenna, Spoleto and Rome. For all that, there's little to see on this mountainous stretch. **Sigillo** has some frescoes by the local painter Matteo da Gualdo in its church of Sant'Anna, and the remains of a small single-arch

Roman bridge at the Ponte Spiano. **Fossato di Vico** was founded as a Roman station along the road, and is now divided into a quiet upper and very medieval quarter and a lower modern town. The upper town has an 11th-century church, San Pietro, and frescoes by an accomplished follower of Ottaviano Nelli in the little Santa Maria della Piaggiola, and one by Matteo da Gualdo of Pope Urban V in San Benedetto. Just west of the Flaminia from here is the pretty hill village of **San Pellegrino**, stalwart preserver of an old fertility rite of spring: on 30 April, two poplar trees are brought to the village and stripped of their branches like maypoles, before they are 'married'. The church has frescoes by Matteo da Gualdo and a triptych (1465) by the fine Marchesi painter Girolamo di Giovanni from Camerino.

Somewhere along the Via Flaminia, between Scheggia and Gualdo Tadino, the deciding battle in the bitter Greek–Gothic war took place in 552. The Goths, led by Totila, were coming up the road from the south, and were met here by the freshly arrived Byzantine forces under the eunuch general Narses, at the time nearly 80 years old. The Goths were outnumbered, and Totila did everything he could to stall battle until reinforcements arrived, even to the extent of ordering his most skilled horsemen to put on a display of dressage to entertain the Byzantines. But Narses was not to be fooled. His troops completely outflanked the Goths; Totila was mortally wounded, and although enough Goths fled to fight one last showdown with the Greeks near Cumae, their show was over. As for the octogenarian eunuch, he continued to besiege and battle and consolidate the position of his emperor Justinian in Italy over the next *nine* years.

## Gualdo Tadino

This stern old town is on the steep slopes under rugged Monte Serra Santa. The ancient Umbrian town of *Tarsinater* was mentioned in no uncertain terms in Gubbio's Eugubine Tables (feelings were such that any citizen of *Tarsinater* caught in Gubbio was liable to be sacrificed). The Romans, who called it *Tadinum,* refounded it down in the plain near the Flaminia; after it was destroyed by the Goths, the few surviving inhabitants took to the hills. The Lombards named it Gualdo di Nocera ('Nocera's wood'), and the present site was resettled in the 12th century. After a brief period of independence Gualdo was taken over by Perugia. It has taken some big blows from earthquakes: the one in 1751 felled many public buildings, and the 1997–98 was pretty bad as well; many people are still living in containers (*see* pp.50–51) and most of Gualdo's churches are still off limits.

In Gualdo's main square, **Piazza dei Martiri della Libertà** (recalling the civilians killed by the Germans in the Second World War) has a squat but well-proportioned **Duomo** with a good façade and rose window of 1256 and three doors, with an inscription mentioning the restoration after the 1751 earthquake; the 16th-century fountain on its side is attributed to Antonio da Sangallo. The 13th-century **Palazzo del Podestà** is here as well, remodelled in Baroque times, as is the former church of **San Francesco**, a copy of the basilica in Assisi, with a luminous interior and frescoes by Matteo da Gualdo, a local boy of the late quattrocento given to brilliant colouring (and, as critics liked to sniff a century ago, 'incorrect drawing') as well as others by the school of Ottaviano Nelli. Another work by Matteo, a glowing triptych of the *Virgin and Child, with SS. Sebastian and Roch* can be seen in the church of **Santa Maria dei Raccomandati** over on Piazza XX Settembre. Gualdo's castle, the **Rocca Flea**, was restored and improved by Emperor Frederick II, and is considerably larger than its name suggests (*open April–June, Fri–Sun, 10.30–1 and 3.30–6.30; July–Sept,*

*Tues–Sun, 10.30–1 and 3.30–6.30; Oct–Mar, Sat and Sun, 10.30–1 and 3–5.30; free).* Restored before the quake, it contains ceramics (like Gubbio, Gualdo has made them for centuries), archaeological finds, and the town's painting collection, with a sumptuous polyptych by Niccolò Alunno, a *Coronation of the Virgin* by Sano di Pietro and more Matteo da Gualdo.

There's fine walking country in the mountains above Gualdo: take the road 8km east to **Valsorda**, a resort 3333ft up and the base for the pilgrmage walk to the 12th-century sanctuary of **Santissima Trinità** on Monte Serra Santa, now part of Monte Cucco park.

Gualdo has preserved four 13th-century gates, and in the last week of September the townspeople from the four quarters, or 'gates', of Gualdo, don their medieval glad rags to play the *Giochi de la Porte*—archery and slingshot competitions, and pellmell donkey races around town.

## Nocera Umbra

South of Gualdo Tadino, the hill town of Nocera Umbra was at the epicentre of the 1997–98 earthquakes, and it's a mess—virtually a ghost town. The *centro storico* is cordoned off with access only during the day. Inside the barrier, every other building seems to be propped up with heavy scaffolding or steel girders. It makes you wonder how it could possibly be rebuilt. Some 6,000 people, as well as offices and banks, are accommodated in containers and prefab housing. The surrounding hills are dotted with cranes, abandoned buildings, prefabs and building sites.

Nocera was an ancient Umbrian town, and later the Roman *Nuceria Camellaria*. It became an important Lombard city (its three Lombard cemeteries yielded a number of treasures, now in Rome's Museo dell'Alto Medioevo), and in the Middle Ages it was under the Trinci family of Foligno. In more recent times, Nocera Umbra has been best known for the fizzy mineral water it ships all over Italy, and it still has enough left over for two small spas in nearby Bagni di Nocera and the Terme del Centino.

The **Pinacoteca** in the church of San Francesco has an excellent *Nativity* by Niccolò Alunno, works by Matteo da Gualdo, a 13th-century crucifix, and a set of Roman milestones, but was badly damaged in the quake. Further up is the 15th-century **Duomo**, and what remains of the once tall tower of the castle. East, above Nocera, there's cross-country skiing at 5154ft **Monte Pennino.**

# The Valle Umbra: Spello to Spoleto

| | |
|---|---|
| Spello | 134 |
| Foligno | 139 |
| Bevagna | 143 |
| Montefalco | 145 |
| Around Montefalco: Into the Monti Martani | 148 |
| Trevi and the Tempietto del Clitunno | 148 |
| Spoleto | 152 |

Between Assisi and Spoleto spreads one of the largest patches of open country in the region. The sunny Valle Umbra, or Vale of Umbria as it is sometimes known, encompasses the valleys of the Teverone and the Topino ('Little Mouse River'), and has much in common with parts of southern Tuscany; the magnificent landscape seems almost consciously arranged by some geomantic artist to display each olive grove, vineyard, city and town to the best advantage. One Grand Tourist, the Abbé Barthélemy, wrote of the area: 'It is the most beautiful countryside in the world. I do not exaggerate.'

This area is littered with fascinating Roman and Lombard relics, thanks to that vital ancient thoroughfare, the Via Flaminia (SS3), the two branches of which joined in the remarkable but often overlooked town of Foligno before heading north to Gualdo Tadino. Besides some of Umbria's most beautiful hill towns, Spello, Montefalco and Trevi, the Valle Umbra is home to that unique relic of the Dark Ages called the Tempietto del Clitunno, and to glorious Spoleto, a genuine capital in those times, one of the most fascinating art towns in Italy, and now one of the trendiest, thanks to its famous festival of the Two Worlds.

## Spello

Lovely medieval Spello (pop. 8,000) could be Assisi's little sister, done in the same pink and cream Umbrian stone, lounging on the same sort of gentle hillside under Mount Subasio, overlooking the Valle Umbra. It has a similar history, first as an Umbrian settlement, then as the Roman city with a fancy name, *Splendidissima colonia Iulia Hispellum* or just *Hispellum* for short. The Lombards destroyed it, then made it part of the Duchy of Spoleto. In the Middle Ages, as a *comune*, Spello fought to keep free of Assisi the same way Assisi resisted domination by the Perugians. This earned it a thumping from Frederick II when he passed through, and when he was dead and gone Spello was swallowed up by Perugia.

There's so much to see in nearby Assisi that relatively few tourists find their way up here, but like most little sisters Spello has some charms of her own.

---

### *Getting Around*

Spello is linked by rail (station 1km from town) and bus to Assisi, Perugia and Foligno.

---

### *Tourist Information*

Piazza Matteotti 3, ✆/🖶 0742 301009, *prospello@libero.it*, *www. comune.spello.pg.it*

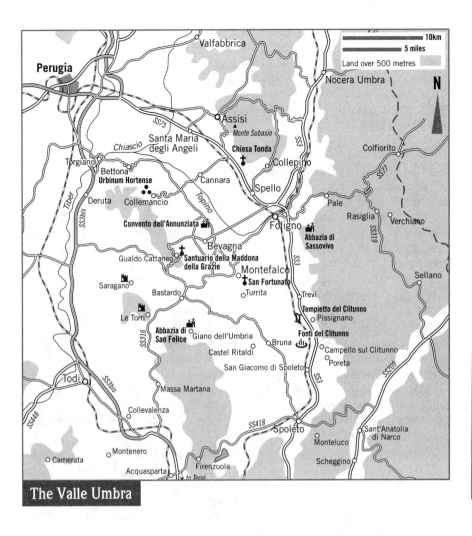

The Valle Umbra

---

The **Festa dell'Olivo e Sagra della Bruschetta** is the town's celebration of its olive oil production, on the last weekend before Mardi Gras.

**Corpus Domini**, in late May or early June, sees the town decked out with intricately designed carpets of flowers, an *Infiorata*—come in the early morning to see the blooms at their best.

135

## Porta Consolare

Spello has three excellently preserved Roman gates, including the main entrance to the town, the Porta Consolare, with three arches and three well-worn statues from the time of the Roman republic, placed here in the 1600s after their discovery by the amphitheatre; in the Middle Ages it was incorporated into the walls, and given a lofty tower to keep it company with a bushy tree growing out the top.

## Pinturicchio *et al*

From the gate, Via Consolare winds up into the centre, following the old Roman main street or *cardo*, passing an open chapel, the **Cappella Tega**, with faded Renaissance frescoes by Alunno. Where Via Consolare meets Via Cavour stands Spello's chief monument, the late 13th-century church of **Santa Maria Maggiore** (*open daily, summer 8.30–12.30 and 3–7; winter 8.30–12.30 and 3–6*), with its original Romanesque campanile and some 11th-century stone-carving incorporated into its 17th-century façade. The interior was renovated at the same time, when it was given its fancy stuccoes and a hodge-podge of Baroque altars. The two holy water stoups are ancient Roman columns, and there are two late and mediocre frescoes by Perugino on the pilasters either side of the apse, an excellent pulpit with grotesques of 1545 sculpted by Simone di Campione, and fine inlaid choir stalls (1520), and *baldicchino* by Tommaso di Rocco.

Best of all, however, is the **Cappella Baglioni**, commissioned in 1500 by Troilo Baglioni, scion of Perugia's gangster family, and brilliantly frescoed by Pinturicchio (make sure you have L1,000 notes to activitate the lighting). The three scenes, an *Annunciation, Nativity* and *Dispute in the Temple*, are delightful, full of colour and incident, and include Pinturicchio's self-portrait hanging under the *Annunciation*. The floor is made entirely of painted ceramics from Deruta (1516). More by Pinturicchio can be seen in the **Cappella del Sacramento**, a fresco of the *Madonna and Child* and an *Angel.*

The adjacent Palazzo dei Canonici contains the **Pinacoteca Civica** (*open daily exc Mon 10.30–1 and 3–6, summer 4–7; adm*), which opened in 1994 as a repository of works from the churches of Spello: there's woodcarving from the 13th and 14th centuries, especially a fine *Madonna and Child,* by an anonymous Umbrian sculptor, gold and silver work (a beautiful enamelled silver cross of 1398, by Perugian goldsmith Paolo Vanni), a portable diptych by Cola Petruccioli from the 1390s and Umbrian paintings by Alunno and his circle. Marcantonio Grecchi's *Madonna and Child with St Felice Vescovo and the Blessed Andrea Caccioli* has a fine view of early 17th-century Spello in the background.

For yet more Pinturicchio (he spent all of 1501 in Spello), the nearby 13th-century church of **Sant'Andrea** (*open 3–6 and sometimes 8–12.30, depending on the priest*) has a large painting of the *Madonna, Child and Saints* to the right of the crossing that he painted with another of Perugino's students, Eusebio di San Giorgio. There are 13th–16th-century frescoes as well, and an attractive high altar with a *Crucifix* attributed to a follower of Giotto.

## Souvenirs of Roman *Hispellum*

Walking the narrow, cobbled streets, hidden archways and stairways of Spello is a joy, although they're a bit steep. Press on past the rather anonymous Piazza della Repubblica, where the **Palazzo Comunale** (*damaged in the 1997 earthquake and closed for restoration, but due to reopen summer 2000: daily exc Sun 8–2, Mon and Thurs also 3.30–6.30*) bears only traces of its original work from the 1200s and contains a small archaeological collection in the atrium. Just off the piazza, the Romanesque **San Lorenzo** (*c.* 1160) has an unusual façade full of bits from Roman and early medieval buildings and some curious paintings within by a 16th-century painter from Brussels, Frans van de Kasteele.

From here ambitious climbers can continue up Via di Torre Belvedere to the top of Spello for the **Belvedere** and lovely view over the Vale of Umbria. There are ruins of the 14th-century **Rocca**, built by the indefatigable Cardinal Albornoz. The small **Roman Arch** nearby was the entrance to *Hispellum*'s acropolis.

A circumnavigation of Spello's walls will show you the two other Roman gates: the **Porta Urbica** (near the Porto Consolare, by a well preserved stretch of 1st-century AD walls), and best of all the **Porta Venere**, a beautiful, almost perfectly preserved monumental gate from the time of Augustus, flanked by a pair of tall cylindrical towers, a relic even more remarkable than the famous Arco di Augusto in Perugia.

## Outside the Walls of Spello

The Porta Venere is plainly visible from the road to Assisi and Perugia. Look the other way and you'll see the overgrown ruins of the **Roman Amphitheatre**, perhaps more impressive when viewed from the Belvedere in the city than from ground level; it once seated 15,000, drawing in gladiator fans from up and down the Via Flaminia. Just to the north of Spello is the charming, resolutely asymmetrical Romanesque church of **San Claudio** from the 12th century. Already in bad condition in 1997, it was almost destroyed that year by the earthquake; it is now closed for long-term restoration. Just beyond this, set in a lovely Italian garden, the **Villa Fidelia** was built in the 1500s but has been often fiddled with over the years; it now contains the **Collezione Straka-Coppa** (*open April, May, June and Sept, Thurs–Sun 10.30–1 and 3–6; July–Aug daily 10.30–1 and 4–7; Oct–Mar, Sat and Sun only, 10.30–1 and 3–6; adm*), an ensemble of late Renaissance, Baroque and early 20th-century art, with a few big names sprinkled throughout (including a 16th-century *Madonna and Child* by Vicenzo Catena of Venice, Italy's first amateur painter) as well as silver and ceramics. Some 2½km further on the same road, set in the lovely countryside around Spello, the **Chiesa Tonda**, or Santa Maria Rotonda, another geometric Renaissance temple (1517), has quirky Umbrian frescoes by Mezzastris inside (although it's now privately owned and off limits).

A kilometre northeast of Spello, beyond the 18th-century Porta Montanara, the cemetery church of **San Girolamo** is another good Renaissance work (1474), its portico and interior decorated by various students and followers of Pinturicchio. Another road from the same gate continues up to the slopes of Monte Subasio and the walled medieval village of **Collepino**. Above town, the Romanesque church of **San Silvestro** was founded by St Romualdo in 1025; it has an interesting crypt and an altar carved out of a Roman sarcophagus. From here, a majestic and panoramic if unpaved road continues over Subasio to the Eremo delle Carceri in Assisi (*see* p.105).

## West of Spello: Cannara and Urbinum Hortense

The fertile plain of Foligno along the banks of the river Topino was much appreciated in ancient times. **Cannara** was founded as a satellite of the large Roman town of Urbinum Hortense to the west, but has survived the centuries in better nick; it is known for its unique Vernaccia di Cannara, a sweet red dessert wine. Two churches have good paintings of the *Virgin, Child and Saints* by Nicolò Alunno, one in **San Matteo** (1786) and the other in **San Giovanni**. The Municipio has fresco fragments and other finds from *Urbinum Hortense*.

West of Cannara, in a beautiful setting, the tiny walled village of **Collemancio** has a Romanesque church and Palazzo del Podestà in its core. From the public garden, a road leads up in half a kilometre to the romantic ruins of *Urbinum Hortense*, whose inhabitants enjoyed lovely views. Mentioned by Pliny the Younger, it has been partially excavated; so far a temple, baths and a basilica have been discovered, but to see the colourful mosaic found here you'll have to go to the Museo Nazionale Romano in Rome.

### *Where to Stay and Eating Out*

#### Spello ✉ 06038

The elegant, frescoed 17th-century ★★★★**Palazzo Bocci**, Via Cavour 17, ✆ 0742 301021, @ 0742 301464, *bocci@abitarelastoria.it* (*moderate*) has beautiful rooms and a hanging garden; dining is *bello* and mellow in Spello under the vaulted ceiling at the hotel's restaurant **Il Molino**, ✆ 0742 651305, just opposite, in Piazza Matteotti—try the home-made pasta or traditional, utterly tender Umbrian meats cooked over the flames with a few glasses of Spello's own wines. *Closed Tues.*
★★★**La Bastiglia**, in a charmingly restored mill on Via dei Molini, ✆ 0742 651277, @ 0742 301159 (*expensive–moderate*) stands out for its pleasant rooms, beautiful terrace, views and good restaurant. ★★★**Altavilla**, Via Mancinelli 2, ✆ 0742 301515, @ 0742 651258 (*moderate*) also has a pleasant terrace and 24 well-furnished rooms run by the Prioetti family. ★★★**Albergo del Teatro**, Via Giulia 24, ✆ 0742 301140, @ 0742 301612, *hoteldelteatro@mclink.it* (*moderate*), so-called because of its situation near the Teatro Comunale, is a quiet and cheerfully furnished hotel with 11 well-equipped and comfortable rooms and wonderful views from the breakfast veranda. ★★**Il Portonaccio**, Via Centrale Umbra, ✆ 0742 651313, @ 0742 301615, is a sound, *inexpensive* choice. Rooms at ★★**Il Cacciatore**, Via Giulia 42, ✆ 0742 651141, @ 0742 301603 (*moderate*) are a bit more, but will save you a walk to its very popular restaurant, with beautifully prepared homemade pasta and other dishes at decent prices. *Closed Mon.* At **La Cantina**, Via Cavour 2, ✆ 0742 651775 (*moderate*), the menu is seasonal: you may be offered *oca al sagrantino e castagne* (goose braised with chestnuts in Sagrantino wine), or *agnello al limone* (lamb cooked with lemon) or, in summer, lighter dishes such as fresh grilled trout. *Closed Wed.*

#### Cannara ✉ 06033

Outside town, English-owned **Case delle Volpi**, Vocabolo Ducale 50, ✆/@ 0742 720361 (*inexpensive*) offers self-catering in a traditional farmhouse, with spacious garden and excellent views over rolling hills to Assisi. *Minimum one week stay.*

In Foligno (pop. 54,000), Umbria's third city, they point out the exact centre of a billiard table in the centre of a bar that stands in the centre of town, which is in the centre of Umbria, which is in the centre of Italy, which is in the centre of the Mediterranean, a sea whose very name means the middle of the world. Tragically, in September 1997, Foligno was in the middle again, this time of the earthquake. The whole world watched on the news as its medieval Torre Comunale collapsed in one of the aftershocks, while the Folignati wept and vowed to rebuild it just as it was as soon as possible *dov'è era, com'è era* ('where it was, as it was'—the battle cry of major Italian restoration projects). Many townspeople are still living in containers, but should be back in their own homes or wooden chalets before the end of 2000. The tower will take longer.

Even before the disaster not many people stopped for Foligno; in a sense the town centre has also been a victim of its post-war prosperity, and the ring of factories and modern suburbs that surrounds it is enough to discourage most travellers. But to pass on by is to miss one of the most distinctive Umbrian towns, not as archaic or as cute as Assisi, but memorable in its own way, a minor medieval capital with a pinch of grandeur and an air of genteel dilapidation that the tremors have aggravated. For the next few years the churches will be leaning on their crutches; ring the tourist office to see what has reopened.

## History

Foligno was the ancient Roman *Fulginum* that grew up near the junction of the two branches of the Via Flaminia. This key location brought Christianity early to Foligno, thanks to St Felicianus, who was martyred in the 3rd century. In spite of its location on a plain, the city never disappeared in all the troubles that followed the crack-up of the Roman Empire: it survived attacks by the Saracens and Magyars to pop back up in the 12th century as a free *comune* with strongly Ghibelline tendencies. St Francis was a frequent visitor, and not long afterwards it was the home of the Blessed Angela (1248–1309), a mystic whose direct communion with God and visions were recorded by her spiritual director in her autobiographical *Book of Divine Consolation*.

The Blessed Angela was 12 when the man suspected of being the Antichrist, Emperor Frederick II, with his exotic Saracen army and dancing girls, held his parliament in Foligno, in defiance of the pope who had excommunicated him. This got the Folignati into trouble after his death, and the period of wars and civil disorders that followed resulted in the Trinci family's assuming power in 1305. Their rule, which saw Foligno dominating Assisi, Spello, Montefalco, Bevagna and Trevi, lasted until 1439, when in a moment of upheaval Pope Eugenius IV sent in an army under Cardinal Giovanni Vitelleschi. Vitelleschi came from a family who hated the Trinci, and he had no qualms about executing the last lord and his followers, and instituting direct papal rule. There was one bright spot before the town nodded off, when German printers brought their presses to Foligno in 1470, only six years after the first books were printed in Italy; the first printed edition of Dante's *Divina Commedia*—which was also the first printed book in the Italian language—came out in Foligno the following year.

### Getting Around

Foligno, 36km/30mins from Perugia and 158km/2½hrs from Rome, is one of the principal **rail** junctions for eastern Umbria. **Buses** (the bus station is just up Viale Mezzetti) link it to Colfiorito, Montefalco, Bevagna, Trevi and Spoleto; FS bus services connect Foligno to Assisi, Perugia and Siena three times a day. Hire a **bike** from Associazione Gaia, Via Monte Cervino 6, ✆ 0742 20502 or ✆ 0742 818608. There is underground **parking** near Porta Romana, handy for the tourist information office.

### Tourist Information

Corso Cavour 126, ✆ 0742 354459/0742 349854, 🖷 0742 340545, *www.umbria2000.it*

### market day

Tuesday and Saturday, in Via Nazario Sauro.

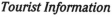

## Piazza della Repubblica

Piazza della Repubblica marks the centre of Foligno, with the Duomo facing the **Palazzo Comunale**—a rare architectural catastrophe. This was a genuine 12th-century monument, until in the early 1900s someone had the bright idea of pasting a neoclassical façade on it, mercifully disguised by scaffolding at present. The tower survived with its original lantern with Ghibelline crenellations as one of Foligno's proudest landmarks, before it collapsed in the earthquake.

The Folignati can't leave well alone; in the 18th century they commissioned Luigi Vanvitelli, court architect to the Kingdom of Naples, and the town's own Giuseppe Piermarini, designer of La Scala in Milan, to modernize their already grandiose **Duomo**. Fortunately they didn't tamper with the two façades, on either side of the L-shaped piazza: the **east front** (1133) is pink and white in the Perugian style, with some 1900s Venetian mosaics and other modern improvements, but the **south front** remains in its original state, and has one of the finest portals in Umbria (1201). It's also one of the least orthodox, a strange memorial of the syncretic religious and philosophical currents of that age. The sculpted reliefs include figures of the zodiac, a wild and comprehensive medieval bestiary, and long panels with geometric patterns and grapevines. Frederick II himself appears to the left of the door in one of only two existing likenesses in Italy. At the bottom, two stout porphyry lions hold up the doorway, and at the top of the arch, barely visible, is the most surprising bit of all: a Muslim star and crescent. More fantastical animals—including some pigs and cats—can be seen in the frieze above the portal, along with a good rose window.

The portal was brand new when young Francis of Assisi came here in 1205 and sold his father's stock of cloth and packhorse to raise money for the restoration of San Damiano (*see* p.104). He wouldn't, however, recognize the Duomo's interior, where the Cappella dell'Assunta is all that remains of the 12th-century original. The best art is in the sacristy, with a painting of the *Madonna and St John* by Alunno and busts of Bartolomeo and Diana Roscioli that have recently been attributed to the great Bernini. The cathedral also houses, or housed, a remarkable life-sized silver statue of St Feliciano, seated on a throne; much of it was taken to bits and stolen in 1982.

At the western end of the piazza, the much-altered **Palazzo Trinci** was home to Foligno's *signori* and still has its elegant original Renaissance courtyard behind a neoclassical façade. Nearly all the interior, however, dates from the period of Foligno's greatest *signore*, Ugolino III Trinci (ruled 1386–1415), who commissioned a precocious humanistic cycle of late Gothic frescoes for the second floor. They are not only an early example of the reawakening of interest in the Classical past, but are especially notable for being far from the centre of action in Florence. The frescoes were under restoration for years before the earthquake, and emerged unscathed (*open Tues–Sun 10–7; adm*). The palace **chapel** has frescoes on the *Life of Mary* (1424) by Ottaviano Nelli of Gubbio, who also painted the heroic Roman figures in the Sala dei Giganti. Frescoes in the loggia show the founding of Rome: most curious of all is a half-completed fresco and sinopia of *Rhea Silvia Being Buried Alive*; Rhea was the Vestal Virgin who gave birth to Romulus and Remus. The **Sala delle Arti Liberali e dei Pianeti** have allegorical figures of the liberal arts represented by women seated on thrones, and allegories of the planets. The corridor, which once provided the Trinci with private access to the Duomo, has frescoes of ancient heroes and the Seven Ages of Man. Ugolino also collected ancient art: there's a rare high relief of the games in the Circus Maximus, busts of the emperors, and a statue of Cupid and Psyche, with an inscription devised by Ugolino. The building also houses the **Pinacoteca Comunale** (*same hours as Palazzo*), with an *Annunciation* attributed to Gozzoli, works by Pierantonio Mezzastris of Foligno, and detached trecento frescoes.

## Down Via Gramsci

Palazzo Trinci is only the first of a long line of Folignati palaces, stretching down Via Gramsci. Most of the noble residences were built in the 1500s, and most were under restoration and scaffolding after long years of neglect even before the earthquake. The one nearest Palazzo Trinci, the 16th-century **Palazzo Deli**, is the most beautiful. Foligno's other churches are well endowed with art: **San Niccolò** in Via Scuola d'Arti e Mestieri with virtuoso (but not always interesting) works by Foligno's own Niccolò di Liberatore, better known as Alunno; In Piazza San Domenico at the end of Via Gramsci, **Santa Maria Infraportas** is one of Foligno's oldest churches, with unusual 12th-century windows and portico, and frescoes by Mezzastris and others; the large, deconsecrated church of **San Domenico** has good trecento frescoes, recently discovered under the whitewash. There are more Renaissance palaces along Via Mazzini and along Via Garibaldi, its northern extension: in Via Garibaldi the oratory known as the **Nunziatella** has a fresco by Perugino (*open daily exc Sun, 10–12.30*).

## Up the Menotre Valley

Directly east of Foligno, you can penetrate the valley of the little Menotre river into the mountains, a beautiful but seldom visited corner of Umbria that extends as far as the border with the Marche. This area was especially hard hit by the quake. Some of the collapsed buildings in the little villages have already been cleared, but scaffolding, rubble and cranes are everywhere. Inhabitants of the numerous container villages had little before, and what little they had has been lost. A number of modest roadside stalls sell the lentils, chickpeas, red potatoes and onions indigenous to the region.

The SS77 from Foligno follows the valley but, just after it crosses the Via Flaminia, a side road to the right (signposted Casale) heads in 5km up to the **Abbazia di Sassovivo** (*being restored, but it is possible to visit by arrangement, © 0742 350473), an 11th-century Benedictine abbey with a remarkable cloister; its variegated double columns are reminiscent of those in St Paul's Outside the Walls in Rome. The main road twists up into the mountains, passing some interesting caves and a pretty waterfall on the Menotre at **Pale**, 8km from Foligno, a village in a dramatic setting wedged between the rocks. Paper was milled here ever since the 13th century, and there's some good art in the church, although like most of the buildings it's closed tight.

On the heights, just before the border with the Marche, the mountains level out to form the lovely broad meadow or *valico* of **Colfiorito**, where the lofty green marshlands, 2400ft above sea level, are a favourite spot of migrating birds; other parts of the *valico* are used for growing beans and lentils. Sadly, most of the hamlets around its rim have been abandoned since the earthquake. By the road, the rugged 11th-century church, **Santa Maria di Pistia**, has porticoes on two sides to accommodate the country fairs held here in the Middle Ages. A side road before Colfiorito (24km) heads south into pristine mountain scenery around Rasiglia, where the little **Santuario della Madonna delle Grazie** (*closed since the earthquake*) has walls covered with well-preserved, colourful quattrocento frescoes, many of them painted as ex votos. Further up is **Sellano**, in a beautiful setting but again almost abandoned since the earthquake.

### Activities

Knights from ten rival districts of Foligno joust every second and third Sunday in September at the *Giostra della Quintana*, a custom dating back to the 17th century. The event is accompanied by plays performed in 300-year-old Umbrian dialect (of which you won't understand a word), and a more accessible historic cooking competition as well as other games, a fair, parades, outdoor taverns, and so on. Besides jousting, Foligno is one of Umbria's gliding and hang-gliding centres (*contact the Aeroclub, © 0742 670201*); there's a riding stable as well at Verchiano (*Centro Ippico CO.GI.VE, © 0742 632846*).

*Foligno* ✉ *06034*                              ### Where to Stay and Eating Out

The first recorded visit to an inn here was by the irascible Tobias Smollett, who described it in his *Travels through France and Italy* (1766):

> *In choosing our bed at the inn, I perceived one chamber locked, and desired it might be opened; upon which the cameriere declared with some reluctance: 'Bisogna dire a su' eccelenza; poco fa, che una bestia è morta in questa camera, e non è ancora lustrata.' 'Your excellency must know that a filthy beast died lately in that chamber, and it is not yet purified and put in order.' When enquired what beast it was, he replied, 'Un'eretico Inglese.' 'An English heretick.'*

Such was life in the Papal States; these days heretics and English travellers alike are welcome at the 17th-century ***Villa Roncalli**, just south of the centre on Viale Roma 25, © 0742 391091, @ 0742 391001 (*moderate*), a fashionable villa-hotel with a shady garden, pool, garage and comfortable rooms, and the city's finest restaurant (*expensive*) serving Umbrian dishes with a gourmet flair. *Closed Mon and two weeks in August*. Near the station, the family-run ★★**Belvedere**, Via Ottaviani 19, ☏ 0742 353990, ✉ 0742 356243 (*moderate–inexpensive*) is more than adequate, with pleasant rooms and breakfast, but no restaurant. ★★★**Le Mura**, Via Mentana 25, ☏ 0742 357344, ✉ 0742 353327 (*moderate*) is a comfortable, modern hotel on the northwest side of town with a good restaurant in the basement where you can watch the chef grilling meat or cooking *cialde* (wafer-thin layers of pizza-ish dough stuffed with cheese, vegetables or ham prepared on the griddle).

The classic place to eat, for the past four generations, is **Da Remo**, in a Liberty-style villa near the train station at Via Filzi 10, ☏ 0742 340 522 (*moderate*) serving tasty *strangozzi* (fat, homemade spaghetti) and roast kid simmered in Montefalco's Sagrantino wine. *Closed Sun evening and Mon*. **Osteria del Teatro**, Via Petrucci 8, ☏ 0742 350745 (*expensive*), is a delightful restaurant with vaulted ceiling, theatre posters on the walls and a garden where you can eat courgette fritters, deep-fried sage, ravioli filled with pumpkin and excellent lamb and beef (the *tagliata* is particularly good). *Closed Wed*. Wine lovers can while away an evening over their favourite bottles, cheeses and other snacks at the cosy **Bacco Felice**, Via Garibaldi 73, ☏ 0742 341019. For a light snack, coffee or *aperitivo*, try **Barbanera** in Piazza della Repubblica, an old *drogheria* complete with a wonderful old counter.

## Bevagna

Located under the Martani hills, on the original westerly route of the Via Flaminia, Roman *Mevania* has survived as Bevagna (pop. 2,400), a quiet, unspoiled, friendly town, where the main crops are flax and wine. Although low-key, it has some artistic gems. During its period as a free *comune* in the Middle Ages, before being taken over in 1371 by the Trinci family of Foligno, it built two of Umbria's best Romanesque churches. The earthquake left a number of people homeless and damaged the churches, which are now undergoing lengthy restoration.

*Tourist Information*

Piazza Silvestri 1, ☏ 0742 361667.

## Piazza Silvestri

Bevagna's pride and joy is its perfect **Piazza Silvestri**, a medieval and theatrical *pièce de résistance* which shows that the Bevanati tried hard to keep up with their bigger neighbours. It has a Corinthian column, a fountain and the impressive Gothic **Palazzo Comunale** of 1270, which was damaged by an earlier earthquake, in 1832, and restored with a charming little theatre inside.

An archway connects it to the delightful church of **San Silvestro**, built by an architect named Maestro Binello (who signed his work) and currently being restored with funds raised by Prince Charles. The simple façade incorporates bits of Roman buildings, an 1195 inscription to Emperor Henry VII and a frieze over the door. The interior is essentially Romanesque, all muscular stone and subtle geometry. Like many 12th-century buildings, it features a raised presbytery, leaving room for twin pulpits (*ambones*, now vanished) on either side of the steps, and a small crypt underneath. The real surprise is the style of the capitals—they're in the Egyptian order, representing papyrus leaves the way Ionic and Corinthian capitals recall the leaves of the acanthus. Such columns are common in this area, but their presence has never been explained. One possible guess: that they were copied from the ruins of some Roman-era temple to Isis or Serapis. Like the Parthenon, they are slightly curved, in *entasis* to look straight. (*Closed. Call© 0742 361667 for an update.*)

Across the piazza, the big, late 12th-century church of **San Michele Arcangelo** (*also closed*) has a few Egyptian capitals, recycled from older buildings. Binello and Rodolfo built this one about the same time as San Silvestro, and to the same interior plan. St Michael and his dragon figure prominently on the façade, along with some re-used Roman friezes, a Cosmatesque arch, and a menagerie of cows, cats and such, similar to the portal in Foligno (by the same architects), while the large crypt under the raised presbytery is supported by ancient Roman columns and capitals. The church houses two processional statues of Bevagna's patron saint Vincenzo, one of wood and the other of silver.

The third church on the piazza, **Santi Domenico e Giacomo** (*closed, but due to open in summer 2000*), has a Baroque interior with what must be the biggest alabaster window in Italy behind the altar. Of the church's original decoration, little remains but a radiant trecento *Virgin of the Annunciation* in the choir; there are also works by the Bevagna-born artist Il Fantino ('the Jockey,' Ascensidonio Spacco, d. 1646). From here, Corso Matteotti follows the route of the old Via Flaminia, passing by an 18th-century pharmacy and 18th-century *municipio*, its ground floor the home of a new **Museo della Città** (*open April–Sept, Tues–Sun 10.30–1 and 2.30–5, closed Mon; Oct–Mar, Sat and Sun only, 10.30–1 and 2.30–5; adm*). This houses a fine collection of Roman artefacts and coins, busts and architectural fragments found in and around Bevagna; a collection of medieval manuscripts, including a papal bull issued by Innocent IV, and a model of the Santuario della Madonna delle Grazie (*see* opposite); and works by Dono Doni, Il Fantino, and an *Adoration of the Magi* by Corrado Giacinto.

## The Rest of Town

More remnants of Roman *Mevania* can be seen a few blocks further up the Corso, turning at Via Crescimbeni, where a **Roman Temple** was partially conserved when its columns were bricked in long ago. Nearby, in Via Porta Guelfa, there's a marine **mosaic** featuring a big lobster, sea horses, and Tritons, once part of the 2nd-century baths (*ring the bell at No.2*). A picturesque crescent of houses traces the curve of the amphitheatre, in Via dell'Anfiteatro, and there's a house at the end, in Via Dante Alighieri, with a fine Roman frieze.

At the highest point in Bevagna, the 13th-century church of **San Francesco** (*closed since the earthquake*) has, near the altar and protected by a grille, the stone on which Francis stood when he preached to the birds at Pian d'Arca, north of Bevagna. Steps from the church lead down to Piazza Garibaldi and Bevagna's best preserved medieval gate, **Porta Cannara**.

## Around Bevagna

More bits of Roman *Mevania* can be seen off the old Via Flaminia to Foligno (the SS316): the fossil-like imprint of another amphitheatre in a field, and two ruined tombs. Here too, the big medieval **Torre di Montefalco**, near an old mill and canals, is a pretty place for a picnic. Just north of Bevagna, the **Convento dell'Annunziata** has more works by Il Fantino and a pretty terracotta altarpiece of the *Annunciation*. A path from the convent leads down to a charming spring-fed lake. To the southwest of Bevagna stands yet another 16th-century shrine to the Virgin Mary, the **Santuario della Madonna delle Grazie**, designed by Valentino Martelli with a handsome octagonal dome and a pretty view over the area.

---

*Bevagna* ✉ *06031*                          ***Where to Stay and Eating Out***

In the centre of town, **L'Orto degli Angeli**, ✆ 0742 360130, 🖷 0742 361756, *orto.angeli@bcsnet.it*, *www.ortoangeli.it* (*expensive –moderate*), must be almost unique in that the property contains both a 2nd-century temple to Minerva (forming one wall of the restaurant), and the ruins of a Roman theatre, part of the delightful hanging garden. The Antonini Angeli Nieri Mongelli family opened their historic home to guests a couple of years ago, having decorated each of the bedrooms and suites in keeping with the style of the house. It is full of lovely family antiques and pictures. The restaurant (*expensive–moderate; closed Tues*) serves creative versions of Umbrian classics. ★★★**Palazzo Brunamonte** in Corso Matteotti 79, ✆ 0742 361932, 🖷 0742 361948 (*moderate*) is another old palazzo, newly restored but more modestly furnished, with 16 comfortable bedrooms and frescoed public rooms.

Bevagna offers a simple but attractive lunch stop at **Da Nina**, Piazza Garibaldi, ✆ 0742 360161 (*moderate*), serving truffles, and good pasta dishes with porcini mushrooms and wild boar flavoured with tarragon—fancy dining for these parts. *Closed Tues*. Mario Siena is the smiling host at **El Rancho**, Via Flaminia 53, ✆ 0742 360105 (*inexpensive*), serving a tempting array of local dishes and products at down-to-earth prices, consumed outside in fair weather. *Closed Mon*. For something a little more upmarket, try **Ottavius**, Via Gonflone 4, ✆ 0742 360555 (*moderate*). *Closed Mon*.

## Montefalco

Only 7km from Bevagna but located much higher up in the hills, Montefalco (pop. 5,500) is another unspoilt gem. Known as the '*Ringhiera* (balcony-rail) *d'Umbria*', the town offers splendid 360° views to Assisi and Perugia and down the entire Valle Umbra as far as Spoleto. Another nickname, '*il lembo di cielo caduto in terra*' (heaven's hem fallen to earth) refers to its reputation as a factory for saints, extraordinary even by Umbrian standards; the celestial hosts count no fewer than eight former Montefalconesi. Until 1240 it was known as Coccorone, and when Frederick II destroyed it and rebuilt as a Ghibelline town he named it after his imperial eagle. It later became part of the Trinci family's domains, and then part of the Church's; today it is practically synonymous with its fine Sagrantino wines.

At the museum, Via Ringhiera Umbra 1, ✆ 0742 379598.

## San Francesco

Appropriately enough, the town of heaven's hem wears a monk's tonsure on top: central, circular and partially arcaded **Piazza del Comune**, from where streets radiate down like spokes. One of these, Via Ringhiera Umbra, takes in the lovely valley of the Clitunno while descending to Montefalco's pride and joy, the collection of frescoes in the deconsecrated 14th-century church of **San Francesco**, now converted to a museum (*open daily exc Mon; 10.30–1 and 2–6 in spring and autumn; 3–7 in summer; 2.30–5 in winter; adm*). The earthquake caused some structural damage to the apse, and although the frescoes themselves were unharmed, it was deemed a good moment for a complete restoration; work is due to finish in July 2000, but there are plans to leave the scaffolding in place for a limited period after the reopening to give a better view.

Benozzo Gozzoli spent two years here (1450–52), painting the apse with the ***Life of St Francis***. Montefalco's Franciscans did not let Gozzoli put in many of his usual fancies—though there are a few moppet children grinning out from the corners. Gozzoli does, however, indulge in his favourite cityscapes, including views of Montefalco (where Francis visited after preaching to the birds around Bevagna), and of Arezzo (where he cast out the devils). The panels along the bottom of the apse show portraits by Gozzoli of great Franciscans—a distinguished company of saints and popes and philosophers, including Duns Scotus. The cycle makes a fascinating contrast to the earlier and much better frescoes in Assisi, but it cannot be denied that Gozzoli's rather facile, charming and sentimental figures struck a deep chord in the mid 15th century, because they became a model for a good deal of later Umbrian painting. Gozzoli also frescoed the first chapel, a triptych with the *Madonna and Saints and Crucifix*.

The other Renaissance fresco here is by Perugino, a run-of-the-mill *Nativity* with Lake Trasimeno, restored in 1999. The aisles contain fine trecento painting, including a vivid and unique version of the *Temptations of St Anthony*; there is a fond painting by Tiberio d'Assisi of a local favourite and exemplar of spiritual first aid, the *Madonna del Soccorso*, in which Our Lady is about to whack a devil with a big club, when he comes to snatch a child whose exasperated mother had exclaimed 'May the Devil take you!'

The **Pinacoteca** at San Francesco has an 18th-century statue of Foligno's Quintana Saracen, another *Madonna del Soccorso*, a *Madonna and Child* by the school of Melozzo da Forlì, and a beautiful painting of *SS Vincent, Illuminata and Nicolas of Tolentino* by Antonizzo Romano; another section has an ancient marble statue of Hercules found in the town, a medieval lion, and a Renaissance river god.

## The Rest of Town

Montefalco's people are a cheerful lot, contentedly looking down from their balcony on to the rest of Umbria. Most of them live in tiny low houses jammed into narrow lanes; when it's nice they sit out front in garden chairs fostering Umbria's leading industry—talking about the weather. After San Francesco, sights are few; two other churches contain frescoes by 14th–16th-century Umbrian painters—**Sant'Agostino** and **Sant'Illuminata**, the latter with a lunette of the *Madonna della Misericordia* (1500) over the door. Montefalco retains its medieval walls, including the two interesting gates of **Porta Sant'Agostino**, with a fresco of the Virgin and saints, and **Porta Federico II**, decorated with the eagle.

## Outside the Walls

Just outside the Porta Federico II, the large 17th-century church of **Santa Chiara da Montefalco** was built around a much earlier chapel of Santa Croce. This has beautiful Sienese-inspired Umbrian frescoes of 1333 on the life of Montefalco's most venerated saint, Clare of the Cross (*c.* 1268–1308). Clare was a follower of St Francis, a mystic visionary and special devotee of the Passion of Christ, famous for her charity, learning and prophecy; after she died, her heart was found to be branded with the sign of the cross.

The Franciscan convent of **San Fortunato**, just over 1km to the southeast of Montefalco's Porta Spoleto, enjoys a beautiful setting and still shelters a handful of friars; the thick ilex forest that surrounds it was planted as insulation against the winter winds. The church, dedicated to Fortunatus (d. 400), a priest famous for his charity to the poor, was founded over a Roman basilica in the 5th century. In the 16th century it was rebuilt, and later Baroqued inside, although preserving interesting fragments of frescoes by Gozzoli: a lunette over the door, an *Adoration of the Child* and the *Enthroned St Fortunatus*. The cloister reuses Roman columns, and has a chapel frescoed by Tiberio d'Assisi on the *Life of St Francis*. In the little village of **Turrita**, the parish church has an array of votive frescoes; just outside the town, there's a very fancy 19th-century **Santuario della Madonna della Stella**, built in honour of a miracle-working 16th-century fresco.

---

*Montefalco* ✉ *06036*                    ***Where to Stay and Eating Out***

The delightful ★★★★**Villa Pambuffetti**, Via della Vittoria 20, ✆ 0742 378823, 🖷 0742 379245, *villabianca@interbusiness.it* (*expensive*) is a 19th-century villa owned by a local noble family who now run it as a beautifully kept inn, with 15 rooms, all decorated differently, some with family antiques. The villa is set in a lovely park with huge trees and an outdoor pool. A cheaper but comfortable choice just under Piazza del Comune, ★★**Ringhiera Umbra**, Corso G. Mameli, ✆/🖷 0742 379166 (*rooms inexpensive, meals moderate*) has en suite baths in some of the rooms, and a good restaurant, too.

Montefalco is perhaps best known for a couple of red wines, Sagrantino and Rosso di Montefalco. Sagrantino is a bit special, with a delicate aroma of blackberries; both are sold in many shops around town. **Coccorone**, off the central square at Vicolo Fabbri, ✆ 0742 379535 (*inexpensive*) is an elegant, understated place with tempting crêpes and *tagliatelle al tartufo* as a starter and *faraona ai salmi* (braised woodcock) and grilled pigeon as main dishes. *Closed Wed.* For a similar price, **Il Falisco**, Via XX Settembre 14, ✆ 0742 379185 (*inexpensive*) offers local specialities such as *filetto al sagrantino*, beef fillet cooked in Sagrantino wine. *Closed Mon.* **Enoteca Federico II** in Piazza del Comune, ✆ 0742 378902, is a pleasant place for a snack and a glass of local wine.

At Montefalco begins a range of hills and lofty plateaux known as the Monti Martani, separating the Valle Umbra from the Tiber. This is a quiet area, well off the main tourist trails: Umbria may be the 'Green Heart of Italy' but this heart has some surprisingly empty quarters once you leave its main arteries. Places like **Gualdo Cattaneo**, a windy drive west of Bevagna, knew their peak of importance under the Lombards (the name Gualdo comes from the German *Wald*, or wood). Its big cylindrical castle dates from the 1494—the work of Pope Alexander VI, built after his fiery son Cesare Borgia barnstormed through the area to show the Umbrians who was boss. When Gualdo's church was rebuilt in 1804, stonework from its 13th-century predecessor was preserved on its façade; the crypt is original as well. The apse has a fine *Last Supper* by Bevagna's early 17th-century master Fantino.

A pretty drive just west of Montefalco leads to a little market town bearing the rather unfortunate name of **Bastardo**. Bastardo is the gateway to other forgotten castles to the west: **Le Torri** (a poor man's San Gimignano), Renaissance **Barattano**, and a rare Lombard fort in good nick at **Saragano**.

Southeast of Bastardo, amid the olive groves on the slopes of the Monti Martani, the walled village of **Giano dell'Umbria** is one of several in the area founded by Norman knights who were granted the land after fighting as mercenaries for Pope Gregory VII in the 1080s—the whole area extending to Castel Ritaldi was known as *Normandia* in the Middle Ages. Originally it consisted of two fortified villages (hence the curious town plan) and has two 13th-century churches on the same piazza, but only a single Palazzo Pubblico; until the 1300s Giano managed to remain independent in spite of being circled by all the local sharks. Of the churches, the Pieve has a Baroque interior and a recently restored painting by Andrea Polinori of the *Madonna and Child* (1620) who keeps company with a much venerated *Madonna and Child* painted 300 years earlier.

Just north of Giano, the red stone **Abbazia di San Felice** was founded by some of Umbria's early cenobitic monks, who had a good eye for serendipitous locations. In the 8th century the Benedictines moved in and rebuilt it, and since 1815 it has been reoccupied by a congregation dedicated to mission work. The current Romanesque church, from the 12th century, has a handsome portal topped by a three-light window and an impressive apse with a gallery. Under the raised presbytery, the crypt has quaint old Roman and early medieval capitals and an ancient sarcophagus, holding the remains of the martyred bishop of Martana. San Felice's cloister, with frescoes, is especially pretty.

Another possible destination, **Castel Ritaldi** (14km south of Montefalco), has a castle from the 1200s. Just outside the village, don't miss the **Pieve di San Gregorio** (1140) and its charming sculpted façade, decorated with elaborate interwoven designs inhabited by little monsters; it is currently being restored by funds raised in New York. Nearby **Bruna** has a Renaissance church in the shape of a trefoil called **Santa Maria della Bruna** (1510).

## Trevi and the Tempietto del Clitunno

No small town in Umbria makes a grander sight than Trevi (pop. 7,400), a nearly vertical village reminiscent of Positano on the Amalfi coast, hung on a steep and curving hillside draped with olive groves above the Via Flaminia. If you were wondering, it has no connection with the famous fountain in Rome outside of the fact that both were at the intersection of three roads, or *tre vie*. Trevi was part of the Duchy of Spoleto and seat of a bishop, and was destroyed by the Saracens and Magyars. Briefly an independent *comune*, its strategic position along the Flaminia made it a prize fought over by Perugia and Foligno. Joining the Papal States in 1439 brought it prosperity, at least in the short run, as well as the fourth printing press in Italy in 1470. These days there are no flies on Trevi: like its sister hill towns it may look medieval, but it also dallies on the wild side of the international avant garde.

### Getting Around

Trevi can be reached by bus several times a day from Foligno (Società Spoletina, ✆ 0742 670746).

### Tourist Information

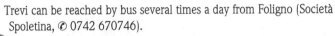

**Trevi:** Piazza Mazzini, ✆ 0742 781150, *www.protrevi.com*

## Two Churches, Two Art Museums

Trevi's credentials as a free *comune* in the Middle Ages are in its small but proud **Palazzo Comunale** in Piazza Mazzini, built in the 14th century, with numerous later additions. From here, the stepped street Via Beato Placido Riccardi leads up past the Piazza della Rocca, lined with quattrocento palaces; further up, at the highest point in town, stands the domed cathedral, **Sant'Emiliano**. Emiliano, an Armenian monk, served in the 4th century as bishop of Trevi, and he has been solemnly celebrated every 27 January since the Middle Ages with a procession of the Illuminata. His church (damaged by the quake) has three Romanesque apses and a 15th-century portal, with the good bishop and a pair of lions carved in relief. The interior was last redone in the 19th century, but contains a beautiful altar of 1522, carved by Rocco di Tommaso. Next to the Duomo, the handsome Renaissance **Palazzo Lucarini** now hosts the **Trevi Flash Art Museum**, a joint endeavour of *Flash Art* magazine and the *comune*, offering a permanent collection of contemporary Umbrian, Italian and foreign artists, as well as changing exhibitions (*open Wed–Sun 10–1 and 3–6, for exhibitions only—call ✆ 0742 381818 for information; adm*).

For the older stuff, make your way to **San Francesco**, a huge church built in the mid 14th century with some original frescoes, on the site where Francis's preaching was drowned out by the braying of an 'indomitable ass'. 'Brother ass, do hush and let me preach to these people,' Francis said, and the animal 'put its head down on the ground and knelt, and remained silent until Francis had finished, much to the wonder of the people'. There are some fine Renaissance tombs inside, and a Roman sarcophagus holding the remains of St Ventura (d. 1310).

Access to the church is by way of its equally enormous convent, now home to the **Museo Civico** or Raccolta d'Arte di San Francesco (*open in summer daily exc Mon; April, May and Sept, 10.30–1 and 2–6; June and July, 10.30–1 and 3.30–7; Aug, 10–1 and 3–7.30; Oct–Mar, Fri–Sun only, 10–1 and 2.30–5; adm*). There are some good paintings by local Umbrian artists, including an *Incoronazione di Maria* by Lo Spagna and various small scenes of the *Life of Christ* from polyptychs by Giovanni di Corraduccio, a charming 15th-century painter from Foligno. In 1999, a **Museo della Civiltà dell'Ulivo** was opened in the same convent. Trevi is famous for its olive oil: its conical hill is wrapped with some of the most majestic olive trees in Italy, including a few specimens believed to be well over 1,000 years old (especially the so-called Olivo da Sant'Emiliano, 3km south of Trevi at Bovara). Olives made it to Umbria by the 5th century BC, having been introduced by the Greeks in the Bay of Naples; like many Greek things they were quickly adapted by the Etruscans, and the rest is history.

## Around Trevi

Although the medieval town is stockpiled with little churches, the two worth going out of your way to see are just outside town. From modern Piazza Garibaldi, just outside of the gate of the *centro storico*, Via Ciuffelli leads to the 14th-century Capuchin monastery and church of **San Martino** (*usually open mornings*). Over the door is a charming lunette by Tiberio d'Assisi, a painter who is also represented inside with a *St Martin and the Beggar*; the other prize painting is a *Madonna* by Pierantonio Mezzastris. Make sure to ask one of the friars to open the little chapel in the courtyard, containing one of Lo Spagna's finest works, the *Assumption with SS Jerome, John the Baptist, Francis and Anthony of Padua*, in which the Virgin ascends to heaven over Foligno.

The second church is south of Trevi, in the middle of an olive grove. The votive church of the **Madonna delle Lacrime** was built in 1487 to house a weeping statue of the Virgin— the first of the many Renaissance churches that went up in Umbria during the great Marian renewal, inspired by the sermons of San Bernardino. The church, shaped like a Latin cross, has a fine sculpted portal by Giovanni di Gian Pietro of Venice; when it reopens after the earthquake damage has been repaired you'll be able to see the beautiful frescoes: the *Adoration of the Magi* by Perugino, an anonymous *Madonna and Child* of 1483, and others by Lo Spagna, including a good *Deposition*. Many members of the locally prominent Valenti family have impressive tombs from the 1500s and 1600s.

## The Fonti del Clitunno and the Tempietto

Just south of Trevi are the springs of the pretty little river Clitunno. This has been considered one of Umbria's great beauty spots for some 2,300 years; it was sacred in Roman times and probably ancient Umbrii times as well. Through the elegiac poetry of Virgil and Propertius, all Rome knew of Clitumnus and its eponymous river god, and the big snow-white oxen raised here, not to pull ploughs but to serve as temple sacrifices. It was one of the great sights of the Grand Tour, and in the 19th-century it inspired Carducci to write one of his best known poems, which baptized Umbria green for evermore:

> *Salve, Umbria verde, e tu del puro fonte*
> *nume Clitumno! Sento in cuor l'antinca*
> *patria e aleggiarmi su l'accesa fronte*
> *gl'ital iddii.*

> Hail, green Umbria, and you, Citumno, genius of the pure spring!
> I feel in my heart the ancient fatherland, and the Italic gods
> alighting on my fevered brow.

> Giosuè Carducci

A score of underground springs rise up at the **Fonti del Clitunno** (*open 9–12, 2–dusk*) forming a landscape of lagoons and islands, planted with weeping willows and poplars. It is at its best if you come off season, or late in the day when the coachloads of tourists are gone. Byron devoted a few stanzas of *Childe Harold's Pilgrimage* to the place (Canto 4), but today the proximity of the busy Via Flaminia and the railway tracks keep the springs from being quite the idyllic paradise evoked by the poets. It's still a popular resort for the locals, and well stocked with trout for those who follow that favourite Umbrian pastime of beating the prices at the local fish market.

The Roman villas and temples that once stood here are long gone, but bits of them were reassembled in a mysterious little building called the **Tempietto del Clitunno** (*open daily exc Mon, 9am–8pm in summer, 9am–2pm in winter*). Two centuries ago, this was commonly believed to be a pagan temple converted to Christian use; Goethe, almost alone in his opinion, dissented, believing it to be an original Christian work. For once this most misinformed of all geniuses got it right. The most recent studies put the Tempietto somewhere in the 6th century, or even as late as the 8th, making this obscure, lovely building in a way the last work of classical antiquity, Christian enough, but an architectural throwback to a world that was already lost.

The little track that runs below the temple was the original Roman Via Flaminia; travellers between Ravenna and Rome would look up and see the beautiful façade, with its two coloured marble columns and ornate pediment, in an exotic, half-oriental late Roman style. The entrance, however, is round the side, leading into the portico and from there to the tiny sanctuary, decorated with Byzantine frescoes of the 700s: Saints Peter and Paul flanking the altar, and above them two unforgettable, very spiritual angels inspired by the great mosaics of Ravenna, gazing inscrutably out at you from the depths of the Dark Ages. The dedication remains intact, on the architrave: 'Holy God of the Angels who made the Resurrection.'

The village near here, **Campello sul Clitunno**, is built around the 16th-century **Chiesa della Bianca**, with frescoes by Lo Spagna inside. For a remarkable view over the Valle Umbra, take the steep little road that snakes up and up through the terraces of olives to the **Castello** (or Campello Alto), a tiny old place hunkered down in the walls.

## South of Clitunno: San Giacomo

After Clitunno, the Flaminia passes under a square grim castle in **San Giacomo di Spoleto**, an outpost built in the 14th century by Cardinal Albornoz. Unlike the Cardinal's other Umbrian fortresses, this one was later converted into a residential neighbourhood, with tiny lanes lined with little houses. Opposite the castle walls stands the church of **San Giacomo**, founded in the 13th century and redone in the 16th, the date of its beautiful carved doorway and frescoes. The best of these are by Lo Spagna, and show miracles accredited to St James the Greater that occurred along the road to Compostela: a young man, unjustly hanged, was discovered to be still alive when his parents returned to cut down his body. The parents hurry to tell the judge, who scoffs and says their son is as alive as the roast chickens on his table, whereupon the roast chickens fly away.

## Trevi ✉ 06039

Peaceful **★★Del Pescatore**, Via Chiesa Tonda 50, ✆/✉ 0742 381711 (*inexpensive*) is a good *pensione*, with nine pleasant rooms, located near a babbling brook. Downstairs, the excellent **Taverna del Pescatore**, ✆ 0742 780920 (*moderate*) is run by another branch of the same family, with an imaginative range of menu choices based on meat or fish, both very good value and beautifully prepared. *Closed Wed.* The new **★★Il Terziere**, Via Salerno 1, ✆ 0742 78359, has lovely views and delicious dinners (*moderate*). **★La Cerquetta**, Via Flaminia 144, Loc. Parrano, ✆ 0742 381455 (*rooms and meals inexpensive*) turns out reliable Umbrian food for very honest prices. *Closed Sun.* If you come to Trevi in October, try its famous black celery (*sedano nero*) which packs more punch than any other celery in Italy; every Thursday morning in October there is a market devoted to it.

## Campello sul Clitunno ✉ 06042

Campello sul Clitunno is a quiet alternative to Spoleto if you've come for the festival. Don't be put off by the location of ex-water mill **★★★Il Vecchio Molino**, Via del Tempio 34, Loc. Pissignano, ✆ 0743 521122, ✉ 0743 275097 (*expensive-moderate*). It may be close to the traffic-clogged Perugia–Spoleto road, but, once inside the property the sounds are of gurgling water; two streams run through the garden. Inside, old bits of mill are still in evidence and the bedrooms are decorated with antiques. **★★Fontanelle**, Via d'Elci 1, ✆ 0743 521091, ✉ 0743 275052, is a lovely hotel and restaurant (*both moderate*) surrounded by refreshing greenery. Rooms are comfortable, and all equipped with bath; the restaurant serves Umbrian specialities like country prosciutto, *strangozzi* (homemade pasta) and platters of tender lamb, chicken and pigeon. At the Fonti del Clitunno, **★★Ravale**, Via Virgilio, ✆ 0743 521320 (*rooms and meals moderate*) has simple rooms, as well as a modestly priced *ristorante-pizzeria*. In Loc. Pettino above Campello (*follow the road northeast to Colle Pian Fienile and Monte Serano*), family-run **Pettino da Palmario**, ✆ 0743 276021, has an excellent reputation for its truffles at affordable prices. *Closed Tues.*

## Spoleto

When composer Giancarlo Menotti was dreaming up the Festival of Two Worlds in the 1950s, he spent months travelling across central Italy looking for just the right spot, some pretty town where the best of modern culture could be displayed against a background that recalled the best of the past. Spoleto (pop. 36,000) was almost unknown then, a rather austere town of grey stone and cobbled streets, buried in one of the most obscure corners of darkest Umbria. But more than any Umbrian city, this one has a remarkable past; after its prominence in classical times, Spoleto became the seat of one of the most powerful states in Italy at the very beginning of the Middle Ages. It remained splendid enough through the golden years of the high Middle Ages and Renaissance to acquire its share of lovely monuments, and then it pricked its finger on a spindle and dozed like Sleeping Beauty. Shelley called it 'the most romantic city I ever saw'.

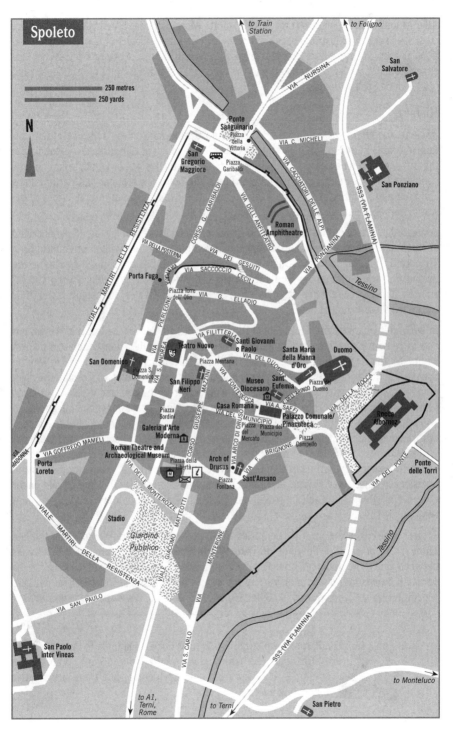

After its long sleep, Spoleto was ready for Menotti. More than ready, perhaps: even after the musicians pack their instruments and go, they leave behind a Spoleto full of special exhibitions and art workshops, its streets littered with jarring chunks of abstract sculpture. This experimental marriage of trendy art and the medieval hill town is not always a happy one, but it's done Spoleto no harm.

## History

Ancient *Spoletium* was one of the Umbrii's most important cities. It was resettled as a Roman colony in 242 BC, only 24 years before an over-confident Hannibal came pounding at the gates, expecting an easy victory after his rout over the legions at Lake Trasimeno (*see* pp.85–6). But *Spoletium* remained loyal to Rome and heroically repulsed the Carthaginians and their allies, and Hannibal, who had intended to move straight on to Rome from there, was discouraged enough to make a fatal detour into the Marche instead.

Strategically located on the Via Flaminia midway between Rome and the late Imperial capital of Ravenna, Spoleto was one of the rare towns to prosper in the twilight of empire. King Theodoric built it up for the Ostrogoths; Justinian's general, Belisarius, did the same for the Byzantines; the Goths under Totila made the city into a fortress, while the Lombards, arriving in 569, made it the base of their power, a duchy that at its height in the 700s controlled most of central Italy.

In 890, after Charlemagne, Duke Guido III made an armed play for the Imperial crown, but had to be content with crowning himself King of Italy at Pavia. After Guido and his son Lamberto, the duchy fell into decline, and in the 11th century the popes began to lean on Spoleto, claiming authority through that famous forgery, the 'Donation of Constantine'. Not until 1198, though, was Innocent III successful in capturing the city, and in 1247 it became part of the papal domains once and for all. But not without occasional complications: in 1499 Spoleto was briefly ruled by Lucrezia Borgia, a 19-year-old just married to the second of three husbands by her scheming papal father. By all accounts, Lucrezia ruled well, but was sent off two years later to marry a bigger fish—Alfonso d'Este of Ferrara. Under the popes, it became a favourite resort of the papal nobility, who filled it with fancy palaces and occasionally entertained visiting celebrities: the chronicles record lavish banquets laid on for Queen Christina of Sweden in 1655, and for Maria Casimira, widow of the hero John Sobieski, in 1699.

Spoleto is next heard from three centuries later, thanks to Giancarlo Menotti and the late Thomas Schippers. The **Festival of Two Worlds** takes place for around three weeks between mid June and mid July. Festival information, programmes and tickets can be obtained by writing, phoning or visiting the offices of the Associazione Festival dei Due Mondi, Piazza del Duomo 9, ✆ 0743 45028, 🖷 0743 220321, *www.spoletofestival.net.*

### Getting Around

The Rome–Ancona railway follows the Via Flaminia to Spoleto. There are also some 10 **trains** daily to Perugia (63km/70mins); the station is a bit far from the city centre, but there are regular connecting buses.

Spoleto has its own intercity **bus** company, the Società Spoletina Trasporti (SSIT, ✆ 0743 212211) with connections from Piazza Garibaldi on the western edge of town to Assisi, Terni, Perugia and nearby villages. There are also regular buses to Norcia and Foligno, and one a day to Rome and to Urbino in the Marche.

Long term **parking** in the city centre is next to impossible; there's a convenient car park outside Porta Loreto on the west end of the city, a free one in Via Don Bonilli, by the stadium and Roman theatre, and another just south of the city walls along Viale Cappuccini.

**Bikes** can be hired at Scocchetti Cicli, Via Marconi 82, ✆ 0743 44728.

### Tourist Information

Piazza della Libertà 7, ✆ 0743 220311, 🖷 0743 46241.

**Post office**: Piazza della Libertà 12, ✆ 0743 43752.

### market day

Friday, in Via Cacciatori delle Alpi; also daily farmers' market in Piazza del Mercato.

## Remnants of Roman *Spoletium*

Like Perugia, Spoleto is a city of many ages, all jammed together cheek by jowl in a fascinating collage of time and space. Thanks to the festival, the 20th century gets its say, too: if you arrive in Spoleto by train you'll be greeted by a huge iron sculpture, the *Teodolapio* by Alexander Calder, a relic of the 1962 festival now used to shade a taxi stand. Buses from the station leave you at central **Piazza della Libertà**, which is also the usual approach if you arrive by car. Just across from the tourist office, the open side of the piazza overlooks the **Roman theatre**, built in the 1st century AD. In the 1950s it was restored as a venue for concerts and ballets during the music festivals; most of the theatre's impressive substructure of arches and tunnels has survived, as well as the pretty marble pavement in the *scena*.

In the Middle Ages, the stage building was replaced with the formidable church, charming cloister and Benedictine monastery of **Sant'Agata**. This too has been restored, and the convent now houses Spoleto's **Archaeological Museum** (*theatre and museum open daily 9–7; closed 1 Dec, 1 Jan and 1 May; adm*) with inscriptions and architectural fragments, busts of Julius Caesar and Augustus and other distinguished Romans, and a stone found in what had been a sacred grove dedicated to Jupiter, warning against profaning the place (or chopping wood). The convent refectory has a good cinquecento fresco of the *Last Supper*.

Continue east through Piazza Fontana and turn left, and you'll pass under the travertine **Arch of Drusus**, erected in AD 23 by Tiberius's son (Drusus would have made a good emperor—but he died, and the Roman world got Caligula instead). The arch marked the entrance to the Forum, and on the adjacent modern building you can see the outline of the columns of a temple, as well as its actual foundations underneath. The church of **Sant'Ansano**, built over a Paleochristian church built in turn over a Roman temple, incorporates more ancient fragments, although its original medieval appearance was sacrificed for fashion in the late 18th century. The 11th-century **Crypt of San Isacco**, however, has stayed the same, decorated with rare frescoes in the Byzantine style: the *Beheading of John the Baptist, Christ in Glory*, the *Last Supper*, and the *Life of St Isaac the Hermit*, a 5th-century Syrian monk who took refuge near Spoleto. The crypt's columns are Roman, and the capitals Lombard. Via Arco di Druso empties into the Roman forum, now the **Piazza del Mercato**, where the glistening tomatoes and aubergines compete for your attention with the 18th-century **Fonte di Piazza**, a provincial version of Rome's Trevi Fountain, which incorporates Carlo Maderno's monument to Urban VII of 1626.

## Pinacoteca Comunale and the Roman House

From the fountain, walk north past some more questionable modern sculpture into the narrow Piazza del Municipio. Enter the town hall, the **Palazzo Comunale**, report to the Spoleto police in an office on the right, and they'll sell you a ticket for the **Pinacoteca** on the first floor (*open daily exc Mon 10–1 and 3–6; adm*). The pictures have been hung in the same place since 1910: among the highlights are works by Spoleto-born Lo Spagna, including his finest, the Raphaelesque *Madonna, Child and Saints* (1512) painted for the Rocca Albornoz. Another of his commissions, an allegory of *Charity, Mercy and Justice*, was painted for Julius II even though they were hardly that pope's strong points; in 1824 the work was adjusted to fit a bust of another pope, Leo XII, a Spoleto native whose main concern was to eliminate every single Napoleonic reform in the Papal States. There are portraits of the Teutonic dukes of long ago and coins from the days of the Lombard duchy, as well as a beautiful crucifix reliquary and painting of Christ in a a lavish filigree frame by the Maestro di Sant'Alò, who worked in Spoleto at the end of the 1200s. There's a bejewelled Byzantine-style icon from the 13th century, and frescoes on the *Lives of SS Peter and Paul*. Readers of that classic conspiracy book, *Holy Blood, Holy Grail*, may want to take a close look at the best painting, a *Magdalene*, by Guercino. Plans are in (slow) motion to move this museum into the Rocca Albornoz (*see* below) when restorations are completed.

The same ticket will get you into the 1st-century BC **Casa Romana**, around the corner on Via di Visiale, believed, perhaps fancifully, to have been the address of Emperor Vespasian's mother, Vespasia Polla. The atrium and well head, bedrooms and bath survive along with some beautiful mosaic floors.

## Piazza Campello, the Rocca and the Ponte delle Torri

From Piazza del Municipio, Via Saffi climbs up to panoramic **Piazza Campello**, where you'll find another good fountain, the 17th-century **Mascherone**, with a huge, grotesque face spitting out the water from the Roman and medieval aqueduct. The monument on the square is from 1910, built to honour all the Spoletines who fought to free their city from the Papal States.

The symbol of the oppression looms just above: the **Rocca Albornoz** (*open 15 Mar–31 May, Mon–Fri 10–12 and 3–7, Sat and Sun 10am–7pm; June–Sept, Mon–Fri 11am–8pm; Sat and Sun 10am–9pm; Oct, Mon–Fri 10–12 and 3–6, Sat and Sun 10am–7pm; Nov–Dec, Mon–Fri 2.30–5, Sat and Sun 11am–5pm; Jan–14 Mar, Mon–Fri 2.30–5, Sat and Sun 10–5; adm*), the impressive, six-towered citadel by Gattapone from Gubbio, commissioned in 1359 by that indefatigable papal enforcer Cardinal Albornoz, who made this his personal headquarters. Most of its stone is at least third-hand, first used in the Roman amphitheatre, then cannibalized by the Goth Totila for his fortress, then dragged up here. When Spoleto was firmly in the papal pocket, the Rocca became a popular country resort for the popes, frequented in particular by Julius II, accompanied on occasion by Michelangelo, who loved the peace of the surrounding hills. Until recently the Rocca served as a prison (one of the last inmates was Mohammed Ali Agca, the would-be assassin of Pope John Paul II); now that its long restoration is nearing completion, there are plans to install a museum dedicated to the Duchy of Spoleto, a laboratory for the restoration of books and art, an exhibition and conference area and an open-air theatre. Ruins of a 7th-century church of **Sant'Elia** have been found on the hill, which will be a public park; there are beautiful views of Spoleto and the valley below.

The pedestrian-only **Via del Ponte** from Piazza Campello leads down to one of the greatest engineering works of the 1300s, the spectacular 755ft **Ponte delle Torri**, a bridge and aqueduct of ten towering arches built by Gattapone for Cardinal Albornoz, to guarantee the water supply to the Rocca. It dizzily spans the 260ft-deep ravine of the Tessino river far far below, and was one of the unmissable sights for Grand Tourists, all of whom thought it was Roman; Turner painted a fine picture of it. The bridge does stand on a Roman foundation; you can walk across it to the towers that gave it its name, to Monteluco's San Pietro (*see* p.161). From here Via del Ponte circles around under the Rocca back to Piazza Campello.

## Sant'Eufemia and the Museo Diocesano

Behind the Palazzo Comunale (*see* above), on Via Saffi, an archway leads into the small courtyard of the archbishop's palace, facing one of the finest Umbrian Romanesque churches. **Sant'Eufemia** (*open winter 8–12.30 and 2.30–6; till 8 in summer*), completed about 1140. It has a plain façade but its interior is remarkable, in luminescent white stone. Fragments of Roman buildings are built into the walls and columns in surprising ways, and it has an anachronistic *matroneum*, the Byzantine-style second-floor gallery where women were segregated during Mass—although this was a common practice in Rome and Ravenna, it's the only *matroneum* in Umbria. The altar, brought here from Spoleto's first cathedral, is a good piece of Cosmatesque work, with symbols of the four Evangelists surrounding the Paschal lamb.

Part of Sant'Eufemia's convent, built over an important and still partly visible 1st-century Roman structure, became the Palazzo Arcivescovile, now home of the **Museo Diocesano** (*closed for restoration but due to open Easter 2000*). This has works garnered from the diocese, with an array of good early painted *Crucifixes* and trecento Madonnas, including a beautiful one by the First Master of Santa Chiara di Montefalco. Highlights among the later works are an *Adoration of the Child* by Domenico Beccafumi of Siena, the *Madonna delle Neve* by Neri di Bicci, and a *Madonna and Child with SS Montano and Bartolomeo* by Filippino Lippi. One room contains an excellent collection of medieval Umbrian sculpture, and there's a fascinating assortment of popular ex-votos from the 16th to 19th centuries.

## Via dell'Arringo

Via dell'Arringo, a grand, shallow stairway behind Sant'Eufemia, opens into the Piazza del Duomo. Here in early medieval times the Spoletani gathered to make communal decisions by acclamation, after hearing speeches (*harangue* comes from *arringo*). It must have been this naturally theatrical ensemble that sold Menotti on Spoleto, with its naturally tiered seating over the piazza, and the lovely cathedral façade and the Umbrian hills for a backdrop. Among the fine buildings along the sides, there's the **Teatro Caio Melisso**, an exquisite little late 19th-century theatre, named after the Spoleto-born dramatist and librarian of the Emperior Augustus, the pink and white striped **Casa dell'Opera del Duomo** (1419), and an octagonal church, **Santa Maria della Manna d'Oro**, built after 1527, as a votive after the Sack of Rome, with four paintings by Sebastiano Conca. On the right, note the Roman sarcophagus used as a fountain, the memorial to American conductor Thomas Schippers, who loved the view and festival so much that he asked to be buried here. Nearby is the 16th-century **Palazzo Rácani**, designed by Giulio Romano—with faded graffito decoration, in dire need of restoration.

## The Duomo

*Open daily Nov–Feb, 7.30–12.30 and 3–5; Mar–Oct, 7.30–12.30 and 3–6.*

The magnificent Duomo was rebuilt after Emperor Frederick Barbarossa, the most powerful of papal enemies, razed its predecessor to the ground in 1155; it was consecrated by the most powerful of medieval popes, Innocent III, in 1198. It has several unusual features. A graceful Renaissance portico, added in 1491, incorporates two pulpits; four rose windows and four circular emblems of the Evangelists adorn its façade like slightly but charmingly mismatched buttons, surrounding a gold-ground Byzantine-style mosaic of *Christ Enthroned with Mary and John the Baptist* (1207), signed by Solsternus. The lower middle *rosone* is an exceptional example of the Cosmatesque work imported from Rome—stone or enamel chips arranged in sinuous, intricate patterns—that is so common in this part of Umbria. The huge campanile is built out of Roman odds and ends.

The earthquake damaged the cathedral but it has remained open during repair work. The Latin cross **interior** was unfortunately redone in the 1630s, a misguided gift to the city by the Barberini family of Rome: Maffeo Barberini had been Cardinal of Spoleto before he was elected Urban VIII in 1623, and his nephew, another Cardinal of Spoleto, funded the works and commemorated his uncle with the bronze bust by Bernini located just inside the central door. Several treasures survived the interior re-designers, including the fine Cosmati pavement in the central nave. Pinturicchio, not on one of his better days, painted the frescoes of the *Madonna and Saints* in the first chapel on the right, but not without his usual amusing detail, such as St Jerome's lion frisking about the landscape. His pupil Jacopo Siculo painted the frescoes in the next chapel. In the right transept, a Baroque chapel by Giambattista Mola holds the 12th-century *Santissima Icone*, a highly venerated icon from Constantinople donated as a peace offering to Spoleto by the church-burning Frederick Barbarossa. The chapel has two paintings by the Cavalier d'Arpino, who painted the dome of St Peter's.

In the apse are the exquisite, richly coloured **frescoes of the *Life of the Virgin*** (1467–69) by Fra Filippo Lippi of Florence, a masterpiece that has recently been beautifully restored. Not only did Lippi paint larger-than-life figures, but he expertly fitted them into the large space, through a canny use of perspective and architectural features, including columns and friezes from Spoleto itself. The splendid *Coronation of the Virgin*, in the upper part of the apse, is the best preserved fresco of the cycle, crowded with the angel musicians and female figures that Lippi loved to paint, here in the guise of Sibyls and women from the Old Testament. Lippi portrayed himself (in a white habit with a black hat), his son Filippino (the young angel) and his assistants among the mourners in the central scene of the Virgin's death. The fun-loving monk from Florence (he ran off with a nun, but was permitted to leave his order and marry her) died in Spoleto while working on the project, and the *Nativity* scene was finished by his chief helpers, Fra Diamanti and the Umbrian painter Pier Matteo d'Amelia. When Lippi's great patron Lorenzo de' Medici asked that the artist's body be returned to Florence, the Spoletini refused, claiming they had no notable dead while Florence had so many. Lorenzo had to be content with commissioning a handsome Florentine tomb for him, now in the right transept.

In the left aisle, the original sacristy was converted into a chapel of reliquaries in the 1560, with lavish intarsia cupboards, mostly made by local craftsmen, although the two with architectural perspectives are by the great Fra Giovanni da Verona; the most important relic is a very rare letter in the hand of St Francis to Fra Leone. Hanging in the first altar on the left is a large and colourful *Crucifix,* dated 1187 and signed by Alberto Sotius, the first Umbrian artist whose name has come down to us.

## Lower Spoleto

Some of the city's contemporary art has found a home in the Palazzo Collicola on Via Collicola, now the **Galleria d'Arte Moderna e Contemporanea** (*closed April–Sept 2000 while it relocates from another palazzo in town*). Founded in 1953, the collection has works by Italy's top 20th-century masters (Pomodoro, Burri, Guttoso, Accardi) and showcases Spoleto's own Leoncillo Leonardi (1915–68), who evolved a distinctive and colourful style of art executed in highly textured glazed terracotta. The custodian of the gallery keeps the key for **Santi Giovanni e Paolo**, a little church by Via Filitteria, consecrated in 1178. It has excellent frescoes; on the left wall, note the scene, attributed to Alberto Sotio, of the *Martrydom of Thomas à Becket,* canonized only five years previously (1170).

From here Via Tobagi will take you to Spoleto's fanciest Baroque church, **San Filippo Neri**, with an ornate façade and lofty dome, designed by a local architect named Loreto Scelli who studied in Rome. Although closed since the last earthquake, it has a fine Baroque bust of St Philip Neri by the Bolognese sculptor Alessandro Algardi and paintings by Sebastiano Conca and Gaetano Lapis da Cagli.

Via Filitteria leads into Via Sant'Andrea, site of another grand theatre, the **Teatro Nuovo**, headquarters of the Two Worlds festival and the even older September Festival of Experimental Opera. Down the steps from here, the colourful pink and white striped preaching church of **San Domenico** was built in the 13th century; the interior has been restored to its original medieval appearance, and has a colourful *Crucifix* hanging in the centre of the nave. The walls are decorated with interesting if fragmentary 13th–15th-century frescoes: the first chapel has an especially good *Triumph of St Thomas Aquinas* from the early 1400s, representing the triumph of Aquinas' scholastic philosphy; a little chapel in the right transept has a pretty *Life of Mary Magdalene* and there's a beautiful *Madonna and Child* behind the high altar, both from the early 15th century. The *Crucifix* over the altar is 14th-century. Near here is a fine fresco of the *Pietà*, and a painting of *St Peter Martyr*, the overly efficient Dominican inquistor who was axed in the head for his trouble.

From San Domenico, walk down Via Leone to the tall-towered 13th-century **Porta Fuga** ('Put-to-flight-gate'—as the tablet attests, it happened to Hannibal here, in 217 BC) and then along Via Saccocchio Cecili, where you can take in an excellent stretch of Spoleto's **walls**, with their *millefeuille* layers of history. The Umbrii built the 6th-century BC cyclopean base of huge polygonal blocks, which were heightened by the Romans and all the other occupants of Spoleto up to the 15th century. The street ends in Piazza Cairoli; from here Via dell'Anfiteatro descends past the ruined 2nd-century AD **Roman amphitheatre**, turned into a fortress by Totila and still part of a military barracks (the bored soldiers can sometimes be persuaded to show visitors around it).

Further down, on Piazza Garibaldi there's the fine 12th-century church of **San Gregorio Maggiore**; through the gate are the ruins of the Roman **Ponte Sanguinario** ('bloody bridge'), supposedly named after the Christians martyred in the amphitheatre, although in reality it seems to be a corruption of the Latin name of a nearby gate, the Sandapilarius. It was built in the 1st century BC to carry the new route of the Via Flaminia over the river, and was rediscovered in 1817.

## Outside Spoleto: San Ponziano and San Salvatore

From the bridge and Piazza Vittoria, it's a short drive or an unpleasant 15-minute walk on the road under the *superstrada* to the cemetery, passing by way of 12th-century **San Ponziano** (*open 9–12 and 3–6*). Ponziano is Spoleto's patron, martyred here in 169. The façade of his church, once faced with marble, is divided horizontally by a cornice, and has a pretty Cosmatesque door and a round window surrounded with symbols of the Evangelists. The interior was redone by Giuseppe Valadier in 1788, but has preserved the original crypt. This is one of the most fascinating in a region full of fascinating crypts: this one has an upside Roman column, two turning posts (*metae*) from a Roman circus, three ancient sarcophagi and some pretty fresco fragments. In the corridor, embedded like fossils in the wall, are huge Corinthian columns.

Even more Roman material went into building the charming **San Salvatore**, just down from San Ponziano by the cemetery. Spoleto's oldest church, built in the 4th century, San Salvatore preserves much of its original lines and simplicity (the façade and the apse) despite subsequent rebuildings and loss of its marble facing; the three doors still have fine marble architraves and three curious old windows. The elegant, fluted Corinthian columns in the interior originally supported a Roman temple; the fresco of the jewelled cross in the apse is from the 8th or 9th century.

## Monteluco

Just east of town, beautiful, forested Monteluco is Spoleto's holy mountain. The name is derived from *lucus* (sacred wood), and in Roman times it was forbidden to chop down the trees. In the 5th century, Isaac the Hermit from Antioch founded the first cenobitic community here; the Benedictines and the Franciscans followed, the latter in the footsteps of their founder.

You can get to Monteluco by car, by bus from Piazza della Libertà, or by foot over the Ponte delle Torri (*see* p.157). Near the bottom of the mountains stands the great Romanesque church of **San Pietro**, with a magnificent romp of a façade dating from the 12th century, the last hurrah of the Lombard Dukes of Spoleto (if you can, come in the late afternoon when the light is at its best). If you've ever visited the medieval cathedrals in northern Italy you'll recognize the vigorous animals, real and imaginary, that the Lombards delighted in portraying: here is a fox playing dead to capture some too-curious chickens, battles with lions, oxen, peacocks, eagles, a wolf in monk's clothing, animals devouring one another and the occasional armoured knight; devils contest souls, and St Michael slays his dragon. On the top level are two bulls, statues of St Peter and St Andrew and reliefs of Christ washing St Peter's feet and the Christ calling SS Peter and Andrew. An elaborate frieze of vines and plants around the doors link various allegorical scenes; on the left, the pious could compare the various post-mortem destinies of the righteous and the sinful. The interior was Baroqued in 1699.

A steep, hairpinning road leads up through beautiful ilex forests to reach the lonely 12th-century church of **San Giuliano**, with a façade incorporating some 6th-century elements of its predecessor (the restaurant next door has the key). In the 7th century, anchorites and hermits, refugees from the wars in the Holy Land, settled here and set up early monasteries; St Francis, who tried to emulate them, came to meditate here, and in 1218 founded the tiny monastery of **San Francesco** near the summit of the mountain, a serene spot overlooking the surrounding countryside. Monteluco now has more summer villas and hotels than hermitages, but it's still a cool and tranquil place to spend an afternoon, and a good place to look for accommodation when Spoleto is jammed solid.

## San Paolo Intervineas

A kilometre or so southwest of Spoleto, San Paolo Intervineas is one last church of interest (take Via San Paolo off Via Martiri della Resistenza). Founded in Paleochristian times and mentioned in the 6th century by St Gregory the Great, it was rebuilt in the 10th century and again in 1234, when it was consecrated by Gregory IX as a church for a convent of Clarisse. It has a pretty façade with a rose window and frescoed lunette over the door; the interior contains a good series of frescoes from the period, including an account of the *Creation*, and an old altar. At the time of writing, it is closed for restoration after earthquake damage.

During the Festival of the Two Worlds accommodation is tight in Spoleto and in the surrounding area from Foligno to Terni, so reserve months in advance. The tourist office in Spoleto has a list of private rooms to rent, but again, don't count on finding one on the spot: it's essential to book ahead.

The tourist office can also provide a list of the *agriturismo* farmhouse accommodation in the area.

### expensive

Spoleto itself has several fine hotels, of which the most spectacular is the bijou ★★★★**Gattapone**, Via del Ponte 6, ✆ 0743 223447, ✉ 0743 223448, located in a stone house, clinging to the slope near the Rocca and the Ponte delle Torri, with fabulous views; even during the festival rush it remains serene. Its eight rooms are spacious and finely furnished. Just outside the historic centre near the Piazza della Libertà, the ★★★★**Albornoz Palace**, Viale Matteotti, ✆ 0743 221221, ✉ 0743 221600, *info@albornozpalace.com*, is refined and stylish and has a pool. Nearby, ★★★★**Dei Duchi**, Viale Matteotti 4, ✆ 0743 44541, ✉ 0743 44543, an attractive contemporary hotel, is popular among visiting artists and performers. The beautiful and central 16th-century **Palazzo Dragoni**, Via del Duomo 13, ✆ 0743 222220, ✉ 0743 222225, has kept much of its original atmosphere during its renovation into a *residenza d'epoca*. Another recently opened hotel in the historic centre, ★★★★**San Luca**, Via Inaterna delle Mura 21, ✆ 0743 223399, ✉ 0743 223800, offers a sophisticated 19th-century ambience and a chance for self-indulgence, if you book a room equipped with a hydromassage.

### moderate

★★★**Charleston**, Piazza Collicola 10, ✆ 0743 220052, ✉ 0743 222010, is in a pretty 17th-century palazzo, with 18 comfortably furnished rooms in the *centro storico*. ★★★**Clarici**, Piazza della Vittoria 32, ✆ 0743 223311, ✉ 0743 222010, is more modern, in the lower part of town, but still decorated with taste and style. ★★★**Nuovo Clitunno**, Piazza Sordini 6, ✆ 0743 223340, ✉ 0743 222663, is a good, fairly central hotel.

There are two good choices up at Monteluco: ★★★**Paradiso**, ✆ 0743 223427, ✉ 0743 223082, with a garden, great views and peace and quiet. Near the top of Monteluco, ★★★**Michelanglo**, ✆ 0743 47890, ✉ 0743 40289 has large rooms and very friendly staff. *Open April–Oct.*

### inexpensive

Still in Monteluco, ★★**Ferretti**, ✆ 0743 49849, ✉ 0743 222344, is a *pensione* with plenty of charm; some rooms have balconies looking out on to the pretty tree-shaded piazza (*rooms with en suite baths may be moderate*). In Spoleto itself, ★★**Dell'Angelo**, Via Arco di Druso 25, ✆/✉ 0743 222385, offers seven good double rooms near the centre of the action. **La Macchia**, Loc. Licina 11, ✆/✉ 0743 49059, just north of the town centre off the Via Flaminia, is a quiet hotel offering good value for money. The style is modern, but the furniture in the 12 bedrooms is rustic and made by local craftsmen. The restaurant specializes in the local *cucina spoletana*, and there is a nice garden. Also try **★★Due Porte**, Piazza della Vittoria 5, ✆/✆ 0743 223666, or **★★Il Panciolle**, Via Duomo 4, ✆ 0743 45677, with a good restaurant (*moderate*) where meat is grilled over an open fire. *Closed Wed.*

About 12km from Spoleto in Strettura, on the scenic SS3 to Terni, the **Pecoraro**, ✆ 0743 229697, is a very pretty and above all welcoming *agriturismo*, where guests are treated like one of the family by owners Sandro and Illy Montefalchesi. There is also a small outdoor pool, a luxury in these parts. Very good home cooking and wickedly strong homemade *grappas* make this a memorable place to stay or eat (*rooms inexpensive, meals moderate*).

## Eating Out

Truffle in Italian means **Tartufo**, Piazza Garibaldi 24, ✆ 0743 40236 (*expensive*) and here the black diamonds of the Valnerina appear in various forms of pasta and eggs; other dishes include grilled lamb, kid and veal. Prices depend on whether or not you indulge. *Closed Sun evening and Mon.* A 12th-century Franciscan convent houses the romantic dining rooms of **Apollinare**, Via S. Agata 14, ✆ 0743 223256 (*expensive–moderate*), although the former occupants wouldn't recognize the elaborate concoctions that come out of the kitchen; a change of pace, although you may want to stick to the least elaborate choices on the big menu. *Closed Tues; they also have a few rooms.*

A favourite festival rendezvous near Piazza della Libertà, **Pentagramma**, Via Martani 4, ✆ 0743 223141 (*moderate*) is a warm and welcoming place in a former stable, owned by the daughter of Arturo Toscanini, serving perfectly prepared local dishes: *garbanzo* soup, *stringozzi di Spoleto* (flat homemade pasta, with olive oil, garlic, tomato and basil), truffles, lamb and trout. *Closed Mon and in part of July and Aug.* Another old Spoleto favourite, **Sabatini**, Corso Mazzini 54, ✆ 0743 221831 (*moderate*) has good traditional Umbrian fare, served indoors and out. *Closed Mon.*

In the heart of Spoleto, the **Trattoria del Festival**, Via Brignone 8, ✆ 0743 220993 (*moderate*) has a pretty dining room, with arched ceilings and a blazing fireplace in winter. As well as truffle dishes of every kind, the chef has a winning way with desserts and gives regulars membership cards which guarantee them a 10 per cent discount off the already very reasonable prices. *Closed Fri.* Tucked off Via Porta Fuga, **Trattoria Pecchiarda**, Vicolo San Giovanni, ✆ 0743 221 009 (*moderate– inexpensive*) serves delicous dishes prepared with olive oil from the owner's grove, served with the owner's own white or red Colli Spoletini wine. *Closed Thurs except in summer.* Nearby in Via Porta Fuga, **Il Fratello d'Annibale** has decent food and piano keys tickled by Gianni on Friday and Saturday night. Another central choice is **Sportellino**, Via Cerquiglia 4, ✆ 0743 45230 (*moderate*), with a simple, homely atmosphere; try the generous mixed *antipasti*, gnocchi with truffles, grilled meats or ossobuco with peas. *Closed Thurs.*

### Outside Spoleto

Some 10km south on the Via Flaminia, **Il Capanno**, Loc. Torrecola 6, ✆ 0743 54119 (*moderate*) is situated on the top of a hill covered in oak trees. The menu is Umbrian, with some surprises such as ravioli flavoured with lemon, mint and courgettes. Meat is big here: wild boar, venison, and pork—all, of course, prepared with truffles. *Closed Mon*. Also on the SS3 to Terni, **Madrigale**, ✆ 0743 54144 (*expensive–moderate*) offers a gourmet *menu degustazione* of Umbrian specialities; just sit down and a wonderful succession of pasta and meat courses will arrive at your table. *Closed Tues*. Along the same road, in Strettura, the **Palazzo del Papa** (*inexpensive*) is a mere trattoria in spite of its name, but serves some of the best home cooking in the region.

# The Tiber Valley: Todi, Orvieto, Amelia

| | |
|---|---|
| Todi | 166 |
| Around Todi | 175 |
| Orvieto | 176 |
| Hills, Lakes and Gardens Around Orvieto | 190 |
| Amelia | 194 |
| Around Amelia | 196 |

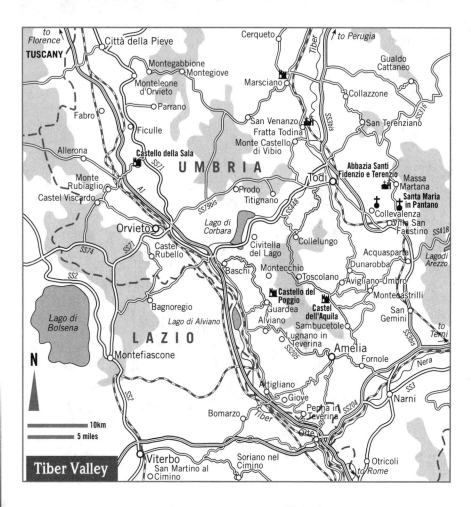

Tiber Valley

South of Perugia, Old Father Tiber flows below the proud medieval eagle's eyrie of Todi, then swells to form the Lago di Corbara and takes a sharp left under lofty hills to form the border with Lazio. This corner of Umbria closest to Rome has a character all its own, much of it concentrated in Orvieto, where mementos of Etruscans rub elbows with those of medieval popes and the papal nobility, under the shadow of one of Italy's great cathedrals. Amelia, wrapped in walls built by the ancient Umbrii, is the third important hill town in the area, charming but often overlooked. In between the three big hill towns are vineyards and steep wooded ridges, a score of smaller villages and lovely churches, and a handful of unexpected oddities, from a fossil forest of sequoias at Dunarobba to a tiny jewel box theatre at Monte Castello di Vibio to the bizarre gardens of La Scarzuola at Montegiove.

Todi (pop. 17,200) may be small, but it has everything it needs to rate as a self-respecting central Italian hill town. There's the hill, of course, in a gorgeous setting, a cathedral upstaged by exceptional medieval public buildings, one great Renaissance monument, a long and tortuous history, a saint (uncanonized, this time), and a proud *comune* escutcheon, a fierce eagle over the inevitable device '*SPQT*'. In the past few years, it has consistently been voted the world's most livable-in town by the University of Kentucky, an accolade which has brought American tycoons rushing to buy up its villas and castles and convert them into holiday retreats. But even before they came, Todi was a sophisticated little place, famous for its carpentry and woodworking. In April it hosts one of Italy's major antique fairs, the Rassegna Antiquaria d'Italia, and in Aug and Sept is a *Mostra Nazionale dell'Artigianato*, a national crafts fair. Since 1986, the Tudertini have also added the latest fashionable ingredient: a festival, which brings the town opera, ballet and stage companies in late Aug–early Sept.

## History

It was the eagle that showed the ancient Umbrii where to build the city they called the 'Border' or *Tuter*, high atop modern Todi, on what is now the Rocca. The border was an uncomfortable one with the Etruscans, who founded a settlement lower down around Piazza del Popolo, and it didn't last; one day the Etruscans became kings of the whole hill when they surprised, slaughtered and enslaved their Umbrian neighbours. As *Colonia Julia Fida Tuder*, appropriately dedicated to the war god Mars, the town prospered through Roman times, and its nearly impregnable site kept the barbarians out remarkably well; there's no evidence that Todi was ever part of the Lombard duchy of Spoleto, and indeed it may have maintained its independence all along.

By the 1200s Todi had accumulated a little empire, including Terni and Amelia, and its soldiers were kept in trim by constant dust-ups with their peers in Spoleto, Narni and Orvieto. In 1227, their *podestà* was the notorious Mosca dei Lamberti, who had been exiled from Florence after the vendetta killing of Buondelmonte dei Buondelmonti (*see* pp.51–3); Dante would consign him to the Eighth Circle of Hell. But Todi's special pride was its good deeds. In 1249, the *comune* founded the Ospedale della Carità, where the poor were treated for free—even Florence wouldn't have the like until 1316—and it produced one of the greatest Italian poets of the Middle Ages in Fra Jacopone (*see* pp.170–73). By the end of the century both the government and the political effectiveness of the free *comune* were failing. The Atti family established themselves as *signori* in the early 1300s, but were pushed out by visiting bosses, the Malatesta of Rimini and Francesco Sforza of Milan among others, until the pope gobbled up the town definitively for the Papal States in the 1460s.

### Getting Around

Todi is linked by **bus** with Terni (33km/45mins), Perugia (41km/1hr), and Rome (130km/2½hrs), and by the FCU's little **trains** to Perugia and Terni. Trains and coaches (to Perugia, Terni, Rome and Orvieto) come and go from down below, at Ponte Rio, © 894 2092, linked to the centre by city bus. Unfortunately there's only one bus a day between Todi and Orvieto, a route that takes in the lovely scenery over the Tiber valley.

## Tourist Information

Piazza Umberto I 6, ✆ 075 894 3395, 🖷 075 894 2406. There's also a little office in Piazza del Popolo, ✆ 075 894 2526.

## Piazza del Popolo

Todi's streets converge on its magnificent 13th–15th-century Piazza del Popolo, the centre of civic life since the Etruscans and Romans. In the 15th century, as Todi's existence as an independent city state came to an end, the square was preserved in aspic, leaving a medieval pageant in grey stone. The sternest building, the **Palazzo dei Priori** (1293–1337), has square battlements with a chunky tower, while the **Palazzo del Popolo** (1213), with the swallow-tail crenellations, and its adjacent **Palazzo del Capitano** (1290) are all grace by comparison; these two, connected by a grand Gothic stairway, make up one of the most remarkable medieval town halls in Italy. These outer stairs, so common in Umbria's *comunale* buildings, emphasized how easy it was for the citizenry to have access to their local government, who invariably held their meetings on the first floor.

They now provide access to Todi's attic, the **Museo Civico Pinacoteca** (*open 10.30–1 and 2–4.30, till 6 in the summer, closed Mon; adm; beware that the stairs can be slippery when wet*). Located on the fourth floor of the Palazzo del Popolo, this is full of fond civic memories: retired eagles, archaeological bits and bobs, 16th-century scenes of charity by local painter Pietro Paolo Sensini, among portraits of saints and worthies connected to the city, a model of the Tempio della Consolazione from *c.* 1570, a fine *Coronation of the Virgin* by Lo Spagna, and paintings by a 16th-century so-so painter named Ferraù da Faenza, who spent a lot of time in town. Todi is especially proud of a saddle made in town for the ailing and pregnant Anita Garibaldi.

To the right of Palazzo del Capitano, a cypress was planted in 1849 in honour of Garibaldi's visit—it was a fleeting one, as the republic of Rome had just fallen to the French allies of the pope and they were in hot pursuit of the hero, his wife, and a handful of loyal garibaldini. This is now **Piazza Garibaldi**, and has views over much of central Umbria.

On the far side of the Piazza del Popolo, the squarish **Duomo** is enthroned atop another distinguished flight of steps. Begun in the 12th century and finished 200 years later, it has a handsome flat screen façade, fine rose window and delicately decorated portal, while the interior is embellished with good capitals, a Gothic arcade by a fourth aisle, and a 14th-century altarpiece; parishioners who turned round to gossip during Mass were confronted by a not-too-terrifying vision of the *Last Judgement* by Ferraù da Faenza, a decaffeinated reworking of Michelangelo's in the Sistine Chapel. The large crypt has been turned into a lapidary museum (*adm*), containing bells, a copy of Todi's patron deity *Mars*, now in the Vatican, and fragments of statue groups by the school of Giovanni Pisano.

To the left of the Duomo stands the 16th-century **bishop's palace** and the **Palazzo Rolli**, attributed to the younger Antonio da Sangallo; it was once the home of Paolo Rolli (d. 1765), who translated Milton into Italian.

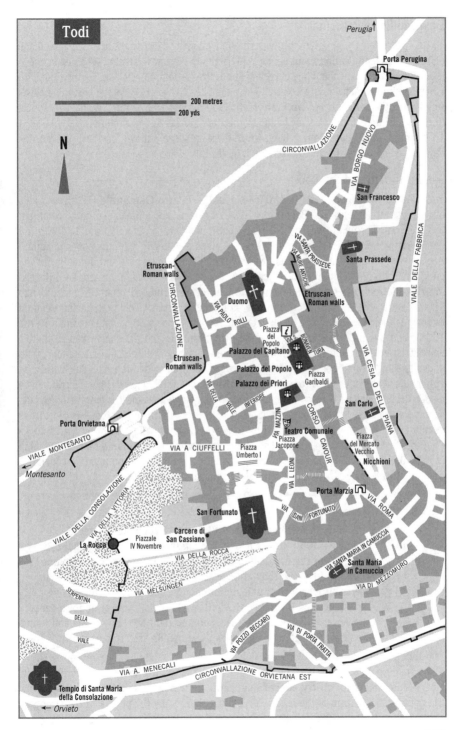

169

## Down to Porta Perugina

To the right of the Duomo, the road twists around, allowing a view of its beautiful apse. Some of Todi's **Etruscan-Roman walls** survive near here, off Via Mure Antiche. Via Santa Prassede leads down to the pink and white church of **Santa Prassede**, from the 14th century, but with a Baroque interior. The early medieval town ended here; beyond, Via Borgo Nuovo descends steeply past the monastery of **San Francesco**, also from the 14th century, with an allegorical fresco on *Salvation* from the same period by the altar. Further down, a round tower marks the 13th-century **Porta Perugina**, through which there are views out over the lovely countryside around Todi. The only hitch is walking back up the hill.

## San Fortunato and the Rocca

From Piazza del Popolo, Via Mazzini leads past the **Teatro Comunale** (1872) to Todi's other great monument, **San Fortunato** (1292). Located atop a broad stair in a prominent position, San Fortunato was one of many churches built during the late 13th-century Franciscan spending spree, when the Order received permission from the popes to administer as well as 'use' the substantial property it had received as gifts and donations of the pious. In Todi they built on a grand scale, but the façade remains unfinished; according to scurrilous legend, when the Orvietani heard that the Tuderini had commissioned Lorenzo Maitani to decorate it, they had the sculptor murdered to prevent Todi from having a church as good as their cathedral. The lovely late Gothic central portal was completed only in the 1400s, and has little figures hidden among the acanthus and decorative bands: there's St Francis receiving the stigmata and the damned in hell with a little salamander, who doesn't seem to mind because salamanders were believed to be fireproof. The statues on either side of the door are of the *Annunciation*; the beautiful angel has been attributed to Jacopo della Quercia. The airy, luminous and remarkably wide Gothic interior is one of the best in central Italy, divided into three naves of equal height. Large fragments of frescoes decorate many of the chapels, including a *Madonna and Child* (1432) by Masolino da Panicale, his only work in Umbria. The fine wooden choir is by Antonio Maffei of Gubbio (1590). But for the Tuderini the focal point is the tomb of the poet and mystic Jacopone da Todi in the crypt, the subject of much local if unofficial devotion.

## God's Fool

 Todi in its golden age was the home of Jacopo dei Benedetti (1228–1306), the greatest of the *laudesi*, or medieval Franciscan poets. For the first half of his life, however, Jacopone was anything but saintly: a worldly, money-grubbing notary, his one good point was his love for his wife, whom he married in 1267. But the next year she died in a freak accident, when a platform set up for a dance collapsed. Mad with grief, Jacopone brought her body home and found that, under all the finery he had made her wear, she had dressed in a hair shirt.

The shock of her death and discovery of her secret piety made him repent—slowly. The wrestling match with his soul lasted for ten years, which he amply documented in a new-found talent for poetry. Rather than Latin, he wrote in Todi's dialect, employing the popular ballad form of the *laude*, the hymns chanted by the people in the streets, modelled on St Francis' great *Canticle of All Things Created*. Jacopone's previous career taught him the virtues of brevity and getting straight to the point—his staccato verse stands in marked contrast to the younger Dante's courtly measured Italian. Jacopone was the first to make the *laude* an art form, the perfect vehicle for communicating to the uneducated his message, of love for Christ, warnings of death, of the conflicts in his own soul, of the foibles of the worldly great and proud—he was a satirist almost by nature. His language is vivid and unconventional: in coming to terms with his unworthiness, for instance, he begs for sickness and even death, with his grave in the belly of a wolf, so his relics would be nothing but excrement.

His well bred family in Todi disowned him. As a wandering penitent, a *bizocone*, he became 'Big Jim' the town eccentric, liable to do anything. He followed the medieval countercultural example of Francis himself in acting out his inner life, becoming 'God's fool': when his brother asked him not to show up at his wedding reception and ruin it with his usual follies, Jacopone crashed the party in the middle of the dance, naked and covered all over with honey and brightly coloured feathers.

In 1278, Jacopone joined the Franciscans at San Fortunato, although at first they were reluctant to accept him, convinced that he was mad. Jacopone had reservations about Todi's friars as well; although the first Franciscan convent, founded in 1220, had been a very humble place outside the walls, in 1254 they had traded houses with the wealthy Vallombrosians of San Fortunato in the centre to town, and were constantly in the courts arguing over the considerable lands and possessions they had amassed in Todi.

Franciscans by then had become learned scholars and priests, but Jacopone followed Francis's path and remained a friar, one who constantly upset his fellow brothers. To combat his gluttonous urges, for instance, he hung up a piece of meat in his cell, and let it rot until the whole convent stank; his peers threw him in the latrine for revenge, which he claimed to enjoy. This was the period of his most famous and unique poem, *Donna del Paradiso*, a dramatic dialogue on the grief of Mary at the Crucifixion; it quickly spread throughout Italy and developed into Passion plays, the first theatrical representations in Italy since Roman times (although Jacopone is often credited with the *Stabat Mater*, which has a similar theme and appeared at the same time, its Latin elegance shows that it is by another hand).

As a Franciscan, Jacopone soon found his niche with the Spirituals, the most unworldly branch of the order, which sought to keep to the letter of Francis's ideals of poverty. This involved Jacopone in the big events of the day, when the pro-Spiritual 'angel pope', Celestine V, was in 1294 compelled to resign by the irascible lawyer Cardinal Benedetto Gaetani, whose subsequent election as Boniface VIII was regarded by many as illegitimate. Boniface abrogated all of Celestine's acts, imprisoned the old man until he died (he was canonized in 1313) and forced the Spirituals back into the Franciscan fold. He then got down to the serious business of enriching his family, embezzling Church funds and spending the equivalent of two years' worth of the Curia's income, a tremendous sum, to buy up land around Rome.

Threatened by his acquisitiveness, the great Roman family of the Colonna became his sworn enemy, and Jacopone, who knew the pope well (he had lived in Todi for a long time), joined in the fray, signing a Colonna statement that declared that Boniface was not the true pope. Holed up in Palestrina with the Colonna, Jacopone let the pope have it in his vitriolic *Lauda LVIII*, listing his vainglorious and greedy acts, accusing him of being a desperado and heretic. When the pope's forces proved to be too strong for the Colonna in 1298, Jacopone was seized, excommunicated and tossed in prison, where he would remain in solitary confinement until Boniface died in 1303, mad and paranoid after the famous 'Slap of Anagni' administered by Sciarra Colonna.

When he was freed from prison by the next pope, Jacopone retired to a small friary in Collazzone, where he spent his last three years; Todi wanted no part of the old rebel. Now at peace, beyond good and evil, he wrote his greatest mystical poetry on divine love and joy, including the famous *Amor de Caritate*. His hometown's attitude to him began to change when he became a hero for the new back-to-basics Observantist movement, founded in Umbria by Paolo de' Trinci in the 1360s; later the famous preacher Bernardino of Siena would be a great exponent of Jacopone's *laude*.

With his revolt against Boniface, Jacopone may have blown all hopes of ever being canonized, although Todi regards him as a saint and in 1906, on the 600th anniversary of his death, erected the bronze **statue** in the niche at the bottom of San Fortunato's steps. Next to San Fortunato stands the **Palazzo Ludovico Atti**, built for the town's *signore* and attributed to Galeazzo Alessi. From the garden to the right of the church, a lane leads up to the top of the town and the massive round tower of the **Rocca**, all that remains of Todi's 14th-century citadel; the public gardens and magnificent belvedere offer an unforgettable view of the valley of the Tiber and the Tempio della Consolazione, and make a lovely spot for a picnic. Here too is a Roman cistern converted into a chapel, and known as the **Carcere di San Cassiano** for an account that it also at one point served as St Cassian's prison cell.

## Piazza Mercato Vecchio and Santa Maria in Camuccia

The most impressive survival of Roman *Tuder* is in the **Piazza Mercato Vecchio**; to get there, take the picturesque stepped Via San Fortunato down to Via Roma, walk through the handsome medieval **Porta Marzia** (made of Roman pieces) and turn left. A temple of *Tuder*'s patron Mars once stood near here, and in the old medieval market square there is a series of imposing arches with a Doric frieze called the **Nicchioni** (niches) from an Augustan-era basilica. Below the piazza is the sweet little Romanesque church of **San Carlo** and the **Fontana Scarnabecco**, built in 1241 by a *podestà* from Bologna.

If you return to the Porta Marzia, carry a bit further down Via Roma and turn right, you'll come to **Santa Maria in Camuccia**, a 13th-century church with Roman columns by the door; if it's open, you can see the 12th-century wooden statue of the *Virgin and Child* known as the *Sedes Sapientiae* ('Seat of Wisdom'). From here you can walk down to the Tempio della Consolazione (but only if you don't mind the long slog back up the hill); you can also reach it by car on the ring road around Todi.

## Tempio di Santa Maria della Consolazione

*Open April–Sept daily, 9–1 and 2.30–6; Oct–March daily, 10–12.30, Sat and Sun only, 2.30–6.*

This is the most ambitious attempt in Umbria to create a perfect Renaissance temple, and it makes a remarkably beautiful ornament for Todi, an ivory-coloured essay in geometric forms, isolated near the bottom of the hill in a lovely setting amid wooded slopes and farmlands. Dedicated to an apparition of the Virgin, the Tempio della Consolazione was begun by the otherwise unknown Cola da Caprarola in 1508 but shows the strong influence of the great Roman architect Bramante, who may indeed have helped with the design. Scholars attempting to unravel the building's origins found only more puzzles, as a picture of the temple was discovered among the architectural sketches of Leonardo da Vinci from 1489.

Begun in 1508, the church was not completed until 99 years later. By that time every celebrity architect of the late Renaissance had stuck his oar in, including many who worked on St Peter's: Antonio da Sangallo the Younger, Baldassare Peruzzi, Vignola and Sanmicheli among others. In 1589 a Perugian architect, Valentino Martelli, designed the drum and dome. But unlike St Peter's in Rome, too many cooks did not spoil this broth; the Tempio's purity of form, geometrically harmonious restraint, patterns of semicircles and triangles, and careful proportions of the fine dome and four apses (three polygonal and one semicircular) came out as if the work of a single architect. Four Tudertini eagles guard the corners of the terrace, and the classical interior, white and spacious and serene in the form of a Greek cross, contains good Baroque statues of the twelve Apostles and an elaborate altar with a venerated 15th-century fresco of the *Madonna della Consolazione*.

## Montesanto

Another sacred site outside Todi's walls, the 13th–14th-century fortified **Convento di Montesanto**, is on Viale Montesanto, a kilometre below the Porta Orvietana. A famous Etruscan bronze statue of Mars (probably made in Orvieto) was found here in what was probably an Etruscan temple. The great lime tree by the entrance is one of the oldest in Italy, planted in 1428 during a visit by San Bernardino of Siena. The church contains a massive 16th-century fresco of the *Nativity*, and another by Lo Spagna, and there are lovely views over the Tempio della Consolazione.

---

*Todi* ✉ *06059*

The **Relais Todini** is a 14th century palazzo superbly furnished with antiques on the road to Collevalenza di Todi, ✆ 075 887521, 🖅 075 887182, with a heated pool, tennis, elegant restaurant, and beautiful views up to Todi; the 750-acre park is home to camels, kangaroos, zebras and penguins; there are horses or carriages to ride, or boats for puttering about on the four lakes (*some rooms very expensive*).

Just outside town, ★★★★**Bramante**, Via Orvietana 48, ✆ 075 894 8381 🖅 075 894 8074, is in a former 13th-century convent, with air-conditioned rooms, but although the setting is lovely, service and décor have become a bit run-down in recent years. In the historic centre, near Piazza Jacopone, the 18th-century ★★★★**Fonte Cesia**, Via L. Leoni 3, ✆ 075 894 3737, 🖅 075 894 4677, is stylish and comfortable.

**San Lorenzo Tre**, Via S. Lorenzo, ✆ 075 894 4555, occupies a listed palazzo in town, with atmospheric 19th-century furnishings. ★★★**Villa Luisa**, Via A. Cortesi 147, ✆ 075 894 8571, 🖷 075 894 8472, is a pleasant place near the centre, with parking and a large garden; all rooms have TVs and frigo bars. **La Palazzetta**, a few km southwest at Asproli, ✆ 075 885 3219, 🖷 075 885 3358, is an exceptional *agriturismo* villa—a grand old house in the country with comfortable rooms all with bath and colour TV, or two suites frescoed in 1920, a good pool and a pretty restaurant. An unusual choice in the same area is **Poggio d'Asproli**, Loc. Asproli 7, ✆/🖷 075 885 3385; artist Bruno Pagliari has opened up his farmhouse home (with 7 double rooms and 2 suites) to guests, and filled it with a mixture of antiques and his own art. There is a pool, a lovely terrace, and in the summer there are musical and theatrical evenings. Arty and comfortable. Dinner is available on request. Up in Monte Castello di Vibio, ✉ 06057, the cinquecento ★★★**Il Castello**, Piazza G. Marconi, ✆ 075 878 0561, 🖷 075 878 0561, is the only place to sleep and eat, and it's as charming as the village.

*inexpensive*

No hotels, but there are some *agriturismo* places on the periphery of Todi: try **L'Arco**, at Cardigliano, ✆ 075 894 7534 (shared baths); **Poponi**, Via delle Piagge 26, ✆ 075 894 8233 (similar); or **Castello di Porchiano**, at Porchiano, ✆ 075 885 3127.

---

### Eating Out

In Todi, local specialities in the kitchen range from the usual pigeon, lamb and *porchetta*, though here the homemade fat spaghetti is called *ombricelli*, served by preference *alla boscaiola* (tomatoes, piquant black olives and hot peppers); the wine to look for, dating back to the days of the Roman Republic, is the dry white Grechetto di Todi. For fine Umbrian cuisine with an enchanting Umbrian view, eat at—where else?— the **Umbria**, under the stone arches just off the Piazza del Popolo at Via S. Bonaventura 13, ✆ 075 894 2737 (*expensive–moderate*). Meals begin with a delicious variety of *antipasti*, followed perhaps by *spaghetti alla tudertina*, and succulent grilled meat and fish, ranging from trout to boar. *Book for a table with an unobstructed view, closed Tues.* Otherwise, try **Jacopone**, in Piazza Jacopone, ✆ 075 894 2366 (*moderate*) with similar Umbrian specialities, served in an attractive dining room by friendly staff. *Closed Mon.*

**Lucaroni**, Via Cortesi 57, ✆ 075 894 3572 (*expensive–moderate*) offers more sophisticated dishes, such as a delicious risotto with pigeon, black truffles and port and an excellent linguini with crab—a refreshing change after so many Umbrian meat dishes. *Closed Tues.* Tucked away down a narrow alley off the main piazza, **Italia**, Via del Monte 27, ✆ 075 894 2643 (*moderate*) is an unpretentious but welcoming trattoria, with cheerful red tablecloths and a rustic feel. The kitchen offers the usual fare, plus a few specialities, most notably the *capriccio*, a pasta dish cooked in the oven, a bit like lasagne. *Closed Mon.* **Antica Hosteria de la Valle**,

Via Ciufelli 19, © 075 894 4848 (*moderate*) is an atmospheric restaurant with a creative menu—be sure to book ahead. The *antipasto della casa* is recommended: cheese fondue flavoured with truffles, rustic pâté and a selection of *bruschette*. Seasonal vegetables, fruit and aromatic herbs feature strongly and result in dishes such as lamb cooked with orange. *Closed Mon.*

Three km from the centre at Ponte Naia, you can enjoy a fine view up at Todi from the garden at **La Mulinella**, © 075 894 4779, a reliable old favourite, that will fill you up with tagliatelle with goose sauce, gnocchi with mushrooms, roast pigeon or lamb with porcini or artichokes, for around L35,000. *Closed Wed.*

# Around Todi

## North of Todi: the Smallest Theatre in the World

The surroundings of Todi are lovely and dotted with minor attractions. If you have to choose just one destination, make it **Monte Castello di Vibio**, 10km northwest, a walled medieval hill town high over the Tiber valley that hosts an American art school. Monte Castello always disliked Todi's bossy ways, and when it became its own master under Napoleon the village's nine leading families decided to commemorate the Revolution by pooling their money together to build the delightful **Teatro della Concorda**, a miniature version of La Scala with its boxes and decorations, and all of 99 seats. In 1950 it closed, but in 1993 it was beautifully restored (*open at weekends, 9.30–12 and 3–6 in winter, 4–7.30 in summer; to visit at other times, call © 075 878 0307*).

## Beyond Monte Castello

Just north of Monte Castello, the little hill town of **Fratta Todina** was a bone of contention between Perugia and Todi before it became a favourite country retreat of the rich families of Todi; it has a handsome Franciscan convent called La Spineta. Seven km further north, there's a 12th-century castle at **Marsciano**, built by its *signori* the Bulgarelli, who gave their fief to Perugia rather than let it fall into the grasping talons of Todi. North again, there's a beautiful part of a fresco of *St Sebastian and the Plague Saints*, by a young Perugino (1478) in the parish church of **Cerqueto**.

There's a bridge over the Tiber at Marsciano to charming **Collazzone**, a still very intact walled medieval hill town that was once a Perugian outpost. Like Todi, it enjoys a lovely setting among olive groves and forests, so perhaps Jacopone, who spent his last years here in the monastery of San Lorenzo, wasn't too homesick. The monastery was restored by Todi's bishop Angelo Cesi, and is now Collazzone's town hall. South, little **San Terenziano** is another charming place, with a handsome Palazzo Cesi and a pink Romanesque church outside the centre; don't miss the crypt with its funny old capitals.

## East of Todi: Massa Martana and Around

These days, when art and devotion rarely coincide, pilgrims in the Todi area ignore the Tempio della Consolazione and Montesanto, preferring the **Santuario dell'Amore Misericordioso**, 6km east of Todi in **Collevalenza**; founded in 1955 by Mother Speranza Alhama Valera (d. 1983), it proved so popular that it had to be enlarged ten years later.

Six km further east, set in lovely country, lies **Massa Martana**, behind a 10th-century gate and 13th-century walls; it was founded as *Vicus ad Martis*, a way-station along the western branch of the Via Flaminia. Unfortunately Massa was the epicentre of the first earthquake—back in May 1997—of the many that would shake Umbria for the next two years, and it will be a long time before its *centro storico*, and its houses, town hall and theatre are repaired. The fact that the little town, like Orvieto, is built on a *rupe*, or spongey bluff made of tufa, adds to the difficulty; it requires major infrastructure work and buttressing as well as the more obvious repairs to walls and roofs. Just outside the centre, the late Renaissance church, the octagonal **Santa Maria della Pace**, is a minor jewel, with an interior reminiscent of the Tempio della Consolazione (*now being restored*). West of Massa, in a beautiful setting, the pink and white 11th-century **Abbazia Santi Fidenzio e Terenzio** is built over the tomb to Umbria's first saints, who came all the way from Syria to spread the Good Word and were martyred for their trouble under Diocletian. The campanile stands on an impressive twelve-sided pedestal made out of big tufa blocks, cannibalized from a Roman structure; if it ever reopens it has an unusual crypt and Lombard reliefs, and a pretty marble pulpit from the 1200s.

South of Massa, **Santa Maria in Pantano** (*key in the house next door*) was built in the 7th or 8th century out of a Roman structure along the Via Flaminia. The oldest section is the apse; the adjacent campanile was converted from a medieval defensive tower. Inside are Roman bits and a Roman altar, columns erected in the 12th century (one made partly of a giant Corinthian capital, to create a charming magpie effect) and frescoes from the 14th century and earlier; it also has a beautiful wooden Christ on the cross, hanging halfway down the nave. Further south, the little walled town of **Villa San Faustino** is synonymous in Umbria with its bottled mineral water. Just outside the walls, the **Abbazia di San Faustino** (*key next door*) was also built out of Roman stone, this time in the 12th century. But this is an old mysterious place, set among other buildings cobbled together over the centuries. One was a Paleochristian funerary chapel, built over **catacombs** dating back to the 4th century AD and decorated with the Christian symbols of the fish and lamb. These have recently been restored and are open to the public (*Tues, Thurs, Sat, Sun, 9–1*).

## Orvieto

There's no mistaking Orvieto (pop. 20,700), a remarkable town that owes much of its success to an ancient volcano. First it created the city's *rupe*, its magnificent pedestal of golden tufa—a 1066ft, sheer-cliffed mesa that wouldn't look out of place in the American southwest—and then it enriched the hillsides below with a special mixture of volcanic minerals that form part of the secret alchemy of the eponymous wine that has made the place famous well beyond Italy.

On top of this unique crag, the town, made out of the same tufa, looks much the same as it has for the last 500 years, crowned by its stupendous candy-striped cathedral. Because of this, and its proximity to the Rome–Florence *autostrada*, Orvieto gets more visitors than most hill towns in Umbria, and you may want to time your visit for a weekday to avoid the worst crowds.

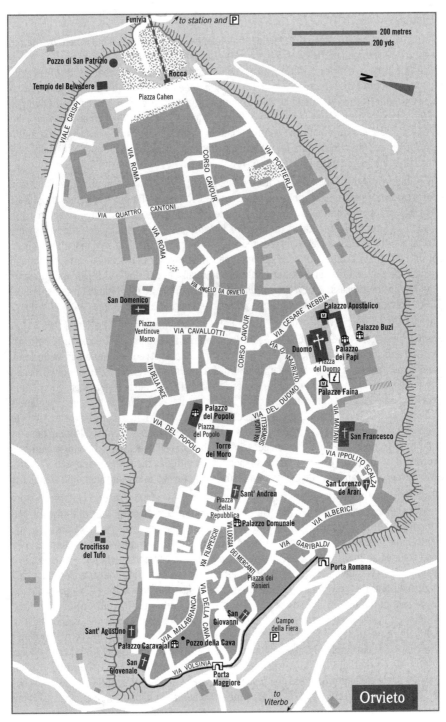

Orvieto

# History

Attracted by Orvieto's incomparable natural defences, the Etruscans settled here by the 6th century BC and named their city *Velzna* (or *Volsinium* as the Romans pronounced it). It was one of the twelve cities of the Etruscan confederation, and the probable site of its main shrine, *Fanum Voltumnae*, where the usually independent-minded Etruscan gathered to discuss issues of mutual defence and to compete in sacred games; it was their Olympia, although the site has never been identified. Unlike Umbria's other great Etruscan city, Perugia, *Velzna* was a major art centre, noted in particular for its fine bronze work, and it prospered into the 4th century BC, although increasingly at odds with Rome, especially after the latter conquered nearby *Veii* in 396.

The Romans first invaded the territory of *Velzna* in 294 BC, and although the Gauls and Etruscans of Vulci came to their aid, the city was conquered and put to the sack in 280 BC. The historians record the Romans carting home 2000 bronze statues as their swag, many of which had probably decorated the *Fanum Voltumnae*. The Roman victory led to severe social turmoil: Velzna's plebeians revolted against the aristocrats, and demanded the right to sit in the Senate and even to wed noblewomen. The Etruscan élite appealed to the Roman senate for aid, and the senators sent in troops to quell the uprising and incidentally destroy the city in the process. A new *Volsinium* was founded for the inhabitants on the shores of Lake Bolsena, and the old site remained uninhabited until the fall of Rome.

By the 5th century AD, the easily defensible butte was resettled as the 'Old City' (*Urbs Vetus*, hence Orvieto). The Goths took it, Belisarius captured it, Totila took it back, the Lombards settled and it became a *comune* early on in the Middle Ages, sometimes allied with Rome and sometimes with the new power up the road to the north—Florence. It was often visited by popes, especially popes whose polls were down with the fickle Romans or when Rome was occupied by foreign armies; it was here that Pope Gregory X received England's Edward I in 1271 after the Eighth Crusade. For most of the Middle Ages, however, Orvieto was embroiled in wars with its neighbours and internal wars between two leading families and their factions, the Guelph Monaldeschi and the Ghibelline Filippeschi, whose feud was recorded by Dante in his *Purgatorio* as being just as bitter as the struggle between Verona's Montecchi and Cappello families, whom Shakespeare turned into Montagues and Capulets.

The event that tipped their quarrel into the worst incident of bloodshed in Umbrian history was the announced visit in 1313 by Henry VII, Count of Luxembourg, King of Germany, and uncrowned Holy Roman Emperor, who was making his way to Rome with a German army. The Ghibellines began to swagger, thinking their moment had come and all the wrongs they had suffered at the hands of the Monaldeschi would soon be righted, while the Guelphs, in a panic, offered to give the city to the Ghibellines on the condition that the German army remained outside the town walls. The Ghibellines refused to accept the terms, precipitating two days of fighting in the streets, in which the Ghibellines came out on top. But then Guelph reinforcements arrived and the battle started anew, and when it seemed the Ghibellines would have to give up, reinforcements arrived from Spoleto, Terni, Todi and Amelia. Now outnumbered, the Bishop of Orvieto surrendered the city to the Ghibellines, who insisted that all the Guelphs leave town. As they filed out of the gate, the Perugian cavalry came to their rescue and the battle began again, and this time the Guelphs came out on top. In the fury, some 4000 Ghibelline men, women and children were massacred, many hurled off the cliffs. Their houses were burnt, and for the next few years the Monaldeschi and their Guelph junta systematically destroyed all Ghibelline property it laid its hands on, and Guelph and papal rule was never threatened again. As for Henry VII, he never made it to Orvieto after all; while the Orvietani were killing each other, he died in Siena.

Over the last 20 years the big news in Orvieto has been the shoring up of its fantastical perch. Tufa is soft and the *rupe* absorbs water, then starts to break up. A few small landslides set off the alarm bells in the 1980s, and since then much of the bluff has been encased in scaffolding while the *rupe* was reinforced and a whole new waterworks and sewer system were dug for the town—another, if rather unglamorous, reminder of how expensive Italy is to keep up.

## Getting Around

Orvieto, or at least its lower version, Orvieto Scalo, lies on the main **railway** between Florence (152km/2hrs) and Rome (121km/2hrs); from Perugia it's 86km and just over an hour. Orvieto is also linked by ATC **coach**, ✆ 0763 301224, with Terni and Todi (48km/2hrs), a magnificently scenic journey down the SS79bis made only once a day, and far more frequently with Viterbo in Lazio; all coaches depart from Piazza XXIX Marzo.

If you're driving, there are **car parks** in Piazza Cahen and at the ex-Campo della Fiera under the cliff (from where you can take a lift up to the church of San Giovanni, or Bus C to Piazza della Repubblica). If you book a table at a restaurant in the historic centre, you are allowed to park for free in Via Roma: the restaurant will give you a voucher to stick on the dashboard.

Often the easiest thing to do is park for free by the station. From there, bus no.1 makes the steep trip up a couple of times a day, or take the scenic **funivia** (built in 1888, when it ran on water power, restored in 1990 to run on electricity) that runs every 15 minutes (7.15am–8.30pm, Sun 8am–8.30pm) from the station to Piazza Cahen next to the Fortezza and Etruscan temple. From here shuttle bus A will take you directly to the cathedral, or bus B will take you around the *centro storico* (if you save your tickets, you get a discount at the Museo Faina).

**Car hire** can be arranged with Avis, Viale I Maggio 46, ✆ 0763 393007, or Hertz, Strada dell'Arcone 13, ✆ 0763 301303. Hire pedal or motor **bikes** at Via Montemarte 47, ✆ 0763 344303. For **bike tours** of the surrounding countryside, contact Natura e Avventura, Piazza del Popolo 17, ✆ 0763 342484.

## Tourist Information

Piazza del Duomo 24, ✆ 0763 0763 341772, ✉ 0763 344433, *www.umbria2000.it* or *www.comune.orvieto.tr.it*, email: *info@iat. orvieto.tr.it*. Enquire about their money-saving *Carta Orvieto Unica*: it costs L20,000 and covers entrance fees to four of the main sights (the Duomo, Museo Faina, Orvieto Underground, and the Torre del Moro) and includes a free round trip on the funivia plus minibus A or B or five hours' free parking in the Campo della Fiera car park and lifts to the city centre. It can be bought from the tourist office, from the museums concerned or at the booth in the car parks.

**Post office**: Via Cesare Nebbia, just off Corso Cavour, ✆ 0763 340914.

# The Duomo

*Closed for visits Sun morning, and between 12.45 and 2.30. For Cappella di San Brizio, see below.*

The 13th century may have been an age of faith, but it certainly wasn't an age of fools. The popes were having trouble putting over the doctrine of transubstantiation, an archaic, genuinely pagan survival that many in the Church found difficulty in accepting. But then the necessary miracle occurred, and it just happened to happen during a visit to Orvieto by Pope Urban IV in the 1260s. A Bohemian priest named Peter, while on his way to Rome, was asked to celebrate Mass in Bolsena, just to the south. Father Peter had long been sceptical about the doctrine of the Host becoming the body of Christ, but during this Mass the Host itself answered his doubts by dripping blood on the altar linen.

Marvelling, Peter took the linen to the Pope, who declared it a miracle and instituted the feast of Corpus Christi. St Thomas Aquinas, also in Orvieto at the time, was asked to compose a suitable office for the new holy day, while Urban IV promised Orvieto (rather unfairly to poor old Bolsena) a magnificent new cathedral to enshrine the blood-stained relic. The cornerstone was laid by Pope Nicholas IV in 1290, and the nave was built in the Romanesque style, probably to a design by Arnolfo di Cambio, the builder of Florence cathedral. In 1300, the plan was changed into Gothic by a local architect named Giovanni di Uguccione, who replaced the stone vaults for an open truss roof. When the walls began to sway dangerously in 1305, master architect and sculptor Lorenzo Maitani of Siena was summoned to remedy the situation. Maitani built four lateral flying buttresses and made the apse into a square to stabilize the building, and then designed the façade. The grateful Orvietani made him a citizen, gave him the privilege of carrying arms in the city, and let him choose his own assistants. Subsequent architects included his son, followed by such luminaries as Nicolò and Meo Nuti, Andrea and Nino Pisano, Andrea Orcagna, and Michele Sammicheli; Ippolito Scalza of Orvieto oversaw the works for fifty years, until 1617.

The end result is one of Italy's greatest cathedrals, visible for miles around, with a stunning, sumptuous 170ft façade resembling a giant triptych. This is Maitani's masterpiece, the 'Golden Lily of Cathedrals' or 'the greatest polychrome monument in the world,' as Burckhart called it, masterly designed as an architectural and decorative whole, the simple geometric forms and gables emphasized to make them strong enough to take the lavish detail. Colour it certainly has, especially when the late afternoon sun enflames the dazzling Technicolor **mosaics** that fill every flat surface, although artistically there's not much to say about them—all were replaced after the façade was struck by lightning in 1795, except for the restored *Nativity of Mary* (1364) over the south door. The magnificent **rose window** (1360) is by the great Florentine artist Orcagna, and is surrounded by 16th-century statues of the Apostles.

Close up, the richness and beauty of the sculptural detail is simply breathtaking. It is said that 152 sculptors worked on the cathedral but it was Maitani himself who contributed the best work—the remarkable design and execution (along with his son Vitale, and Nicolò and Meo Nuti) of the **bas reliefs** (1320–30) on the lower pilasters that recount the story of the *Creation* to the *Last Judgement*. This Bible in stone captures the essence of the stories with vivid drama and detail—the *Last Judgement*, in particular. Maitani also cast the four bronze symbols of the Evangelists, the ox, eagle, man and winged lion, all ready to step right off the cornice of the façade, and the bronze angels in the lunette over the central portal, who pay homage to a *Madonna* by Andrea Pisano (*removed for restoration*). The bronze doors, portraying the *Works of Mercy* (1965) are by Emilio Greco. The 16th-century Sibyls on the corners of the façade were sculpted by Fabiano Toti and Antonio Federighi.

In contrast with the soaring vertical lines of the façade, the cathedral's sides and little rounded chapels are banded with horizontal zebra stripes of yellow tufa and grey basalt. On the right (south side) is the oldest door, the Porta di Postierla, while on the left, the Porta del Corporale had three statues by Andrea Pisano in its lunette, which have also been removed for restoration.

One of the best times to come to Orvieto is in May for the Pentecost **Festa della Palombella**, a tradition founded by the Monaldeschi in 1404: a steel wire is suspended from the roof of the church of San Francesco (*see* below) to a wooden tabernacle on the porch of the cathedral, and exactly at noon a white dove tied with red ribbons on an iron wreath-like contraption gets the ride of its life hurtling down to the tabernacle, its arrival greeted with a round of firecrackers, symbolic of the flames of the Holy Spirit that lit up over the heads of the Apostles. The dove is later presented to the last couple wed in the cathedral, who are charged to keep it as a pet until the end of its natural days. Another high day, **Corpus Christi** in early June, occasions a procession of the *Corporale* in its glittering reliquary through Orvieto, accompanied by the Orvietani in all their trecento finery.

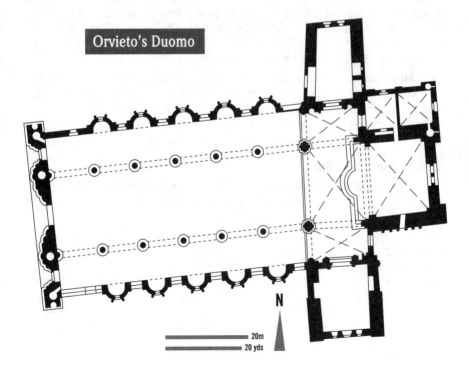

Orvieto's Duomo

N

20m
20 yds

## The Interior

Filtered through stained glass and alabaster windows, the muted light adds to the serene beauty of the striped Romanesque nave, divided into three by fine columns and capitals and rounded arches, topped in turn by a clerestory. The lack of clutter—much of the art has been stowed away in the Museo dell'Opera del Duomo—reveals the lovely proportions and the subtle asymmetries that give the interior its unique dynamism. Note how neither the five semicircular chapels on each wall nor the windows are centered between the arches of the aisles, nor are the upper clerestory windows. The floor rises gently towards the altar, and each striped column is slightly shorter as you approach—the whole produces a magical effect as you walk down the nave.

Of the details that remain, look for Gentile da Fabriano's delicate fresco of the *Madonna and Child* (1426) by the left door, near the beautiful baptismal font of 1407. Many of the side chapels have remains of votive frescoes. In the left transept, there's a *Pietà* (1579) by Ippolito Scalza, its four figures carved from a single block of marble. Beyond is the **Cappella del Corporale**, built *c.* 1350 between the flying buttresses to house the famous relic. Nearly all of its decoration is by Sienese masters: the frescoes of the *Miracle of Bolsena* and *Crucifixion* by Ugolino di Prete Ilario (1360s) and, in a niche in the right wall, the exquisite large panel of the *Madonna dei Raccomandati* (1339) by Lippo Memmi of Siena, the brother-in-law of Simone Martini. The altar, with a Gothic tabernacle by Nicola da Siena and Orcagna, shelters the venerated blood-stained linen. To the left, in a show case, is the fabulous silver gilt **Reliquario del Corporale** (1338), echoing the façade of the cathedral and decorated with twelve enamelled scenes from the *Life of Christ* by goldsmith Ugolino di Vieri, also of Siena. In the nave is the cathedral's magnificent **organ**, built in 1584 and the second largest in Italy; for a real ear-opener, attend a musical Mass.

The **choir** frescoes, by Ugolino di Prete Ilario and other Sienese painters, have recently been restored. The intarsia **stalls** are by another Sienese, Giovanni Ammannati, and the **stained glass** is by Giovanni di Bonino from Assisi (1334). To the right is Ippolito Scalza's last work, an *Ecce Homo* (1608). In the little south transept, the **altar of the Magi** was sculpted by a young Sammicheli, before he went on to his career as Venice's great military architect.

## The Cappella di San Brizio

*Open Mon–Sat, 10–12.45 and 2.30–7.15, Sun and hols 2.30–5.45; buy tickets at the tourist office or souvenir shops in Piazza del Duomo; to reserve tickets, call ✆ 0763 342477. Only 25 people admitted at a time.*

This contains one of the finest and most powerful fresco cycles of the Renaissance, but, as in the case of the cathedral's building, its genesis was hit and miss. In 1408, the Monaldeschi financed the construction of the Cappella Nuova or what became known as Cappella di San Brizio for the pretty 14th-century altarpiece of the *Madonna di San Brizio*. In 1447, they hired Fra Angelico to fresco it and he began with the ceiling vaults, completing two scenes in the first bay near the altar—the serene *Christ in Judgement* and the *Prophets*—while his pupil Benozzo Gozzoli contributed the hierarchies of angels. Then the pope summoned the Angelic one to Rome, and he died before he returned to finish the project.

Years later Perugino was commissioned to complete the work, but he left after a few days. Finally, in 1499, Luca Signorelli of Cortona, a student of Piero della Francesca and a painter already sufficiently famous to have painted a fresco in the Sistine Chapel, was hired to complete the vaults. The patrons liked what they saw, and commissioned him to fresco the walls. Driven by the turbulent *fin de siècle* mood in Italy at the time, Signorelli made the end of the world his theme, and worked on the project until 1504. This chapel is in many ways the stylistic and psychological precursor of Michelangelo's *Last Judgement* in the Sistine Chapel; Signorelli's remarkable draughtsmanship and foreshortening, his dynamic male nudes inspired by Antonio Pollaiolo and the lessons he learned from Piero on simplifying nature and architecture into essential geometrical forms, give the frescoes tremendous power.

There are six scenes in the Cappella di San Brizio, iconographically taken from the *Divine Comedy* and St Augustine's *City of God.* The first, the *Preaching of the Antichrist,* is a rare subject in art and evokes the confusion and turmoil in Florence that followed in the wake of the Dominican preacher Savonarola, who was burned at the stake in 1498. If you look in the crowd attending the Antichrist (whose words are prompted by the Devil), you can see Dante's beaky profile and red hat standing with Petrarch and none other than Christopher Columbus—symbolic of the beginning of the modern era—while in the background, around the Temple of Solomon, chaos and catastrophe are busy at work in the last throes of the Middle Ages. Far to the left of the Antichrist, the artist has portrayed himself and Fra Angelico dressed in black, watching the anarchy with a quiet detachment that seems almost chilling. Signorelli's mistress jilted him while he painted this, so he put her in the scene as the prostitute taking money. Overhead St Michael keeps the Antichrist from ascending to heaven.

Next to this is the *End of the World*, where a prophet foretells doomsday: the sea floods, the earth shakes, the stars fall from the firmament, and the darkened sky is shot with streaks of fire. Signorelli gives us the *Resurrection of the Dead* in unforgettable, literal detail as the corpses and skeletons pull themselves out of the earth and form new coats of flesh. After the *Separation of the Elect and the Damned* comes another powerful scene, a crowded writhing *Inferno* that seems to echo Sartre's 'Hell is other people'; even the devils are more or less human, except for their colour (Signorelli made sure to put his mistress here too, caught in the embrace of a blue devil). The Blessed get to go to *Paradise* with the lovely angels. Below the frescoes Signorelli painted medallions of Cicero, Homer (although since the restoration, he's been identified as Statius), Dante, Virgil, Ovid, Lucan and pre-Socratic philosopher Empedocles (to the right of the entrance). He also painted the scenes from the *Divine Comedy* and myth in the tondi, and the *Deposition*, where one of Christ's mourners is Pietro Parenzo, who served Orvieto as *podestà* in the 13th century and was killed by heretics.

## Piazza del Duomo

The cathedral shares the piazza with Ippolito Scalza's handsome **Palazzo Buzi** (1580) and the deteriorating neoclassical church of **San Giacomo Maggiore**, as well as other palazzi housing Orvieto's five museums. Opposite the cathedral, the 19th-century Palazzo Faina contains two of these, the **Museo Claudio Faina e Museo Civico** (*open Oct–Mar 10–1 and 2.30–5, closed Mon; April–Sept daily, 9.30–6; adm*). The ground floor, the Museo Civico, has terracotta decorations from the Belvedere temple—male figures, including a warrior, a horse, and the goddess Artemis that show a strong Greek influence. The Venus of Cannicella, an Archaic Greek statue made of Naxos marble from the 6th century BC, was found in Orvieto's oldest tombs; a giant warrior's head from the same period came from the

Crocifisso del Tufo. A 4th-century BC sarcophagus is decorated with gruesome scenes from the Trojan War, of Achilles sacrificing Trojan prisoners to Patroclos, and Neoptolemos killing Polyxena, Priam's daughter, on Achilles' tomb.

The Museo Claudio Faina, one of Italy's top private archaeological collections, was garnered in the last century by the Faina counts and donated to the city in 1954. It fills the two upper floors, and is rich in finds from Orvieto's necropoli: there are 3,000 ancient coins, Etruscan gold, an excellent Etruscan collection of vases and bronzes, a beautiful selection of the black and red figure Attic vases that the wealthy Etruscans imported like crazy, *bucchero* ware, and an Etruscan sarcophagus still bearing traces of its bright paint. The top floor enjoys one of the best views of the cathedral. Concerts are held in the garden in summer.

This museum is one of the few you will came across which has a specific children's 'programme'. Kids are given a special brochure (written in English and Italian) with information and descriptions of the various exhibits plus a history of the museum, and explanations on: What is archaeology? What does an archaeologist do? How did the exhibits get here? There is then a quiz which will test how much of the museum they have taken in.

The south side of the cathedral was the heartbeat of papal Orvieto. The austere, crenellated tufa **Palazzo dei Papi** (or Palazzo Soliano) was begun by Boniface VIII in 1297, who didn't think the slightly older Palazzo Apostolico (*see* below) was up to snuff. It was finished in the 1500s and contains the **Museo dell'Opera del Duomo** (*closed for restoration until kingdom come*), with works that once filled the cathedral—statues by grand masters like Arnolfo di Cambio and Andrea Pisano, grand statues by little-known hands, especially the colossal *Apostles*, and two early Baroque figures of the *Annunciation* by Bernini's teacher, Francesco Mocchi. Paintings include a *Crucifixion* by Spinello Aretino, a *Madonna* by 13th-century master, Coppo di Marcovaldo, a *Self-portrait* and a *Magdalene* by Signorelli (very much like the one painted by his master Piero, in Arezzo), a reliquary of San Savino's head by Ugolino di Vieri, and, most beautiful of all, two lovely, richly coloured *Madonnas* by Simone Martini. There are two beautiful sketches on parchment of the cathedral façade, one by Maitani, and an older one attributed to Arnolfo di Cambio. The ground floor houses the **Museo Emilio Greco** (*open 10.30–1 and 3–7, winter 2–6, closed Mon; adm; combination ticket available with the Pozzo di San Patrizio*), with a large collection of works from 1947 up to the 80s, donated to Orvieto by the sculptor—although there are plans to relocate this by the end of 2000.

Adjacent, the 13th-century **Palazzo Apostolico** (or Palazzo Papale), begun by Urban IV and finished in 1304, has been restored to hold the **Museo Archeologico Nazionale** (*open Tues–Sat, 9–1.30 and 2.30–7, Sun 9–1, closed Mon; adm*) with another excellent collection, especially Etruscan: bronzes, vases (including some fine Greek ones), mirrors, a whole suit of bronze armour, and a fresco of an Etruscan butcher's stand. Best of all are two painted 4th-century BC tombs from Settecamini, reconstructed here and offering a little window into life not long before the Roman conquest. Both represent scenes of the banquet that all good Etruscans expected to find when they went into the underworld: those in the first tomb, of the Leinie, show scenes of the kitchen, as servants (all carefully named) prepare the meat. On the opposite wall the banquet takes place, presided over by the gods of the underworld, Pluto in a wolfskin cap and spear decorated with a serpent, and Persephone, holding a sceptre topped by a bird. The dead guest of honour arrives in a chariot with a demon.

## Orvieto Underground

From the days when it was still Etruscan *Velzna*, the residents of the *rupe* have excavated a shadow, alternative city in their obliging tufa, an underground labyrinth of galleries (or *grotte*) containing wine cellars, silos, wells, cisterns, ovens, aqueducts, little religious shrines, medieval rubbish pits, dovecotes and more. Guided tours of this curious subterranean world, departing from the tourist office at Piazza del Duomo 24, are run daily (*scheduled visits at 11, 12.15, 4 and 5.15, and extra visits when required; call © 0763 3733 2764 about tours in English; adm exp*).

## Piazza del Popolo and Around

In contrast to its heavenly cathedral (Pope John XXIII said that on Judgement Day the angels would bear it up to Paradise), the rest of Orvieto is unpretentious and worldly, a solid, bourgeois, medieval town, dotted with substantial palazzi built for Roman and local bigwigs by many of the architects who worked on the cathedral. **Corso Cavour** was Orvieto's main street since Etruscan times, and where it meets Via del Duomo towers the 137ft **Torre del Moro**, built in the 12th century and affording a sublime view over the city and its surroundings (*open summer 10–8, winter 10.30–1 and 2.30–5; adm*). The big bell, decorated with 24 symbols of Orvieto's guilds, was cast in 1316 and has been marking the hours ever since; the cathedral builders timed their workday by clanging. Adjacent, the **Palazzo dei Sette** (1300) was built for the seven magistrates elected by the guilds to govern the *comune*.

One block to the north, in Piazza del Popolo is the attractive **Palazzo del Popolo**, a tufa palace begun in 1250, with mullioned windows and an open loggia in the Lombard style. Turned into a prison and warehouse by the popes, the building has just undergone a complete restoration and conversion into a conference centre. The restoration uncovered more secrets in Orvieto's soft underbelly—the sacred area of an Etruscan temple, a medieval aqueduct, and cistern. Another palace in the piazza, Palazzo Simoncelli, is to be the site of a new museum,-the **Museo delle Ceramiche Mediœvale Orvietane**, due to open in October 2000. Orvieto was an important centre for the production of ceramics in the Middle Ages.

From here, Via della Pace leads back to a big piazza with the church of **San Domenico**, built in 1233, just after St Dominic's canonization, making it the first Dominican church ever built. St Thomas Aquinas taught at the former monastery here and is recalled with several mementoes in the **Cappella Petrucci**, built by Sammicheli below the church. None of these claims to fame, however, spared the church from a savage amputation of its naves in 1934 to make room for a barracks. The surviving transept held an elaborate, elegant *Tomb of Cardinal de Braye* (1285), by Arnolfo di Cambio, but even that has now vamoosed.

### Four Churches and a Palazzo

From the Torre del Moro, Corso Cavour leisurely winds down through 16th-century palazzi and medieval buildings to **Piazza della Repubblica**, Orvieto's main square and site of the Etruscan and Roman forums. Standing on the corner is the 12th-century church of **Sant'Andrea** with its unusual twelve-sided campanile, pierced by mullioned windows and topped by bellicose crenellations. The mosaic pavement of a 6th-century church was discovered underneath Sant'Andrea, and on an even lower level there's an Etruscan street and buildings (*the sacristan has the key to the excavations*). Decorated with 14th-century frescoes, Sant'Andrea was the most important church in Orvieto before the construction of the cathedral, and basks in the memory of the important events that took place within its walls: here Innocent III proclaimed the Fourth Crusade, and here in 1281 Charles of Anjou and his glittering retinue attended the coronation of Martin IV.

Piazza della Repubblica's 13th-century **Palazzo Comunale**, hidden behind a late Renaissance façade, is the starting point for exploring Orvieto's most picturesque medieval streets, such as Via Loggia dei Mercanti, lined with tufa houses; at its end, beyond Piazza dei Ranieri, the octagonal church, **San Giovanni**, was first built in 916 and rebuilt in 1687; it has a 14th-century detached fresco of the *Madonna* from the original church, and a handsome cloister used for exhibitions. At this point, Orvieto's volcanic pedestal is almost sheer, and a narrow lane follows along the edge down and around to the oldest corner of the town and the delightful **San Giovenale**, begun in 1004, equipped with a fortified square tower, and full of frescoes from the 12th–15th centuries and charming old bits of ancient sculpture. The big adjacent Gothic church of **Sant'Agostino** with a handsome door has been restored as an exhibition space.

## To Porta Maggiore

Picturesque Via Malabranca leads back to the centre by way of the 16th-century **Palazzo Caravajal**, designed by Ippolito Scalza, with a handsome portal and inscription in Spanish, informing passers-by that the house was built for the comfort of the owner's friends. Here too is the 15th-century **Palazzo Filippeschi** (or Pietrangeli), the most beautiful in Orvieto, Florentine rather than Roman in style, with such a lovely courtyard and portico that it has been attributed to Bernardo Rossellino. From here Via della Cava descends to the old gate, **Porta Maggiore**; at the restaurant at Via della Cava 26, you can peer into the depths of the **Pozzo della Cava**, a deep public well excavated by the Etruscans and used from 1428 to 1546 (*open summer 8am–8pm, closed Mon; adm*).

## San Lorenzo and San Francesco

The 13th-century Romanesque church of **San Lorenzo de Arari**, reached by Via Ippolito Scalza from Corso Cavour (or on Via Maitani from the Piazza Duomo) was named for its venerable altar (*ara*), supported by a cylindrical Etruscan altar, the whole protected by a lovely 12th-century stone ciborium. The Byzantine-style frescoes in the apse add an ancient feel, especially the elongated figures and staring eyes of *Christ enthroned with Saints*, while other frescoes, from the 1330s and restored with more good will than skill, depict the *Life of St Lawrence*, who retains his sense of humour even while being toasted on the grill ('Turn me over, I'm done on this side,' he said). In the Middle Ages, when no body part was too kinky to stick in a reliquary, some churches claimed to have vials containing his melted fat.

Nearby in Piazza dei Febei, the large 13th-century preaching church of **San Francesco** has been much changed over the centuries. Its size came in handy for important events—it was here that Boniface VIII canonized St Louis of France in 1297. Inside, it has a wooden *Crucifixion* attributed to Maitani or a close follower, and some recently discovered 14th-century frescoes in the sacristy.

## The Citadel, a Temple, and St Patrick's Well

Orvieto's northeastern end and funicular terminus, **Piazza Cahen**, is dominated by the ruins of the **Rocca**, a citadel built in 1364 by Cardinal Albornoz. The people of Orvieto, always willing to host a pope or two (some 33 spent extended periods in the city) showed their appreciation of this direct attempt at papal domination by destroying it in 1390, so that only the walls, a gate and a tower survive, now encompassing a garden of umbrella pines. Views from the ramparts stretch from the shallow Paglia river to the Tiber valley. Next to the citadel lies the massive podium of an Etruscan temple, the 5th-century BC **Tempio del Belvedere**, made of travertine: it had a double row of columns in front, a pronaos, and three *cellae*, a perfect example of the typical Etruscan-Italic temple described by Vitruvius. The podium was rediscovered by accident in 1828, and fragments of its terracotta decoration are in the Museo Civico.

Much of the temple's stone was cannibalized for the building of a nearby well, but it's hardly any old well: the ingenious **Pozzo di San Patrizio**, designed in the 1530s by Antonio da Sangallo the Younger, is the most celebrated of all Orvieto's subterranean wonders. Its name comes from St Patrick's well in Ireland, where according to legend Patrick found paradise after passing through the depths of hell.

The well was built on the orders of the calamitous Medici pope Clement VII. After surviving the sack of Rome—and sneaking out of the city disguised as a greengrocer—Clement became understandably paranoid about the security of the papal person. He commissioned this unique work of engineering to supply Orvieto in the event of a siege; to reach the spring below, Sangallo had to dig the equivalent of seven storeys. To haul the water to the surface he built two spiral stairs of 248 steps in a brick double helix—one for the water-carriers and their donkeys going down, another for going up, meeting at a narrow bridge at the base of the well. The stairs are lit by 72 windows on the central shaft. Bring a sweater; it is surprisingly cold and damp at the bottom (*open summer 10–7, winter 10–6; adm*). Despite the labour that went into its construction, the well was never needed. But it didn't harm the Church as much as another decision the hapless Clement made during his stay in Orvieto—his refusal to annul Henry VIII's marriage to Catherine of Aragon.

## Around Orvieto

The base of Orvieto's bluff is pocked with **Etruscan tombs** that have been excavated off and on for centuries, and back in the finders-keepers age of archaeology, many of the most beautiful finds went to the Louvre and British Museum. Unlike Perugia's impressive Ipogeo dei Volumni, few of these have any decoration at all; the tombs resemble streets of low houses, each sparsely furnished with a pair of benches where the urns of the departed were arranged. The most impressive is the 6th-century BC **Crocifisso del Tufo**, on the SS71 north of Orvieto; by foot leave from the Porta Maggiore (*open daily, 9–an hour before sunset; adm*), where the austerity of its large tufa blocks are relieved by the velvety moss and soft grassy roofs. Excavations began here in the 1800s and continue slowly apace. So far over 100 rectangular chamber tombs have been found, one per nuclear family, sharing walls, each with a little entrance with the family and given names inscribed on the lintel. Originally they were closed with a stone door. Piles of clay and earth sealed the roofs, which would be topped with a *cippus*—the head of the warrior in the Museo Civico was one of these. By the unique wealth of inscriptions found here, it seems that *Velzna* was unusually multicultural for an Etruscan town—the oldest burials were of Greek origin, while other families have Latin, Umbrian and even Gothic names.

Still on the SS71, about 2½km south from the Porta Romana, the 12th–13th-century Benedictine abbey of **Santi Severo e Martirio** (now partly a hotel, *see* below), retains much of its original work—a Cosmatesque pavement and some trecento frescoes, as well as another dodecagonal campanile similar to the peculiar one at Sant'Andrea. Further south, there's the painted Etruscan **Tomb of the Hescanas**, near **Castel Rubello** (*open by request; the custodian lives nearby*) while just over the border in Lazio, medieval **Bagnoregio** is piled on a smaller version of Orvieto's tufa pedestal.

## Orvieto's Wine, in Legend and in a Glass

When Signorelli drew up his contract to fresco the Cappella di San Brizio, he made sure to add a certain clause: 'that he be given as much as he wanted of that wine of Orvieto'. And, fuelled on the stuff, Signorelli never painted better. First made by the Etruscans and Romans, and shipped down the Tiber at Palianum, near Baschi (where archaeologists have recently found large caches of amphorae), the wine legendarily saved the city from the barbarians, who partook so generously of the golden nectar that they found in the city's temples that all the locals had to do was gather up the drunks in the middle of the night and give them the old heave-ho.

Now refined over the centuries, Umbria's most famous wine is grown in 16 designated areas in Terni and Viterbo provinces, and consists of a careful mixture of grapes, with Tuscan Trebbiano and Verdello dominant. Light straw-coloured Orvieto DOC comes in four different varieties: dry (Orvieto *secco*), which now predominates because of the market, although you can still find the more authentic moderately dry (*abboccato*, often served with appetizers), medium sweet (*amabile*) and sweet (*dolce*), made like a sauterne from noble rot (*muffa nobile*). If made in the oldest growing zone, right near Orvieto, it's called Classico; these were traditionally aged in the tufa cave cellars. In the 19th century Orvieto was also known for its reds, and in recent years a few estates have renewed the tradition.

Possibly the best place to taste local wines in the city is at the **Enoteca Regionale**, situated in the old cellars of the ex-convent of San Giovanni. There are tours of the cellars and wine tastings accompanied by appropriate nibbles, while the first floor hosts art exhibitions (*building open Mon–Sat 9–1 and 3–7; wine tastings and wine tours daily, 15 April–15 Sept at 11am and 5pm; 16 Sept–14 April at 11am and 4pm; adm*). Wines can be tasted and bought at *cantine* around town, including the following: **Di Mario**, Via della Pace 26, © 0763 342527; **Foresi**, Piazza Duomo 2, © 0763 341611; **La Bottega del Buon Vino**, Via della Cava 26, © 0763 342373; **Vinovino**, Via Loggia dei Mercanti 21, © 0763 344308 (*all closed Tues*). A number of vineyards also welcome visitors: the three closest to Orvieto are **Tenuta Le Velette**, at Le Velette near Orvieto Scalo, © 0763 29090 (*open Mon–Sat, ring ahead*); the **Cooperative Vitivinicola** at Cardeto, Sferracavallo, © 0763 341286, (*open year round Tues–Fri except during the harvest*) and **Palazzone**, at Rocca Ripesena 68, © 0763

344921 (*open year round Mon–Sat*); the **Consorzio Tutela Vino** at Corso Cavour 36, ✆ 0763 343790, has information on visiting the area's estates, with a list and map. Many of the vineyards also sell their own olive oil.

*Orvieto* ✉ *05018*

**Where to Stay**

### expensive

Orvieto's hotels have more character than most, including the sumptuous, luxurious ★★★★**Palazzo Piccolomini**, in the historic centre on Piazza dei Ranieri 36, ✆ 0763 341743, ✆ 0763 391046, a superbly restored medieval palace, opened in late 1997. ★★★★**Maitani**, Via Maitani 5, ✆/✆ 0763 342012, just opposite the cathedral, has comfortable rooms all with bath, air-conditioning and TV, and there's parking. In the aforementioned abbey of Santi Severo e Martirio, ★★★★**La Badia**, set in the hills 5km south on the Bagnoregio road, ✆ 0763 301959, ✆ 0763 305396, has lovely views up to the tufa-crowned citadel. Renovated in the 19th century, it preserves much of its original ambience—the rooms are still a bit monkish in their amenities—and in the grounds there's a pool and tennis court. Or stay in the 16th-century ★★★★**Villa Ciconia**, set in an oasis of green bordered by two rivers in the ugly sprawl of Orbetello Scalo, north on the SS71, ✆ 0763 305582, ✆ 0763 302077, with well-equipped rooms and a finely frescoed restaurant serving equally fine food.

### moderate

★★★★**Aquila Bianca**, Via Garibaldi 13, ✆ 0763 341246, ✆ 0763 342273, is an old-fashioned hotel, not particularly luxurious but with a good central position, a garage and a wine cellar for the all-important business of tasting Orvieto. In a recently refurbished trecento building, ★★★**Virgilio**, Piazza Duomo 5/6, ✆ 0763 341882, ✆ 0763 343797, is just across from the cathedral. Near San Domenico, in a 16th-century house, ★★★**Valentino**, Via Angelo da Orvieto 32, ✆/✆ 0763 342464, is well furbished with mod cons, and a garage.

### inexpensive

None of these is special, but the price is right (there are also lots of excellent *agriturismo* farms in the area; ask at the tourist office for a list). In the historic centre, right off Corso Cavour, ★★**Posta**, Via Luca Signorelli 18, ✆ 0763 341909, has a garage and a patch of garden to sit out in, or there's the basic ★★**Duomo**, near the cathedral at Via di Maurizio 7, ✆ 0763 341887. Near the station in Orvieto Scalo, try ★★**Pergoletta**, Via Sette Martiri 5, ✆/✆ 0763 301418, with a garage and TV in each room, or the even cheaper ★★**Picchio**, Via G. Salvatori 17, ✆/✆ 0763 301144, with similar facilities.

### Eating Out

There are plenty of good restaurants in Orvieto to suit all budgets, although the bus-loads of day trippers from Rome have over the years helped to keep some mediocre and often overpriced venues in business—choose your restaurant with care. Besides the town's famous wine, local specialities to look for are *cinghiale in agrodolce* (sweet and sour boar) and *gallina ubriaca* (Umbrian 'drunken chicken').

**La Taverna de' Mercanti**, Via Loggia dei Mercanti 34, ℓ 0763 393327 (*expensive–moderate*) is in the basement of the Hotel Piccolomini, serving up creative variations on regional *cucina* in the stylish setting of the old cellars. *Closed Tues*. In the *moderate* range, there's **Le Grotte del Funaro**, in one of Orvieto's prettier corners at Via Ripa Serancia 41, ℓ 0763 343276, an elegant restaurant in a set of tufa caves that dishes up good, solid Umbrian cuisine, with especially good pasta and mixed grilled meats, and pizza at night. *Closed Mon, exc in July and Aug*. More inspired Umbrian pasta and other dishes can be had at **Maurizio**, Via Duomo 78, ℓ 0763 341114, a long-time favourite. *Closed Tues*. Another good bet, **Sette Consoli**, Piazza Sant'Angelo, ℓ 0763 343911, uses the best local ingredients with imagination (pappardelle with duck sauce, gnocchi with zucchini and mint, etc.) and has a good choice of wines, with dining outside in the summer and a good L50,000 *menu degustazione* with three wines. *Closed Wed*. Another restaurant using local ingredients with flair, **Osteria dell'Angelo**, Corso Cavour 166, ℓ 0763 341805 (*moderate*), offers dishes such as tongue and goose liver terrine, ravioli with a pecorino and nettle sauce, rack of lamb roasted with aubergine and good desserts. The wine list is particularly good. *Closed Mon*.

Tops among the tratts, **Etrusca**, in a cinquecento building near the cathedral at Via Lorenzo Maitani 10, ℓ 0763 344016, serves lovely traditional food, *except on Tues*. Another, **La Volpe e l'Uva**, Via Ripa Corsica 1, ℓ 0763 341612 (*inexpensive*), has a frequently changing menu, with some unusual *secondi. Closed Mon and Tues and Jan*; busy. Family-run **La Palomba**, Via Cipriano Manente 16, ℓ 0763 343395 (*inexpensive*) is popular with the locals, just off Piazza dell Repubblica. *Bruschette* are generously doused with local oil, pasta is homemade and the price is right. *Closed Wed*. In a narrow lane off Piazza del Popolo, **L'Asino d'Oro** (the 'Golden Ass'), Vicolo del Popolo 9, ℓ 0763 344406 (*inexpensive*), is a wine bar with a few outside tables where you can have a snack or something more substantial accompanied by a glass of local wine.

## Hills, Lakes and Gardens Around Orvieto

### North of Orvieto

The rather empty territory high in the hills to the north of Orvieto on either side of the *autostrada* isn't one of Umbria's better known regions—which you may find part of its appeal. It also has one of the most curious gardens in Italy at La Scarzuola (*see below— although to visit you must ring ahead and make an appointment before you set out*).

**Castel Viscardo**, 13km from Orvieto, in an isolated setting to the northwest, takes its name from a really fancy, if crumbling, castle, an archaic sort of family palace built for the Monaldeschis of Orvieto in the 1400s—it's still privately owned and not open to visitors. It was later owned by the Spada family, one of whom was a cardinal and received a beautiful ivory *Crucifix* from Louis XIV, which is now by the high altar of the parish church. The village is known for its brick-production—the paving of the Campo in Siena was made here.

**Monte Rubiaglio,** the next village north, has a 13th-century castle now converted into apartments, as well as something you don't find every day in Umbria: a church from the early 1900s, with an Art Nouveau interior. **Allerona,** north by indirect roads, is another out-of-the-way spot, the westernmost *comune* in Umbria, and the site of some well-preserved stretches of a minor Roman aqueduct. Two old gates, named Sun and Moon, and a few walls remain of Allerona's castle, demolished by Charles VIII of France in his ill-omened Italian tour of 1495; in nearby Selva di Meana park, don't miss another Art Nouveau work, the Villa Cahen.

Other possible destinations are along the winding, scenic SS71 towards Città della Pieve: walled medieval **Ficulle,** founded by the Lombards and long home to potters who make earthenware wine pitchers (*panate*), oil containers (*ziri*) and bean pots (*pignatte*), which you can purchase. All the houses in Ficulle have little terracotta numberplates by the doors. The Collegiata in town was designed by Ippolito Scalza, while the little church of **Santa Maria Vecchia,** outside the walls, has 15th-century frescoes and preserves an ancient *cippus* from a mithraeum. Other residents of Ficulle are the Marchesi Antinori, who make the finest Orvietos and live 6km south at the imposing, beautifully preserved **Castello della Sala,** built by the Monaldeschi in the 1300s; it has a Gargantuesque cylindrical tower, linked to the square castle by a covered gallery (*open for visits if you call ahead, ✆ 0763 86051*). **Parrano,** to the northeast, has a castle begun in the year 1000 and in the vicinity a number of *Tane del Diavolo* ('Devil's Lairs')—not that old Nick spends more time here than anywhere else, but the peculiar shape of these water-carved caves led the locals to suspect a supernatural origin. Back in the Upper Palaeolithic era, these lairs were home sweet home for the first Umbrians for thousands of years.

**Fabro,** west of the A1, also has a castle for a landmark, occupied by the Germans in 1944, which made both castle and town a target for bombers. Further north, **Monteleone d'Orvieto** is better preserved, a pleasant hill town founded by Orvieto in the 11th century. It once had a fortress which went through a score of owners before it bit the dust in a battle between the Papal States and the Grand Dukes of Tuscany, in 1643. The houses are packed densely on three parallel streets over the surrounding cliffs, and the Collegiata dei SS Pietro e Paolo has paintings by Perugino's followers. Città della Pieve is just north (*see* p.88).

## The Dream Garden of La Scarzuola

East of Monteleone, there's yet another Art Nouveau church in **Montegabbione,** and near **Montegiove,** up a signposted unpaved road through a forest, lie the gardens of **La Scarzuola** (*by appointment only, ✆ 0763 837 463; adm exp*). In 1956, the architect Tomaso Buzzi (1900–81) purchased a 13th-century Franciscan convent and its grounds to create a garden based on the beautiful woodcuts and descriptions in the celebrated *Hypnerotomachia Polifili* (Polyphilus' Dream of the Strife of Love), a nearly incomprehensible philosophical romance on love, beauty and architecture written by a Dominican friar named Francesco Colonna, and published in Venice in 1499 (and now on the Internet, at *www.mitpress.mit.edu/e-books/HP/hyp000.htm*).

Buzzi's fantasy garden is very much in the offbeat Italian tradition: Renaissance gardens often had follies and water games, and not far from here, just over the border in Lazio, is the ultimate crazy garden, the 16th-century Monster Park at Bomarzo, while in southern Tuscany you can find another new one still under construction, Nikki de Sainte-Phalle's Giardino dei Tarrochi. At La Scarzuola, Buzzi has created a series of ruins and stage sets meant to be viewed by following a special itinerary: there's even a transparent pyramid (predating the one at the Louvre) and a musical staircase. Although it's unfinished, Buzzi's nephew is continuing the project according to his plans. You can also see the Franciscan church, with a fresco portrait of St Francis from the mid 13th century.

## East and South of Orvieto: Lakes Corbara and Alviano

Between Orvieto and Todi, a modern dam stops up the Tiber to form the **Lago di Corbara**, backed up into the wooded hills; this is Umbria's second largest lake and popular with fishermen. Both of the Orvieto–Todi routes are scenic drives: the slower SS79bis passes by **Prodo**, with its pretty pink medieval castle and by the turn-off for **Titignano**, a 16th-century fortified villa connected to a hamlet; the more southerly SS448 passes along the lake shore and **Civitella del Lago**, nationally known for its restaurant Vissani (*see* opposite). The little convent by the lake was founded by St Francis in 1218, on land donated by the prominent Baschi family, and was rebuilt in 1703.

Nearby, at the confluence of the Paglia and the Tiber, stands their eponymous fief, **Baschi**, a hill town with a medieval centre enjoying spectacular views, in spite of its location directly over the Autostrada del Sole. Below lie the ruins of the ancient Roman port of *Palianum*, from where Orvieto's wine would be shipped down to Rome. Baschi's church of **San Nicolò**, designed by Ippolito Scalza (1584) has a lovely triptych by the Sienese painter Giovanni di Paolo and a Murano chandelier.

From Baschi, the SS205 climbs high over the valley of the Tiber, taking in splendid scenery on the way to **Montecchio** and the 15th-century **Castello del Poggio** (*open second Sat and third Mon of the month*) set on a wooded hill overlooking the village of Guardea, with beautiful views over Lakes Corbara and Alviano. This now peaceful area was a busy place in the Greek–Gothic wars; the castle was founded by the Byzantines and later occupied by the Normans, when they took over the Greek lands of southern Italy; it was restored by Antonio Sangallo the Younger and is now being restored again as a cultural centre and residence.

To the south, just off the SS205 is medieval **Alviano**, where St Francis hushed the swallows that drowned out his preaching. Alviano has a strong, square and perfectly preserved **castle** (1495–1506), with a fine Renaissance courtyard, built by the *condottiere* Bartolomeo d'Alviano. A scion of the Liviani family, Bartolomeo was employed by the Republic of Venice and gave such satisfaction that he was made the lord of the Venetian city of Pordenone. In 1651, his castle was purchased by the grasping Olimpia Pamphili, the sister-in-law of Pope Innocent X; in 1920 her family donated the castle to Alviano, which now uses it as a town hall. On the round tower, note the Medusa head designed to ward off enemies. The **chapel** in the castle courtyard is frescoed with scenes of St Francis and the swallows, while in the old storage cellars there's a little ethnographic museum dedicated to farm tools from the good old days (*open mornings by request*). Alviano's charming parish **church** (1505) has kept most of its original features and has Umbria's only fresco (the *Madonna and Saints*) by the painter Pordenone. The commission came from Pentesilea Baglione, the widow of the *condottiere*; she is the elderly woman on the right. The church also contains one of Niccolò Alunno's finest paintings, the *Madonna in Gloria* (1480s).

The Tiber has been dammed near here to create another small artificial lake, the **Lago di Alviano**; its banks are nothing to look at now, but come back in a century or so. The surrounding marshes are protected as a nature reserve, complete with blinds where you can sit and watch the herons, bitterns and ducks (*morning guided tours Sept–April; contact the WWF in Orvieto, ✆ 0763 903715*).

## Where to Stay and Eating Out

### Ficulle ✉ 05016

One of the nicest of the numerous *agriturismo* places around is **La Casella**, an old hamlet in Ficulle near Parrano, ✆/✉ 0763 86684, set in a 1,000-acre forest; lodgings are in 12 stone houses, and there are horses and a riding school, pool, tennis, mountain bikes, an antique billiards table, and a good restaurant; one favourite summer activity is riding in the moonlight followed by a candlelit dinner in the forest. *Half pension per person L140,000.*

### Titignano ✉ 05010

**Fattoria di Titignano**, Loc. Titignano, ✆ 0763 308022, ✉ 0763 308002, is a simple guesthouse in a rural setting, on a working farm owned by the Corsini family. Bedrooms and self-catering apartments are either in the main house or in cottages in the grounds, and there's a pool (*half board L120,000*). The restaurant (*inexpensive; non-residents need to book*) serves wonderful rustic food: lasagne with porcini mushrooms, *gallina ubriaca*, wild boar with olives.

### Baschi ✉ 05023

On the shore of Lake Corbara, **★★★Villa Bellago**, on the SS448, ✆ 0744 950521, ✉ 0744 95024 (*expensive*) is a handsome complex of three old farmhouses, set in its own grounds with a pool and terrace restaurant, specializing in giant *bistecca alla fiorentina*. On a 350-acre farm which produces wine, oil, honey and jams, fruit, *agriturismo* **Pomurlo Vecchio**, Loc. Pomurlo Vecchio (5km east of Baschi on the Montecchio road), ✆ 0744 950190, ✉ 0744 950500 (*half board from L105,000 per person*) has five apartments in the house—actually, a tower—and 14 simply decorated double rooms in outbuildings (in better condition than the apartments), as well as a good pool. Horse riding is offered. An ideal choice for families. There is a good restaurant serving dishes using produce from the estate.

What Baschi is best known for is the restaurant gourmets rank as one of Italy's top five: **Vissani**, on the SS448 towards Civitella del Lago, ✆ 0744 950206. In this almost passionately religious inner sanctum of *cucina altissima*, you may dip your fork (but only if you've diligently reserved a table in advance) into such marvels as oysters with roast onions and thyme sauce, suckling pig with bilberries, or lobster in broccoli leaves; each dish is accompanied by a specially prepared bread. A fabulous array of Italian and French cheeses and exquisite wines will help make your meal unforgettable, though so too will the bill. *From L200,000; closed all day Wed, Thurs lunch and Sun evening.*

## Montecchio ✉ 05020

High in the woods above Montecchio, in the medieval hamlet of Melezzole, **Semiramide**, Via Pian dell'Ara, ✆ 0744 951008 (*moderate*) is a fine place to tuck into *bruschette*, homemade pasta with asparagus, pigeon and other Umbrian favourites, at the right price. *Closed Tues and 20 days in Sept.*

# Amelia

Authorities as important as the Elder Pliny and Cato claimed that *Ameria* was among the oldest cities in Italy—perhaps founded in the 12th century BC, a good three centuries prior to Rome itself. It didn't take advantage of its head-start, but was an important Roman *municipium* by 90 BC, and gave its name to the Via Armerina, linking Perugia and Todi to southern Etruria. When it became a *comune* in the Middle Ages, its sympathies lay with the Ghibellines, even after it was officially incorporated into the Papal States; in 1571 the whole town was excommunicated for refusing to pay a war tax the popes had levied to fight the Turk. In a beautiful setting on the ridge dividing the valleys of the Tiber and Nera, modern Amelia (pop. 11,200) is far enough off the busy *autostrada* to Rome to retain its tranquility, at least in its *centro storico*, even if the surroundings are gritty and prosperous. Once you get there, reward yourself with one of the town's famous candied figs, made with cocoa and almonds.

### Getting Around

Amelia is on the ATC bus routes from Terni, Orvieto, and Orte. Less frequent buses from Amelia go on to Lugnano in Teverina, Attigliano and Alviano. Cars are forbidden in Amelia's centre on weekdays; leave your vehicle in one of the car parks outside the Porta Romana and catch the minibus into the centre.

### Tourist Information

**Amelia**: Via Orvieto 1, ✆ 0744 981 53, 🖅 0744 981566.

**Pro Loco**: Via della Repubblica 2, ✆ 0744 982559.

## The Walls, San Francesco and the Archeological Museum

The great age attributed by the Romans to Amelia is most tangible today in the portions of its **Mura Poligoni**, the 5th-century BC Cyclopean walls built by the Umbri. Built without mortar, a section remains substantially intact, 12ft thick in places and standing some 25ft high near the Renaissance **Porta Romana**. These walls are about the only thing to survive after the Goths devastated the town in 548, although parts of the Roman town can be seen here and there, in the bits of ancient masonry and columns in some of the houses; sections of Roman street paving have recently been revealed along Via della Repubblica.

Near the Porta Romana, the **Museo Archeologico** will open in Palazzo Boccarini in the near future. It is all set to go, but opening has been delayed by a tug-of-love bronze statue of Germanicus, father of Caligula, which was found near the town in 1963. It has been restored and is on show in the Museo Nazionale Archeologico in Perugia, but Amelia wants it back as there is now somewhere to put it. Perugia is hanging on to it...and so the battle goes on.

Just off Via della Repubblica, Piazza Vera opens up with the town war memorial and the church of **San Francesco** (or SS Filippo e Giacomo), built in 1287 and remodelled inside in the 18th century. The one chapel that was left alone houses six fine Renaissance tombs of the Geraldini family, one of which (Matteo and Elisabetta) is by Agostino di Duccio, exquisite although somewhat worse for wear. The best known member of the family, Alessandro Geraldini (1455–1525), lobbied in the court of Ferdinand and Isabella for Columbus' voyage, and was rewarded with the appointment of the bishopric of Santo Domingo, the first in the New World.

## To Piazza Marconi and the Duomo

Continuing up Via della Repubblica, take the narrow stepped alley under the arch to the left to Amelia's most impressive palace, the **Palazzo Farrattini** (1520), designed by Antonio da Sangallo the Younger as a smaller version of the Palazzo Farnese in Rome; it incorporates two Roman mosaics inside. After this Via della Repubblica continues up steeply past more Renaissance palazzi to the **Arco della Piazza**, made up in the Middle Ages of Roman fragments and a frieze. Through here is Amelia's charming old main square, the rectangular **Piazza Marconi**, with its original paving, more proud Renaissance palaces, and the **Loggia dei Banditori**, the pulpit from where public proclamations were read. The **Pinacoteca** is here, in Palazzo Petrignani (*open Mon–Fri 5–7pm, Sat and Sun 10.30–12.30 and 5–7; adm*) with frescoed mannerist and Baroque rooms.

From here, Via Duomo ascends steeply towards the cathedral, passing by way of pretty Via Pellegrino Carleni as it rises into the medieval part of town. At the summit, the **Duomo** (*open 10–12 and 4–6.30*) was almost completely rebuilt in 1640 with a brick façade. The handsome dodecagonal **campanile** was built in 1050 as a Torre Civica, reusing Roman stones and a portion of another frieze. The cathedral keeps a worn Romanesque column, where Amelia's patron saint Firmina is said to have been bound and tortured to death under Diocletian, in 303. It also contains reliefs by Agostino di Duccio's followers, in the tomb of another Bishop Geraldini (1476), in the first chapel on the left. Another Duccio, this time the great Sienese Duccio di Buoninsegna, painted the cathedral's finest painting, an *Assumption*, but you have to come in May or between 15 and 20 August to see it on display. In the right transept there's a *Last Supper* by Francesco Perini of Amelia (1538) and in the Oratorio del Sacramento two recently restored paintings by Niccolò Pomarancio. The octagonal chapel in the right aisle is said to be the work of Antonio da Sangallo and there are two Turkish flags captured in the Battle of Lepanto in 1571—most peculiar for a town that was excommunicated for refusing to contribute its share to the Christian cause. There are lovely views from the nearby belvedere.

## Sant'Agostino to Piazza Matteotti and the Roman Cisterns

From the Duomo, Via Geraldini descends to the church of **Sant'Agostino** with a good, squarish Gothic façade rebuilt in 1477, a beautiful ogival doorway and a large rose window. The interior (*open mornings only*) was enthusiastically Baroqued and frescoed by Francesco Appiani in 1747–62. The first altar to the right has a *Vision of St John at Patmos* by Pomarancio. Of the older church, only the pavement remains, but recent work in the sacristry revealed some very curious sinopie from the 11th century. A sinopia is the rough sketch made for a fresco in red earth pigment: these show saints, floral patterns and stars in the vault that were never completed.

From here Via Poserola descends to a little 13th-century gate of the name, passing the large convent of **San Magno**; the church has a rare old organ of 1680 that has recently been restored and is used for concerts. Heading the opposite way, Via Garibaldi passes a nest of medieval alleys and leads into Piazza Matteotti, home of Amelia's delightful **Palazzo Comunale.** Fragments of Roman *Ameria* decorate the courtyard, and a *Madonna with Saints* presides in the Sala Consigliare (*open by request*), painted by Pier Matteo d'Amelia (d. 1508) who through art history sleuthing has been identified with the so-called Master of the Gardner Annunciation. In 1996, a steep stair was built to allow access to the remarkable vaulted **Roman cisterns** underneath (*open Sat 4.30–7.30, Sun 10.30–12.30 and 4.30–7.30; during the week by appointment, © 0744 976220*). These were built for emergencies in the 1st century BC, and consist of ten chambers into which rain water was channelled; another channel was used to release the waters periodically to keep them fresh. They could hold over 4,000 cubic meters.

Amelia has an especially delightful little theatre, the **Teatro Sociale**, located under Piazza Matteotti. Built in 1783 on the model of La Fenice in Venice, its boxes and stalls are well preserved and still in use from November to May; at other times, especially at weekends, you may find the custodian who shows visitors around. Note how some of the boxes are equipped with cupboards for food; in the late 18th century only a magnificently sung aria had the power to make an audience shut up or stop eating.

The surrounding hills are famous for their figs and wine: visit the Cantina dei Colli Amerini near Amelia at **Fornole**, © 0744 989721 (*open Tues–Sat 8–1 and 3–7, year round*). On the first Sunday in October, the wine is miraculously made to pour from Amelia's fountains.

*Amelia* ✉ *05022*                                                 ***Where to Stay and Eating Out***

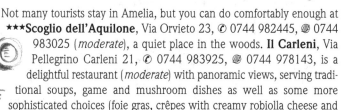

Not many tourists stay in Amelia, but you can do comfortably enough at ★★★**Scoglio dell'Aquilone**, Via Orvieto 23, © 0744 982445, ✆ 0744 983025 (*moderate*), a quiet place in the woods. **Il Carleni**, Via Pellegrino Carleni 21, © 0744 983925, ✆ 0744 978143, is a delightful restaurant (*moderate*) with panoramic views, serving traditional soups, game and mushroom dishes as well as some more sophisticated choices (foie gras, crêpes with creamy robiolla cheese and spinach). *Closed Mon and Tues*. The owners have recently expanded their business to include a lovely hotel in the same palazzo; comfortable, rustic rooms (*moderate*), some of which have a little kitchenette.

## Around Amelia

### Lugnano in Teverina

Four km south of Amelia, **Lugnano in Teverina** (pop. 1,650) is a walled town built along a ridge that was long a bone of contention between the *comuni* of Amelia, Orvieto and Todi; in 1503 it was sacked by Cesare Borgia. Now it attracts a few Romans and foreigners for summer holiday *villeggiatura*. The huge **Palazzo Pennone** in the centre was built in the 1500s by wealthy cardinals for clerical *villeggiatura*; now converted into the town hall, the palace has a little **antiquarium** on the first floor (*open Sat and Sun only, 10–12.30 and 3–7; closes earlier in winter; outside these times, call © 0744 904425 to visit*) containing fragments of frescoes and mosaics from a 1st-century BC Roman villa at Poggio Gramignano. Excavations were started in 1988 in collaboration with the University of Tucson, Arizona. Among the finds was what is believed to be the only infant cemetery of its kind—dozens of babies died from malaria and were buried in a series of amphorae; their skeletons (still in the vessels) can be seen among the artefacts in the antiquarium.

Lugnano's main attraction is one of the finest, most exotic Romanesque churches around, the 12th-century **Collegiata di Santa Maria Assunta**. It has a striking roof and columned portico or pronaos, added in 1230 reusing older columns, on a design derived from the ancient Roman basilica. The shallow arches above still bear a few traces of their once glorious Cosmati decoration, and there is a fine large window in the form of a double wheel. On the wall to the left of the portico, a curious three-headed figure represents the Trinity.

The barrel-vaulted interior, not remodelled to everyone's taste, still retains its fine proportions. Like so many churches of the period, the presbytery at the end of the central nave is raised over the crypt. The pavement is beautifully worked, and there are fine carved capitals along the nave; the third one to the left shows a scene of a Byzantine-style Mass and a man with a snake coming out of his mouth, symbolic of evil, almost like an editorial comment on the Great Schism. There are finely carved *ambones* (twin pulpits), and transennas from the original choir, with bas reliefs showing St Michael killing the dragon and two men exchanging the kiss of peace, and a rare ciborium restored in 1937. The apse has a fine triptych of the *Assumption* by Nicolò Alunno, while the mannerist painter Livio Agresti from Forlì checks in with a rather surprising *Beheading of John the Baptist* of 1571, in a chapel to the right.

---

*Lugnano in Teverina* ✉ *05020*      ***Where to Stay and Eating Out***

The best place to stay and eat here is ★★**La Rocca**, Via Cavour 60, © 0744 902129 (*inexpensive*), a small, pleasant little inn in the centre, with parking and good home-style cooking in the restaurant (*moderate*). The only other option is a new youth hostel, due to open in Easter 2000, with 120 beds in a 15th-century ex-convent on the road to Alviano (*phone tourist office for details*).

**La Frateria dell'Abate Loniano**, Loc. San Francesco, © 0744 902180 (*moderate*) is an atmospheric restaurant in an ex-convent just outside Lugnano. It serves Umbrian fare in the restored 13th-century refectory; some evenings are dedicated to dishes with medieval origins. *Closed Wed.*

---

## South of Amelia: Penna in Teverina, Giove, and a Dip into Lazio

Southeast of Amelia towards the Tiber and the big road and rail junction at Orte, **Penna in Teverina** is a charming old fortified town with houses built directly into the walls. It was disputed by Rome's eternal Punch and Judy factions, the Colonna and Orsini families, until the Colonna got tired of the show and simply sold it to the Orsini, who constructed a Palazzo

Orsini in town with a fine 19th-century Italian garden attached (still privately owned). Other relics of that century are the Mammalocchi, allegorical herms in travertine that stand at the entrance to another large villa, on the road to Amelia.

North of Penna are a pair of crumbling medieval villages. **Giove** was smashed in 1503 by the troops of Cesare Borgia, who dismantled the walls and castles; what was left was rebuilt in the next century as an imposing and elegant **Palazzo Ducale** overlooking the Tiber; it was built by the Mattei, a great Roman family, and is still privately owned by their heirs. Members of great Roman families can be on the lazy and decadent side; one of the original features of this palace is the proto-parking garage ramp spiralling up to the first floor, big enough for horse drawn carriages. The nearby hamlet of **Attigliano** is all but abandoned.

Most of the truly remarkable sights in these parts are over the border in Lazio—the **Monster Park** in the woebegone village of **Bomarzo**, a mad garden of colossal cinquecento sculptures that brings the neurosis of late Renaissance Italy right to the surface. Just to the south, the pretty Cimini hills shelter fine towns like **Soriano nel Cimino** and **San Martino al Cimino**, as well as beautiful, unspoiled **Lake Vico**, an ancient volcanic crater. **Caprarola**, nearby, sits in the shadow of one of the greatest, strangest and most arrogant of all Renaissance palaces, the Farnese, built with papal booty by Perugia's arch enemy Paul III.

## North of Amelia

Much of the lovely countryside north of Amelia towards Todi is *terra incognita*; today hamlets stand abandoned but in Roman times it was important enough for a road, the Via Falisca Armerina. There are traces of this and a Roman bridge by **Sambucetole**; the modern hamlet is under the abandoned old medieval town. Further north the road passes the tower of the medieval **Castel dell'Aquila**, and then the road forks: to the west, surrounded by forests, is the unusual circular walled village of **Toscolano**, once owned by Todi (note the eagle over the gate), now the summer base for the Centro Europeo Tuscolano, dedicated to the renewal of popular Italian music among other things. Just outside the centre, the chapel of the **Santissima Annunziata** has recently restored frescoes attributed to Pier Matteo d'Amelia. A scenic road continues north to **Collelungo**, the last outpost of the Monaldeschi, on the frontier of Todi. The recently restored church has a Lombard-era altar and frescoes from the late 1200s.

The east fork of the road from Castel dell'Aquila leads to **Avigliano Umbro** with a landmark castle-like water tower. North of here, little **Dunarobba**, with its big 16th-century castle, stood on the banks of the prehistoric Lago Tiberino that once filled the Tiber Valley to the brim. In the 1980s, in a quarry on the Montecastrilli road, the diggers came upon 40 impressive specimens of the 200,000-year-old ancestors of the sequoia that once stood on the lake shores. The mighty trunks of this **Foresta Fossile**, some standing 25ft high, were so well preserved that they were found still standing upright in a thick bed of clay. They are the most important palaeobotanical finds in the region, and a research centre has been set up next door to study them (*to visit, enquire at the* municipio *in Avigliano*). The surrounding countryside is lovely, whether you head north towards Todi or east towards **Montecastrilli,** a traditional fortified Umbrian hamlet that was an outpost of Todi for centuries.

# The Valnerina: Narni to Norcia

| Narni | 201 |
| Terni | 208 |
| Up the Valley and Into the Mountains | 214 |
| Cascia | 219 |
| Norcia and the Monti Sibellini | 221 |

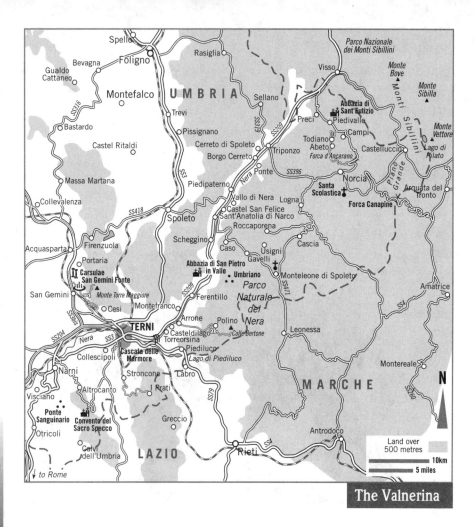

The Valnerina

The clear river Nera, one of the main tributaries of the Tiber, flows east off the slopes of the mighty Monti Sibillini across the southern edge of Umbria. *Nera* means 'black' in Italian, but the name actually derives from Naharkum, the tribe of the Umbrii who were the valley's first known inhabitants, although one of the very few facts we do know about them is that they did not get along at all with their cousins in Gubbio.

The Nera is the region's special river: 'There would be no Tiber if the Nera did not give it to drink,' is an old Umbrian saying; the Umbrians have long memories and know deep in their hearts that the ancient Romans learned all their simple and honest virtues from their ancestors, before they started conquering the world and running amok. Much of the Valnerina is still an Italian secret, although its black truffles and its saints (Benedict, Valentine and Rita) enjoy international reputations, and its superb, unspoiled and often dramatic natural beauty is now protected under the auspices of a natural park.

## Narni

Once an important station on the Via Flaminia, Narni (pop. 21,000) is a fine old hill town in a dramatic position, guarding the steep gorge at the entrance to the Valnerina.

Originally an Umbrian town called *Nequinum*, it renamed itself *Nahar* or *Narnia* after the river when it changed its allegiance to Rome in 299 BC. Pliny wrote of its unassailable defences—'*nec vi nec munimento capi poterat*'. The Emperor Nerva was born here in AD 32, and the city can also claim a pope, John XIII (965–72) as well as one of the greatest of all *condottieri*, Gattamelata (1370–1443), who went on to fame and fortune in Venice.

For all its art and interest and lovely views, Narni tends to be overlooked; many people never bother to breach the modern industry and electro-carbon plant at Narni Scalo in the river valley to discover the fine town within—which, *pace* Foligno, is in reality the closest to the geographic centre of Italy.

### Getting Around

Narni is easily reached by **train** from Rome (89km/1hr), Terni, Spoleto, or Assisi on the main Rome–Ancona line; it is only 15km from the main Florence–Rome rail and *autostrada* junction at Orte. Frequent buses link the railway station with the city on the hill; ATC **buses**, ✆ 0744 715207, also departing from the station, make connections to Amelia, Terni, Otricoli, and surrounding hamlets. You can **hire a car** at Auto Maggiore, Via Tuderte 10, ✆ 0744737997.

### Tourist Information

Piazza dei Priori 3, ✆/✉ 0744 715362. Ask here about visits *inside* the narrow tunnel of the Ponte Cardona, part of a 1st-century Roman aqueduct located 3km east of town.

## To Piazza Garibaldi

The sight in Narni that most engaged the Grand Tourist of the past two centuries, the romantically ruined **Ponte d'Augusto** (27 BC) is now just visible from the bridge at lower, industrial Narni Scalo or from the train window when you approach from the south. This lofty massive arch standing in the river is all that survives of the bridge that was famous even in Roman times for its size—it stretched 425ft and stood 90ft high—built to carry the newer route of the Via Flaminia towards Terni and Spoleto. It fell into ruins in the Middle Ages, and until 1855 it had two arches, and a much more picturesque setting. If it looks familiar, you may have seen the famous painting by Corot, in the Louvre.

Many of Narni's old city gates are intact, especially the eastern **Porta Ternana**, with its twin round towers built by Sixtus IV where the Via Flaminia entered Narni proper. This bustling ancient road served the city well throughout history, except in 1527, when the brutal mercenary troops of Charles V, having sacked Rome, were marching home and stopped to sack and pillage Narni thoroughly as well, just for spite. The Flaminia (here called the Via Roma) leads to Narni's main crossroads: the busy, colourful, irregularly shaped **Piazza Garibaldi**, overlooked by the side door of the cathedral and a neoclassical palace.

Below, its recently restored 15th-century **fountain** is decorated with imaginary animals. The whole square was original a Roman *piscina* (its medieval name was Piazza del Lago). Steps from the fountain descend into a 12th-century cistern.

## The Duomo and Around

From Piazza Garibaldi, main Via Garibaldi squeezes round the corner to the front of the **Duomo** and its elegant quattrocento portico, adorned by a classical frieze. Consecrated in 1145 by Pope Eugenius III, the cathedral's interior is an Old Curiosity Shop; it originally had three naves, separated by a wide variety of capitals and columns reused from other buildings. A fourth nave was added in the 15th century, when most of its art was commissioned, although you can still see remnants of original frescoes here and there. There's a charming 15th-century fresco of the *Madonna and Child* by a local artist by the door. On the right, the third chapel has a Cosmati mosaic pavement, and a Renaissance architectural perspective by a northern artist named Sebastiano Pellegrini.

The next chapel, the **Sacello dei Santi Giovenale e Cassio,** predates the cathedral by almost eight centuries, founded around the tomb of Narni's first bishop, San Giovenale. Its marble screen was pieced together in the Renaissance from palaeo-Christian and Romanesque reliefs and Cosmati work, and on the upper wall there's a mosaic of the Redeemer from the 9th century. The niches contain 15th-century statues of Giovenale and a German-made *Pietà*. The inner chapel is made in part from the old Roman wall and contains the 6th-century sarcophagus of the saint; there's an excellent picture of him as well on the pilaster, by the Sienese artist Vecchietta. The eleborate high altar was completed in 1714; there are a pair of marble pulpits and choir stalls from 1490, and, in the left nave, a large polychrome wooden statue of *Sant'Antonio Abate* by Vecchietta (1474). There are two good Renaissance funerary monuments to the left as well; the one to Pietro Cesi has been attrib- uted to Bernardo da Settignano.

Opposite the Duomo, in little Piazza Cavour, is the **Museo Cittadino**, a new museum due to open in summer 2000 in Palazzo del Vescovile. There will be a picture gallery containing newly restored paintings owned by the cathedral and town, including an *Annunciation* by Benozzo Gozzoli. Tucked behind Piazza Cavour is the **Roman arch**, reworked into a medieval gate. To the right of the cathedral, off Via Garibaldi, arched Via del Campanile leads to the sturdy Roman base of the cathedral's **bell tower**; the upper section was added in the 1400s and adorned with colourful ceramic plates. The 14th-century church of **San Francesco**, with an elaborate Gothic portal, stood near the top of the next street to the left until it burned down in 1998; it occupied the site of an oratory founded by St Francis in 1213.

## Piazza dei Priori

Via Garibaldi, the main street since Roman times (note the pretty 19th-century restored Teatro Comunale here), widens to form narrow Piazza dei Priori, the centre of Narni's civic life in the Middle Ages. This is the address of the **Palazzo del Podestà** (14th–15th centuries), now the seat of the *comune,* an old tower melded with three medieval tower houses, and decorated with four bas reliefs depicting a joust, a lion and dragon, the beheading of Holofernes, and a hunt with falcons. In the Sala del Consiglio (*has been closed for restoration, but due to open in May 2000; opening hours to be decided*) hangs Narni's finest painting, a magnificent *Coronation of the Virgin* (1486) by Florentine Domenico Ghirlandaio, in a beautiful frame with a predella showing *St Francis Receiving the Stigmata,* a *Pietà* and *St Jerome.*

The pretty circular **fountain**, reminiscent of Perugia's, dates from 1303. Opposite is the medieval **Casa Sacripanti**, with more reliefs, and the **loggia** and **clock tower** of the once massive 14th-century Palazzo dei Priori, built by Matteo Gattapone. This is all that survived the sack of Charles V's *Landsknechten* in 1527; the exterior pulpit was used for the reading of public proclamations.

At the end of the piazza and the beginning of Via Mazzini is the beautiful Romanesque façade of **Santa Maria in Pensole** (1175), fronted with a handsome portico made with columns borrowed from older buildings and three beautiful doors with elaborate if weathered marble decoration. Other reused columns line the three naves, many with charming capitals. The church was built over the vaults (*in pensole*) of an 8th-century Benedictine church and a Roman cistern once believed to be a temple of Bacchus, which you can visit by appointment with the local caving club, the Associazione Culturale Subterranea, *©* 0744 722 292. Opposite the church are two attractive palaces, the **Palazzo Bocciarelli** (17th century) and the **Palazzo Scotti** (16th century).

The iron fixtures you see in the walls, here and all around Narni, hold torches for the medieval pageant that takes place on the night of the second Saturday in May, in honour of San Giovenale. The festivities culminate the next day in the *Corsa dell'Anello*, the Tournament of the Ring, in which knights from three neighbourhoods of Narni compete to pierce a ring suspended over the street with their lances—a popular medieval joust that tested the skill of a knight, with springtime fertility rite undercurrents that once associated the success with the outcome of the year's crops. The *Corsa dell'Anello* remains one of the most colourful festivals in Umbria, when the streets are festooned with flowers and tavernas staffed by waiters in costume, serving platters of pasta and jugs of wine on big trestle tables.

## San Domenico

Further down tower- and palace-lined Via Mazzini, the large deconsecrated 12th-century pink and white church and campanile of **San Domenico** now serves as Narni's public library and archives, and is open weekdays during office hours. The door is decorated with worn medallions of the twelve apostles, and inside the walls are covered with 13th- to 16th-century fresco fragments, resembling a house where no one could agree on the wallpaper. On the east end an attractive wall memorial is still in place (1494) near a tabernacle by the workshop of Agostino di Duccio; on the left side are faint frescoes by the Zuccari family and the tusk of a prehistoric elephant, found on the banks of the Nera in 1988.

The Dominicans' convent, demolished in the 1950s, has been replaced by the **Giardino di San Bernardo**, with ruins of a lofty tower and an excellent panorama across to the Romanesque Abbey of San Cassiano over the narrow wooded gorge of the 'pale Nera', as Virgil described it; near Narni the river takes on a natural if peculiar shade of robin's-egg blue from the copper and lime deposits in the surrounding soil. The aforementioned Associazione Culturale Subterranea discovered an earlier church under the apse of the San Domenico, dating from the 1100s with interesting frescoes, another Roman cistern and a prison cell covered with 18th-century graffiti left by poor souls imprisoned by the Dominican-run Inquisition; the ensemble is known as the **Sotterranei della Chiesa di San Domenico** *(open Sun and hols 11–1 and 3–5, or by appointment, © 0744 722 292)*.

## Lower Narni, and the Rocca

At the end of Via Mazzini, in the Piazza Marzio, is the 15th-century well, the **Pozzo della Comunità**; from here you can follow the lines of the 15th-century walls along Via della Mura, or cut down the steps of Vicolo degli Orti to the most picturesque section, around the tall tower of the **Porta della Fiera**. From here Via Gattamelata continues back to the centre, passing the so-called **House of Gattamelata** (No.113). The 'Honeyed Cat' (Erasmo da Narni) was born here in 1370 to a baker, and from these modest beginnings he went on to become such a successful, reliable, and honest *condottiere* for Venice that he received the highest honour that the usually stingy Republic ever bestowed on anyone: a paid funeral and an equestrian statue by Donatello, the first since Roman times and one of the jewels of Padua.

Via Gattamelata continues to **Sant'Agostino**, its unusual severe façade decorated with a faded fresco in a niche, attributed to Antoniazzo Romano. The interior has good quattrocento frescoes, a *Crucifixion* by the school of Antoniazzo Romano and a Madonna by Pier Antonio d'Amelia; a fine Renaissance wooden crucifix and a lofty carved ceiling holding a 16th-century painting on the *Triumph of St Augustine* by Carlo Federico Benincasa of Narni. From here a right turn will return you to Via Garibaldi.

From Piazza Garibaldi, Via del Monte winds up through a picturesque medieval neighbourhood, eventually (although it's much easier to drive up, by way of Via XX Settembre) to the great foursquare **Rocca Albornoz** that dominates all views of Narni from the plain of Terni. Built in the 1370s by the indefatigable Cardinal Albornoz, the Rocca's seemingly eternal restoration programme has just recently been completed; the views, not surprisingly, are far and wide.

## South of Narni

South of Narni, the ancient Via Flaminia (SS3) continues towards the Rome of the Caesars, no longer the main highway of Empire, but a back road in one of the more obscure corners of Umbria. At about the 83km mark, it passes through a small plain with rugged cliffs near the road, an ancient holy site that has somehow acquired the name **Grotte d'Orlando** (Roland's cave). Some badly worn Roman reliefs can be made out on the rocks, and there are remains of an altar called 'Roland's Seat'. On a steep slope below the hamlet of **Visciano,** southwest of Narni off the Otricoli road, there's a lovely 11th-century church dedicated to Santa Pudenzia, a small church surrounded by trees, with an exceptionally tall slender campanile. The portico has two Roman columns with fine capitals, and other Roman bits embedded in the walls. The polygonal apse is similar to those in Ravenna. Where the road branches off for Calvi, you'll see scanty remains of another Roman bridge, the **Ponte Sanguinario**.

The first Umbrian town a Roman would find along the Via Flaminia was **Otrícoli** (16km from Narni), a thriving town of the Umbrii that was destroyed by the Romans in the Social War in the 1st century BC. It was later rebuilt down on the then-navigable Tiber as the city and port of *Ocriculum*. When this became swampy in the Middle Ages, the inhabitants moved back up to their hill, and what was once a thriving city became by the 18th century a wretchedly poor village where Grand Tourists moaned about the less than grand level of accommodation on offer—many of the porticoed houses on the main street began as inns. The rest of Otrícoli is concentrated in a walled hill town with medieval streets, built of cannibalized Roman stone. The constantly rebuilt and reworked parish church of Santa Maria seems to have something from every century, somewhere, from Roman columns within to a 19th-century campanile.

The ruins of **Ocriculum** (*always open*) are a mile below town, overlooking the Tiber. Excavations began under Pope Pius VI in 1776 and enriched the Vatican museum with an enormous head of Jupiter and other pieces, but little has happened since, and many of the ruins, including the big baths, a theatre, amphitheatre, funerary monuments and a section of the original Via Flaminia, are overgrown and crumbling from exposure.

There are fine oak forests and lovely scenery around **Calvi dell'Umbria** (directly south of Narni, or 11km east of Otrícoli). This is the southernmost *comune* of Umbria right on the border of Lazio, and was a prosperous place before much of the population died of the plague in 1527. It was the home of Bernardo da Calvi, an early follower of St Francis, who was martyred in the first Franciscan mission to Morocco; the church of San Francesco is built on land Bernardo donated to Francis. The pride of the village, however, is the *presepio* of unusually large terracotta figures from the 16th century, in the church of Sant'Antonio; the neoclassical façade was designed by Ferdinando Fuga.

To the southeast, 13km from Narni beyond Altrocanto and Sant'Urbano, the **Convento del Sacro Specco**, was founded in 1213 by St Francis, who often stayed in a nearby cave; the legend goes that once when he fell ill here, an angel came to comfort him with sweet violin music. It was rebuilt in the 1300s and remains one of the most authentic and evocative Franciscan monuments in Italy, isolated in the deep forest. In recent years it has been reoccupied by friars living according to the saint's First Rule (*guided tours 8–11.30 and 3–4.45*).

Most of the hotels are down by the river and station at Narni Scalo; in the centre, the finest is ★★★**Dei Priori**, Vicolo del Comune 4, © 0744 726843, ✆ 0744 726844 (*moderate*), located in a medieval palace on a narrow lane, with very comfortable rooms; its restaurant, **La Loggia**, © 0744 722744 (*moderate*) predates the hotel and has long been on the maps of visiting gourmets, although of late its reputation isn't quite what it was. *Closed Mon.* For something on the outskirts and a touch of the Arabian Nights, ★★★**Il Minareto**, in a Moorish-style villa at Via Cappuccini Nuovi 32, © 0744 726343, ✆ 0744 726284 (*moderate–inexpensive*), has eight pretty rooms near a tiny lake and garden.

Outside town, towards Terni, **Cavallino**, Via Flaminia Romana 220, © 0744 761020, is a good old-fashioned inn, with a few *inexpensive* rooms and solid Umbrian cookery that has kept them coming back for more for over 30 years. *Closed Tues, and part of July.* **Monte del Grano 1696** at Loc. San Vito, some 15km south of Narni on the SS3bis, © 0744 749143 (*expensive*) is an elegant yet welcoming restaurant serving delicious, creative dishes made with the best local ingredients including truffles. Desserts—such as chocolate terrine with coffee-flavoured zabaglione or hazelnut ice-cream with hot caramelized fruit—are worth leaving room for. *Open Tues–Fri evenings only, Sat and Sun lunch and evenings. Closed Mon.*

## San Gemini, Carsulae, Acquasparta and Cesi

North of Narni, the main SS3bis up to Todi passes two little towns known for their waters since the Etruscans. The first, **San Gemini**, keeps its spa a few kilometres to the north, while the old centre remains the essential little Umbrian hill town, despite being thoroughly wrecked on two occasions, by the Saracens in 882, and by the Imperial mercenary army of the Constable of Bourbon in 1527, who was practising for the Sack of Rome. There's a convenient car park near the church of **San Francesco** (1291), with a carved portal and wooden doors from the 14th century and frescoes from the 15th–17th centuries. In the medieval centre (take narrow Via Casventino), in little Piazza Palazzo Vecchio, the recently restored 12th-century **Palazzo Pubblico** has the usual external stair and encompasses an older defensive tower converted into a campanile in the 1700s; here too is the 13th-century **Oratorio San Carlo**, housing a striking ciborium covered with frescoes. Further along, the curious-shaped parish church of **San Giovanni Battista** started out in the 12th century as an octagon; it has a lovely Romanesque door on its left side, with scant remains of its Cosmati decoration and an inscription of 1199. Near San Gemini's monumental 18th-century **gateway** stands its **cathedral**, with a simple façade and a tarted-up 19th-century interior.

Outside the gate, set in a pretty garden, the church of **San Nicolò** (*open Fri–Sun 9–1 and 2–5, summer 3–6*) was built as a dependency of the once mighty abbey of Farfa near Rieti, and is now privately owned; the frieze and lions of its portal are copies of the originals, which are now ensconced in the Metropolitan Museum in New York. The columns in the interior have fine sculpted capitals, several of which came from *Carsulae*, and among its 13th-century frescoes, most of which are detached, is the only known work of Rogerino da Todi.

The spa, **San Gemini Fonte**, is in a pretty park full of old oaks, where you can try the little carbonated diuretic waters from May to October. Near here, in a beautiful setting under the steep green hills, are the remains of Imperial-era ***Carsulae*** (*always open*), one of the Roman cities that was abandoned and never rebuilt, in this case after an earthquake in the 800s. In its day *Carsulae* was famous for its waters and wines, and enough has survived over the centuries to give a fair idea of its layout. From the handsome gate built by Trajan (the locals' favourite spot for wedding photos) you can follow a stretch of the original Via Flaminia, dotted with funerary monuments, among them two large and well preserved tombs. There are the remains of a residential district, theatre and amphitheatre; in the forum are the bases of twin temples that may have been dedicated to the heavenly twins, the Dioscuri, and the basilica used as a council house or Curia. One temple was rebuilt in the 11th-century to become a little chapel of **San Damiano**.

North of San Gemini, the little village of **Portaria** is known for its restaurants, and for possessing one of the oldest post boxes in Italy (1674, located under the clock tower).

Further north, **Acquasparta** (Latin *Ad Aquas Partas*) is another quiet spot to sort out your digestive problems, recommended by no less than St Francis; today the waters Amerino and Furapane are bottled here. Thursday is market day. In the centre of town, the **Palazzo Cesi** (1565) has Renaissance frescoes and a beautiful courtyard filled with ancient inscriptions. Here the Roman prince, Federico Cesi, established a country branch of the scholarly Accademia dei Lincei that he founded in Rome in 1609; his friend Galileo came out to visit for a month, in 1624. Although the Accademia died with the prince, the idea caught on across Italy, and most towns of any consequence managed to create a little academy of their own, although typically the ones in Umbria never amounted to much. These days the University of Perugia uses the Palazzo Cesi for conferences and seminars, but if nothing's shaking, you can visit (© *075 585 2222 for an appointment*). Normally peaceful and very Umbrian, the town alarms its neighbours every summer by hosting, of all things, a German *lieder*-singing competition.

From Acquasparta, you can follow a pretty mountain road, SS418, which will lead you across to Spoleto—just don't think you've somehow got lost in Tuscany when you see signs for Arezzo and Firenzuola. There are pleasant picnic spots along the way, overlooking deep-set **Lake Arezzo**, and near that a Romanesque church with an unusual portico at a country crossroads called **Firenzuola**.

Six km east of San Gemini Fonte, on the last craggy slope of the Monti Martani, **Cesi** thrived between the 12th and 16th centuries, although it lies under a much older town of the Umbrii. The entrance, through the Porta Ternana, leads up into the medieval centre and the parish church of **Santa Maria Assunta** (1515–25), where the sacristy used to house a *Virgin and Child*, the key work of the early 14th-century Maestro di Cesi; now there's a trecento wooden sculpture of the *Virgin and Child*, and underneath, a room that belonged to a former church on the site, frescoed with a *Crucifixion* of 1425 by Giovanni di Giovannello of Narni. Outside the second gate, the Porta Tudertina, a small piazza has a handsome little church of **Sant'Andrea**, built of Roman stones from *Carsulae*, as well as another impressive

16th-century Palazzo Cesi, owned by the leading family of Acquasparta. A twisting road up Monte Eolo leads to the site of the ancient town, with remains of the 6th-century BC walls and splendid views. **Sant'Erasmo**, a 12th-century church with a pretty window, stands near remains of the medieval fortress. From here, an unpaved road continues to the top of **Monte Torre Maggiore** (3677ft).

---

*San Gemini* ✉ *05029*          ***Where to Stay and Eating Out***

★★★**Antica Carsulae**, SS3bis, at San Gemini Fonte, ✆ 0744 630163, ✇ 0744 333068 (*moderate*) is a pleasant little place to stop to sleep or eat well along the road. In the centre of town, ★★**Duomo**, Piazza Duomo 4, ✆ 0744 630015, ✇ 0744 630336 (*moderate*) has beds and a restaurant.

## Terni

> *Welcome to California.*
>
> graffito at Terni train station

Sprawling, mouldering, modern—you may not want to spend much time in southern Umbria's provincial capital, but at least some respect for Terni's accomplishments is in order. As the city closest to the geographical centre of Italy, it was purposed in 1867 to make it the nation's capital (this was before Rome was wrested from the occupying French) but even so the idea flew like a penguin. If Italy's politicians couldn't appreciate Terni's location, far from the country's vulnerable coasts and frontiers, the military certainly did. Its location on the river Nera, and the vicinity of the Cascata delle Marmore, Europe's highest waterfall, sealed its destiny. In the 1870s, the beautiful thundering waters were diverted for cheap hydroelectric power, and Italy's first steel mill went up to build ships for its navy to pester Africa, pushing Umbria, lurchingly and belatedly, into the Industrial Revolution (Italy has no iron ore to speak of, and the steel mill has never made a profit, but it's still there). The population doubled in less than a decade, then tripled, and today hovers around 110,000. Before the First World War the city employed a third of Umbria's workforce, and what had been an insignificant medieval town before Unification became Umbria's second city after Perugia, the Manchester of Italy.

In the 1920s Terni scientists astounded the world with the first practical plastic. Terni also has an armaments works (the rifle that killed John Kennedy was manufactured here); these three industries together proved enough of an attraction during the last war for Allied air forces to smash the place flat. They also keep Terni an ardently Communist town, the heart of Red Umbria, and a fun place to be on 1 May, occasion for a parade of humorous floats made by towns in the province.

And don't imagine that Terni has been sitting on its gritty laurels: for the past few years it has hosted an Easter holiday instalment of the Umbrian jazz festival, with a special emphasis on gospel and spirituals. Even more importantly, as Italian film makers grow estranged from the high costs and confabulations of Rome and Cinecittà, they are falling under the seduction of Terni: cheap, spacious, and just over an hour's drive away from the capital. Some of Italy's best special effects gizmos and wizardry are concentrated in the increasingly important Centro Multimediale di Terni, which lent its support to Roberto Benigni's *Life is Beautiful*, much of which was shot in the suburb of Papigno.

## Getting Around

SS209 from Terni to Visso is the main thoroughfare of the upper Valnerina; you can reach Norcia and Cascia by turning off at either Sant'Anatolia di Narco or Triponzo, the latter offering the prettier routes. Both towns have frequent SSIT **buses** to Spoleto. From Terni ATC, ✆ 0744 492711, leave from the park near the station for Narni, the Cascata delle Marmore (bus 21), Piediluco (bus 24), Arrone, Ferentillo, Spoleto, Orvieto, Viterbo and Scheggino; another bus picks up passengers along the SS209 daily to Rome. Terni is the terminus of the FCU **train** line through Todi, Perugia and Città di Castello to Sansepolcro, ✆ 0744 408319, and a stop on the FS's Rome–Ancona line, though from Rome you'll often have to change at Orte; coming from Assisi and points east usually requires a change at Foligno. For **bike** hire, contact 'To bike or no (sic) to bike', Viale C. Dentato 34a, ✆ 0744 428942.

## Tourist Information

Viale C. Battisti 7a, ✆ 0744 423047, ✆ 0744 427259.

**Post office:** Via del Plebiscito, ✆ 0744 440 1839.

### market day

Wednesday, off Piazza Briccialdi, near the stadium.

## St Valentine's City

Well watered and set in a fertile plain, Terni is no spring chicken. During the building of the steelworks, bulldozers uncovered an important Iron Age necropolis, and the mysterious Umbrii Naharkum were on the scene by the 7th century BC. Terni's name derives from their *Interamna Nahars* (from *inter amnes*, 'between two rivers', namely the confluence of the Nera and the torrential Serra). *Interamna* was conquered by the Romans in the 3rd century BC, and grew into a major station along the newer, easterly route of the Via Flaminia. It was traditionally considered the birthplace of the historian Tacitus, although scholars now quibble that Terni's was a more meagre Tacitus, Claudius Tacitus, one of the many Roman emperors for a day.

More certainly identified with the city is its martyred first bishop, St Valentine, who was beheaded in 273. There are several stories that attempt to explain how he became the patron saint of lovers and the greetings-card industry: one claims that he miraculously united a 4th-century Romeo and Juliet, a Christian and a pagan (who of course converted after matrimony), another that his feast day just happened to coincide with the traditional mating day of Umbrian birds. He was buried in a cemetery 2km south of the centre, and not long afterwards the first chapel was built; in the 17th century this was rebuilt rather modestly as the **Basilica di San Valentino.**

There was considerable consternation when Valentine's mummified head was stolen in 1986, but when it was found three years later, unharmed, wrapped in newspaper under a park bench at the Cascata delle Marmore, Terni decided to celebrate. Until then the city seemed blissfully unaware of the fame of its patron abroad. Now every 14 February it hosts not only the traditional Mass, market, and fireworks, but a full range of international chocs and schlock, as well as a jewellery exhibition and prize for the best piece dedicated to St Valentine. An 'Act of Love' prize is solemnly awarded by the city to a person or organization who performed one (in 1996 it was dedicated to the memory of Itzhak Rabin), while modern lovers get to strut their stuff at an all-night Latino dance party.

## In the Heart of the City of Love

Much of the rest of Terni has relatively little to show in spite of a history of over 2,500 years. The post-war rebuilding, however, was left in the expert hands of architect Mario Ridolfi, (d. 1984) who, after working on the reconstruction of Rome, moved here and laid out Terni's more pleasant residential districts, and filled in the gaps left by the bombs. Of Roman Terni only part of the **amphitheatre** of 32 AD remains as a souvenir, on the south end of the city by the pretty public gardens; where gladiators once tussled to the death before a crowd of 10,000, pensioners now play *bocce*.

The **Pinacoteca Comunale** is currently closed and being transferred to Palazzo Gazzoli in Via del Teatro Romano; it's due to open in its new location in October 2000. Most of its paintings are by Anonymous (a strange 16th-century *Circumcision*; a portrait of *St Charles Borromeo*, bright light of the Counter-Reformation, but here almost caricatured, with an enormous nose; and then, in the same Counter-Reformation vein, a neurotic, nightmarish scene of Franciscan martyrdoms in the Low Countries). There's a triptych of the *Madonna, Child and Saints* by Pier Matteo d'Amelia, a *Marriage of St Catherine* (1466) by Benozzo Gozzoli, inspired by his master Beato Angelico, a gonfalon from Siena and another painted by L'Alunno, a triptych by the late 14th-century Maestro della Dormitio di Terni, as well as small works by Chagall, Picasso, Carrà, Gino Severini, Joan Mirò, Kandinsky and Léger.

Best of all, there's a large collection of the works of Terni's own **Orneore Metelli** (1872–1938), a shoemaker who spent his evenings under a 100-watt bulb, drinking quarts of coffee and painting, as Bernard Berenson said, the most naïve of naïve art. Metelli is Umbria's Grandma Moses, and the two rooms of his paintings here make a trip to this industrial city worthwhile: disarming, colourful scenes of Terni, its steel mill and its surroundings, of shoemakers, of Mussolini's motorcade, of Dante, even the Venus of Terni. Apparently all of his paintings not in this gallery are in Tokyo.

Nearby, the **Duomo,** founded in the 6th century, rebuilt in the 12th and completely redone in the 17th century, has a handsome portico and a pair of original portals, the front one topped with a 12th-century frieze. The interior has an elaborate high altar and ornate 17th-century organ; its most valuable painting is a *Circumcision* by Livio Agresti. The 10th-century crypt, with Roman columns and altar, was given a heavy restoration treatment in 1904. There's a pretty 16th-century fountain in the cathedral square, and, from the same century, Terni's most elegant palace, the **Palazzo Bianchini-Riccardi.**

From here, Via Aminale leads around to Terni's old main street, **Via Roma**, where a number of old palazzi survived the boming; a tower house marks the crossroads. Turning left here will take you into amorphous Piazza Europa. The south end of this square is closed off by the massive **Palazzo Spada** (1546) by Antonio da Sangallo the Younger, perhaps his least inspired effort (some scholars have actually absolved him from all responsibility) and now used as Terni's town hall. To its right, set in a little garden, the charming round church of **San Salvatore** is the oldest building in Terni, from the 5th century. Like Perugia's round Sant'Angelo, it is believed, perhaps on equally shaky grounds, to have been a Roman temple dedicated to the Sun. In the 12th century a nave and some fragmented frescoes were added.

From Piazza Europa, Via Cavour leads past the severe medieval **Palazzo Mezzancolli** back to Via Febbraio; off this is the Knights of St John's 12th-century church of **Sant'Alò**, with a pretty exterior, incorporating Roman and medieval fragments. Turn off on to Via Fratini, follow it north to Via Noblini and turn left for the 13th-century **San Francesco**. Its landmark campanile with colourful ceramic edgings (1345) is by Angelo da Orvieto, and inside, in the Cappella Paradisi, are the Dominican friar Bartolomeo di Tommaso's fascinating and recently restored 15th-century frescoes based on Hell, Purgatory and Paradise as described in the *Divine Comedy*.

Piazza della Repubblica, the northern extension of Piazza Europa, is the starting point for modern Terni's main thoroughfare, **Corso Tacito**, which passes through the piazza of the same name, decorated with a fountain by Mario Ridolfi (1932) with mosaics of astrological signs. The train station is just north. Alternatively, from Piazza della Repubblica take its curving predecessor, the Corso Vecchio, past other signs of medieval Terni, around to **San Pietro in Trivio**, a church built in the 14th century and rebuilt in the 1700s, and rebuilt again after the war, somehow managing to retain some of its original frescoes in spite of the odds. The houses opposite are by Mario Ridolfi, while the nearby **Palazzo Carrara** is a 17th-century reconstruction of a medieval palace, containing some of the Iron Age artefacts discovered under the steel mills (*open 8.30–1 and 4–7, Sat 8.30–1, closed Sun*). Another church along the Corso Vecchio, **San Lorenzo**, has Terni's oddest interior, with one short and one tall nave, and contains a good 16th-century painting on the *Martyrdom of San Biagio*. Opposite are a set of medieval tower houses known as the **Case dei Castelli**.

One last church of interest, **Santa Maria del Monumento** (*open 8.30–9.30am only*), is west of town, near the cemetery, 1½km out along the extension of Via Cavour (Viale di Porta Sant'Angelo); it is partly built from a Roman funerary monument, and was enlarged in 1474. The curious frescoes within are on the legend of the golden apples, while a niche holds an early 16th-century *presepio*.

## Around Terni

Overlooking Terni to the southwest, but slowly being engulfed in sprawl, hilltop **Collescìpoli** with its regular late medieval plan was long a defensive outpost of the city. Among the churches, **Santa Maria Maggiore** has a handsome Renaissance door and one of the most beautiful Baroque interiors in Umbria, lavishly decorated with stuccoes and an unusual painting on the *Death of St Joseph*. There are some good popular votive frescoes and a *Coronation of the Virgin* (1507) painted by Evangelista Aquili in **San Nicola da Bari,** a church of Romanesque origins. By the cemetery, the church of **Santo Stefano** has an odd bell tower, a *Crucifixion* and a rare inscription from 1093 on its façade.

Eight km south of Terni, the pretty, old walled village of **Stroncone** lies at the crossroads up to a series of alpine meadows and chestnut forests called **I Prati**, a popular resort of the Ternani on hot summer weekends. There are grand views over Terni's plain from the highest point, **Cimitelle** (2756ft).

# The Cascata delle Marmore and Lago di Piediluco

*The roar of waters!—from the headlong height*
*Velino cleaves the wave-worn precipice;*
*The fall of waters! rapid as the light*
*The flashing mass foams shaking the abyss;*
*The hell of waters! where they howl and hiss,*
*And boil in endless torture; while the sweat*
*Of their great agony, wrung out from this*
*Their Phlegethon, curls round the rocks of jet*
*That guard the gulf around, in pitiless horror set*

Byron, *Childe Harold's Pilgrimage IV, 69*

Terni, appropriately enough as the city of St Valentine, has its own Niagara Falls for honey-mooners: the 413ft green and misty **Cascata delle Marmore**, 6km east of the city. Falling in three stages, this is one of Europe's tallest, most beautiful and most photographed water-falls—when it's running, that is. Surprisingly, the Cascata is an artificial creation, albeit an ancient one; in 271 BC Curius Dentatus, best known as the conqueror of the Sabines, first dug the channel to drain the marshlands of Rieti, diverting the river Velino into the Nera, which until the last century also diverted Rieti's flooding problems to Terni. Although the falls are usually swallowed up by hydroelectric turbines, the thundering waters are let down on the following schedule (after dark they are brilliantly illuminated):

**16 Mar–30 April:** *Mon–Fri 12–1 and 4–5, Sat 11–1 and 4–9, Sun 10–1 and 4–9*
**May:** *Mon–Fri 12–1 and 4–5, Sat 11–1 and 4–10, Sun 10–1 and 3–10*
**June:** *Mon–Fri 4–5 and 9–10, Sat 11–1 and 3–10, Sun 10–1 and 3–10*
**July–Aug:** *12–1, 5–6 and 9–10, Sat 11–1 and 3–10, Sun 10–1 and 3–10*
**Sept:** *12–1, 4–5 and 9–10, Sat 11–1 and 4–9, Sun 10–1 and 3–9*
**Oct:** *Sat 11–1 and 4–8, Sun 10–1 and 3–8*
**Nov–15 Mar:** *Sun and hols only, 3–4pm*

There are two places from which to view the falls—from the Belvedere Inferiore down below on the SS209, or from the Belvedere Superiore, in the village of Marmore. A path through the woods connects the two, although it's steep, prone to be muddy in the off season, and much nicer to walk down than up (the path at the bottom begins 100 yards downstream from the falls). There are some pleasant places to swim near the bottom, but you can't use them when the falls are on (the siren sounds 15 minutes before the falls are turned on to warn swim-mers). Both top and bottom of the falls are easily reached by bus from Terni. For a closer encounter, contact **Centro Canoa e Rafting Le Marmore**, ℂ 0337 729154, which orga-nizes guided canoeing and rafting down the Corno and Nera rivers.

Up near Marmore, lovely **Lago di Piediluco** zigzags in and out of wooded hills, one of which is crowned by a 12th-century fortress. There are a couple of beaches, but unfortu-nately the lake is better to look at than swim in—the water is cold, a bit dirty, and has dangerous undercurrents. There are other diversions; in recent years the lake has become the capital of sport rowing in Italy and the site of international competitions. On its shores, the medieval village and modest resort of **Piediluco** is named after a sacred Roman grove of trees (*lucus*) and has a fine late 13th-century church, **San Francesco**, up a flight of steps.

The bricked up main door has a striking frieze decorated with knots and lions; inside, the walls are decorated with 16th-century frescoes, among them a *Madonna and Two Saints* by Marcantonio di Antoniazzo. The stoup was a Roman capital, and there's a fine Roman statue of a lady in a niche, who looks perfectly at home. Above the church is a ruined castle built by Cardinal Albornoz in 1364.

Perched high above the east shore of the lake is the lovely village of **Labro**, former nest of noblemen on the run, and now colonized by Belgians after a Belgian architect bought and restored the entire village. Below the lake, the Arrone road passes by **Villalago**, which has an outdoor theatre used for summertime events and lovely grounds for picnicking.

---

*Terni* ✉ *05100*                                              ### Where to Stay

Terni can be a good base for visiting the Valnerina if you're dependent on public transport; it's also a good place to look for lodgings if Spoleto is filled up for the Two Worlds festival. In the centre, ★★★★**Valentino**, Via Plinio il Giovane 3, ✆ 0744 402550, 📠 0744 403335, has comfortable modern rooms, all air-conditioned (an important consideration in the summer) and one of Terni's classiest restaurants, **La Fontanella** (*expensive–moderate*) with a menu featuring fresh, natural ingredients in tasty and imaginative dishes: watch them grill your chops through the glass.

Near the motorway exit, the contemporary ★★★★**Garden**, Via Bramante 6, ✆ 0744 300041, 📠 0744 300414 (*expensive*) is Terni's prettiest hotel, with plant-filled balconies, a pool and all the usual mod-cons. By the station, ★★★**Hotel de Paris**, Viale Stazione 52, ✆/📠 0744 58047 (*moderate*) is convenient, and has just had a complete facelift. ★★★**Allegretti**, Strada dello Staino 7b, ✆ 0744 426747, 📠 0744 401246 (*inexpensive*) is a little way from the centre of town, immersed in green; rooms are adequate, with little balconies. Near the Nera and the Corso del Popolo, ★★**Brenta II**, Via Montegrappa 51, ✆/📠 0744 273957 (*moderate–inexpensive*) has nice modern rooms, all with bath, in one of Terni's shady, anonymous neighbourhoods.

Up at Lake Piediluco, there's ★★★**Casalago**, at Mazzelvettam, ✆ 0744 368421, 📠 0744 368425 (*moderate–inexpensive*), a largish hotel with a garden overlooking the water, or the newly opened ★★★**Vecchia Osteria**, in a suberb panoramic position just below Villalago, ✆ 0744 369111, with one of the loveliest swimming pools in the region, but no restaurant.

---

### Eating Out

Besides the Fontanella, you can dine well and fashionably at the 18th-century **Villa Graziani** (where Byron stayed), 4km from the centre in Papigno, ✆ 0744 67138 ( *moderate*), on a mix of Umbrian specialities and Italian classics. *Closed Sun evening and Mon.* Popular **Lu Somaru** on the west edge of the centre at Viale Cesare Battisti 106, ✆ 0744 300486, offers Umbrian specialities at *moderate* prices, out in a garden in the summer. *Closed Fri.* In the old part of town, **La Piazzetta**, Via del Leone 34, ✆ 0744 58188 (*inexpensive*) offers a change of pace—marinated fish *antipasti* or lamb *cacciatora* with potatoes and truffles. *Closed Sun.* It's easy to eat cheaply in Terni, where the pizza-by-the-slice and snack competition is fierce. And be sure to try viper juice—Viparo, the local *aperitivo* with all the charm of flat rum and Coke.

## Stroncone

The family-run **Taverna di Portanova**, ✆ 0744 60496 (*moderate*) occupies a 14th-century building and serves an unusual speciality—a grain and vegetable *minestra*, from a medieval Franciscan recipe, as well as the more usual Umbrian favourites and a good wine list. *Open evenings only, closed Wed.*

## Piediluco

Piediluco's lakeside restaurant **Tavoletta**, Vocabolo Forca 4, ✆ 0744 368196, off the SS79 (*moderate*), serves food which lives up to the setting. Fish, both from the lake and the sea, not surprisingly figures strongly on the menu, but there is also plenty of meat. *Antipasti* and pasta dishes based on fish are especially good. Try the fresh tagliatelle served with a *ragù* of lake fish and the trout with peppers, but leave room for a fabulous *torta di cioccolata. Closed Wed.*

# Up the Valley and into the Mountains

The further you head up the Valnerina, the more wild and beautiful the scenery becomes, and the tastier the truffles. The Parco Naturale del Nera begins at the Cascata delle Marmore. This part of Umbria had just about finished repairs after tremors in 1979 had damaged its remote villages, when the 1997 earthquake caused fresh damage and closed a number of roads; all have since been reopened.

---

***Tourist Information***

**Ferentillo**: Via della Vittoria 61, ✆ 0744 780990.

---

## Arrone and Ferentillo

After the Cascata delle Marmore, the SS209 passes under the pretty hill townlets of **Torreorsina** and **Casteldilago** before arriving at the more substantial and picturesque market village of **Arrone**, spilling over its isolated rock. In the centre, the church of **Santa Maria** has remarkably good frescoes, including a *Life of the Virgin* in the apse, by Vincenzo Tamagni and Giovanni di Spoleto, inspired by Lippo Lippi's work in Spoleto's Duomo. The *Madonna della Misericordia* (1544) by Jacopo Siculo is to the right of the main altar, and there's a *Supper at Emaus* by Caravaggio's school. In the apse to the left of the altar is an elegant Renaissance terracotta *Madonna Suckling the Child, Between Two Saints.*

In the good old days Arrone and its neighbours indulged in some fierce C Division warfare. The *signori* of Arrone, who built the landmark tower on top of the town (with a tree growing out of its top), were the bitter enemies of the lords of Polino. This is located up a pretty 10km winding road, passing at **Rosciano** under the great white arch of a Mussolini-built aqueduct known as the Ponte Canale. In recent years this has become a popular and not-too-scary **bungee jump pad** between March and October. Further up, past the ricocheting bodies,

**Polino** takes a certain pride in being Umbria's tiniest *comune*, but it too has its feudal tower, as well as a monumental Baroque fountain and a road up to the **Colle Bertone** (1232m), a modest winter sports and summer picnicking area.

The biggest rivals of the lords of Arrone were the powerful abbots of **Ferentillo**, the next town up the Valnerina, guarded by twin 14th-century citadels on dramatic rocks that dominate the narrow valley like matching book ends; their sheer walls are as popular now with rock-climbers as Arrone's aqueduct is with rubber-banded leapers. In Precetto, the oldest quarter of Ferentillo, the crypt of **Santo Stefano** contains something you don't expect to find in Umbria: **mummies**. Accidentally preserved by the soil and ventilation, a desiccated vulture mummy points the way inside with its wing to the mummified Chinese newly-weds (minus a head, swiped perhaps by the same mummy fetishist who got St Valentine's) who came here in the last century for a honeymoon and got cholera instead; two French prisoners who were hanged in the Napoleonic wars; and a pyramid of skulls. Unfortunately, the mummies are now imprisoned in glass display cases, undermining much of their bizarre fusty charm (*open daily 10–12.30 and 2.30–5; knock on door marked* custode *opposite*).

## San Pietro in Valle

The former Benedictine abbey of Ferentillo, **San Pietro in Valle,** is 4km further up the valley, on the beautiful slopes of Monte Solenne, and you won't find a more charming abbey to visit—or stay in, as it has recently been converted into an *agriturismo* hotel and restaurant (*see* below). Founded *c.* 710 by the Duke of Spoleto Faraoldo II, the abbey is on the site of a Syrian hermitage from the 6th century, and it came in handy in 720 when Faraoldo took refuge here after he was deposed by his son.

The church (*open 10.30–1 and 2.30–5*) has a lovely and ornate 12th-century campanile embedded with 8th-century fragments, in a style more common to Rome than Umbria. It is full of rare treasures. The nave is covered with recently restored **frescoes** from 1190, a rare and important early example of the Italian response to the Byzantine style—here, already moving away from the stylized hierarchy to a more natural 'Latin style' where figures are individuals rather than types; the only comparable frescoes of the period are in the Roman church of San Giovanni a Porta Latina. The left wall has Old Testament scenes (note especially *Adam Naming the Animals* and *Noah*) and there are New Testament scenes on the right. The high **altar** (*c.* 740) is an equally rare example of Lombard work, sculpted on both the front and back, complete with a self-portrait of the sculptor, signed *Ursus Magester.* Duke Faraoldo was reputedly interred in the lovely 3rd-century Roman sarcophagus decorated with scenes of Dionysian revels. The apse contains good 13th-century frescoes, with a pretty *Madonna* by the school of Giotto. At the back there's a cylindrical altar, said to be Etruscan but now used for monetary rather than animal offerings. Among the stone fragments arranged on the wall is a real rarity—a bas relief of a monk with oriental features, believed to be one of the two Syrian monks who set up a hermitage here. Ask the custodian to visit the charming two-storey **cloister**, built in the 12th century; the two 11th-century figures guarding the lateral door of the church here are Peter and Paul.

Faraoldo deserves credit for choosing a lovely spot, with views across the valley to the abandoned citadel of **Umbriano**, the legendary first city of Umbria (you can walk up there for equally grand views towards San Pietro, but make a lot of noise to scare off any unsuspecting vipers). It also makes an unforgettable place for a picnic.

## Up the Valnerina: Scheggino to Triponzo

**Scheggino**, the next town up the valley, occupies both banks of the Nera and is laced with tiny canals full of trout and a rare species of crayfish (*gamberettini*) imported from Turkey; it is also the fief of Italy's truffle tycoons, Paolo and Bruno Urbani, who thanks to the foresight of their grandfather Carlo control about 70% of the Valnerina's black gold. Scheggino has 12th-century walls that famously repelled the notorious brigand Girolamo Brancaleoni in 1522. There are late frescoes by Lo Spagna in the apse of the church of **San Nicolò**, along with a *Madonna del Rosario* by Pierino Cesari and other late 16th-century works.

Three km from Scheggino, on the left bank of the Nera, **Sant'Anatolia di Narco** is another bailiwick of the black truffle. It is an ancient place: in the 19th century, a necropolis of Naharkum was discovered here, going back to the 8th century BC, making it one of the oldest of all Umbrii sites. Now fewer than 600 people live in its 14th-century walls. Its glory days as a medieval *comune* are recalled in an archway with a relief of a knight, all that survives of the 13th-century Palazzo del Comune. Nearby, the medieval church of **Sant'Anatolia** has recently been restored (*key in the house opposite*). Just outside the west gate, the Porta di Castello, the pretty church of **Santa Maria delle Grazie** has a façade of 1572 and popular votive frescoes, as well as a beautiful fresco in the presbytery of the *Madonna and Child* by the 15th-century Master of Eggi (*if it's locked, get the key in the church opposite Sant'Anatolia*).

Just up from Sant'Anatolia, the medieval hamlet of **Castel San Felice** is a pretty little place on its hill, completely restored after 1979. At Via Orichelle 34 you can pick up the key to visit the delightful 12th-century church of **San Felice in Narco**, located on an unpaved road at the foot of the village. The façade has an intricate rose window surrounded by symbols of the Evangelists, sculpted columns and capitals, Cosmatesque decoration, and reliefs on the life of St Felice, who moved here with his father Mauro from Palestine in the 5th century. At the time the local inhabitants were having serious problems with a dragon; with the help of an angel, Felice despatched it for them and performed other miracles. When he died, his father Mauro built an oratory over his grave. The interior is just as beautiful, with a pair of transennae with remains of Cosmatesque work, and early 15th-century frescoes; the crypt has the ancient sarcophagus of SS Mauro and Felice.

High over the left bank of the Nera, walled **Vallo di Nera** could be used as a medieval film set with its twisting steep cobbled streets, little piazzas and stone houses, all well restored. It has two churches with frescoes: the 13th-century **Santa Maria**, with a Gothic portal and frescoes by Cola di Pietro from Camerino and Francesco di Antonio, painted in 1383. Other frescoes are votive, and feature some delightful pigs. But even better are the beautifully coloured frescoes in pink and white **San Giovanni Battista** at the top of the village (*key kept next door*), these, on the *Life of the Virgin* (1536), are by Pinturicchio's talented Sicilian assistant, Jacopo Siculo.

This upper part of the Valnerina has been decidedly less remote since the opening of a new road and tunnel from Spoleto to Piedipaterno, replacing the old narrow winding road. The next village, **Borgo Cerreto**, lies at an important crossroads and has a late 13th-century Franciscan church, San Lorenzo, which was badly damaged in the earthquake. Above it, splendid on its high hill, tiny **Ponte** overlooks the confluence of the Tissino and the Nera. In the 9th century this puny village was big news, a major Lombard stronghold that ruled both Cascia and Norcia. The views from Ponte across to Cerreto di Spoleto are lovely, and the **Pieve di Santa Maria Assunta** (1201) is well worth a look; it has a beautifully carved rose window with symbols of the Evangelists and a telemon on its tall flat screen façade, and a fine apse decorated with hanging arches and funny little heads. The handsome interior (the custodian lives in Via Nortosce) was restored in 1940 and contains ancient fragments and a fine old pavement, and damaged frescoes by the Umbrian school. From here you can make the steep but pretty walk up to the ruined castle.

Across the valley and just off the main valley road, **Cerreto di Spoleto** sits high on its spur, and offers equally splendid views towards Ponte. It was the birthplace of the humanist and Latin poet Giovanni Pontano (1426–1503), better known as Pontanus. When he was attending university at Perugia, his family's home in Cerreto was burned, so he moved in with some relatives in Naples and stayed there, advising the court and running the literary academy that later took his name, the Accademia Pontana. Cerreto has several fine palazzi, and a pretty main piazza with a 15th-century **Palazzo Comunale** and fountain; just beyond is the tall 15th-century **Torre Civica**. The churches were all damaged in 1997 and are closed; one of these, **San Giacomo**, on the edge of the hill, has beautiful 15th-century frescoes.

**Triponzo**, the last Umbrian village in the Valnerina, was the epicentre of the 1979 earthquake, and is still practically empty. The road continues to Pontechiusita, where you can pick up the road to Preci and Norcia (*see* below).

---

### Activities

**Valnerina Verticale Sport**, Piazza Vittorio Emanuele 9, Ferentillo, ✆ 0744 302451, organizes rock-climbing at various levels around Ferentillo, Montefranco and Arrone.

---

### Where to Stay and Eating Out

**Arrone** ✉ 05031

**★★Rossi**, on the SS209, ✆ 0744 388372, 🖷 0744 388305 (*inexpensive*) has 16 modern rooms, all with bath, and one of the best restaurants in the area (*moderate*), with excellent *crostini*, spaghetti with truffles, the usual grilled meats and a wide variety of trout dishes, served in a pretty garden in summer. *Closed Fri.* Just down the road, the **Grottino del Nera**, Via Valnerina 21, ✆ 0744 389104 (*inexpensive*) is an old country inn that never disappoints with its big platters of *antipasti* and other delights. *Closed Wed.*

There's the reliable, *inexpensive* **Mola Bella** just up the Polino road, for pizza and the basics, and further up by the aqueduct, the **Rema** (*inexpensive*) is a fine little trattoria with an outdoor grill, and the usual Umbrian fare at old-fashioned prices; try the *ciriole* (homemade spaghetti) with mushrooms and grilled lamb *scortaditta* ('burn your fingers'). *Closed Mon.*

### Ferentillo ✉ 05034

On SS209, towards Ferentillo in the *comune* of Montefranco, ★★★**Fontegaia**, ✆ 0744 388621, 🖷 0744 388598 (*hotel and restaurant moderate*) has the most pretensions in the Valnerina; rooms are very comfortable; there's a playground for the children and beautiful gardens for dining *al fresco*; the restaurant is a favourite for locals going out for a special occasion, if a bit heavy-handed with the cream sauces. On the mummy road, an old mill was beautifully converted in 1997 into a hotel, the ★★★**Monterivoso**, ✆/🖷 0744 780725 (*moderate*), where antique furnished rooms look out over the lawn—a pool is planned but the municipal one in Ferentillo, only 3 minutes away, is especially nice; the restaurant is good, too. **Abbazia San Pietro in Valle**, ✆ 0744 780129 (*moderate*), has opened as a hotel and restaurant in the former abbey (*see* above), with well furnished rooms in the old monks' quarters—a very peaceful spot. **Piermarini**, Via della Vittoria 53, ✆ 0744 780714 (*moderate*) is a wonderful restaurant to taste local dishes, prepared as 'La Nonna' (granny) would have prepared them. There's *coratina di agnello* (lamb's innards) with wild asparagus, homemade pasta with truffles, delicate lamb cutlets '*scottadito*' served with olive focaccia, fresh-water trout and river crayfish. In autumn, mushrooms and chestnuts appear on the menu.

### Scheggino ✉ 06040

One hotel, charming little ★★**Del Ponte**, Via Borgo 15, ✆ 0743 61253, 🖷 0743 61131 (*inexpensive*), right on the Nera river, offers 12 rooms with bath, and, in the restaurant (*moderate*), delicious meals based on Scheggino's two specialities, crayfish and truffles. For a trip to Umbrian heaven, try the fettuccine with a sauce that combines both ingredients. *Closed Mon.*

### Sant'Anatolia di Narco ✉ 06040

There are simple *inexpensive* rooms at the ★★**Tre Valli**, ✆ 0743 613118, and excellent ravioli filled with ricotta, and lamb on the spit at **Da Franchina Ripanti**, ✆ 0743 613144 (*inexpensive*). *Closed Tues, exc in summer.*

---

## Towards Monteleone di Spoleto and Cascia from Sant'Anatolia

A spectacular mountain road rises east of Sant'Anatolia di Narco for the tiny hamlet of **Caso**, with a pair of interesting churches: **Santa Maria delle Grazie** with frescoes by the school of Lo Spagna, and outside the village the little Romanesque **Santa Cristina**, its walls coated with frescoes from the 14th–16th centuries, although it's usually kept locked. Futher along, the road rises and rises to **Gavelli** (3780ft), a tiny hamlet on the cliff with a 15th-century church of **San Michele Arcangelo**, beautifully frescoed by Lo Spagna and his school (*key next door*). One of the surprises in this area is **Usigni**, a tiny hamlet signposted off the main road, in a remote valley, but with a remarkable 17th-century Roman Baroque church, **San Salvatore** (*open Sun only*) attributed to Bernini. It was commissioned by Fausto Poli, who was born here and became a cardinal in the court of Urban VIII; in Umbria he is best remembered for promoting the beatification of St Rita.

Further south, high above the Corno valley, remote little **Monteleone di Spoleto** has a pretty setting that has been inhabited for centuries: a large 6th-century BC cemetery on the road from Usigni was discovered in 1902 and yielded a wooden chariot of Etruscan manufacture, decorated with magnificent bronze reliefs of the life of Achilleus (now in the Metropolitan Museum in New York). Monteleone was ruled by Spoleto until 1559, but has suffered from earthquakes in 1703 and 1979. In the upper, almost deserted part of town, a couple of fine quattrocento palazzi and a porticoed **Palazzo dei Priori** are testimony to its former importance. Here too is the massive 13th-century church and convent of **San Francesco** with a beautiful Gothic door. The recently restored interior has a fine high altar, an 18th-century painted ceiling decorated with symbols of the Madonna, and fascinating remains of 15th-century frescoes, especially a magnificent *Christ in Majesty*. The arcaded cloister has more frescoes, as does the lower church, with a nice one of *St Anthony Abbot and the Animals*. For stupendous views over much of southern Umbria, take the remote SS471 south through the mountains to Leonessa in Lazio and follow the signs west to Labro, Lake Piediluco and the Cascata della Marmore near Terni.

## Cascia

On the other hand, if you take the narrow SS471 north from Monteleone (the alternative route, off the SS396 from Triponzo to Norcia, is less hairpinny), you'll end up near the top of Cascia (pop. 4,000), a hill town that sees more pilgrims than truffles; more pilgrims, in fact, than any Umbrian town except Assisi. Santa Rita, the matronly 'Saint of Impossibilities', was born near here in 1381, but had to wait until 1900 to be canonized, and then hold on until the inauspicious period of 1937–47 for her sanctuary. Poor Rita! After a wretched marriage to a roughneck, who was killed by his many enemies, she persuaded her two sons not to take vengeance; when they died soon afterwards of disease, she became a nun, only to develop such a foul-smelling sore on her forehead that none of the other sisters would come near her. Then she received the Stigmata and spent the rest of her life in pain.

Cascia itself has known more than its share of bad luck. Originally the Roman *Cursula*, it was wiped out by an earthquake and refounded on a different site. This did not prevent other earthquakes from periodically destroying it, in 1599, 1703 and 1979. The Lombards and Saracens sacked it in the three digit years. Afterwards, Cascia was a freewheeling *comune* like the others, sometimes under Spoleto's sway, sometimes under the Emperor or the Trinci family in Foligno. When it came under the Church with the rest of Umbria, it rebelled, in 1516, but was soon put in its place.

### Getting Around

The Società Spoletino, © 0743 221991, runs buses from Norcia, Spoleto, Terni, Foligno and Perugia to Cascia.

### Tourist Information

**Cascia**: Via G. da Chiavano 2, © 0743 71401, @ 0743 76630. Piazza Garibaldi, © 0743 71147.

### market day

Wednesday.

## The Basilica of Santa Rita

You can't miss it. The **Basilica di Santa Rita** has been described as the most vulgar in Christendom, a proto-Disney castle with a pseudo-Byzantine interior decorated throughout with ghastly frescoes. Rita's dried up, age-darkened body is displayed in a glass coffin, surrounded by votive offerings from the Terni and Rome football clubs, while every year tens of thousands of fervent if unhappily married women and other victims of inordinate bad luck come to pray for relief. An attempt to insert some art into the basilica, the high altar by Giacomo Manzù, doesn't really stand a chance. The **Monasterio di Santa Rita**, to the left of the basilica, marks the spot where she spent her 40 years as a nun (*open for guided tours, year round*); the 15th-century cloister, her cell, and miraculous rose bush.

## The Rest of Town

Other spots around Cascia may receive less devotion, but offer more substance in the art department. The **Museo di Palazzo Santi**, in Via G. Palombi (✆ 0743 751 010, *open Jan–Mar, Fri, Sat and Sun 10–1; other times, 10.30–1 and 4–6, closed Mon; adm*) is housed in a 17th-century palace, with an archaeological collection and works of art from the town's churches, including some beautiful early medieval sculpture. There's a lovely carved doorway and rose window on the Gothic church of **San Francesco** in Piazza Garibaldi, Cascia's main square; inside are frescoes from the 15th and 16th centuries, a fancy Baroque pulpit, Gothic choir stalls and the last painting by Niccolò Pomarancio, an *Ascension* (1596). There are more good frescoes by Nicola da Siena and others and a pretty 14th-century statue of the *Virgin and Child* in the nearby **Collegiata di Santa Maria**, a large church founded in 856 and rebuilt several times since; one of the Romanesque lions that original held up a porch is now a fountain, while the other looks out from a niche over the door.

Below Piazza Garibaldi, the austere little church of **Sant'Antonio Abate** is part of the museum (*open the same hours as the Palazzo Santi*). Despite frequent earthquake repairs over the centuries, it preserves in the apse a delightful 14th-century fresco cycle on the *Life of St Anthony Abbot*, attributed to the Maestro della Dormitio di Terni. The nun's choir contains another fine fresco cycle, on the *Passion of Christ* (1461) by Nicola da Siena. But most beautiful of all is the painted 15th-century wooden statue of the *Archangel Raphael with Tobias* by the workshop of Antonio Rizzo.

## Around Cascia

Above Cascia (follow the signs for Monteleone) are the ruins of its 15th-century citadel, destroyed by the papal army after the town's revolt. Below this, the pink and white 14th-century **Convento di Sant'Agostino** has more good 15th-century frescoes. The last site on the Rita trail is her birthplace, at **Roccaporena**, 6km west of Cascia in the Corna valley. The setting, under a mighty rock renamed the Scoglio della Preghiera ('the cliff of prayer') looks exactly like the kind of slightly other-worldly place where a saint would be born. Rita's house was transformed into a church in 1630 by Cardinal Fausto Poli, the chief promoter of her beatification; a little chapel crowns the big rock like a cap.

*Cascia* ✉ *06043*

**Where to Stay and Eating Out**

The top place to stay and eat, ★★★**Cursula**, Via Cavour 3, ✆ 0743 76206, 📠 0743 76262 (*moderate*) has extremely pleasant rooms and good Umbrian home cooking in the restaurant (*moderate*). As its name suggests, ★★**Centrale**, Piazza Garibaldi 36, ✆ 0743 76736 (*inexpensive*) is in a handy location. ★★**Mini Hotel La Tavernetta**, Via Palombi, ✆/📠 0743 71387, is a family-run establishment with clean comfortable rooms (*inexpensive*) and a good restaurant (*moderate*) serving well-cooked local dishes based on wild mushrooms, salami, trout and lamb. *Closed Tues.*

## Norcia and the Monti Sibillini

Umbria has no lack of grandiose scenery, but here in its southeast corner in the shadow of the Monti Sibillini it achieves its highest heights and widest open spaces. Norcia, in ancient times the northernmost of all Sabine towns, stands battered yet proud on its high plain, famous across Italy for its saint and its butchers. One result of the frequent earthquakes here was an 18th-century law limiting the height of buildings to two storeys, and the result looks like no other town in Umbria.

**Getting Around**

Società Spoletino **buses** to Norcia run from Spoleto, Cascia, Perugia, Terni, Foligno, Rome and Ascoli Piceno in the Marche, ✆ 0743 221 991 for schedules. **Bikes** can be hired from March to September from Giuseppina Terenzi, Porta Romana, ✆ 0743 76533.

**Tourist Information**

**Norcia**: in the Municipio, ✆ 0743 828044. There is also an information office for the Monte Sibillini National Park, the Casa del Parco, at Norcia, Via Solferino 22, ✆ 0743 817 090, and at Preci, Via Santa Caterina, ✆ 0743 99145.

**market day**

**Norcia**: Thursday.

## Norcia

Old Norcia (pop. 4,900), or, as the gate reads, VETUSTA NURSIA, is not an easily definable place, and depending on when you visit it can seem bright and cheerful or morose and gloomy, barricaded like a Foreign Legion outpost in its 14th-century walls on the edge of the lofty Piano di Santa Scolastica, surrounded by mountains on all sides. Virgil called it *Frigida Nursia*, so one can imagine when he visited. But the last Roman emperor was still warm in his grave when this old cold town gave the world St Benedict (480–543), the father of Western monasticism, which would go a long way in filling the vacuum of pan-European civilization left by the fall of Rome.

In the Middle Ages, Norcia was a *comune* to be reckoned with. Nor was it long before the Nursini lost their early reputation for sanctity; they were known at various times for witch-craft (there was a sorcerers' college here in the Middle Ages, when *nursino* or *norcino* became synonymous with wizard), as well as pork butchersy and surgery. Practitioners of both the latter were renowned for their expert knife work—after all, in the days when doing autopsies on cadavars was illegal, the famous surgeons of Preci (*see* below) practised on pigs. To this day Norcia is synonymous with prosciutto (from both domestic pork and wild boar) and the best *charcuterie* in Umbria, as well as fine cheeses.

As a sideline to all this, the Nursini were also experts in the art of keeping male voices unnaturally pure and sweet. The parents of a boy with operatic potential would bring him to Norcia, where he would be drugged with opium and put in a very hot bath until he was quite insensible, when the dirty deed was done (the ducts leading to the testicles were severed, so that the organs would eventually shrivel and disappear). Too bad for the lad whose voice never made the grade, but those who did became the darlings of society and quite wealthy besides. Some were such charming primadonnas that Casanova wasn't the only one who kept falling in love with them. One of the last 'graduates' of Norcia, Domenico Mustafa (d. 1912), was director of the Sistine Chapel choir and stayed around long enough to cut the only recording by a castrato.

## Piazza San Benedetto

Norcia keeps its chief monuments on the rounded **Piazza San Benedetto**, presided over by a stern, no-nonsense statue of St Benedict from 1880. Directly behind him stands the 13th-century Gothic **Basilica di San Benedetto**, with a charming portal, framed by statues of Benedict and Scholastica and painted angels, with a Madonna on top and a rose window. On the side of the church, a portico shelters 16th-century grain measures and ends at a sturdy campanile. The interior, blandly remodelled in the 18th century, decorated with unexceptional paintings and restored for the 2000 Jubilee, seems unduly modest for the shrine to the Patron Saint of Europe. Down in the crypt you can study the ruins of a late Roman house, which tradition says belonged to Europroprio Anicio and Abbondanza Reguardati, parents of twins Benedict and Scholastica, the first Western monk and nun.

The handsome **Palazzo Comunale**, also in the piazza, has a 13th-century campanile and portico of 1492, and a **Cappella dei Priori** containing a 15th-century silver reliquary of St Benedict. Next door are the boar and truffle gastronomic speciality shops. These are Norcia's real attraction for Italians: turd-like whole truffles, crusty salami tied up in string and tough weathered hams still sprouting tufts of black bristles (*Two years old and never been in a refrigerator!* proclaims one sign).

The other side of the piazza is occupied by the square **Castellina**, built over the ruins of an ancient temple. Designed in 1554 for Pope Julius III by his favourite architect Vignola, its upper floor now houses the **Museo Civico Diocesano** (✆ 0743 817209, *open daily exc Mon, 10–12.30 and 3.30–6.30*). This holds pretty and precious things, including a late 12th-century painted *Crucifixion* with the two Marys standing on either side of Christ, a not uncommon Romanesque conceit; originally there were two others, but they fell off. Another remarkable *Cross*, signed Petrus, was made half a century later. There's an especially good life-sized *Deposition* group in wood dating from the late 1200s; high reliefs of the *Madonna* *and Child*, and paintings of the same by Antonio da Faenza and others in the Salone, under its handsome panelled ceiling, along with a *Risen Christ* by Nicola da Siena. Another room has stone sculptures by Giovanni Dalmata (1469) from an altarpiece formerly in San Giovanni, and further on are two terracotta statues of the *Annunciation*, by the younger Luca Della Robbia. The loggia is dedicated to detached frescoes.

Next to the Castellina is Norcia's **Duomo**, built by Lombard masons in 1560 and remodelled in the 1700s; the massive campanile was rebuilt in 1859. At the top of the left aisle is the prettiest thing to see: the 17th-century chapel of the Madonna della Misericordia, sheltering a venerated 16th-century fresco of the *Madonna between SS Scholastica and Benedict* set in an elaborate confection of coloured marble and intarsia.

## Elsewhere in Norcia

From the Castellina, Via Battisti leads to the 14th-century Gothic church of **San Francesco**, with a rose window and handsome portal; the interior has 16th-century frescoes and a fine painting by Jacopo Siculo of the *Coronation of the Virgin*. Opposite is the building, now occupied by a restaurant, that once held the public pawn shop, the Monte di Pietà, founded in 1466. Just east of here runs Norcia's straight main street, Corso Sertorio; the town's recently rebuilt theatre is here, in Piazza Vittorio Veneto, on the north end of the Corso by the handsome 19th-century **Porta Romana**. Just outside this, a new partially underground building is slated to house the **Cripto Portico**, an archaeological museum housing finds from the area (*due to open May 2000; phone tourist office for opening times*).

From Corso Sertorio, Via Gioberti leads to the 15th-century church of **San Giovanni**, with its bell tower built into the walls. This is one of the most important churches in Norcia, with a good interior and art, but it has long been closed. From nearby Piazza Carlo Alberto with a fountain, turn down Via Umberto to see the most curious building in Norcia, the square limestone **Tempietto**, built on the street corner by local stonemason Vanni Tuzi in 1354. No one is quite sure what it was used for, but it has pretty reliefs. Via Umberto continues past here to Via Anicia, where a left turn will take you to the 13th-century Gothic church of **Sant'Agostino**, with an ogival portal and a frescoed lunette from 1368, and good 15th- and 16th-century frescoes inside. The **Oratorio di Sant'Agostinuccio**, further up Via Anicia, belongs to a local confraternity and has a charming interior covered in fine woodwork of the early 1600s.

Three km south of Norcia, the cemetery church of **Santa Scolastica** was built not long after the lifetime of the holy twins, according to tradition on the site of their mother's house. Much rebuilt in the 17th century, it has a late 14th-century fresco cycle illustrating the *Life of St Benedict*, discovered in a 1978 restoration. After the 1997 earthquake more of the same is urgently needed.

---

*Norcia* ✉ *06046*   **Where to Stay and Eating Out**

**★★★Nuovo Hotel Posta**, Via C. Battisti 10, ✆/✉ 0743 817434, is a fine hotel and restaurant (*both moderate*), where the pleasant rooms all have bath and they serve the famous, hearty, robust fare of Castelluccio lentils, boar salami, *tortellini alla norcina* (with ricotta), lamb with truffles, topped off, if you dare, by a tumbler of Norcia's nasty *grappa* flavoured with black truffles. ★★★**Grotta Azzurra**, on Via Alfieri, ✆ 0743 816513, ✉ 0743 817342 (*moderate*) also makes a good stopover but offers a different approach to local culinary traditions in its restaurant: a lighter touch, perhaps, its mandatory truffled dishes competing with a tasty risotto with crayfish from the Nera, or fettuccine with trout, or delicious grilled mushrooms. *Closed Tues.* **Dal Francese**, Via Riguardati 16, ✆ 0743 816290 (*moderate*) is the ideal place for a bumper meal in this corner of Umbria, where the truffle is king. Try the smoked turkey and homemade salami for *antipasto*, followed by a pasta medley of *tris al tartufo, gnocchi al tartufo* or *tortellini con crema di tordi* (thrushes) *e tartufi*; for a main course choose between trout dishes, tender grilled lamb or the unusual *braciola in agrodolce con tartufi* (chop in sweet-and-sour sauce with truffles). Good wine list. *Closed Fri exc in summer.* Restaurant **Granaro del Monte**, Via Alfieri 12, ✆ 0743 816513 (*moderate*) specialises in grilled meats prepared before your very eyes on the large open fire. Precede this with pappardelle with truffles and ricotta or a velvety lentil soup.

## North of Norcia: the Valcastoriana

North of Norcia, the rugged and green Valcastoriana is one of the most remote valleys in Umbria. This made it a favourite residence for hermits in the early Middle Ages, and in addition to its natural beauty it has a fine collection of small churches, villages and an important abbey, all of which have unfortunately suffered in the last two earthquakes. The east side of the valley is now part of the Monti Sibillini National Park.

The road from Norcia (follow the signs for Visso) rises through the pines to the 3307ft pass, the **Forca d'Ancarano**. As it descends into the Valcastoriana it passes the delightful church of **Santa Maria Bianca** (*signposted to the right; pick up the key at the nearby house*). Like many, it has been rebuilt and added to over the centuries: early Romanesque capitals support a 15th-century loggia, and there's a funny old campanile. Inside, it has old paving and an ancient font. The high altar shelters the eponymous white *Madonna* (1511), a marble in high relief attributed to the Florentine Francesco di Simone Ferrucci, while the walls are decorated with votive frescoes.

The valley road continues towards Campi, although before reaching it, on the right, you'll see a sign for **Campi Vecchio**, a tiny hamlet with a pretty public wall fountain, all restored after 1979. Its handsome church, **Sant'Andrea**, has a prominent portico that acts as a belvedere over the valley. Two rather sweet lions guard the Gothic door; pick up the key at Via Entedia 15 to visit the attractive 16th-century interior, lined with a hodge-podge of votive paintings and gilded altars. **Campi Basso**, back on the main road, is equally proud of its church of **San Salvatore** out by the cemetery. This has a lovely old asymmetrical façade with a pair of rose windows; inside are fine frescoes by Giovanni and Antonio Sparapane (1464) and an old immersion baptismal font.

To the north just beyond Piedivalle, you'll see the sign for the **Abbazia di Sant'Eutizio**, up in its own little sub-valley. In the early Middle Ages Sant'Eutizio owed much of its success to its remoteness: the story, as told by St Gregory the Great, goes that it was founded by hermits Eutizio and Spes in the late 400s, who were visited by the young St Benedict. It became an abbey under Benedictine rule, and between the 800s and 1200s it prospered under the Dukes of Spoleto, who, along with emperors and popes, gave it large grants of land, so that by the first millennium the abbey owned over a hundred villages and churches. Its library was famous (it had, among other things, Umbria's oldest examples of vernacular Italian, from the 11th century) and an infirmary famous for the skill of its doctors, a skill that was passed on to Preci in the early 1200s when the Benedictines were barred from practising surgery.

The abbey enjoys a beautiful setting, hugging the steep wooded mountain, with its campanile set high on a rock over the cloister. The Romanesque **church** with its rose window and handsome portal was rebuilt in 1190 by a Master Petrus, who gave it a majestic and beautiful interior, with a single nave culminating in a lofty presbytery over the crypt. A fine funerary monument to St Eutizio stands behind the altar, attributed to Rocca da Vicenza (1514), and the intarsia choir stalls date from the 16th century. The abbey has been restored as a hostel for pilgrims of the 2000 Jubilee; from the courtyard, you can visit the grottoes where the first hermits lived.

**Preci**, just up the road, was badly damaged in the earthquakes of 1979 and 1998, and much of it remains structurally unsound and off limits. A small fortified village rebuilt after an attack by Norcia in 1528, it has proud palaces built by its famous surgeons, who learned the art from the Benedictines and passed it down through generations into the 18th century. They had very sharp knives and tools (another speciality of Preci) and specialized in eye operations: when Queen Elizabeth I of England needed a cataract operation in 1588, Cesari Scacchi of Preci was summoned to do the job. A long list of popes and royalty similarly turned to Preci's surgeons; another patient was Sultan Mehemet.

From Preci, you can circle around back to the Valnerina by way of Triponzo, or go back to Norcia by way of the even more remote but wonderfully scenic **Valle Oblita**, where only a handful of people live year round at **Abeto** and **Todiano**, both with handsome palazzi and parish churches holding important Baroque canvases that attest to its importance in past centuries, when the inhabitants made their fortunes as itinerant pork butchers in Tuscany.

## The Piano Grande and Castelluccio

Since 1993, all the territory east of Norcia has been encompassed in the majestic **Monti Sibillini National Park**, which Umbria shares with the Marche. A protected area of some 70,000 hectares, it is off the tourist track, remote and wildly beautiful.

You can see some of the most spectacular scenery by way of the narrow old road from the church of Santa Scolastica south of Norcia (*see* above), which winds a magnificent 21km up to **Forca Canapine** (5055ft), a pass high enough to support a modest ski station in the winter, with a refuge and a hotel. If you're in a hurry to get to Ascoli Piceno and the Adriatic, there's a new road and a long tunnel but it cuts out the glorious scenery.

On the same Forca Canapine road, 18km from Norcia, a road descends into one of the most poetic landscapes in all these pages, the best possible ending to a journey in Umbria. This is the sublime **Piano Grande**, a karstic basin, former glacial lake and now an extraordinary meadow measuring 16 square km, surrounded by bare rolling hills and mountains that look as if they were covered with velvet in the late spring, when the entire meadow explodes into swathes of wildflowers that go on and on for miles, reaching their peak in June. It is a rarefied dream landscape (used by Franco Zeffirelli in his Franciscan film *Brother Sun, Sister Moon*), large enough to distort distances; the flocks that produce Norcia's famous cheese graze here, and its fields produce the famous minute lentils of Castelluccio, which come in three colours and are among the tastiest and rarest in Italy.

A long straight road crosses the Piano Grande, then rises to the lentil village of **Castelluccio**, perched over the valley at 4763ft, the highest and altogether loneliest settlement in Umbria. Castelluccio had 700 inhabitants in 1951 and now has around 40; not so long ago it was often cut off from the rest of the world by the winter snows, a problem now alleviated by ploughs. It is also the one old village in Umbria with no pretence to charm, but it does attract hikers, hang-gliders and cross-country skiers.

## The Rooftop of Umbria: the Monti Sibillini

Castelluccio lies near an important crossroads under the dark and legendary **Monti Sibillini**, the most dramatic mountains in the Apennines. They are still the haunt of wolves and now of bears, who have migrated up from the Abruzzo. There is the odd wildcat and marten, and about 50 pairs of royal eagles (the entire Italian population of this bird is estimated to be only about 300). In late May and early June they are covered with wildflowers and orchids, including some rare ones.

East of Castelluccio a secondary road skirts the slopes of **Monte Vettore** (8123ft), the tallest in the Sibillini, covered with snow from October until June. Its summit (the usual approach is from the east, from the hamlet of Foce near Montemonaco in the Marche) is one of the very few places on the Italian peninsula where both the Adriatic and Tyrrhenian seas are visible, at least on a clear day.

On the slopes of Monte Vettore, the uncanny **Lago di Pilato** lies on the border of Umbria and the Marche, a four-hour trek from Foce. The lake is associated with Pontius Pilate, who either threw himself into its waters to drown in remorse, or according to another story was condemned to death by Tiberius and asked for his body to be placed in a cart, to be driven by oxen to go where they would, and they dumped his body in this lake. Other say a lake as red as blood formed here at the moment of the Crucifixion (the lake really does turn red on occasion, thanks to a species of algae). Peaks and crags in these parts are named after Christ, the Devil, and right by the lake there's a rock called 'the Policeman' to keep mischief to a minimum. Originally, however, this was the lake of the Sibyl. Amulets and weird carvings were found on its shores, left by Norcia's college of sorcerors, who would trudge up here to baptize their grimoires to double their powers. But that's not all they did up here.

## The Sibyl of the Mountains

 One of the most popular medieval Italian romances was *Guerino il Meschino* ('Guerino the Wretch') written in 1391 by Andrea da Barberino. Guerino, a bold and clever young orphan in search of his parents, meets the Devil in a mountain pass above Norcia. The Devil, playing the role of a pimp, advises Guerino to go up into the mountains and seek out Sibilla, a lovely fairy whose cave is a bower of bliss. The price of her charms, of course, is his soul.

But Guerino doesn't hesitate, and finds that Sibilla is everything the Devil promises. He also finds out her true identity: she is the Cumean Sibyl from Campania, the most famous of the dozen prophetic wise women who were honoured by the Church for their predictions of Christ's birth and Passion, thus earning a place on Michelangelo's Sistine Chapel ceiling, on Siena Cathedral's inlaid floor, and elsewhere before the Counter-Reformation put on the brakes. In the *Aeneid*, the Cumean Sibyl was visited by Aeneas on his way to founding Rome and offered him a brief tour of hell; she was later visited by the last king of Rome, Tarquin, who came to her to purchase the nine Sibylline books of prophesy. When he try to dicker down the price, the Sibyl threw three of the precious books into the fire; when he still tried to bargain, she threw in three more, until, in a panic, he paid the original price for the last three. In *Guerino il Meschino* we learn something else about her: that she had expected God to have chosen her to be the virgin mother of His son and was miffed when He chose Mary, then a nobody. When the new Christianity she had predicted took hold, the Sibyl left her cave in Campania and took refuge in a cave in the mountains that were named in her honour.

Guerino in the nick of time discovers that Sibilla and her ladies turn into monsters on Saturdays, and after spending a year in their pleasant company he goes to Rome to seek the Pope's absolution. The humanist Aeneas Sylvius (the future Pope Pius II) identified Sibilla as the goddess Venus, and the popular tale inspired several variants, all casting their spell of magical eroticism and forbidden knowledge over the Monti Sibillini. The most famous story these days, thanks to Wagner, is *Tannhäuser*. Soon so many amorous pilgrims and necromancers were making their way to Norcia, the lake, and the cave (near Montemonaco), that by the 1490s, Rome threatened to excommunicate anyone who went to visit the Sibyl. So many people continued to defy the pope with their profane pilgrimages that the long corridors that descended into the magical realm of the Sibyl were filled in in the 17th century, and dynamited in the 19th to keep all the wickedness within from ever escaping. But in Montemonaco they still know where it is, if you're interested.

### Activities

Outdoor activities abound: trekking (both on foot and in the saddle), mountain-biking, hang-gliding, delta-planing, rock-climbing, canoeing, rafting and, in winter, skiing (downhill and cross-country). For overnight stays in the mountains, there are plenty of *rifugi* or refuges—huts offering modest accommodation and food for equally modest prices (for information, contact the park's headquarters: **Parco Nazionale dei Monti Sibillini**, Largo G.B. Gaola Antinori 1, Visso (Mc). ✆ 0737 95526, ✉ 0737 95532, email *ente@parcosibillini.sinp.net*). For mountain bike excursions and horse trekking, try **Associazione Piangrande**, Castelluccio, ✆ 0743 817279, or **Cooperativa Monte Patino**, Via Foscolo 2, Norcia, ✆ 0743 817487; the latter also organizes hiking trips. For rafting, contact **Rafting Centre Monti Sibillini**, c/o Ristorante dei Cacciatori, Biselli di Norcia, ✆ 0742 23146. **Prodelta**, Via delle Fate 3, Castelluccio, ✆ 0743 821156, is a paragliding and hang-gliding school.

You can spend a rural medieval interlude at the ⋆**Sibilla**, ✆ 0744 870113; its 11 rooms each have showers (*rooms inexpensive; restaurant moderate*). *Closed Tues.* The **Taverna Castelluccio**, Via dietro la Torre, ✆ 0744 821100 (*moderate*) has the best food in town, with good Norcia-style *antipasti* and the village's famous lentils in soup or with sausages. It also has a few *inexpensive* rooms to rent. *Closed Wed, but open daily in summer.*

The fathers of modern Italian were Dante, Manzoni and television. Each played its part in creating a national language from an infinity of regional and local dialects; the Florentine Dante, the first to write in the vernacular, did much to put the Tuscan dialect into the foreground of Italian literature. Manzoni's revolutionary novel, *I Promessi Sposi*, heightened national consciousness by using an everyday language all could understand in the 19th century. Television in the last few decades has performed an even more spectacular linguistic unification; although many Italians still speak a dialect at home, school and work, their TV idols insist on proper Italian.

Italians are not especially apt at learning other languages. English lessons, however, have been the rage for years, and at most hotels and restaurants there will be someone who speaks some English. In small towns and out-of-the-way places, finding an Anglophone may prove more difficult. The words and phrases below should help you out in most situations, but the ideal way to come to Italy is with some Italian under your belt; your visit will be richer, and you're much more likely to make some Italian friends.

## Pronunciation

Italian words are pronounced phonetically. Every vowel and consonant is sounded. Most consonants are the same as in English, exceptions are the c which, when followed by an 'e' or 'i', is pronounced like the English 'ch' (*cinque* thus becomes cheenquay). Italian g is also soft before 'i' or 'e' as in *giro*, or jee-roh. H is never sounded; r is trilled, like the Scottish r; z is pronounced like 'ts' or 'ds'. The consonants sc before the vowels 'i' or 'e' become like the English 'sh'; ch is pronouced like a 'k' as in Chianti; gn as 'nya' (thus *bagno* is pronounced ban-yo); while gli is pronounced like the middle of the word million (Castiglione, pronounced Ca-stil-yohn-ay).

Vowel pronunciation is as follows: a is as in English father; e when unstressed is pronounced like 'a' in fate as in *padre*, when stressed it can be the same or like the 'e' in pet (*bello*); i is like the 'i' in machine, o, like 'e', has two sounds, 'o' as in hope when unstressed (*tacchino*), and usually 'o' as in rock when stressed (*morte*); u is pronounced like the 'u' in June. But beware of the Venetian accent where vowels and consonants are often slurred into a porridge of 'u's, 'v's, 'x's (pronounced 'sh') and 'z's.

The stress usually (but not always!) falls on the penultimate syllable.

# Language

## Useful Words and Phrases

| yes/no/maybe | *sì/no/forse* | Speak slowly | *Parla lentamente* |
|---|---|---|---|
| I don't know | *Non lo so* | Could you assist me? | *Potrebbe aiutarmi?* |
| I don't understand | *Non capisco* | Help! | *Aiuto!* |
| (Italian) | (*italiano*) | Please | *Per favore* |
| Does someone here | *C'è qualcuno qui che* | Thanks (very much) | (*Molto*) *grazie* |
| speak English? | *parla inglese?* | You're welcome | *Prego* |

| | | | |
|---|---|---|---|
| It doesn't matter | *Non importa* | Why? | *Perché?* |
| All right | *Va bene* | How? | *Come?* |
| Excuse me | *Mi scusi* | How much? | *Quanto?* |
| Be careful! | *Attenzione!* | I am lost | *Mi sono smarrito* |
| Nothing | *Niente* | I am hungry | *Ho fame* |
| It is urgent! | *E urgente!* | I am thirsty | *Ho sete* |
| How are you? | *Come stai?* (informal) | I am sorry | *Mi dispiace* |
| | *sta* (formal) | I am tired | *Sono stanco* |
| Well, and you? | *Bene, e Lei?* | I am sleepy | *Ho sonno* |
| What is your name? | *Come si chiama, Lei?* | I am ill | *Mi sento male* |
| Hello | *Salve* or *ciao* | Leave me alone | *Lasciami in pace* |
| | (both informal) | good | *buono/bravo* |
| Good morning | *Buon giorno* | bad | *male/cattivo* |
| | (formal hello) | It's all the same | *Fa lo stesso* |
| Good afternoon, | *Buona sera* (also | slow | *lento/piano* |
| evening | formal hello) | fast | *rapido* |
| Good night | *Buona notte* | big | *grande* |
| Goodbye | *ArrivederLa* (formal) | small | *piccolo* |
| | *Arrivederci* (informal) | hot | *caldo* |
| What do you call | *Come si chiama* | cold | *freddo* |
| this in Italian? | *questo in italiano?* | up | *su* |
| What? | *Che cosa?* | down | *giù* |
| Who? | *Chi?* | here | *qui* |
| Where? | *Dove?* | there | *lì* |
| When? | *Quando?* | | |

## Shopping, Service, Sightseeing

| | | | |
|---|---|---|---|
| I would like ... | *Vorrei ...* | money | *soldi* |
| Where is/are?. . . | *Dov'è/Dove sono?...* | museum | *museo* |
| How much is it? | *Quanto via questo?* | newspaper (foreign) | *giornale* (*straniero*) |
| open | *aperto* | chemist | *farmacia* |
| closed | *chiuso* | police station | *commissariato* |
| cheap | *a buon mercato* | policeman | *poliziotto* |
| expensive | *caro* | post office | *ufficio postale* |
| bank | *banca* | sea | *mare* |
| beach | *spiaggia* | shop | *negozio* |
| bed | *letto* | telephone | *telefono* |
| church | *chiesa* | tobacco shop | *tabacchaio* |
| entrance | *entrata* | WC | *toilette/bagno* |
| exit | *uscita* | men | *Signori/Uomini* |
| hospital | *ospedale* | women | *Signore/Donne* |

## Time

| | | | |
|---|---|---|---|
| What time is it? | *Che ore sono?* | today | *oggi* |
| month | *mese* | yesterday | *ieri* |
| week | *settimana* | tomorrow | *domani* |
| day | *giorno* | soon | *fra poco* |
| morning | *mattina* | later | *più tardi* |
| afternoon | *pomeriggio* | It is too early | *E troppo presto* |
| evening | *sera* | It is too late | *E troppo tardi* |

## Days

| | | | |
|---|---|---|---|
| Monday | *lunedì* | Friday | *venerdì* |
| Tuesday | *martedì* | Saturday | *sabato* |
| Wednesday | *mercoledì* | Sunday | *domenica* |
| Thursday | *giovedì* | | |

## Numbers

| | | | |
|---|---|---|---|
| one | *uno/una* | twenty | *venti* |
| two | *due* | twenty-one | *ventuno* |
| three | *tre* | twenty-two | *ventidue* |
| four | *quattro* | thirty | *trenta* |
| five | *cinque* | thirty-one | *trentuno* |
| six | *sei* | forty | *quaranta* |
| seven | *sette* | fifty | *cinquanta* |
| eight | *otto* | sixty | *sessanta* |
| nine | *nove* | seventy | *settanta* |
| ten | *dieci* | eighty | *ottanta* |
| eleven | *undici* | ninety | *novanta* |
| twelve | *dodici* | hundred | *cento* |
| thirteen | *tredici* | one hundred and one | *cent'uno* |
| fourteen | *quattordici* | two hundred | *due cento* |
| fifteen | *quindici* | thousand | *mille* |
| sixteen | *sedici* | two thousand | *due mila* |
| seventeen | *diciasette* | million | *milione* |
| eighteen | *diciotto* | billion | *miliardo* |
| nineteen | *diciannove* | | |

## Transport

| | | | |
|---|---|---|---|
| airport | *aeroporto* | port station | *stazione maritimma* |
| bus stop | *fermata* | ship | *nave* |
| bus/coach | *autobus/pulmino* | automobile | *macchina* |
| railway station | *stazione (ferroviaria)* | taxi | *tassi* |
| train | *treno* | ticket | *biglietto* |
| train/platform | *binario* | customs | *dogana* |
| port | *porto* | seat (reserved) | *posto (prenotato)* |

## Travel Directions

| | | | |
|---|---|---|---|
| I want to go to . . . | *Voglio andare a …* | When does the next train leave? | *Quando parte il prossimo treno?* |
| How can I get to…? | *Come posso arrivare a …?* | From where does it leave? | *Da dove parte?* |
| The next stop, please | *La prossima fermata, per favore* | How long does the trip take? | *Quanto tempo dura il viaggio?* |
| Where is … / where is it? | *Dove … /Dov'è?* | How much is the fare? | *Quant'è il biglietto?* |
| How far is it to …? | *Quanto siamo lontani da … ?* | Have a good trip! | *Buon viaggio!* |
| What is the name of this station? | *Come si chiama questa stazione?* | near | *vicino* |
| | | far | *lontano* |

| | | | |
|---|---|---|---|
| left | *sinistra* | south | *sud/mezzogiorno* |
| right | *destra* | | (the South of Italy) |
| straight ahead | *sempre diritto* | east | *est/oriente* |
| forward | *avanti* | west | *ovest/occidentale* |
| back | *indietro* | around the corner | *dietro l'angolo* |
| north | *nord/settentrionale* | crossroads | *bivio* |
| | (the North of Italy) | street/road | *strada* |
| | | square | *piazza* |

## Driving

| | | | |
|---|---|---|---|
| car hire | *noleggio macchina* | breakdown | *panna* |
| motorbike/scooter | *motocicletta/Vespa* | driver's licence | *patente di guida* |
| bicycle | *bicicletta* | driver | *guidatore* |
| petrol/diesel | *benzina/gasolio* | speed | *velocità* |
| garage | *garage* | danger | *pericolo* |
| This doesn't work | *Questo non* | parking | *parcheggio* |
| | *funziona* | no parking | *divieto di sosta* |
| mechanic | *meccanico* | narrow | *stretto* |
| map/town plan | *carta/pianta* | bridge | *ponte* |
| Where is the | *Dov'è la strada* | toll | *pedaggio* |
| road to . . . ? | *per. . . ?* | to slow down | *rallentare* |

# Italian Menu Vocabulary

## Antipasti

These appetizers can include almost anything, among the most common are:

| | | | |
|---|---|---|---|
| *antipasto misto* | mixed antipasto | *gamberi ai fagioli* | prawns with beans |
| *bruschetta* | toast with garlic and | *mozzarella* | cow or buffalo |
| | tomatoes | *(in carrozza)* | cheese (fried with |
| *carciofi (sott'olio)* | artichokes (in oil) | | bread in batter) |
| *crostini* | liver pâté on toast | *olive* | olives |
| *frutti di mare* | seafood | *prosciutto* | raw ham |
| *funghi (trifolati)* | mushrooms (with | *(con melone)* | (with melon) |
| | anchovies, garlic | *salame* | cured pork |
| | and lemon) | *salsiccia* | sausage |

## Minestre e Pasta

These dishes are the principal first courses (*primi piatti*) served throughout Italy.

| | | | |
|---|---|---|---|
| *agnolotti* | meat-filled pasta | *minestrone* | soup with meat, |
| *cacciucco* | spiced fish soup | | vegetables and pasta |
| *cappelletti* | small ravioli, often | *orecchiette* | ear-shaped pasta, |
| | in broth | | often served with |
| *crespelle* | crêpes | | turnip greens |
| *fettuccine* | long strips of pasta | *panzerotti* | ravioli filled with |
| *frittata* | omelette | | mozzarella, |
| *gnocchi* | potato dumplings | | anchovies and egg |
| *minestra di verdura* | thick vegetable soup | *pappardelle alla* | flat pasta ribbons |
| | | *lepre* | with hare sauce |

| | | | |
|---|---|---|---|
| pasta e fagioli | soup with beans, bacon and tomatoes | spaghetti alla carbonara | with bacon, eggs and black pepper |
| pastina in brodo | tiny pasta in broth | al pomodoro | with tomato sauce |
| penne all'arrabbiata | pasta tubes in spicy tomato sauce | al sugo/ragù | with meat sauce |
| polenta | cake or pudding of corn semolina, fried, baked or grilled | alle vongole | with clam sauce |
| | | stracciatella | broth with eggs and cheese |
| risotto | rice cooked with | tagliatelle | flat egg noodles |
| (alla Milanese) | stock, saffron and wine | tortellini al | stuffed rings of |
| spaghetti all' | with tomatoes, bacon | pomodoro/ | pasta filled with meat |
| Amatriciana | and garlic, plus | panna/ | and cheese, served |
| | pecorino cheese | in brodo | with tomato sauce, cream, or in broth |
| | | vermicelli | very thin spaghetti |

## Second Courses—*Carne* (Meat)

| | | | |
|---|---|---|---|
| abbacchio | milk-fed lamb | lepre (in salmi) | hare (marinated in wine, herbs etc) |
| agnello | lamb | | |
| anatra | duck | lombo di maiale | pork loin |
| animelle | sweetbreads | lumache | snails |
| arista | pork loin | maiale (al latte) | pork (cooked in milk) |
| arrosto misto | mixed roast meats | manzo | beef |
| bistecca alla Fiorentina | Florentine beef steak | osso buco | braised veal knuckle with herbs |
| bocconcini | veal mixed with ham and cheese and fried | | |
| | | pancetta | bacon |
| bollito misto | stew of boiled meats | pernice | partridge |
| braciola | pork chop | petto di pollo | boned chicken breast |
| brasato di manzo | braised beef | (alla Fiorentina/ | (fried in butter/ |
| bresaola | dried salt beef served with lemon, olive oil and parsley | Bolognese/ Sorpresa) | with ham and stuffed and deep fried) |
| | | piccione | pigeon |
| capretto | kid | pizzaiola | beef steak with tomato |
| capriolo | roe buck | | and oregano sauce |
| carne di castrato/suino | mutton/pork | pollo | chicken |
| carpaccio | thin slices of raw beef served like bresaola | (alla cacciatora/ alla diavola/ | (with tomatoes and mushrooms cooked in |
| cassoeula | winter stew with pork and cabbage | al Marengo) | wine/grilled/fried with tomatoes, garlic & wine) |
| Cervello | brains | polpette | meatballs |
| (al burro nero) | (in black butter sauce) | quaglie | quails |
| cervo | venison | rane | frogs |
| cinghiale | boar | rognoni | kidneys |
| coniglio | rabbit | saltimbocca | veal scallop with |
| cotoletta | veal cutlet (fried in | | prosciutto and sage, |
| (alla Milanese/ | breadcrumbs/with | | cooked in pieces of |
| alla Bolognese) | ham and cheese) | | beef or veal, usually |
| fagiano | pheasant | | stewed |
| faraona (alla creta) | guinea fowl (in earthenware pot) | stufato | beef braised in white wine with vegetables |
| fegato alla veneziana | liver and onions | tacchino | turkey |
| involtini | rolled slices of veal with filling | trippa | tripe |
| | | vitello | veal |

## *Pesce* (Fish)

| | | | |
|---|---|---|---|
| *acciughe* or *alici* | anchovies | *merluzzo* | cod |
| *anguilla* | eel | *nasello* | hake |
| *aragosta* | lobster | *orata/dorata* | gilthead |
| *aringhe* | herrings | *ostrice* | oysters |
| *baccalà* | salt cod | *pesce azzuro* | various small fish |
| *bonito* | small tuna | *pesce S. Pietro* | John Dory |
| *branzino* | sea bass | *pesce spada* | swordfish |
| *calamari* | squid | *polipi* | octopus |
| *conchiglie* | scallops | *rombo* | turbot |
| *cefalo* | grey mullet | *sarde* | sardines |
| *cozze* | mussels | *seppie* | cuttlefish |
| *datteri di mare* | razor (or date) | *sgombro* | mackerel |
| | mussels | *sogliola* | sole |
| *dentice* | dentex (perch-like | *squadro* | monkfish |
| | fish) | *tonno* | tuna |
| *fritto misto* | mixed fish fry, with | *triglia* | red mullet (rouget) |
| | squid and shrimp | *trota* | trout |
| *gambereto* | shrimp | *trota salmonata* | salmon trout |
| *gamberi* (*di fiume*) | prawns (crayfish) | *vongole* | small clams |
| *granchio* | crab | *zuppa di pesce* | mixed fish in sauce |
| *insalata di mare* | seafood salad | | or stew |
| *lampre* | lamprey | | |

## *Contorni* (Side Dishes, Vegetables)

| | | | |
|---|---|---|---|
| *asparagi* | asparagus | *lattuga* | lettuce |
| (*alla Fiorentina*) | (with fried eggs) | *lenticchie* | lentils |
| *broccoli* | broccoli | *melanzane* | aubergine/eggplant |
| (*calabrese, romana*) | (green, spiral) | (*al forno*) | (filled and baked) |
| *carciofi* (*alla* | artichokes (deep | *patate* (*fritte*) | potatoes (fried) |
| *giudia*) | fried) | *peperonata* | stewed peppers, onions |
| *cardi* | cardoons, thistles | | and tomatoes |
| *carote* | carrots | *peperoni* | sweet peppers |
| *cavolfiore* | cauliflower | *piselli* (*al prosciutto*) | peas (with ham) |
| *cavolo* | cabbage | *pomodoro* | tomato |
| *ceci* | chickpeas | *porri* | leeks |
| *cetriolo* | cucumber | *radicchio* | red chicory |
| *cipolla* | onion | *radiche* | radishes |
| *fagioli* | white beans | *rapa* | turnip |
| *fagiolini* | French (green) beans | *sedano* | celery |
| *fave* | broad beans | *spinaci* | spinach |
| *finocchio* | fennel | *verdure* | greens |
| *funghi* (*porcini*) | mushroom (boletus) | *zucca* | pumpkin |
| *insalata* | salad | *zucchini* | courgettes |

## *Formaggio* (Cheese)

| | | | |
|---|---|---|---|
| *Bel Paese* | soft, white cow's | *fontina* | rich cow's milk |
| | cheese | | cheese |
| *cascio*/ | pale yellow, often | *groviera* | mild cheese |
| *casciocavallo* | sharp cheese | *Gorgonzola* | soft blue cheese |

| | | | |
|---|---|---|---|
| *Parmigiano* | Parmesan cheese | *provolone* | sharp, tangy cheese; |
| *pecorino* | sharp sheep's | | *dolce* is more mild |
| | cheese | *stracchino* | soft white cheese |

## *Frutta* (Fruit, Nuts)

| | | | |
|---|---|---|---|
| *albicocche* | apricots | *mandorle* | almonds |
| *ananas* | pineapple | *melograna* | pomegranate |
| *arance* | oranges | *mele* | apples |
| *banane* | bananas | *melone* | melon |
| *cachi* | persimmon | *more* | blackberries |
| *ciliege* | cherries | *nespola* | medlar fruit |
| *cocomero* | watermelon | *nocciole* | hazelnuts |
| *composta di frutta* | stewed fruit | *noci* | walnuts |
| *dattero* | date | *pera* | pear |
| *fichi* | figs | *pesca* | peach |
| *fragole (con* | strawberries (with | *pesca noce* | nectarine |
| *panna)* | cream) | *pompelmo* | grapefruit |
| *frutta di stagione* | fruit in season | *pignoli* | pine nuts |
| *lamponi* | raspberries | *susina* | plum |
| *macedonia di frutta* | fruit salad | *prugna secca* | prune |
| *mandarino* | tangerine | *uve* | grapes |

## *Dolci* (Desserts)

| | | | |
|---|---|---|---|
| *Amaretti* | macaroons | *panforte* | dense cake of |
| *cannoli* | crisp pastry tube | | chocolate, almonds |
| | filled with ricotta, | | and preserved fruit |
| | cream, chocolate or | *Saint Honoré* | meringue cake |
| | fruit | *semifreddo* | refrigerated cake |
| *coppa* | assorted ice cream | *sorbetto* | sorbet |
| *crema caramella* | crème caramel | *spumone* | a soft ice cream or |
| *crostata* | fruit flan | | mousse |
| *gelato (produzione* | ice cream | *tiramisù* | mascarpone, coffee, |
| *propria)* | (homemade) | | chocolate and |
| *granita* | flavoured ice, | | sponge fingers |
| | usually lemon or | *torrone* | nougat |
| | coffee | *torta* | tart |
| *Monte Bianco* | chestnut pudding | *torta millefoglie* | layered custard tart |
| | with whipped cream | *zabaglione* | whipped eggs, sugar |
| *Panettone* | sponge cake with | | and Marsala wine, |
| | candied fruit and | | served hot |
| | raisins | *Zuppa Inglese* | trifle |

## Drinks

| | | | |
|---|---|---|---|
| *acqua minerale* | mineral water | *latte* | milk |
| *con/senza gas* | with/without fizz | *(magro)* | (skimmed) |
| *aranciata* | orange soda | *limonata* | lemon soda |
| *birra (alla spina)* | beer (draught) | *sugo di frutta* | fruit juice |
| *caffè (freddo)* | coffee (iced) | *tè* | tea |
| *cioccolata* | hot chocolate | *vino (rosso, bianco,* | wine (red, white, rosé) |
| *(con panna)* | (with cream) | *rosato)* | |

## Cooking Terms, Miscellaneous

| | | | |
|---|---|---|---|
| *aceto (balsamico)* | vinegar (balsamic) | *mostarda* | sweet mustard sauce, |
| *affumicato* | smoked | | served with meat |
| *aglio* | garlic | *olio* | oil |
| *ai ferri* | grilled | *pane (tostato)* | bread (toasted) |
| *al forno* | baked | *panini* | sandwiches |
| *alla brace* | braised | *panna* | fresh cream |
| *arrosto* | roasted | *pepe* | pepper |
| *bicchiere* | glass | *peperoncini* | hot chilli peppers |
| *burro* | butter | *piatto* | plate |
| *cacciagione* | game | *prezzemolo* | parsley |
| *conto* | bill | *rosmarino* | rosemary |
| *costoletta/cotoletta* | chop | *sale* | salt |
| *coltello* | knife | *salmi* | wine marinade |
| *cucchiaio* | spoon | *salsa* | sauce |
| *filetto* | fillet | *salvia* | sage |
| *forchetta* | fork | *senape* | mustard |
| *forno* | oven | *tartufi* | truffles |
| *fritto* | fried | *tazza* | cup |
| *ghiaccio* | ice | *tavola* | table |
| *limone* | lemon | *tovagliolo* | napkin |
| *magro* | lean meat/or pasta | *tramezzini* | finger sandwiches |
| | without meat | *in umido* | stewed |
| *marmellata* | jam | *uovo* | egg |
| *miele* | honey | *zucchero* | sugar |

| | |
|---|---|
| **ambones** | twin pulpits (singular: *ambo*), often elaborately decorated. |
| **ambulatory** | an aisle around the apse of a church. |
| **atrium** | entrance court of a Roman house or early church. |
| **badia** | an abbey or abbey church; also *abbazia*. |
| **baldacchino** | baldachin, a columned stone canopy above the altar of a church. |
| **basilica** | a rectangular building, usually divided into three aisles by rows of columns. In Rome this was the common form for law courts and other public buildings, and Roman Christians adapted it for their early churches. |
| **bucchero ware** | black, delicately thin Etruscan ceramics, usually incised or painted. |
| **campanile** | a bell tower. |
| *campanilismo* | local patriotism; the Italians' own word for their historic tendency to be more faithful to their home towns than to the abstract idea of 'Italy'. |
| **cantoria** | singing gallery in a church. |
| **cartoon** | preliminary sketch for a fresco or tapestry. From *cartone*, 'big paper'. |
| **castrum** | a Roman military camp, always neatly rectangular, with straight streets and gates at the cardinal points. Later the Romans founded or refounded cities in this form: Carsulae is an obvious one. |
| **cavea** | the semicircle of seats in a classical theatre. |
| **chiaroscuro** | the arrangement or treatment of light and dark areas in a painting. |
| **ciborium** | a tabernacle; the word is often used for large, free-standing tabernacles, or in the sense of a *baldacchino* (q.v.). |
| **cippus** | a funerary monument resembling an altar. |
| **clerestory** | a row of windows in the upper part of the wall of a church that divides the nave from the aisle, set above the aisle roof. |
| *comune* | commune, or commonwealth, referring to the governments of the free city states of the Middle Ages. Today it denotes any local government, from the Comune di Roma down to the smallest village. |
| *condottiere* | the leader of a band of mercenaries in late medieval and Renaissance times. |
| **confraternity** | a religious lay brotherhood, often serving as a neighbourhood mutual-aid and burial society, or following some specific charitable work (Michelangelo, for example, belonged to one that cared for condemned prisoners in Rome). |

# Architectural, Artistic and Historical Terms

| | |
|---|---|
| *contado* | the county or countryside around and under the control of a medieval *comune*. |
| *convento* | a convent or monastery. |

| | |
|---|---|
| **Cosmati work** | or *Cosmatesque*: referring to a distinctive style of inlaid marble or enamel chips used in architectural decoration (pavements, pulpits, paschal candlesticks, etc.) in medieval Italy. The Cosmati family of Rome were its greatest practitioners. |
| **Cyclopean** | ancient walls made of enormous fitted unmortared stones, which the ancients attributed to the Cyclops. |
| *duomo* | cathedral. |
| **ex voto** | an offering (a terracotta figurine, painting, medallion, silver bauble, or whatever) made in thanksgiving to a god or Christian saint; the practice has always been present in Italy. |
| **forum** | the central square of a Roman town, with its most important temples and public buildings. The word means 'outside', as the original Roman Forum was outside the first city walls. |
| **fresco** | wall painting, the most important Italian medium of art since Etruscan times. It isn't easy; first the artist draws the *sinopia* (q.v.) on the wall. This is covered with plaster, but only a little at a time, as the paint must be on the plaster before it dries. |
| **Ghibellines** | one of the two great medieval parties, the supporters of the Holy Roman Emperors. |
| **gonfalon** | the standard of a medieval free city; the *gonfaloniere*, or flag-bearer, was often the most important public official. Cities or religious confraternities also had gonfalons painted of the Madonna della Misericordia or a plague saint, which would be carried around an afflicted town in the hopes of attracting divine mercy: a number of these survive. |
| **graffito** | originally, incised decoration on buildings, walls, etc.; only lately has it come to mean casually scribbled messages in public places. |
| **Greek cross** | in the floor plans of churches, a cross with equal arms. The more familiar plan, with one arm extended to form a nave, is called a *Latin cross*. |
| **grisaille** | painting or fresco in monochrome. |
| **grotesques** | carved or painted faces used in Etruscan and later Roman decoration; Raphael and other artists rediscovered them in the 'grotto' of Nero's Golden House in Rome. |
| **Guelphs** | (see *Ghibellines*): the other great political faction of medieval Italy, supporters of the Pope. |
| **hypogeum** | a manmade hole in the ground, usually a subterranean tomb and usually Etruscan. |
| **intarsia** | decorative inlaid wood or marble. |
| **loggia** | an open-sided gallery or arcade. |
| **lunette** | semicircular space on a wall, above a door or under vaulting, either filled by a window or a mural painting. |
| **majolica** | tin-glazed ceramics. |

| | |
|---|---|
| **matroneum** | the elevated women's gallery around the nave of an early church, a custom adopted from the Byzantines in the 6th and 7th centuries. |
| **narthex** | the enclosed porch of a church. |
| **palazzo** | not just a palace, but any large, important building (though the word comes from the Imperial *palatium* on Rome's Palatine Hill). |
| **Palio** | a banner, and the horse race in which city neighbourhoods contend for it in their annual festivals. |
| **Pantocrator** | Christ 'ruler of all', a common subject for apse paintings and mosaics in areas influenced by Byzantine art. |
| **pietra dura** | rich inlay work using semi-precious stones, perfected in post-Renaissance Florence. |
| *pieve* | a parish church. |
| *podestà* | in a medieval *comune*, an elected official in charge of law and order, usually from another town in order to ensure his impartiality. He served for an appointed period, usually from six months to a year. |
| **predella** | smaller paintings on panels below the main subject of a painted altar piece. |
| **Presepio** | a Christmas crib. |
| **Pronaos** | porch of a temple; the area between the façade and the *cella* or inner sanctum. |
| **Putti** | flocks of plaster cherubs with rosy cheeks and bums that infested much of Italy in the Baroque era. |
| **Quattrocento** | the 1400s—the Italian way of referring to centuries (*duecento, trecento, quattrocento, cinquecento*, etc.). |
| *sbandieratore* | flag-thrower in medieval costume at a festival; sometimes called an *alfiere*. |
| **sinopia** | the layout of a fresco (q.v.), etched by the artist on the wall before the plaster is applied. Often these are works of art in their own right. |
| **stele** | a vertical funeral stone. |
| **stigmata** | a miraculous simulation of the bleeding wounds of Christ, appearing in holy men like St Francis in the 12th century, and Padre Pio of Apulia in our own time. |
| **thermae** | Roman baths. |
| **tondo** | round relief, painting or terracotta. |
| **transenna** | marble screen separating the altar area from the rest of an early Christian church. |
| **travertine** | hard, light-coloured stone, sometimes flecked or pitted with black, sometimes perfect. The most widely used material in ancient and modern Rome. |
| **triptych** | a painting, especially an altarpiece, in three sections. |
| **tympanum** | the semicircular space, often bearing a painting or relief, above the portal of a church. |

# Further Reading

**Gelmetti, Susanna**, *Italian Country Cooking: Recipes from Umbria and Apulia* (Ten Speed Press, 1996). Written by a chef who runs a cooking school, and lavishly illustrated.

**Goethe, J.W.**, *Italian Journey* (Penguin, 1982). An excellent example of a genius turned to mush by Italy; good insights, but big, big mistakes. Interesting section on Umbria.

**Hutton, Edward**, *The Cities of Umbria* (London, Methuen, 1905). You'll have to go to a big library for this classic of 'Umbria, the true Italia Mystica' from the glorious age of travel writing.

**McIntyre, Anthony**, *Medieval Tuscany and Umbria* (Viking, 1992). Recent account of Umbria's golden age of the *comuni* to the rise of the *signoria*.

**Peck, George T.**, *The Fool of God: Jacopone da Todi* (University of Alabama, 1980). Fine account of his life and times in medieval Todi, along with a sympathetic analysis of his poetry.

**Procacci, Giuliano**, *History of the Italian People* (Penguin, 1973). An in-depth view from the year 1000 to the present—also an introduction to the wit and subtlety of the best Italian scholarship.

**Richards, Charles**, *The New Italians* (Penguin, 1995). An observant and amusing study of life in Italy during and since the political upheaval and the financial scandals in the early 1990s.

**Ross, Ian Campbell**, *Umbria: A Cultural History* (Viking, 1996). Well researched and sympathetic account that explains how Umbria arrived at its current state of affairs.

**St Aubin de Terán, Lisa**, *A Valley in Italy: Confessions of a House Addict* (Penguin, 1994). Life in rural Umbria, and one of the more eccentric but entertaining ex-pat sagas of recent years.

*The Little Flowers of St Francis (I Fioretti): The Acts of Saint Francis and His Companions*, trans. E.M. Blaiklock and A.C. Keys (Hodder & Stoughton, 1985). The poems and original source of the Franciscan legend.

**Vasari, Giorgio**, *Lives of the Painters, Sculptors and Architects* (Everyman, 1996). Readable, anecdotal accounts of the Renaissance greats by the father of modern art history.

**White, John**, *Art and Architecture in Italy 1250–1400* (Yale University Press, 1993). Puts Umbria's golden age into context with the rest of Italy.

**Notes:** Page numbers in *italics* indicate maps

Abbazia di San Felice 148
Abbazia di San Pietro in Valle 38, 45, 215, 218
Abbazia di Santa Maria di Sitria 130
Abbazia di Sant'Eutizio 38, 224
Abbazia Santi Fidenzio e Terenzio 176
Abbazia di Santi Severo e Martirio 188, 189
Abbazia di Sassovivo 141–2
Abbazia di Vallignegno 130
Abeto 34, 225
Accoromboni, Vittoria 126
Acquasparta 207
Agostino di Duccio 67, 68, 72, 75, 195
Agresti, Livio 197, 210
agriturismo 27, 29–31
Alaric 37
Alberto Sotio *see* Sotius
Albornoz, Cardinal Gil 41, 42, 62, 91, 96, 103, 151, 157
Alessi, Galeazzo 67, 81, 89
Alexander VI, Pope 41
Alfani, Domenico di Paride 48, 71, 89
Algardi, Alessandro 159
Allerona 191
Alunno, L' (Niccolò di Liberatore) 46, 101, 102, 136, 141, 210
Alunno, Nicolò 81, 138, 192, 197
Alviano 192
Amelia 16, 21, 34, 194–6
Amelia, Pier Matteo d' 159
Ammannati, Giovanni 182
Andersen, Hans Christian 82
Andrea di Bartolo 118
Andreoli, Mastro Giorgio 124, 126
Angela, Blessed 103, 139
Angelico, Beato *see* Beato Angelico
Angelico, Fra 182
Angelo da Orvieto 116, 124
Antognola 27
Antoniazzo, Marcantonio di 213
Antoniazzo Romano 204
Antonio da Faenza 223
Appiani, Francesco 195
Aquinas, St Thomas 160, 180, 185
archaeology tours 11–12
architecture 237–9
Armenzano 107
Arnolfo di Cambio 68, 180, 184, 185
Arpino, Cavalier d' 158
Arrigo Fiammingo (Heinrich van der Broek) 91
Arrone 214, 217
Asproli 174
**Assisi** 26, *61*, **91–109**, *92–3*
    activities 106
    Basilica of San Francesco 45, 50–51, 91–101, *97*

**Assisi** (*cont'd*)
    Cathedral 102
    earthquakes 44, 50–51, 93–4, 101, 105, 106
    eating out 108–9
    Eremo delle Carceri 105
    festivals 15, 16, 106
    history 35, 50, 91–4
    Piazza del Comune 94, 102
    Porziuncola 53, 105–6
    Rocca Maggiore 91, 103
    San Damiano 53, 104–5
    San Francesco *see* Basilica of San Francesco *above*
    Santa Chiara 103–4
    Santa Maria degli Angeli 105–6
    Temple of Minerva 91, 102
    where to stay 107–8, 109
Atti family 167
Attigliano 198
Augustus, Emperor 37, 61
Avigliano Umbro 198

Badia di San Salvatore 112–14
Baglioni 41, 60, 62, 63, 67, 70, 86, 136
Baglioni, Astorre I 63
Baglioni, Braccio I 63
Baglioni, Giampaolo 63
Baglioni, Malatesta I 63
Barattano 148
Barberini family 158
Barberino, Andrea da 226
Barnoregio 188
Barocci, Federico 123
Bartolomeo di Tommaso 46, 211
Baschi 18, 188, 192, 193
Bastardo 148
Bastia Umbra 15, 109
bears 56, 226
Beato Angelico 46, 68
Beccafumi, Domenico 157
Belisarius 38
Belvedere 119
Benedict, St 37, 221–3, 224
Benedict XI, Pope 62, 75
Benedictines 130, 225
Benincasa, Carlo Federico 204
Bernardino of Siena, St 67, 72, 172, 173
Bernardo da Calvi 205
Bernini, Gian Lorenzo 140, 218
Bettona 109–10
Bevagna 15, 143–5
Bevignate, Fra 66, 123
Binello, Maestro 143
birds 27, 56, 82, 84, 142, 226
Black Death 41, 55
boars, wild 27, 56

Boccati da Camerino, Giovanni 68
Bomarzo 191, 198
Bonfigli, Benedetto 46, 68, 74, 81, 90
Boniface VIII, Pope 171–2, 184, 186
Borgia, Cesare 41
Borgia, Lucrezia 41, 154
Borgo Cerreto 216
Borgo Sansepolcro 46, 121
Bosco 79
Bourbon Del Monte family 119
Bovara 150
Braccio, Carlo 114
Braccio Fortebraccio (Andrea Braccio) 41, 63, 67, 114
brigandage 42
Bruna 148
bungee jumping 214
Buondelmonti, Buondelmonte dei 51
Burri, Alberto 48, 117
bus travel 7–8
Byron, Lord 151, 212, 213
Byzantines 37–8, 45, 131

Calder, Alexander 155
Calvi dell'Umbria 205
Camignano valley 122
Campello Alto 151
Campello sul Clitunno 151–2
Campi Basso 224
Campi Vecchio 224
Campione, Simone di 136
Canada, travel from 4–5
Cannara 21, 138
canoeing 27, 212, 227
Capanna, Puccio 96, 99
Caporali, Bartolomeo 46, 68, 84, 85, 109, 114
Caporali, Cesare 90
Caporali, Gian Battista 90
Caprarola 198
car hire 3, 7, 9
Cardigliano 174
Carducci, Giosuè 44, 150
Carsulae 38, 207–8, 237
Carthaginians 36–7, 85–6
Cascata delle Marmore 27, 208, 212
Cascella, Pietro 86
Cascia 15, 219–21
Caso 218
Castel d'Alfiolo 130
Castel dell'Aquila 198
Castel Rigone 84, 87
Castel Ritaldi 148
Castel Rubello 188
Castel San Felice 216
Castel Viscardo 190
Casteldilago 214

# Index

Castello di Montegualandro 85
Castello del Poggio 192
Castello di Zocco 84
Castelluccio 27, 226, 228
Castiglione del Lago 15, 82–3, 86–8
castrati 222
Catena, Vicenzo 137
Cavallini, Pietro 100
caves 27, 130, 205
Cenerente 79
ceramics 26, 80–81, 191
Cerqueto 175
Cerreto di Spoleto 217
Cesari, Pierino 216
Cesi 207–8
Cesi, Federico 207
Charlemagne, Emperor 38–9
Chiara see Clare
Chiesa Tonda 137
children 3, 58
churches 24
Cimabue 45, 98–9, 101, 106
Cimitelle 211
Cirelli, Vittorio 114
Citerna 120
Città di Castello 16, 47, 115–20
Città della Pieve 15, 16, 88–91
Civitella Benazzone 112
Civitella del Lago 192, 193
Civitella Ranieri 112
Clare, St (Chiara Offreduccio) 103–4
Clare of the Cross, St (Chiara da Montefalco)
    103, 147
Clement VII, Pope 42, 187
climbing see rock
Clitunno river 146, 150
coach travel 7–8
Cola di Pietro 216
Colfiorito 50, 142
Collazzone 172, 175
Colle Bertone 215
Colle Plinio 120
Collelungo 198
Collemancio 138
Collepino 105, 137
Collescìpoli 211
Collevalenza 175
Colli see wines
Colonna family 172–3, 197
Colonna, Francesco 191
comuni 39–41
Conca, Sebastiano 158, 159
condottieri 41
Constantine, Emperor 37
Constantine Rescript 36
consulates 22
Convento del Sacro Specco 205
Convento di Santa Maria della Rocchicciola
    109
Convento di Sant'Agostino 220
Coppi, Fra Elia 86
Coppo di Marcovaldo 184
Corciano 16, 27, 81
Corraduccio, Giovanni di 46
Cosmati work 158, 197, 202
Cospaia 121
Costacciaro 130

country houses 29
courses 11–12
credit cards 22–3
crime 25
crossbow matches 27
Crusades 53–4
cultural tours 11–12
currency 22–3
customs formalities 5–6, 26
cycling 9, 12, 227

Dalmata, Giovanni 223
d'Amelia, Pier Matteo 159
Daniele da Volterra 123
Dante Alighieri 130, 139, 171
Del Monte family 119
Della Corgna family 81, 86
Della Corgna, Ascanio 86, 89
Della Robbia, Andrea 106
Della Robbia, Luca 223
Deruta 47, 80–81
Diamanti, Fra 159
Diocletian, Emperor 37
disabled travellers 9–10
Disciplinati (Flagellants) 62
Donation of Constantine 38
Doni, Dono 48, 110
drink 18, 20–21, 57, 235
    see also wines
driving see car travel
drugs 25
Duccio di Buoninsegna 45, 68, 195
Dunarobba 34, 198

earthquakes 41, 50–51
    1979 quake 50, 217, 219
    1997 quake 44, 50–51, 131, 132, 137,
        139, 141, 142, 143, 150, 176, 214
    see also Assisi
Egidian Constitutions 41, 42
Egyptian influences 144
electricity 25
Elias, Brother 54, 95, 98
Ellera 27
embassies 22
emigration 43
Etruscans 12, 35–7, 71, 73, 82, 109, 178
Eugubine Tablets 35, 124
Eugubini 122
Eusebio da San Giorgio 48, 76, 86, 104,
    125, 136
Eutizio, St 224–5

Fabro 191
Fantino, Il (Ascensidonio Spacco) 144–5,
    148
Fanum Voltumnae 35, 36, 178
farm holidays 29–31
Fascism 44
Felice, St 216
Ferentillo 214, 215, 217
Ferraù da Faenza 168
Ferrucci, Francesco di Simone 224
festivals 14–16, 23
Ficulle 191, 193
Fiorenzo di Lorenzo 46–7, 76, 110
Firenzuola 207

fishing 82, 84
Flash Art 149
Foligno 14–16, 27, 40, 52,
    139–43
Fontecchio 119
Fonti del Clitunno 150–51, 152
Fontignano 91
food 17–20, 24
    menu vocabulary 232–6
Forca d'Ancarano 224
Forca Canapine 27, 225
Fornole 196
Fortebraccio see Braccio Fortebraccio
Fossato di Vico 131
Fraccano 120
Francesco di Antonio 216
Francesco di Castel della Pieve 90
Francis of Assisi, St (Francesco Bernardone)
    39, 44, 52–5, 95–102
    life 52–4, 85, 91, 98, 99–102, 104–6,
        122, 140, 149, 192, 203, 205
    poetry 54, 104, 171, 240
Franciscan order 53–5, 95, 105, 146, 171,
    205
Franks 38–9
Fratta Todina 175
Frederick II, Emperor ('Stupor Mundi') 40,
    52, 86, 102, 131, 139
Frederick Barbarossa, Emperor 40, 122, 158
frescoes 45–6
Fuga, Ferdinando 205

Gaius Flaminius 36–7, 85
Garavelle 119
Garibaldi, Giuseppe 43, 168
Gattamelata (Erasmo da Narni) 201, 204
Gattapone, Matteo 77, 124, 156, 157, 203
Gavelli 218
Gentile da Fabriano 46, 68, 182
Geraldini family 195
Gherardi, Cristofano 121
Ghibellines 39, 40–41, 51–2, 178–9
Ghiberti, Lorenzo 118
Ghirlandaio, Domenico 203
Giannicola di Paolo 48, 70, 126
Giano dell'Umbria 148
Giolio Romano 158
Giotto 45, 55, 98–100
Giovanni di Bonino 182
Giovanni di Corraduccio 150
Giovanni di Gian Pietro 150
Giovanni di Giovannello 207
Giovanni da Gubbio 102
Giovanni di Pian di Carpine, Fra 83
Giovanni di Spoleto 214
Giovanni di Uguccione 180
Giove 198
Giovenale, St 202, 203
gliding 27, 227
Goethe, Johann Wolfgang von 42, 45, 46,
    91, 102, 151, 240
golf 27
gonfalons 75
Gothic art 46, 99
Gozzoli, Benozzo 46, 47, 141, 146, 147,
    182, 203, 210
Grand Tourists 42, 45, 157, 202, 205

Greco, Emilio 181, 184
Greek-Gothic wars 38, 131
Greeks 34, 35, 36, 38
Green Umbria 44, 55
Gregory XVI, Pope 43
Grotte di Monte Cucco 130
Grotte d'Orlando 205
Gualdo Cattaneo 148
Gualdo Tadino 15, 16, 36, 131–2
Guardea 192
Gubbio 121–30
   eating out 129–30
   festivals 15, 16, 27, 127–8
   history 35–6, 42, 60, 121–2
   shopping 26, 123, 128
   where to stay 128–9
Guelphs 39, 40–41, 51–2, 178–9
Guercino 48, 156

hang-gliding 27, 130, 142, 227
Hannibal 36–7, 85–6, 154, 160
Hawkwood, Sir John 41, 69, 74
Henry VII, Emperor 41, 178–9
hiking see walking
holidays, official 23
Holy Roman Emperors 39
horses see riding
hostels 30
hotels 26, 28–9
hunting 27
hydroelectric power 44

I Prati 211
Ikuvini 36
Ilario da Viterbo 106
Innocent III, Pope 40, 53–4
Innocent VI, Pope 41
insects 56–7
insurance 3, 22
International Gothic style 46, 98
Iron Age 34
Isola Maggiore 83, 84–5, 87
Isola Polvese 83, 84
Italian see language

Jacopo di Mino del Pellicciaio 90
Jacopo Siculo 158, 214, 216, 223
Jacopone da Todi, Fra (Jacopo dei Benedetti)
   54, 170–72, 175
jazz festivals 15, 44, 60, 77, 93
jousts 27, 142, 203
Julius II, Pope 156, 157, 222
Justinian, Emperor 38, 131

Knights of Malta 83

La Scarzuola 191–2
Labro 213
Lago di Alviano 192–3
Lago di Corbara 192
Lago di Piediluco 27, 212–13
Lago di Pilato 226
Lago Tiberino 34, 198
Lake Arezzo 207
Lake Trasimeno 21, 61, 82–8
   activities 27, 82, 87
   history 36–7, 82, 85–6

Lake Vico 198
Lamberti, Mosca dei 166
Lamborghini, Ferruccio 87
language 229–36
   courses 11, 77
Lapis da Cagli, Gaetano 159
Lars Porsena 82
Le Torri 148
lentils 226
Leo III, Pope 39
Leo X, Pope 63
Leonardi, Leoncillo 159
Leonardo da Vinci 47, 84
Lippi, Filippino 157, 159
Lippi, Fra Filippo 159
Lo Spagna see Spagna, Lo
Lombards 38–9, 154, 161
Lorenzetti, Pietro 46, 98
Lugnano in Teverina 196–7

Maderno, Carlo 156
Madonna delle Lagrime 150
Maestro di Cesi 207
Maestro della Dormitio di Terni 210, 220
Maestro di San Francesco 68
Maestro di Santa Chiara 103
Maestro di Sant'Alò 156
Maestro della Vele 98
Maffei, Antonio 170
Magione 30, 83, 87
Magyars 39
Maitani, Lorenzo 90, 170, 180, 184
malaria 34, 44, 82
Manetti, Rutilio 126
Manzù, Giacomo 220
maps 8
Marmore 212
Marsciano 175
Martelli, Valentino 145, 173
Martin V, Pope 41, 63
Martini, Francesco di Giorgio 68, 125
Martini, Simone 46, 98–9, 184
Mary, cult of 72, 150
Masolino da Panicale (Tommaso Fini) 46,
   90, 170
Massa Martana 176
Master of Città di Castello 118
Master of Eggi 216
Master Petrus 225
Master of St Francis 45, 68, 96–9
Master of Santa Chiara di Montefalco, First
   157
Matteo da Gualdo 47, 102, 130, 131, 132
medieval sports 27
Melezzole 194
Melissus, Gaius 158
Memmi, Lippo 46, 182
Menotre Valley 141
Menotti, Giancarlo 152–4, 158
Metelli, Orneore 210
mezzadria 42, 4344
Mezzastris, Pierantonio 47, 104, 137, 141,
   150
Michelangelo Buonarroti 47, 48, 157
Michelotti, Biondo 63
Milan, air travel 2
Mola, Giambattista 158

Monaldeschi family 41, 178, 190, 198
Monasterio della Fonte Avellana 130
money 6, 22–3
Mongiovino Vecchio 90
Monte Castello di Vibio 174, 175
Monte Cucco 27, 130
Monte Ingino 127, 129
Monte di Lago 84
Monte Peglia 34
Monte Pennino 132
Monte Rubiaglio 191
Monte Santa Maria Tiberina 119
Monte Serra Santa 132
Monte Subasio 27, 105, 107
Monte Vettore 226
Montecastrilli 198
Montecchio 192, 194
Montecolognola 83
Montefalco 15, 21, 46, 145–7
Montefeltro Dukes of Urbino 42, 122
Montefeltro, Federico da, Duke of Urbino
   125
Montefranco 217, 218
Montegabbione 191
Montegiove 191
Montelabate 112
Monteleone d'Orvieto 191
Monteleone di Spoleto 218–19
Monteluco 161, 162
Monterchi 46, 120
Montesanto 173
Monti Martani 143, 148, 207
Monti Sibillini 221, 226–7
   National Park 224, 225
Montone 16, 114
Morgan, Lady (Sydney Owenson) 43
Morra 114–15
mountain sports 27, 28
mummies 215
museums 24
music:
   castrati 222
   holidays 11
   see also jazz
Mussolini, Benito 44

Naharkum 201, 209, 216
Napoleon Bonaparte 43, 47, 64
Narni 15, 36, 44, 201–6
Narses 131
Nazarenes 45
Nelli, Ottaviano 46, 117, 123, 126, 141
Neolithic era 34
Nera river 36, 201, 204, 209, 211
Neri di Bicci 157
Nicola da Siena 182, 220, 223
Nocera Umbra 132
Norcia 14, 15, 37, 57, 221–4
Normans 148
Nuti, Nicolò and Meo 180
Oasi delle Valle 84
Ocriculum 205
Octavian see Augustus
Oddi family 41, 62, 63
Odoacer 37
olives 26, 150
opening hours 23, 24

Orbetello Scalo 189
Orcagna, Andrea 180, 182
Orsini family 197–8
**Orvieto** 176–90, *177*
  Duomo 45, 180–83, *181*
  eating out 189–90
  festivals 15, 16, 180
  history 35, 36, 41–2, 176–9
  where to stay 189
  wines 21, 188–9, 191, 192
Orvieto Scalo 179, 188
Ossaia 85
Ostrogoths 37–8
Otricoli 205

Paciano 90
packing 24–5
painting courses 11
Palaeolithic era 34, 198
Pale 142
Palianum 188, 192
Paneri, Giacomo (Boldrino di Panicale) 90
Panicale 88, 90–91
Panicarola 87
Papal States 41–3, 52, 156
Parco Naturale del Monte Cucco 27, 130, 132
Parco Naturale del Nera 214
Parco Nazionale dei Monti Sibillini *see* Monti Sibillini
Parrano 34, 191
Passignano sul Trasimeno 16, 82–3, 84, 87–8
passports 5
Paul III, Pope 41, 63–4, 70
Pellegrini, Sebastiano 202
Penna in Teverina 197–8
Pepin the Short, King 38
Perini, Francesco 195
*permesso di soggiorno* 5
**Perugia** 46–7, 60–80, *61*
  Arco di Augusto 73
  Battaglia de' Sassi 62, 67
  Borgo Sant'Angelo 73
  Cathedral (San Lorenzo) 67–8
  Collegio del Cambio 69–70
  Corso Vannucci 69–71, 77
  eating out 79–80
  festivals 15, 16, 60, 62, 77–8
  Fontana Maggiore 66, 68
  Galleria Nazionale 68–9
  history 35, 36, 37, 38, 40–44, 60–64, 73, 77
  Ipogeo dei Volumni 77
  Museo Archeologico Nazionale dell'Umbria 75–6
  Oratorio di San Bernardino 72
  Palazzo dei Priori 66, 68
  Piazza IV Novembre 66–70
  Piazza Matteotti 75
  Piazza Michelotti 74
  Rocca Paolina 43, 70–71
  San Domenico 47, 68, 75
  San Filippo Neri 71
  San Lorenzo *see* Cathedral *above*
  San Pietro 76
  San Severo 74

Santa Colomba 74
Santa Giuliana 77
Sant'Agostino 73–4
Sant'Angelo 74
Torre degli Sciri 71
university 44, 60, 73, 75, 207
Perugino (Pietro Vannucci) 45, 47, 48, 67, 89, 91
Bettona 110
Cerqueto 175
Città della Pieve 89
Corciano 81
Foligno 141
Fontignano 91
Montefalco 146
Panicale 90
Perugia 69, 76
Spello 136
Trevi area 150
Petrignano 109
Petruccioli, Cola 46, 136
Piano Grande 225–6
Piediluco 15, 27, 212–13, 214
Piedmont, Kings of 43
Pier Matteo d'Amelia 48, 196, 198, 204, 210
Piermarini, Giuseppe 140
Piero della Francesca 46, 47, 183
  Borgo Sansepolcro 121
  Monterchi 120
  Perugia 68
Pietralunga 114
Pietro da Cortona 69
Pieve di San Gregorio 148
Pieve del Vescovo 81
Pilate, Pontius 226
Pinturicchio (Bernardino di Betto) 47
  Città di Castello 116
  Perugia 69
  San Martino in Colle 81
  Spello 136
  Spoleto 158
Pisano, Andrea 180, 181, 184
Pisano, Giovanni 66, 68, 75
Pisano, Nicola 66, 88
Pius II, Pope (Aeneas Sylvius) 227
Pius IX, Pope 43, 64
Pius VII, Pope 43
Pliny the Younger 37, 119, 120
Poggio Gramignano 197
Poggiodomo 30
Poli, Fausto 218, 220
Polino 215
Polinori, Andrea 148
Pomarancio, Antonio 48
Pomarancio, Niccolò 48, 86, 89, 90, 91, 112, 120, 195, 220
Pompili, Guido 44
Pomurlo Vecchio 193
Pontanus (Giovanni Pontano) 217
Ponte 216–17
Ponte d'Augusto 202
Ponte Canale 214
Ponte Cardona 201
Ponte Naia 175
Ponte Sanguinario 205

popes 38–9, 40–42, 52, 60
Porchiano 174
Pordenone, Giovanni Antonio 192
Portaria 207
post offices 25–6
potholing 27
Prati, I 211
Pre-Raphaelites 45
Preci 38, 222, 225
Preggio 114
prehistory 34–5
Prodo 192
Propertius, Sextus 37, 91, 104
Punic War, Second 36, 85

Quercia, Jacopo della 170

Raffaellino del Colle 118, 120, 126
rafting 27, 212, 227
Raphael 47, 70
  Città di Castello 47, 117, 118
  Perugia 47, 69, 74
Rasiglia 142
Ravenna, Exarchate of 38
*residenze d'epoca* 29
restaurants 17–18, 232–6
riding 27, 227
Ridolfi, Mario 210, 211
*rifugi* 227
Risorgimento 43, 64
Rita, St 219–20
Rivotorto 108
Rocca d'Aries 114
Rocca Ripesena 188
Rocca Sant'Angelo 109
Roccaporena 220
Rocco di Tommaso 91, 149
rock climbing 215, 217, 227
Rogerino da Todi 207
Romans 36–7
Rome, air travel 2
Romualdo, St 130
Rosciano 214
Rossellino, Bernardo 186
Rosso Fiorentino 48, 116
rowing 27
Rufino, St 91, 102
Ruskin, John 92

sailing 87
salt taxes 41, 64
Salt War 41, 64
Sambucetole 198
Sammicheli, Michele 182, 185
San Damiano *see* Assisi
San Feliciano 84, 87
San Fortunato 147
San Gemini 16, 206–8
San Gemini Fonte 207, 208
San Giacomo di Spoleto 151
San Girolamo 137
San Giustino 121
San Gregorio 108
San Martino al Cimino 198
San Martino in Colle 81
San Paolo Intervineas 161
San Pellegrino 131

San Pietro in Valle 38, 45, 215, 218
San Terenziano 175
San Vito 206
Sangallo, Antonio da the Younger 70–71, 118, 168, 187, 192, 195, 210
Sanguineto 85
Sansepolcro 16, 27
Santa Maria in Pantano 176
Santa Maria di Pistia 142
Santa Maria della Rocchicciola, Convento di 109
Santa Scolastica 223, 225
Sant'Anatolia di Narco 216, 218
Sant'Egidio, Battle of 63
Sant'Eutizio 38, 224
Santissima Trinità 132
Santuario dell'Amore Misericordioso 175
Santuario della Madonna del Belvedere 119
Santuario della Madonna delle Grazie (Bevagna) 145
Santuario della Madonna delle Grazie (Rasiglia) 142
Santuario della Madonna della Stella 147
Saracens 39, 139
Saragano 148
Scalza, Ippolito 180, 182, 183, 186, 191, 192
Scarzuola, La 191–2
Scelli, Loreto 159
Scheggia 130
Scheggino 216, 218
Schippers, Thomas 158
Scholastica, St 222–3
sculpture courses 11
self-catering 11, 29–31
Sellano 142
senior citizen discounts 3, 7, 24, 30
Sensini, Pietro Paolo 168
Sermei, Cesare 96
Settignano, Bernardo da 202
Settignano, Domenico Bertini da (Topolino) 84
Sferracavallo 188
Sguazzino, Lo (G. B. Pacetti) 116
shopping 24, 26
Sibyl, the 226–7
Sienese artists 45–6
Sigillo 15, 16, 27, 30, 130
Signorelli, Luca 48
  Citerna 120
  Città di Castello 118
  Morra 114–15
  Orvieto 182–3, 184, 188
  Perugia 67
  Umbertide 112
skiing 14, 27, 130, 132, 225
Smollett, Tobias 43, 142
Socialists 44
Solsternus 158
Soriano nel Cimino 198
Sotius, Alberto 159
Spagna, Lo (Giovanni di Pietro) 48, 74, 106, 149–50, 151, 156, 168, 216, 218
Sparapane, Giovanni and Antonio 224
specialist holidays 11–12, 30
speleology 27
Spello 14, 15, 35, 36, 37, 47, 134–8

Spenser, Edmund 52
Spinello Aretino 118
Spoleto 11, 152–64, *153*
  festivals 15, 16, 152, 154
  history 36, 37, 41, 154
Spoleto, Duchy of 38, 39, 40, 154, 157, 161, 225
Spoleto, Faraoldo II, Duke of 215
Spoleto, Guido III, Duke of 154
sport 27–8
stamps 25–6
Strettura 163, 164
strikes 6
Stroncone 211, 214
students 3, 5, 11, 30
subterranean excursions 27, 130, 203, 204
Swiss Guards 43, 64
Syrians 38, 215

Tacitus 209
Tamagni, Vincenzo 214
Tane del Diavolo 34, 191
*tartufi see* truffles
Tavernelle 90
taxis 8
telephones 26
Tempietto del Clitunno 151
Terme di Fontecchio 119
Terminillo 27
Terni 15, 44, 46, 208–14
Theodoric, King 38
Tiber Valley 112–32, *113*, 165–98, *167*
Tiberio d'Assisi 48, 71, 104, 105, 106, 110, 146, 147, 150
Tifernum *see* Città di Castello
tipping 17
Tirreni 35
Titignano 192–3
Todi 15, 16, 35, 46, 166–75, *169*
Todiano 225
Tommaso da Celano 53, 54
Topino river 134, 138
Torgiano 21, 80, 82
Torrecola 164
Torreorsina 214
Torriti, Jacopo 100
Toscolano 198
Totila 38, 131
tour operators 11–12, 30–31
tourist information 28
Trasimeno *see* Lake Trasimeno
Trevi 14, 16, 30, 148–52
Trinci family 139, 141, 143, 145, 219
Trinci, Paolo de' 172
Trinci, Ugolino III 141
Triponzo 217
truffles 26, 57, 216, 222
Tuoro sul Trasimeno 82–3, 85–6
Turrita 147
Tursha 35
Tuzi, Vanni 223
Tyrennoi 35

Ubaldo, St 122, 127–8
Ugo of Hartlepool, Fra 96
Ugolino di Prete Ilario 182

Ugolino di Vieri 182, 184
Umbertide 21, 112–15
Umbrian artists 45–8
Umbriano 215
Umbrii 34–7, 102, 124, 166
  *see also* Naharkum
United States of America, travel from 4–5
Urbinum Hortense 138
Usigni 218

Valcastoriana 224
Valentine, St 37, 209–10
Valle Oblita 225
Valle Umbra 55, 133–64, *135*
Vallo di Nera 216
Valnerina 38, 50, 199–228, *200*
Valsorda 132
Vanvitelli, Luigi 140
Vasari, Giorgio 117, 118, 240
  on Perugino and Pinturicchio 47, 89
Vecchietta 202
Venus of Trasimeno 34
Vettona *see* Bettona
Via Armerina 194
Via Flaminia 36–7, 42, 130–31, 134, 151, 160, 202, 205
Vignola, Jacopo Barozzi 86, 222
Villa Fidelia 137
Villa San Faustina 176
Villalago 213
Villanovan culture 34–5
villas 30–31
vipers 56
Virgil 37, 227
visas 5
Visciano 205
Visigoths 37
Vissani 193
Vitelleschi, Cardinal Giovanni 139
Vitelli family 115, 117, 118
Vittorio Emanuele II, King 43
Volsinii Veteres (Orvieto) 35, 36

walking 12, 28
water skiing 87
when to go 14, 24
where to stay 28–32
wildlife 55–7, 193, 226
  *see also* birds; wolves
wines 12, 20–21, 26, 80
  Colli Amerini 21, 196
  Grecchetto di Todi 174
  Montefalco 21, 147
  Orvieto *see* Orvieto
  Sagrantino 21, 147
  Torgiano 21, 80
  Trasimeno 21, 87
  Vernaccia di Cannara 21, 138
wolves 56, 122, 127, 130
World War, Second 44, 48, 122

youth discounts 3, 5, 24
youth hostels 30

Zuccari family 204

# Also Available from Cadogan Guides...

## Country Guides

Antarctica
Belize
Central Asia
China: The Silk Routes
Egypt
France: Southwest France;
    Dordogne, Lot & Bordeaux
France: Southwest France;
    Gascony & the Pyrenees
France: Brittany
France: The Loire
France: The South of France
France: Provence
France: Côte d'Azur
Germany: Bavaria
Greece: The Peloponnese
Holland
India
India: South India
India: Goa
Ireland
Ireland: Southwest Ireland
Ireland: Northern Ireland
Italy
Italy: The Bay of Naples and Southern Italy
Italy: Bologna and Emilia Romagna
Italy: Italian Riviera
Italy: Lombardy, Milan and the Italian Lakes
Italy: Rome and the Heart of Italy
Italy: Tuscany, Umbria and the Marches
Italy: Tuscany
Italy: Umbria
Italy: Venetia and the Dolomites
Japan
Morocco
Portugal
Portugal: The Algarve
Scotland
Scotland: Highlands and Islands
South Africa, Swaziland and Lesotho
Spain
Spain: Southern Spain
Spain: Northern Spain
Syria & Lebanon
Tunisia
Turkey
Yucatán and Southern Mexico
Zimbabwe, Botswana and Namibia

## City Guides

Amsterdam
Beijing
Brussels, Bruges, Ghent & Antwerp
Bruges
Edinburgh
Florence, Siena, Pisa & Lucca
Italy: Three Cities—Rome, Florence, Venice
Italy: Three Cities—Venice, Padua, Verona
Italy: Three Cities—Rome, Naples, Sorrento
Italy: Three Cities—Rome, Padua, Assisi
Japan: Three Cities—Tokyo, Kyoto and
    Ancient Nara
Spain: Three Cities—Granada, Seville,
    Cordoba
London
London–Paris
London–Brussels
London–Edinburgh
London–Amsterdam
Madrid
Manhattan
Moscow & St Petersburg
Paris
Prague
Rome
St Petersburg
Venice

## Island Guides

Caribbean and Bahamas
Jamaica & the Caymans

Greek Islands
Crete
Mykonos, Santorini & the Cyclades
Rhodes & the Dodecanese
Corfu & the Ionian Islands

Madeira & Porto Santo
Malta
Sardinia
Sicily

## Plus...

Bugs, Bites & Bowels
London Markets
Take the Kids Travelling
Take the Kids London
Take the Kids Paris and Disneyland

Available from good bookshops or via, in the UK, **Grantham Book Services**, Isaac Newton Way, Alma Park Industrial Estate, Grantham NG31 9SD, ✆ (01476) 541 080, ✉ (01476) 541 061; and in North America from **The Globe Pequot Press**, 246 Goose Lane, PO Box 480, Guilford, Connecticut 06437–0480, ✆ (800) 243 0495, ✉ (800) 820 2329.